VALIDATION AND VERIFICATION OF KNOWLEDGE BASED SYSTEMS

T0205399

VALIDATION AND VERIFICATION OF KNOWLEDGE BASED SYSTEMS

Theory, Tools and Practice

Edited by

Anca Vermesan
Det Norske Veritas,
Norway

and

Frans Coenen
University of Liverpool,
U.K.

KLUWER ACADEMIC PUBLISHERS
BOSTON / DORDRECHT / LONDON

A C.I.P. Catalogue record for this book is available from the Library of Congress.

ISBN 978-1-4419-5107-6

Published by Kluwer Academic Publishers,
P.O. Box 17, 3300 AA Dordrecht, The Netherlands.

Sold and distributed in North, Central and South America
by Kluwer Academic Publishers,
101 Philip Drive, Norwell, MA 02061, U.S.A.

In all other countries, sold and distributed
by Kluwer Academic Publishers,
P.O. Box 322, 3300 AH Dordrecht, The Netherlands.

Printed on acid-free paper

All Rights Reserved
© 1999 Kluwer Academic Publishers, Boston
Softcover reprint of the hardcover 1st edition 1999
No part of the material protected by this copyright notice may be reproduced or
utilized in any form or by any means, electronic or mechanical,
including photocopying, recording or by any information storage and
retrieval system, without written permission from the copyright owner.

CONTENTS

Ontologies

Safety critical KBS

Knowledge Revision and Refinement

Applications

ACKNOWLEDGEMENTS

The editors would like to thank the following organisations for their sponsorship:

Det Norske Veritas, Oslo, Norway

The Specialist Group on Expert Systems (SGES) of the British Computer Society (BCS)

The editors are also deeply indebted to the many practitioners and scientific researchers who have contributed to this book, and to the following referees and academic advisors for their support:

Agnar Aamodt, University of Trondheim, Norway

Marc Ayel, LIA-University of Savoie, France

Trevor Bench-Capon, University of Liverpool, UK

Sandro Bologna, ENEA CRE-Casaccia, Italy

Jesus Cardenosa, Univ. Polit. De Madrid, Spain

Susan Craw, The Robert Gordon University, UK

Barry Eaglestone, University of Sheffield, UK

Dieter Fensel, University of Karlsruhe, Germany

Rose Gamble, University of Tulsa, USA

Alun Preece, University of Aberdeen, UK

Marie-Christine Rousset, LRI-University of Paris Sud, France

Frank van Harmelen, Vrije Universiteit Amsterdam, The Netherlands

Gheorghe Tecuci, George Mason University, USA

Jan Vanthienen, Katholieke Universiteit Leuven, Belgium

Jeffrey Voas, Reliable Software Technologies, USA

Claes Wohlin, Lund Institute of Technology, Sweden

CONTRIBUTORS

1. Keith Bell, Det Norske Veritas, Norway.

   Email keith.bell@dnv.com

2. *Trevor Bench-Capon*, Department of Computer Science, University of Liverpool, Liverpool, L69 3BX, UK.

   Email tbc@csc.liv.ac.uk

3. *Robin Boswell*, School of Computer and Mathematical Sciences. The Robert Gordon University Aberdeen, AB25 1HG, UK.

   Email rab@scms.rgu.ac.uk

4. *Jesús Cardenos(Õ)osa*, Dpto. de Inteligencia Artificial, Facultad de Informatica, Universidad Politénica de Madrid, Madrid, Spain.

   Email carde@fi.upm.es

5. *Frans Coenen*, Department of Computer Science, University of Liverpool, Liverpool, L69 3BX, UK.

   Email frans@csc.liv.ac.uk

6. *Susan Craw*, School of Computer and Mathematical Sciences. The Robert Gordon University Aberdeen, AB25 1HG, UK.

   Email s.craw@scms.rgu.ac.uk

7. *Juliette Dibie-Barthélemy*, LAMSADE, Université Paris IX — Dauphine, F-75775 Paris Cedex 16, France.

   Email Juliette.Dibie@inapg.inra.fr

8. *Giovanna Dondossola*, ENEL-SRI, Department of Electronic Systems and Automation, Cologno Monzese 20093 Milan, Italy.

   Email dondossola@pea.enel.it

9. *F. Dupin de Saint-Cyr*, LERIA, Université s'Angers, UFR Sciences, F-49045 Angers, Cedex 01, Frans

   Email bannay@info.univ-angers.fr

10. *Barry Eaglestone*, Department of Information Studies,University of Sheffield, UK.

    Email B.Eaglestone@shef.ac.uk

11. *David Escorial*, Dpto. de Inteligencia Artificial, Facultad de Informatica, Universidad Politécnica de Madrid, Madrid, Spain.

    Email escor@fi.upm.es

12. *Roar Fjellheim*, Computas AS, 1327 Lysaker, Norway.

    Email rf@computas.no

13. *Rik Gerrits*, LibRt B.V., Postbus 90359, 1006 BJ Amsterdam, Netherlands.

    Email Rik@LibRT.com

14. *Tomasz Gladysz*, Department of artificial Intelligence Systems, Wroclaw University of Economics, ul. Kormandorska 118/120, 53-345 Wroclaw, Poland.

    Email gladysz@manager.ae.wroc.pl

15. *Éric Grégoire*, CRIL, Universiteé d'Artois, Rue de l'Université SP16, F-62307 Lens Ciedex, France.

    Email gregoire@cril.univ-artois.fr

16. *Frode Høgberg*, Det Norske Veritas, Norway.

    Email frode.hogberg@dnv.com

17. *Ollivier Haemmerlé*, INA-PG, Département OMIP, F-75231 Paris Cedex 05, France.

    Email Ollivier.Haemmerle@inapg.inra.fr

18. *Dean Jones*, Department of Computer Science, University of Liverpool, Liverpool, L69 3BX, UK.

    Email dean@csc.liv.ac.uk

19. *Antoni Ligęza*, Institute of Automatics AGH, 30-059 Kraków, Poland.

    Email ali@ia.agh.edu.pl, ligeza@uci.agh.edu.pl

20. *Luis Laita*, Department of AI, Universidad Politéccnia de Madrid, Boadtlla delMonte, 28660 Madrid, Spain.

    Email laita@fi.upm.es

21. *Luis de Ledesma*, Department of AI, Universidad Politéccnia de Madrid, Boadtlla delMonte, 28660 Madrid, Spain.

    Email ledesma@fi.upm.es

22. *Stéphane Loiseau*, LERIA, Université s'Angers, UFR Sciences, F-49045 Angers, Cedex 01, France.

    Email loiseau@info.univ-angers.fr

23. *Víctor Maojo*, Department of AI, Universidad Politéccnia de Madrid, Boadtlla delMonte, 28660 Madrid, Spain.

Email vmaojo@infomed.dia.fi.upm.es

24. *Albino Marques*, REN — Portuhuese Transmission Network - (EDP Group), 4471 Maia Codex, Portugal.

25. *Per Martinsen*, Det Norske Veritas, Norway.

Email per.martinsen@dnv.com

26. *Nayyer Masood*, Dept. of Computer Science, Bahauddin Zakariya University, Multan, Pakistan.

Email nmdar@yahoo.com

27. *Ana Moreno-Garcia*, Dep. Economía Financiera y Dirección de Op. University of Seville, Secille, Spain.

Email anafi@ibm.net

28. *Malgorzata Ochmańska*, Department of Artificial Intelligence Systems, Wroclaw University of Economics, ul. Kormandorska 118/120, 53-345 Wroclaw, Poland.

Email ochmansk@manager.ae.wroc.pl

29. *Ståle Olsen*, Computas AS, 1327 Lysaker, Norway.

Email so@computas.no

30. *Mieczyslaw Owoc*, Department of artificial Intelligence Systems, Wroclaw University of Economics, ul. Kormandorska 118/120, 53-345 Wroclaw, Poland.

Email mowoc@manager.ae.wroc.pl

31. *Carlos Ramos*, Polytechnic Institute of Porto, Dept. of Computer Engineering, 4200 Porto, Portugal.

Email csr@dei.isep.ipp.pt

32. *Eugenio Roanes-Lozano*, Dept. Algebra, Universidad Complutense de Madrid, Madrid, Spain.

Email eroanes@eucmos.sim.ucm.es

33. *Francisco Ribeiro*, Instituto Superior Técnio. Departamento de Engenharia Civil, 1096 Lisboa Codex, Lisboa, Portugal.

Email loforte@civil.ist.utl.pt

34. *Mick Ridley*, School of Computing and Mathematics, University of Bradford, UK.

Email M.J.Ridley@scm.brad.ac.uk

35. *Jorge Santos*, Polytechnic Institute of Porto, Dept. of Computer Engineering, 4200 Porto, Portugal.

Email jsantos@dei.isep.ipp.pt

36. *Michael Schroeder*, City University London, London EX1V 0HB, UK.

    Email msch@cs.city.ac.uk

37. *Florence Sellini*, PSA Peugeot Citroën, 92256 La Garenne Colombes Cedex, France.

    Email Florence.Sellini@wanadoo.fr

38. *Jarle Sjøvaag*, Det Norske Veritas, Norway.

    Email jarle.sjovaag@dnv.com

39. *Silvie Spreeuwenberg*, LibRt B.V., Postbus 90359, 1006 BJ Amsterdam, Netherlands.

    Email Silvie@LibRT.com

40. *Rune Steinberg*, Computas AS, 1327 Lysaker, Norway.

    Email rs@computas.no

41. *Zita Vale*, Polytechnic Institute of Porto, Dept. of Electrical Engineering, 4200 Porto, Portugal.

    Email zav@dee.isep.ipp.pt

42. *Jan Vanthienen*, Katholieke Universiteit Leuven, Dept. of Applied Economic Sciences, Leuven, Belgium.

    Email Jan.Vanthienen@econ.kuleuven.ac.be

43. *Anca Vermesan*, Det Norske Veritas, DTP343, 1322 Hovik, Norway.

    Email Anca.Vermesan@dnv.com

44. *Jeffrey Voas*, Reliable Software Technologies Corporation, Sterling, Virginia 20166, USA.

    Email jmvoas@rstcorp.com

45. *Nirmalie Wiratunga*, School of Computer and Mathematical Sciences. The Robert Gordon University Aberdeen, AB25 1HG, UK.

    Email nw@scms.rgu.ac.uk

46. *Pierre-Alain Yvars*, ISMCM-CESTI, GRIIEM Research Team, 93407 St Ouen Cedex, France.

    Email payvars@ismcm-cesti,fr

FOREWORD

1.   INTRODUCTION

Knowledge-base (KB) technology is being applied to complex problem-solving and critical tasks in many application domains. Concerns have naturally arisen as to the dependability of knowledge base systems (KBS). As with any software, attention to quality and safety must be paid throughout development of a KBS and rigorous verification and validation (V&V) techniques must be employed. Research in V&V of KBS has emerged as a distinct field only in the last decade and is intended to address issues associated with quality and safety aspects of KBS and to credit such applications with the same degree of dependability as conventional applications. In recent years, V&V of KBS has been the topic of annual workshops associated with the main AI conferences, such as AAAI, IJCAI and ECAI.

This work contains a collection of papers, dealing with all aspects of KB V&V, presented at the Fifth European Symposium on Verification and Validation of Knowledge Based Systems and Components (EUROVAV'99 – http ://www.dnv.no/research/safekbs/eurovav99/) which was held in Oslo in the summer of 1999, and was sponsored by Det Norske Veritas and the British Computer Society's Specialist Group on Expert Systems (SGES).

EUROVAV is the leading European conference dedicated to the advancement of the theory and practice of V&V of KBS. Its objective is to bring together researchers from both academia and industry, not only from Europe, but also from all over the world, encouraging all styles of V&V approaches and a variety of application areas. EUROVAV'99 held in Oslo,

Norway was the fifth in a biannual series, with previous meetings in Cambridge, UK (91), Palma de Mallorca, Spain (93), Chambery, France (95), Leuven, Belgium (97).

The collection of papers presented in this work are organised under the following headings:

– Theory and Techniques
– Ontologies
– Safety critical KBS (the Safe-KBS project)
– Knowledge Revision and Refinement
– Applications
– Certification
– The wider picture

A brief synopsis of each of the papers presented under each of these headings and included in this work is presented in the following sections.

2.   THEORY AND TECHNIQUES

In this first section 6 contributions are presented, the first two are intended to carry out a certain amount of "scene setting", while the remaining four are concerned with more detailed issues. The first paper by **Cardeñosa** and **Escorial** presents a view of KBS V&V in terms of "Quality assessment" and in particular software reliability. In their paper **Cardeñosa** and **Escorial** present a solid review of the "state of the art" including references to a number of significant V&V projects. The authors then go on to consider the process of KBS V&V, and then consider the minimum tasks that a *validation plan* for a KBS must incorporate.

The second paper, by **Owoc**, **Ochmanska** and **Gladysz**, gives an overview/insight of KBS validation, i.e. the knowledge element. The authors present a slightly unorthodox view KBS of V&V with one considered to be a sub-component of the other. The author's principal concern is that of validating knowledge (rather than the structure of KBS). In this regard the authors suggest a number of guiding principals. The paper provides an interesting balance with that of **Cardeñosa** and **Escorial**.

The following paper, by **Grégoire**, is concerned with the validation of KBS concentrating on the possibility of the KB containing contradictory knowledge. The author notes that the checking of logical consistency of rulebases expressed in a clausal propositional logic form is an NP complete (see Cook [5] or Garey and Johnson [8] for further details). To tackle this problem **Grégoire** suggests that consistency checking should be performed incrementally during the development of a KB rather than on completion, and then proposes a mechanism to achieve this based on a depth-limited instantiation schema.

Laita, Rianes-Lozano, Maojo and **de Ledesma's** contribution deals with the automated extraction of knowledge and verification of consistency in Rule-Based KBS. The paper is illustrated with a medical decision making application. To achieve their objective **Laita et al**. defined an algebra that can be applied to many-valued logics (up to seven). The approach has been incorporated into a software system called CONSIST written in the computer algebra language CoCoA. The authors commence by summarising the main ideas of modelling propositional many valued logic with modal operators (interpreted over Lukasiewicz matrices) using polynomial rings over appropriate field (of integers *modulo p*, where p is the number of logical values). The crucial consequence of this construction is the fact that tautological consequence and consistency can be then expressed by the properties of ideals of the corresponding polynomial rings. Given a KBS the system translates the rules and facts contained in the KBS, together with details of integrity constraints and any other additional information into polynomials. The "Normal Form" and "Grobner Basis" are then calculated; if these are 0 and 1 respectively the KBS is considered to be consistent, otherwise it is considered to be inconsistent. The remainder of the paper then comprises an extensive example application using a decision table describing fitness criteria in heart diseases.

Spreewenberg and **Gerrits** present a tool to verify KB using meta-rules to be used within an object-oriented KBS development environment called "Aion". The tool is designed to be used during and after the development of KBSs and focuses on the logical verification of such systems. The tool uses meta rules, meta information and the inference engine of Aion to accomplish this task. By using the same inference engine in the verification process as the inference engine used to evaluate and fire the rules to be verified **Spreewenberg** and **Gerrits** suggest that there can be no discrepancy between the run time logic and the logic used in the validation process.

Much of the work described above is concerned with the standard rule-base representation of knowledge. **Dibie-Barthélemy, Haemmerleé** and **Loiseau**, however, consider the semantic validation of conceptual graphs (Sowa [13]) based on constraints given by experts for validation purposes. Here a KB is then semantically valid if it satisfies all the given constraints (the authors use the term "specification" to describe expert knowledge given for validation purposes).

3.   ONTOLOGIES

The ontologies concept, as applied to KBS, is a fairly recent innovation. Essentially an ontology, in the computer science sense of the word, is a set of definitions of (hierarchically ordered) classes, objects, attributes, relations, and constraints whose main function is to provide a vocabulary for the expression of domain knowledge. Thus an ontology is a knowledge-level description (Newell [12]) in that it is independent of any representational formalism (Van Heijst [11]). Also, an ontology is considered to be a meta-level description because it is a specification of a specification. We could say that an ontology describes the domain knowledge that remains invariant over various knowledge bases in a certain domain (cf. Guarino and Giaretta [9]).

In general, we can say that ontologies may contribute to the following five KBS "development" areas.

1. Domain-theory development
2. Knowledge acquisition
3. Knowledge-system design
4. System documentation
5. Knowledge exchange

The role that the ontologies concept has to play in the evaluation of KBS is examined by **Bench-Capon** and **Jones** who propose a software tool, PRONTO, to support this approach to KBS evaluation. **Bench-Capon** is a well known international figure in the field of KBS V&V and more particularly the maintenance of such systems ([4]).

4.   SAFETY-CRITICAL KBS (THE SAFE KBS PROJECT)

The two papers in this section both describe work carried out as part of the "Safe-KBS" ESPRIT project, the aim of which is to define development and certification methodologies for KBS, especially embedded KBS used in safety critical domains. The particular result of this work has been the definition of a "Safe-KBS" life cycle, designed so that it can be integrated with formal methods and provide appropriate support for software certification methods.

The first paper in this section, by **Dondossola** provides a review of the results of the "Safe-KBS" project. The role of formal methods is discussed with reference to the work of Fensel [7] and van Harmelen [10]. This is then followed by a detailed discussion of the requirements for KBS formal methods within the context of both specification (again with reference to the work of Fensel) and V&V. **Dondossola** considers the impact of KBS formal methods on the KBS life cycle pointing out that life cycle models should be defined independently of specific development methods and techniques. The author then goes on to consider the elements of such a life cycle based on that developed as part of the Safe-KBS project. Finally **Dondossola** gives consideration to the selection and evaluation of KBS methodologies, concluding that no optimum formal method exists appropriate to the full spectrum of KBS development requirements.

Steinberg, Fjellheim and **Vollsveien** contribution also describes results founded on the Safe-KBS project, but concentrating on KBS design issues. The authors argue that, despite the fact that a well designed life cycle will contribute substantially to the confidence in a KBS, there is also a particular need to concentrate on design. The Safe-KBS life cycle is therefore supported by a catalogue of *design patterns* for safety critical KBS which describe design solutions that seek to increase the confidence of using KBS technology in such systems. The nature of these design patterns is then the main focus of this contribution.

5. KNOWLEDGE REVISION AND REFINEMENT

Having established that errors/anomalies exist in a KBS systems the practitioner will wish to revise/maintain the KBS in question. Given that it is possible to automatically detect errors in rulebases, the obvious next step is the automated refinement of such rulebases. Tools to achieve this end are usually labelled as *knowledge refinement* or *knowledge revision* tools. Such tools are typically used to assist knowledge engineers by automatically identifying the locations within a KB where the knowledge may need to be changed and (importantly) suggesting appropriate amendments (Craw [6]).

The first contribution in this section, by **Boswell** and **Craw** describe a suite of KB refinement tools under development as part of the Krust-Works project. Central to this "tool kit" is a set of generic refinement operators and a representation language for KBS rules. Interestingly **Boswell** and **Craw** also suggest that their knowledge hierarchy describing the rule-elements with a KBS may be regarded as an ontology for rule-elements and thus linking back to the previous section, however in this case the ontology is used to "tell" a Krust tool which refinement operators to apply to which element.

The second contribution, by **Dupin de Saint-Cyr** and **Loiseau**, presents a discussion of the distinction/overlap between KBS validation and KBS revision/refinement (maintenance). This is a continuation of similar work studying the overlap between KBS verification and revision (see Bouali et al. [2,3]). In the paper **Dupin de Saint-Cyr** and **Loiseau** define refinement as a "modification of an incoherent KB in order to restore its coherency". Revision in turn is the modification of an inconsistent KB to restore consistency. A coherent rulebase is one which "if and only if with any valid input, contradictory results cannot be inferred".

Vanthienen and **Moreno-Garcia** describe a decision table technique to restructure KBS. Vanthienen is an internationally recognised expert of decision table techniques especially in the context of KBS. The paper is illustrated with a specific application (SEAR — Enterprise Human Resources Advisory System). The aim of SEAR is to optimise human resource management in a social and juridical consultantship context. **Vanthienen** and **Moreno-Garcia** use their technique to restructure the SEAR KBS and then use classic decision table techniques to verify and validate the result.

Finally the contribution by **Wiratunga** and **Craw** looks at the definition of three strategies for revising a Rule Base:

1.   A strategy of backtracking on previous revision
2.   A strategy for re-ordering previously solved examples, thus providing new fault evidence.
3.   A heuristic for re-ordering counter-examples next to each other before starting the refinement.

Essentially the approaches presented are iterative in nature. **Craw** is an internationally recognised expert in the field of rulebase revision, has been involved in a number of high profile KBS V&V projects — VIVA, VALID and VITAL, and is also the driving force behind the KRUST and KRUSTWORKS projects (see above).

6.   APPLICATIONS

Much of the foregoing concentrates on the theory of KBS V&V. In a work of this kind we believe that it is also important to consider the application of the tools and techniques that have been described.

To this end **Ribeiro** presents a discussion of V&V of a KBS system for supporting human experts in assessing applications for the house renovation grant system in Portugal. **Ribeiro** commences by considering the development of the system (called HRGS) and then goes on to consider the particular approach taken to verify and validate this system.

The contribution in this section, by **Santos, Faira, Ramos, Vale** and **Marques** focuses on the V&V of intelligent applications software used by the electricity supply industry. In particular the paper addresses the V&V of a KBS (called SPARSE) used to assist operators of Portuguese Transmission Control Centres in incident analysis and power restoration. Although this is the central theme of the paper the contribution also provides a more general insight into the application of KBS V&V techniques.

Sellini and **Yvars** present a discussion of the verification of product modelling for design aid systems for mechanical sets based on the knowledge of expertise. The paper describes how knowledge used in a design system can be verified. A particular knowledge representation is described and additional constraints are formulated which should conform to this knowledge. The paper makes a useful contribution as an example of "what is/can be/must be done in a realistic KBS application".

The final paper in this section is concerned with the formal verification of workflows and is by **Schroeder**. The author adopts the CCS (Calculus of Communicating Systems) algebra to produce a verification framework. The main contribution of the paper is the link between verification tools and process definitions expressed in the Process Interchange Format (PIF). The approach allows the author to check for liveness and safety properties such as, for example, ensuring that jobs are possibly fixed and necessarily dispatched. Furthermore **Schroeder** shows how checks for deadlocks and livelocks can be made.

7. CERTIFICATION

The certification of software and the associated techniques is an area that is rapidly expanding. Much of the knowledge that has been developed over the past few years is now mature enough to be implemented in industry [14]. Its implementation is an area of particular interest to **Vermesan** who has worked extensively in recent years to apply V&V methods and techniques in the field of software certification. In this section, two papers are presented which deal with software certification, based on product-oriented view.

Voas, in the first paper, notes that the most popular approaches to software certification are founded on *publisher oaths* and auditors (who carry out spot-checks to confirm such oaths and suggests that this approach may be flawed — "Dirty water can run from clean pipes". **Voas** goes on to propose a certification methodology that does not employ auditors and publisher oaths, i.e. independent product certification. **Voas** is a recognised expert in the field of software assessment, having developed amongst other things the theory of inoculating programs against errors as a way to assess the safety of critical software systems.

The second paper in this section, by **Vermesan, Sjøvaag, Martinsen** and **Bell** presents an approach to certifying software contained within systems where its functionality is considered critical within the environment in which it is placed. Two certification methods are described in detail, and the role of V&V in certification of KB components is emphasised. It is argued that as techniques for the evaluation of software systems develop in parallel with the systems themselves, certification bodies must constantly review the requirements that are required from software components in order to achieve safe and dependable systems. The approach presented here is also based on the findings of the SafeKBS European project.

8.   THE WIDER PICTURE

In this final section some wider aspects of KBS V&V are considered, in particular:

– The possible application of KBS V&V to recent database models.
– The contribution that integrity checking techniques current within the database community may have to play with respect to KBS V&V
– The application of conventional software V&V techniques to KBS V&V.

Coenen, **Eagleston** and **Ridley** consider possible future directions for rule base V&V on the presumption that many techniques developed by the rule base V&V community have come out of the "research domain" into what might be described as "the main stream" (Bench-Capon et al. [1]). In particular they consider opportunities for possible "cross-overs" between database integrity checking techniques and a number of rule base V&V strands. Collectively they refer to these techniques as VVI (Validation Verification and Integrity) techniques. They commence by giving an overview of integrity issues, then go on to consider overlaps between database and rule base systems and finish with a discussion of "future directions" in VVI. **Coenen** has worked extensively in the area of KBS maintenance and for many years has been pioneering new ways of representing rule bases, i.e. based on the concept of binary encoded incidence matrices and multi-dimensional spatial representations.

Continuing in this theme the second paper in this section, by **Ligeza**, is concerned with the analysis and verification of data and knowledge (D&K) using a common model founded on an extension of the relational database model. The main focus of the paper is the meta-level analysis of D&K tables to identify problems associated with data representation, sufficiency, internal and external constraints, correctness, equivalence etc. **Ligeza** also goes on to consider various technical problems encountered when implementing the above.

The third paper in this section is by **Masood** and **Eaglestone** and describes some of the issue of concern in the database community in the context of schema integration of federated databases. **Masood** and **Eaglestone** also briefly overviews a semi-automated methodology for the schema analysis phase of schema integration based upon the ontology-based conceptualisation of schema semantics.

The final paper in this section is by **Vermesan** and **Høgberg** and considers the last of the above mentioned aspects. The paper presents an experimental framework, founded within the SafeKBS project, to determine whether a technique is applicable or not, based on concepts found in mutation testing. The framework itself consists of a number of steps guiding the researcher/practitioner in the assessment process. Mutation testing is used to simulate faults in an example program to determine the technique's ability to detect them. The paper concludes that the framework gives basis for qualitative assessment of the applicability and efficiency of applying specific traditional V&V and testing techniques to KBS components. To illustrate their ideas **Vermesan** and **Høgberg** seed a sample KBS with faults through a mutation process, and then use a number of traditional V&V methods to find these faults.

REFERENCES

[1] T. Bench-Capon, D. Castelli, F. Coenen, L. Devendeville-Brisoux, B. Eaglestone, N. Fiddian, A. Gray, A. Ligeza and A. Vermesan (1999). Validation, Verification and Integrity Issues in Expert and Database Systems. Expert Update, Vol 2, No 1, pp31-35.

[2] F. Bouali, S. Loiseau, M-C. Rousset (1997). Verification and Revision of Rule Bases In Hunt, J. and Miles, R. (Eds.), Research and Development in Expert Systems XIV, proceedings of ES'97, SGES publications, pp253-276.

[3] F. Bouali, S. Loiseau, M-C. Rousset (1997). Revision of Rule Bases. Proceedings EUROVAV'97, Katholieke Universiteit Leuven, Belgium, pp193-203.

[4] Coenen, F.P. and Bench-Capon, T.J.M. (1993). Maintenance of Knowledge Based Systems: Theory, Tools and Techniques. Academic Press, London.

[5] S.A. Cook (1971) Complexity of Theorem-Proving Procedures In Proc. of the 3rd Annual ACM Symposium on Theory of Computing, pp151-158.

[6] S. Craw (1998). Krust Works: Developing a Generic Refinement Toolkit. Expert Update, Vol 1, No 2, pp35-47.

[7] D. Fensel (1995). Formal Specification Languages in Knowledge and software Engineering. Knowledge Engineering Review, Vol 9, No4.

[8] M.R. Garey, D.S. Johnson (1979). Computers and Intractability - A Guide to the Theory of NP-Completeness. W.H. Freeman and Co., San Francisco.

[9] N. Guarino and P. Giaretta, Ontologies and knowledge bases: towards a terminological clarification, In: N.J.I. Mars ed., *Towards Very Large Knowledge Bases* (IOS Press 1995).

[10] F. van Harmelen and A. ten Teije (1997). Validation and Verification of Conceptual Models of Diagnosis. Proceedings EUROVAV'97, Katholieke Universiteit Leuven, Belgium.

[11] G. van Heijst, The role of ontologies in knowledge engineering, (Doctoral Thesis, University of Amsterdam, Amsterdam, The Netherlands 1995).

[12] Newell, The knowledge level, *Artificial Intelligence* 18 (1982) 87-127.

[13] J.F. Sowa (1984). Conceptual Structures: Information Processing in Mind and Machine. Addison-Wesley

[14] A.I. Vermesan (1997). Quality Assessment of Knowledge-Based Software: Certification Considerations. In Proceedings of Third IEEE International Software Engineering Standards Symposium (ISESS '97) Walnut Creek, CA.

Oslo and Liverpool, May 1999

KBS First Prototype V&V Process Plan as a Way to Produce Reliable Requirements

Jesús CARDEÑOSA, David ESCORIAL
Dpto de Inteligencia Artificial
Facultad de Informática – Universidad Politécnica de Madrid

Keywords: Knowledge Based Systems; Validation & Verification; Software Reliability; Methods of Processes; Requirements.

Abstract: The Quality Assessment Process is in charge of assuring several performances of the software products and processes. One of them is the Software Reliability, perhaps the closest concept to the more general of Quality. These Quality processes should be integrated with the product development and depend mainly on two issues. One is the development methodology and the other is the type of product. The Knowledge Based Systems (KBS) are products whose software production presents special difficulties for the Validation and Verification (V&) process application. Indeed, the knowledge characteristics they model, often incomplete, imprecise, inconsistent and uncertain, are solved by the application of heuristics whose validation is difficult to carry out without the systematic application of test cases. This makes that often the development of KBS goes through a life cycle based on prototypes to build a consistent core that can be modelled conceptually and formally. This article aims to describe the set of V&V process activities that can be applied to a KBS core, that is, the essential components of a V&V Plan. Indeed although this Plan is often not defined, it is essential to assure the reliability of the system requirements, result of the prototyping phase.

This paper was written with the support and financing of the Spanish Council for Research and Technology (CICYT) [Project TIC96-0883-CE]

1.   INTRODUCTION

The Quality Assessment Process is in charge of assuring several performances of the software Product and Processes. One of them is the Software Reliability, perhaps the closest concept to the more general of Quality [Gillies 92]. Then reliability is always associated to the lack of errors, and above all of critical consequences, but also to the precision in the system response. That is, speaking of reliability implies an idea of robustness of the system, of being hardly responsive to the environment. In all this, there are underlying concepts present in all the Software Quality Processes. However, this area does not only study the processes, Quality Assurance is always associated to the idea of Quality checking, tests and metrics, that is, setting when a product successfully complies with a series of predetermined requirements. Then the metrics are very linked to the products or sub-products derived from the software system.

One of the processes or rather concepts associated to the development of a software system as well as to the Quality Assessment are Validation and Verification [Cardeñosa 94], that are in charge of methodising the early phases of the Quality and Reliability process during the development.

These processes also have to be integrated with the development processes of the product or software system and for this, they essentially depend on two factors. One is the development methodology that integrates the Validation and Verification activities (V&V on the following) in some moment of the development. The other factor is the type of product or sub-product that, after all, is determined by a phase of the life cycle of this one.

Among the software products lacking of a clear definition or with a product taxonomy that qualitatively differ, the Knowledge Based System (KBS on the following) development presents special difficulties when applying the V&V processes. KBS more generally means the systems that separate the knowledge from the processes that handle it (Knowledge Base and Inference Engine respectively). But contrary to the people who have identified these systems as systems whose knowledge is represented in some of its more frequent formalisms (production rules), it is necessary that the no-algorithmic knowledge comes from an expert or an experience-based knowledge body.

Then, these systems, increasingly present in applications in all the fields, whether integrated with other systems or "stand-alone", present a series of peculiarities that affect the knowledge they model. We can summarise them as follows: incompleteness, imprecision, apparent inconsistencies at least, and uncertainty [Cardeñosa et al. 91]. These peculiarities are solved by the incorporation of heuristics whose validation is very awkward, without the systematic application of test cases.

This is one of the main reasons for the KBS development to be directed in many cases by a life cycle for prototypes so as to build initially a consistent knowledge core that can be modelled conceptually and formally [Boehm 88]. This approach of the life cycle aims to define a clear and consistent set of system requirements, question of great difficulty in a previous stage. As the definition of some requirements that assure the reliability of the whole system is essential, the V&V processes on this node are critical to assure that the system development is based on the Quality Assessment standard methods [O'Keefe et al. 87].

In the same way, as in the development of any software system, it is necessary to carry out a Quality Plan in which the V&V activities are included [Cardeñosa et al. 96]. In many cases, when the thing developed is the core to obtain the reliable requirements or prototype, this Plan is not drawn up, that is, no systematic tests are applied to the system. This is often for saving resources and for estimating that the requirement specification methods imply a sufficient validation. In this paper, we aim to describe the set of V&V process activities applicable to a KBS core, that is, the essential components of a V&V Plan for this type of system, obviated most of the time but essential to assure the reliability of the system requirements, result of the prototyping phase. This Plan, even if more reduced and more directed towards the conceptual consistency of the knowledge and the user tests, is essential for the purpose commented before.

2. THE V&V PROCESS

2.1 Preliminary definitions and "State of the Art"

It is not the point of this paragraph to define concepts that, in some way, the reader already understands. The essential concept in this paper is the one of Verification and Validation that have been subject to the more diverse definitions with significant differences if they refer to conventional software systems or to KBS. By "conventional systems", we mean those in which the knowledge they contain is sufficiently complete and precise to assure the absence of errors. These systems are normally those that reflect knowledge related to systems invented by the man, that is, they obey pre-existing and known principles or their grounds are the so-called "first principles". By "no conventional systems", we mean those in which there is one or several characteristics described in before as uncertainty, imprecision, incompleteness or inconsistency, and that end by requiring specific methods of conceptual and formal representation, usually heuristic methods. A prototype of these systems is the KBS whose specificity has been under study for more than ten years. In the early 80s, the inherent necessities of these activities were raised in diverse forums on the Classic Software Engineering point of view. Then Wilburn [Wilburn 85] who followed, in some way, the more classic guidelines drew up a simple but clear definition of the V&V activities. In the late 80s, a North American project, the EVA project [Chang et al. 90], and another of the European Commission, the VALID project [VALID 89], [Cardeñosa 95], dedicated resources to clarify the terminological and methodological questions of these V&V processes. We will not describe them in details but we can say that they did not really impose their taxonomy and definitions, and as a result, some time later, new projects on this subject were raised by the European Commission (all of them within the ESPRIT Information Technologies programme) like the VITAL [Rouge et al. 93] and the VIVA [Craw et al. 95], [VIVA 95]. The later was terminated recently, it is perhaps the clearest and most complete as for the term definitions as well as the methodological questions, and it is compatible with the European Space Agency Standards. The Verification process is associated to a series of activities to carry out during the different phases of the system development so as to check the absence of errors. Therefore, we can say in a very general way that, given that the whole system obeys user requirements and that, as a result, system requirements are defined, by *Verification*, we mean *the set of activities aiming at checking that the system (products and sub-products) is adapted to the system requirements* (question that gathers the physical system correction as well as the lack of errors).

Likewise, by *Validation*, we mean *the set of activities in charge of checking that the system is adapted to the environment and user requirements*, being essential then the tests on the functional requirements among others [IEEE 1012], [IEEE 1008] and [O'Keefe et al. 87].

A specific term of this paper is that of the "**core of a KBS**". The idea of core is not strict but rather intuitive. This idea is also that of "first prototype". We can find some references as [O'Keefe et al. 90] [Gomaa 83]and [Bischofberger et al. 92], but the intuitive idea is easy to understand. A core, particularly in a KBS, is the minimum part of a Knowledge Base that can operate consistently and is able to solve a number of predetermined test cases. The objective is to determine if the study of the knowledge, its conceptual and formal modelling and even its basic implementation are adequate for the rest of the system. Other authors called it "experimental prototype" and it is more than present in the life cycle of this type of systems that integrate the idea of evolutional prototype with the Validation and Verification activities [Bohem 88], [Gomaa 83] and [O'Keefe et al. 90]. As this core is used to study it and check or evaluate its future effectiveness, on rare occasions a **Validation Plan** is drawn up, and then its examination is "ad-hoc" to the situation and often not very rigorous. An example of lack of rigour is when a prototype is developed having in view the requirement of a domain composed by a determined number of cases. Then the only V&V process consists of checking that the program solves correctly and exclusively these cases. The problem of this approach with respect to the V&V process is that generally the program solving these cases has been developed without a methodical analysis process, knowledge modelling nor other tasks proper to the development of a prototype. There is a system, it runs with these cases (and not others) and it works, but some things are lacking. This paper will propose a scheme of how to draw up a V&V Plan for this core so as to assure that the requirements obtained from the Prototype or Core are correct.

The idea of Quality Plan includes among other things the drawing-up of a V&V Plan that, on the other hand, is explicitly quoted on the standards [IEEE 1012] and [IEEE 730]. These plans are almost always applied on processes and products, not on prototypes. A prototype should not be considered as a product and not even as a sub-product with respect to Quality Assurance. By core, we mean an *"embryo system"* but that is not a reason for requiring less to this system. It is important to take into account that the core is the element on which the system can evolve and if the system is not complete, it cannot be tested on real environments. It is maybe why its inspection has to be especially careful.

2.2   The V&V general Process

The V&V process approach has to be made under two points of view or factors. First, there is the observation that this process forms an essential part of the global Quality process of the Organisation with the quality policies adopted. These Quality policies are those that generate a set of documents related to this question, such as the Quality Manual, and within it, the Quality Plan. On the other hand, partly because of these policies and partly because each product has more or less its own method, a development methodology will have been adopted for each type of product or sub-product. Depending on how this methodology is, a series of activities focussing on the process under study will have been selected.

Under these two points of view, this flow is apparently of inverse sense but in fact it obeys the process of refining of the quality objectives of the whole Organisation. We can see a scheme in Figure 1.

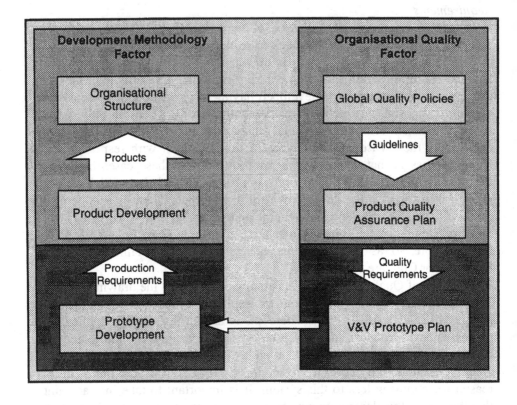

Figure 1. Quality Product Cycle for KBS prototype development

The dark grey parts of the figure are in general the ones that lack a "V&V Prototype Plan", and that make that the Production Requirements are not as reliable as required, that is, the influence of the general procedures is low in the development of the first KBS prototype, since normally the project Engineer adopts a freer and less formal behaviour.

Within the view of the V&V process we are dealing with, the development Methodology is a factor of more influence. Then, it is the first information to consider to situate the V&V Plan in the prototype Workplan. We will not describe methodology methods already very well-known by the readers. Besides, these methodologies have been merging in one way or another towards the previous development of an evolutionary and rarely discardable prototype. The classic activities are the following:

– **Problem identification,** (Global requirements)
– **Conceptualisation,** (Analysis and synthesis)
– **Formalisation,** (Design)

– **Implementation**, (Codification)

And in some occasion, Validation is added gathering all the activities that we call V&V without specifying any moment. Within these four essential phases in the development of KBS prototypes, there is a first phase in which a tentative of system requirements is already made, it is called the Problem Identification phase. A detailed description of the contents and documents to produce in this phase can be found in [Cardeñosa 93]. However, we can summarise briefly its content. Our long and positive experience has been based on the systematic production of three documents before the development of any type of prototype, such as:

Environment document
This document will focus on the detailed description of the organisational environment that has generated the problem and detected the need to solve it using a Knowledge-Based System. This document should contain as many documents as necessary to describe the organisation in which the problem has arisen and should make perfectly clear which department detected the need to solve the problem using a software product.

Problem document
This document deals with the description of the problem itself (the above refers to the environment in which it arises), and it is recommended it contains at least the following points which may be of use in its production:
– Basic description of the problem to tackle. Without going into too many details, this description should give an understanding of the problem.
– Identification of the type of problem. Once the problem has been described, it is studied to see which reasoning methods we estimate we will use to solve it.
– Justification of the need for a prototype. (Should it be deemed most suitable). Here we have assumed that it is the case. However, at this point of the problem analysis, it is impossible to ensure this from the offset.
– Evaluation test. This part of the document focuses on the application of some of the existing techniques that establish whether the application of KBS technology is suited to the problem.

Scope document
The definition of scope applied to the sub-problem that supports the prototype is often considered useless and sometimes immensely difficult. The reason is none other than the fact that prototyping is due to the impossibility of clearly define what is to be done and how to go about it in

the case of the problem selected. Although the idea of scope directly affects the definition of some minimum requirements for the system –and it is pretty difficult to define them at this stage in the development process–, there may already be environmental conditions forcing the developer to assume a minimum compromise.

Considering that the other phases are not strictly sequential but that they have a high degree of feedback and overlapping, the documents are produced on the level of conceptual (or functional) design, physical design (or architecture), and implementation (or codification).

On the other hand, the Workplan obeys a follow-up of the products or sub-products of each phase that obviously depends greatly on the method followed. A first task that we will not describe in details here is to check the existence and contents of the documents associated to each phase of the prototype development, so they will be perfectly defined on the Workplan level. A more detailed description of the contents can be found in [Cardeñosa et al. 96].

To terminate this heading, we have to distinguish between V&V activities independent of the development phase and others depending on it. They will be the basis of the V&V Plan.

3.   VALIDATION PLAN FOR A KBS FIRST PROTOTYPE

In this point, we are going to indicate the minimum specific tasks that this Plan has to propose. We will not follow any determined order since each phase will be executed when the conditions of applications (Input) are fulfilled.

Each task will of this V&V Plan will obey a common format that will be at least:

Table 1. Format of the tasks of the V&V Plan

<Name>:	Name of the task
<Objectives>:	Description of why this task is carried out
<Team>:	Who carries it out
<Entries>:	Pre-conditions that have to be fulfilled for the task to be carried out
<Output>	Product derived from the execution of the task
<Techniques>:	Techniques to use

The general scheme of the Plan has two blocks derived from:

Table 2. Tasks of the V&V Plan

TASKS INDEPENDENT OF THE DEVELOPMENT PHASE				
Name	**Objectives**	**Team**	**Input**	**Output**
Generic Validation of Documentation	To assure a complete, consistent and readable documentation.	Internal to the developer	All the documents produced	Anomaly Report and Changes suggested
V&V Management	V&V Planning and follow-up. Centralisation of the anomaly processing.	Internal V&V Engineer, Head of Project	All the internal reports generated for the V&V tasks	V&V Final Report
Configuration Control	Registering of Anomalies. Change Control and Validation.	Internal V&V Engineer, Knowledge Engineer, Head of Project	Software and Documentation produced according to the Workplan Anomaly Reports	Change Report
TASKS DEPENDING ON THE DEVELOPMENT PHASE				
Name	**Objectives**	**Team**	**Input**	**Output**
Identification	Verification of the system performances and constraints. Inspection of acceptation test cases.	Internal V&V Engineer	Identification Doc.: - Environment Doc. - Problem Doc. - Scope Doc.	V&V Report, Anomaly Reports
Conceptualisation	Validation of the Knowledge acquisition and of the conceptual model	Internal V&V Engineer, Knowledge Engineer, Expert	Acquisition Doc., Conceptual Model (Object-Attribute-Value table, Object Model, Glossary, Process Model and Knowledge Map)	V&V Report, Anomaly Reports
Formal Design	Logic Verification of the Knowledge Base structure. Formalism Validation and user interface design.	V&V Engineer, Knowledge Engineer, (Development team). External V&V Engineer	Formal Design Doc. Knowledge Base	V&V Report, Anomaly Report
Implementation	Checking that the design has been correctly implemented	V&V Engineer, Knowledge Engineer, (Development team).	Formal Design Doc. Software of the core (Documentation, Source code and binaries)	V&V Report, Test Doc. Validation, Report of the core, Anomaly Report

Each one of these tasks is associated to a set of subtasks that are basically of three types:

a) Those that try to assure the tests on the sub-products generated.
b) Those that examine the development processes and sub-processes.
c) Those that focus on the clarity and completeness of the work documentation not specified in the Workplan.

Besides the subtasks, the Plan adds a series of Application and Recommendation procedures.

We will try to illustrate this approach with a small example of some tasks that would belong to the V&V Plan.

A task independent of the development phase would be:

Task: *Generic Validation of Documents*

– Check that there is a format for each type of document and that it is applied correctly.
– Check that the document is in the Workplan.
– Check the document legibility. (All the persons to which it is addressed have to be able to understand it and this implies that each document has, to clearly settle who its addressees are).
– Check that the security and confidentiality have been maintained (A person not entitled should not have accessed it).
– Check the document consistency with the documents generated in previous phases (there should not be contradictions in the contents).

A report from the V&V team associated to this task for a concrete document, could be:

Anomaly-1: In the format of this document, you have to indicate the date associated to the production of each version. This document presents the same version as one with a previous date.
Corrective action: Revise versions and dates according to the defined formats.
Comments: It is maybe due to the use of a template with automatic date updating.
Recommendation: Do not use this type of templates for the documents.

Anomaly-2: The document title does not correspond to anyone defined in the Workplan.

Corrective action: Check if it is a change in the title of some document of the Plan already defined or if this document was not included in the Workplan. Check the possible deviations of the resources.

Comments: It can be a mere change in the title.

Recommendations: A greater follow-up of these details by the persons in charge of the production of these documents.

A task depending on the development phase could be:

Task: *Validation of the Document "Design of the object model and Object/Attribute/Value tables"*

The following aspects should be checked:

– The names of an object attributes have to be the same as those used by the experts. (Check the Dictionary of Terms – Check-List)
– The attributes associated to an object have to strictly characterise this object.
– There should not be repetitions of attributes for different objects of the same class.
– There should not be any object, nor attribute, nor value that do not belong to the problem domain. All of them have to be explicitly collected in the Dictionary of Terms.
– There should not be any attributes without assigned values.
– The validity of the test cases generated artificially has to be corroborated by the experts.
– The values of an attribute have to be completely specified.

The **Anomaly Report** could be:

Anomaly-1: We have found an attribute present in all the members of a same class.

Corrective action: Pass this attribute to the "father" object or class except in case of a justified reason.

Recommendation: Even if it is justified, try to avoid these situations.

Anomaly-2: We have found an attribute that does not define the rank of values, these ones following a continuous function.

Corrective action: Define clearly the rank of values of this attribute or if they cannot be represented in a discrete way, specify the totality.

Recommendation: Define a calculation formula or method associated to the determination of the values.

In short, each document defined in the Workplan, or each development activity of the prototype core will have to be strictly documented in accordance with the Plan. For each activity or task, it is necessary to produce the Anomaly Reports together with the V&V Reports that confirm that the corrective actions proposed have been carried out.

4.   CONCLUSIONS

This paper makes several contributions. Firstly, we have described in a defined way the "Core" of a KBS which is not exactly a prototype but an early stage of this one. We have also shown the crucial importance of the application of the V&V process to this "Core" and we have indicated how it is integrated within the product life-cycle. Thirdly, we have described and expounded in details examples of the application of this V&V Plan. Concretely, we have described the three main documents to produce in the early stages of the KBS Prototype Development (Core) and we have illustrated with two examples the different activities of the V&V process whether they are dependent or independent of the development.

It is worthwhile mentioning a special fact for the implantation of a KBS product such as the certification [Vermesan 87] that is associated to the fulfilment of some organisational or Quality requirements. In this sense, we can say that the "Core" or early KBS Prototype is not a product in itself and thus it is not submitted to certification requirements. However, it is worthwhile observing that the requirements obtained from the rigorous application of the V&V process are really important for the certification of the future product.

ACKNOWLEDGEMENTS

We thank Miss Christèle Legeard for her work of integration and revision of this paper.

REFERENCES

Boehm, B. W. (1988), "A spiral model of software development and enhancement". *IEEE Computer*, pp. 61-72, May.

Bischofberger, W., Pomberger, G. (1992), *Prototyping Oriented Software Development Concepts & Tools,* Springer-Verlarg.

Cardeñosa, J & al. (1991), "The Application of Deep Models in Industrial Expert Systems". *Expert Systems with Applications*, Pergamon, Vol. 2, Number 2/3, pp. 187-194.

Cardeñosa, J. (1993), "Towards a Clarification of Concepts and Terminology for KBS. An Example: Production of User Requirements Documentation". *In: Proc. of TKE'93: Terminology and Knowledge Engineering.* Springer Verlag, Cologne, Germany, pp. 8-15.

Cardeñosa, J. (1994), "Validación de sistemas basados en el conocimiento", *Fronteras de la Informática.* Real Academia de Ciencias Exactas, Físicas y Naturales. D. Maravall Casesnoves y D. Maravall Gómez-Allende (Eds), Madrid, pp 191-210, ISBN: 84-600-8920-7.

Cardeñosa, J. (1995), "VALID: An Environment for Validation of KBS". *Expert Systems with Applications*, Vol. 8, N. 3, pp. 323-331.

Cardeñosa, J.; Pastor, G. (1996), "Towards a Positioning of the VVT Process in the Software Quality Processes". *In: Proc. of the AAAI-96 Workshop on Validation and Verification of KBS and Subsystems,* Portland, USA, August, pp. 109-114.

Chang, C. L.; Combs, J. B.; Stachowitz, R. A. (1990), "A Report on the Expert Systems Validation Associate (EVA)". *Expert Systems with Application,* Vol. 1, N. 3, pp. 217-230.

Craw, S.; Sleeman, D. (1995), "Refinement in Response to Validation". *Expert Systems with Applications*, Vol. 8, N. 3, pp. 343-349. 1995.

Gillies, A. C. (1992), *Software Quality: Theory and Management.* Ed. Chapman & Hall. London.

Gomaa, H. (1983), "The Impact of Rapid Prototyping on Specifying User Requirements", *ACM Software Engineering.* April, Notes 8,2.

IEEE-STD-730. (1995), *Standard for Software Quality Assurance Plans,* Software Engineering Standards Committee of the IEEE Computer Society.

ANSI/IEEE-STD-1008-1987. (1986), *IEEE Standard for Software Unit Testing,* IEEE Computer Society. Software Engineering Technical Committee.

IEEE-STD-1012, Reviewed. (1992). *Standard for Software Verification and Validation,* Software Engineering Standards Committee of the IEEE Computer Society.

O'keefe, R. M.; Balci, O.; Smith, E. P.. (1987). "Validating Expert System Performance". *IEEE Expert,* US, Vol. 2, Num. 4, Winter, pp.81-90.

O'keefe, R. M.; Lee, S. (1990), "An Integrative Model of Expert System Verification and Validation". *Expert Systems with Applications*, Vol. 1, pp.231-236.

Rouge, A.; Lapique, J. Y.; Brossier, F.; Lozinguez, I. (1993), Validation and Verification KADS Data and Domain Knowledge". *In: Proc. of the European Symposium on V&V of KBS.* Palma, Spain, pp. 69-83.

VALID (1989). *Technical Annex.* VALID Project, ESPRIT II n° 2148. European Commission.

Vermesan, A. I. (1997). "Knowledge-Based Systems: Verification and Validation in Support of Certification", *In Proc. of the European Symposium on V&V of KBS 97,* Leuven, Belgium, pp. 71-81.

VIVA. (1995) *Verification, Improvement and Validation of KBS.* VIVA Project, Esprit II 6125. *Deliverable 4: The VIVA Framework for V&V of KBS.* Softlab, Austria.

Wilburn, N. P. (1985), "Software Verification for Nuclear Industry", *In: Proc. of the ANS on computer Applications for Nuclear Power Plant Operation and Control*, September, Tri-Cities (Pasco), Washington. pp. 229-235.

On Principles of Knowledge Validation

Mieczyslaw L. Owoc, Malgorzata Ochmanska and Tomasz Gladysz
Department of Artificial Intelligence Systems. Wroclaw University of Economics
ul. Komandorska 118/120, 53-345 Wroclaw, Poland
E-mail: {mowoc,ochmansk, gladysz}@manager.ae.wroc.pl
Phone: ++4871-3680513, Fax: ++4871-3679611

Motto:*The golden rule is that there are no golden rules. (G.B. Shaw)*

Key words: Knowledge validation, knowledge verification, knowledge evaluation, validation criteria, knowledge validation principles

Abstract: Validation is a critical process in the whole knowledge-based system life cycle. A knowledge base incorporated into such systems has to be verified or (more generally) validated. There have been many approaches to develop specialised procedures and techniques, aimed at assuring the highest level of knowledge quality. Keeping in mind "knowledge validation mappings", we believe a more global view is necessary to facilitate applying the proper techniques, so the paper deals with *practical guidelines of knowledge validation* (KV). Facing the most popular techniques of KV: decision tables-based, decision trees-based or nets-based with the criteria set to be utilised, we try to define certain *principles* useful in the validation procedures referring to two levels: *general and detailed*. The first one refers to paradigms, which arise from interrelationships among the crucial components of the KV process (procedures, approaches and criteria). The detailed principles are addressed to specific forms used for knowledge representations: rules, frames, neural nets and others.

1.   INTRODUCTION

Knowledge and inference are considered to be the crucial components of more intelligent systems. A knowledge base incorporated into such systems has to be verified or (more generally) validated. Five properties of knowledge: *distribution axiom, knowledge axiom, positive and negative introspection axioms and knowledge generalisation rule* (known as S5 properties) have been proposed in [FAHA95], however its applicability is not convincing for more practical approaches. There are some proposals to solve this problem, mostly presented as specialised procedures and techniques, in which knowledge desirable properties have been determined. Completeness and consistency are commonly recognised, though the criterion list should be widened by: knowledge adequacy, reliability and economy ([BONN98] and [OWOC98a]). In spite of the announced "end of science" [HORG96], researchers look desperately for some methodologies and even theories, which can be applied in the defined scopes (including the knowledge validation process).

Keeping in mind the whole "knowledge validation mappings" we believe a more global view is necessary to facilitate applying the proper techniques, so the paper deals with practical guidelines of knowledge validation. Looking at the most popular techniques of KV: graph- tree- or table-oriented, we try to define certain principles useful in the validation procedures referring to two levels: general and detailed. Specific dependence of knowledge verification criteria in contrast to independence of knowledge evaluation criteria are examples of the general principles. Complete validation of procedural forms of KBs or limited validation of neural nets are examples of detailed principles. Naturally, each of the individual techniques can be used for specific, more precisely defined conditions, however more universal principles can be formalised as above.

The initial section of the paper is devoted to the presentation of the approaches, used in practice - they cover two crucial areas: verification and evaluation. Then, assumptions of KV principles are considered: objective, range and structural. The basic part contains discussion on the KV principles, stressing their nature and scope. The principles are grouped at two levels: general and detailed ones. In such understanding, the principles seem to be necessary for knowledge representation in a wider sense or knowledge management [JAOW98].

2.   KNOWLEDGE VALIDATION APPROACHES OVERVIEW

Despite of the still not totally, concluded discussions on knowledge validation interpretations, there is a commonly accepted opinion of its importance in the life cycle of knowledge-based systems. Among the software community, validation is interpreted as *"building the right product"*, verification as *"building the product right"*. After [LAUR92] we assume the validation process can be considered as some determined composition of two kinds of tasks:

– activities that intend to reach the structural correctness of the KB (***verification***),

– activities that intend to demonstrate the KB ability to reach correct conclusions (***evaluation***).

On the other hand, validation refers to different components of a knowledge-based system. We can validate a knowledge base, inference engine, an user interface etc. In our paper we focus on validation of knowledge, especially on validation of a knowledge base. In the validation process, two sorts of activities mentioned – verification and evaluation - are complementary and therefore different methods to reach their goals are applied. Figure 1 depicts some details of a knowledge validation infrastructure.

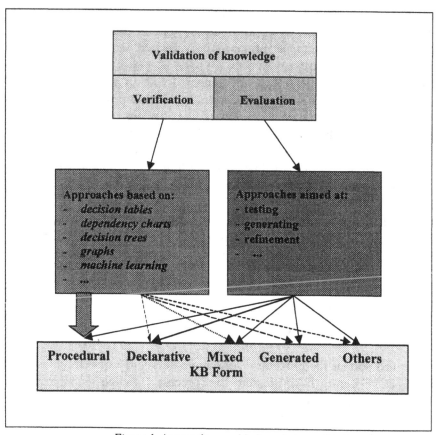

Figure 1. Approaches used in knowledge validation

There are a lot of approaches defined for verification of a knowledge base. They can be supported by specific techniques to facilitate performance of the procedure, basically by transformation of a KB onto decision tables or trees, some graphical forms or even by activation machine learning techniques (see for example: [CRST87], [SUMU94], [VADR93],[LIDI92], [NAZA91], [CODU97] or [LOUN95]). Most of them refer to knowledge bases represented as rules (RB - representative of procedural formalisms), so using the proper KB representation formalism is important. After the transformation of the rules into one of the mentioned indirect form, completeness and consistency tests are defined for the transformed bases. This main stream of interests (verification approaches-procedural form of KB) has been marked with a bold arrow. The other forms of KB representation (declarative, KB generated) are rather not applicable for the described procedure (marked with dashed arrows).

The second group of the approaches belongs to the evaluation procedure. According to the purpose of evaluation - to ensure the KB ability to reach correct conclusions - the main activity of the procedure is testing. As a result we try to satisfy the main criterion of the evaluation process - reliability. During testing, the system performance is compared with that of human expert recorded in test cases.

Then the results of KBS testing are compared with an acceptable level of performance defined in a KBS specification. In this group we can talk about approaches that support the evaluation process. When test cases are not available they can be generated using different methods of test case generation. Thus, random test or structure-based test cases generation is applied. A separate kind of evaluation procedure is refinement, which can be supported by the mentioned generators or an empirical approach may be employed [ZLPR94].

The need for some guidelines arises from this general overview. This is obvious, as not all approaches can be used for any KB form and there are "blank" places on the map of the KV process.

3.   ASSUMPTIONS OF FORMULATING KNOWLEDGE VALIDATION PRINCIPLES

KV is this sort of the process which presents us with some troublesome features. D. O'Leary has stressed the process can be expressed as probabilistic, "fuzzy" and it is performed by team-work. [OLEA94]. All the mentioned characteristics of KV create a rather complex base to determine the practical guidelines of performing the appropriate activities. On the other hand, regarding procedures and techniques supported by knowledge validation criteria (and combined into useful set of approaches) in a structural way, we obtain quite a good position for the more global view. This section is concerned with setting the assumptions essential for principles adequate for KV performing. In other words, we intend to discuss the framework of objectives undertaken in this paper (see: [OWOC99]).

The first issue is to establish acceptable objects which can be considered in the validation process. There are several techniques (or languages) useful for the description of the forms of knowledge existence (starting from domain knowledge via modelling tasks to a coded knowledge base). Undoubtedly, most of the practical approaches are limited to validation of the last form - a knowledge base and moreover rule bases are concerned as the main objective. However, the need for knowledge presentation in many forms (i.e. heterogeneous knowledge representation) is commonly accepted and in such a context we have to respect this. Taking into account all the basic forms of knowledge and all possible formalisms, we assume the following interpretation of knowledge validation objects (the **objective assumption**):

$KV^O \in \sum KS_i$ expressed by some formalism

where:

KV^O - an object of knowledge validation

KS_i - any stage of knowledge; i={domain knowledge, a model of knowledge, a knowledge base}

Obviously, an object of validation has to be chosen rationally, i.e. to fit procedures or approaches to be employed. Thus, knowledge is not limited to a specific stage or its defined form.

The second issue concerns knowledge the validation scopes and it can be understood as a form demarcation referential limits (see details in [OWOC96]). In knowledge validation practice, we focus rather on knowledge items (local) than on the whole formalised and even potential knowledge, which can be applied to generate expertise (global) - [OWOC98]. Considering the *local validation*, we take into account any piece of knowledge as the validation object which leads us to partial verification. Regarding *global validation*, where the whole formalised KB is confronted with potential useful knowledge, we focus on special properties of knowledge (complete evaluation). On the other hand, static and dynamic perspectives must be considered to assure knowledge actuality. The first *static* diversification refers to knowledge forms of a current state. Regarding *dynamic* scope of a knowledge base we deal with its changes in time (see SCGE88]). The views stated above we call the **range assumption** (i.e. both of KV dimensions covering referential aspects, respectively global-local and static-dynamic). Formally the range arrangement can be expressed in the following way:

$$KV^R \rightarrow \{KVP^{rs}, KVP^{rt}\}$$
where:

KV^R - range of knowledge validation

KVP - knowledge validation procedure (verification, evaluation)

^{rs} - scope-oriented reference (local or/and global) of KVP

^{rt} - time-oriented reference (static or/and dynamic) of KVP

In the previous section we have presented approaches applied in validation of knowledge. In order to elaborate the general framework of KV process we need to encompass them into more global sight (reflecting "mappings" of the KV methodology). Therefore we have to set the main components of the KV process, indicating interrelationships among them. In the same way we can define a context of KV principles, which can be regarded as the **structural assumption.**

$$KV^S = \langle Prs, Apps, Crs, KV^{CR} \rangle$$

where:

KV^S - KV components (structure)

Prs - KV procedures (verification and evaluation)

Apps - KV approaches (decision tables, decision trees, ...)

Crs - KV criteria (completeness, consistency, adequacy, ...)

KV^{CR} - KV components relationships (procedure-approach, approach-criterion, procedure-criterion ...)

All the itemised KV components are presented in Figure 2.

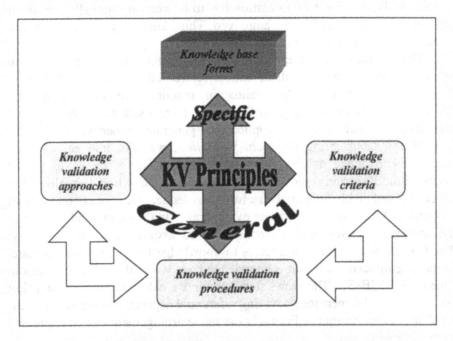

Figure 2. Knowledge validation principles context

The central part of the figure shows the place and sorts of KV principles. Apart from structural assumptions, knowledge base forms complete the crucial determinants of the elaborated principles.

The lower part of the figure shows components of KV which can be a base for the formulation of general principles. They are focused on pointing out some guidelines that arise from the structural assumptions of KV and therefore they are independent of knowledge forms. At the top of Figure 2 the specific principles are marked. These kinds of guidelines can be established as a consequence of knowledge base formalisms that are employed.

4. GENERAL PRINCIPLES OF KNOWLEDGE VALIDATION

To state specific "rules" for knowledge validation, conforming to the established assumptions, we will present a formal description of each of them, together with some comments. The list of these rules is presented in Table 1.

Table 1. General principles for knowledge validation

No	Knowledge Validation Principle
1.	Conformity of knowledge validation procedures and criteria
2.	Specific dependence of knowledge verification criteria
3.	Independence of knowledge evaluation criteria
4.	Unity of practical approaches to knowledge validation
5.	Complementarity of practical approaches for knowledge validation

1. According to the first rule: "conformity of knowledge validation procedures and criteria" particular criteria are assigned to the specific procedure. To be more precise: verification is identified with completeness and consistency, while the others (adequacy, reliability and economics) pertain to the evaluation procedure.
2. The second principle: "specific dependence of knowledge verification criteria" expresses potential interactions between two verification criteria: completeness and consistency. If we start from checking completeness (which can be effected by a rule set modification) and then check knowledge-base consistency, the final results of the verification may be different. Thus, we discover an impact of applied approaches on achieved knowledge base properties.

3. An output of the third principle - "independence of knowledge evaluation criteria" states: knowledge adequacy, reliability and economics can be treated as unconnected properties. As a consequence, the mentioned criteria and evaluation of knowledge can be tested and measured in any order.
4. The fourth rule - "unity of practical approaches to knowledge validation" determines the general assumption of the specific validation method. It arises from the detection of commonly known approaches presented in the third section of the paper. Each method has a strictly defined procedure, with stated input and output streams, which all constitute a unity.
5. According to the fifth general principle: "complementarity of practical approaches for knowledge validation" almost all methods are developed for a very specific purpose. Complete verification and evaluation require the application of more than one method (see: [OCHM98]). There are very few total solutions in this respect.

5.   KB FORM-ORIENTED PRINCIPLES

Apart from the general guidelines that have been expressed in the previous section, some regularities focusing on specific forms of KB can be observed. This part of the paper deals with more specialised principles addressed to particular KB formalisms. The starting point of our research is presented in Table 2.

Table 2. Objectives of KB form-oriented validation

KV Procedure -►	Verification		Evaluation		
KB Form ▼	Completeness	Consistency	Adequacy	Reliability	Economy
Procedural	!	!	!	!	!
Declarative	!	-	!	!	!
Mixed	!	?	!	!	!
Generated KB	?	?	-	!	!
Neural Networks	?	?	?	!	?

Key:
- not applicable (impossible to perform or achieved by nature of a KB form)
! necessary
? disputable

The essential components of the KV process are shown at the top of the table (verification and evaluation procedures with validation criteria pertaining to them), whereas the left column consists of typical KB formalisms. In crossing particular rows and columns, the symbols denote objectives of procedures and criteria assumed for each form of a KB. Instead of the "Others" KB form (compare Fig.1) we have introduced neural nets (NN). "Covering" of the particular KB form is different. In a case of the procedural form (rules) - all the dimensions of KV can be taken into account, while the lowest row, expressing NN - is "poorly" represented.

In Table 3 all principles addressed to the particular KB form have been demonstrated. Short comments for each of them are given follwing the table.

Table 3. Specific principles for knowledge validation

No.	Knowledge Validation Principle
1.	Complete validation of procedural forms of KR
2.	Quasi complete validation of declarative forms of KR
3.	Derivative validation of mixed forms of KR
4.	Originated validation of generated knowledge bases
5.	Partial and indirect validation of neural networks

1. The first specific principle - "complete validation of KB" denotes the possibility (and usually the necessity) of multi-criterial verification and evaluation of a knowledge base expressed by rules. All the developed approaches can be used in many ways to detect the achieved level of rule-based KBs: completeness, consistency, adequacy, reliability and economics. In other words, we have KV techniques good enough to check all the needed features of a KB. There are many concepts of how to transform rules into a more useful form and then how to verify or validate them. On the other hand, RB may suffer from many anomalies, so this "total" validation is reasonable.
2. Quasi complete validation of declarative forms of knowledge representation (i.e. semantic nets or object-attribute-value). Except consistency, which is achieved by nature of any declarative form, the other criteria are relevant to the process.
3. Derivative validation of mixed forms of KB arises from the basic components of frames: rules as well as declarative forms have an impact on the performance verification and evaluation of a KB.
4. Originated validation of generated knowledge bases (i.e. created with classification or genetic algorithms) can be labelled - "speciality of validation approaches applied to generated knowledge bases" and has been introduced to serve special types of knowledge bases (i.e. generated by machine learning means). These knowledge bases are characterised by specific properties (some anomalies are detected), therefore very sensitive approaches should be employed (see: [TACO97] and [OWGA98]).

5. The fifth specific rule - "partial and indirect validation of neural networks (NN)" means that in NN systems, knowledge is represented in the network structure by the connection between neurones and value of neurone weights. So according to the third section of this paper in NN case the object of knowledge validation (KV^O) is an already structured and trained neural network. With this representation of knowledge, nothing can be said about completeness, consistency, adequacy or economics. Testing the neural network by the examples out of a training set, one can check only reliability easily. To check other criteria we have to take neural network with training set and learning method (with specific parameters) as the object of knowledge validation. We can also go a step further. There are some techniques to extract a set of rules from an neural network. An addition these rules to KV^O would make it possible to use all procedures proper to rule bases.

All the proposed principles refer to one part of KB applications – a knowledge base. It is obvious that the proposal has to be confronted with the second component – inference engine to achieve the ultimate goal of KV.

6.   CONCLUSIONS

In this paper we argued the need for the development of some principles aimed at performing the knowledge validation process. Analysing the chosen interrelationships amongst the components, we have formulated principles with a more general range. They describe real and potential references among validation procedures and a set of criteria, stressing some usability aspects. The second group of principles is strictly oriented towards a particular form of knowledge representation. The range of KV activities depends on techniques used for knowledge acquisition and finally expressed with some formalism. A set of general and specific regulations is necessary to perform validation effectively, which stands in contradiction to G.B. Shaw's saying, quoted as the motto. We intend to formulate other principles which can be valuable in more complex environments (heterogenous knowledge-bases, multi-agents and the like) in future research.

REFERENCES

[BONN98] Bonner R.: Economics of Information and Acquisition of Knowledge. AE, Wroclaw. Prace Naukowe AE [Research Papers of the AE] no. 787, 1998.
[CODU97] Coenen F.P, Dunne P.E.: Verification and Validation of Rulebases using Binary Encoded Incidence Matrix Technique. EUROVAV-97, 4th European Symposium on the Validation and Verification of Knowledge Based Systems, Leuven, 1997

[CRST87] Cragun B. J., Steudel H. J.: A decision-table-based processor for checking completeness and consistency in rule-based expert systems. Man-Machine Studies, No. 26,1987.

[FAHA95] Fagin R, Halpern J.Y, Moses Y., Vardi M.Y.: Reasoning about Knowledge. The MIT Press, Cambridge, 1995.

[HORG96] Horgan J.: The End of Science. Facing the Limits of Knowledge in the Twilight of the Scientific Age. Addison-Wesley Publ. Co., 1996

[JAOW98] Jakubczyc J.A., Owoc M.L.: Knowledge Management and Artificial Intelligence. Argumenta OeconomicA, no. 1 (6), Wroclaw University of Economics, 1998.

[LAUR92] Laurent J.P.: Proposals for a Valid Terminology in KBS Validation. ECAI 92. 10th European Conference on Artificial Intelligence. John Wiley & Sons, Ltd., 1992.

[LIDI91] Liu N.K., Dillon T.: An Approach Towards the Verification of Expert Systems Using Numerical Petri Nets. International Journal of Intelligent Systems, Vol. 6,1991.

[LOUN95] Lounis H.: Knowledge-Based Systems Verification: A Machine Learning-Based Approach. Expert Systems With Applications, Val. 8, No. 3, 1995.

[NAZA91] Nazareth D.L., Kennedy M. H.: Verification of Rule-Based Knowledge using Directed Graphs. Knowledge Acquisition, 1991.

[OCHM98] Ochmanska M.: Komplementarnosc metod wartosciowania wiedzy [Complementarity of Knowledge Base Validation Methods]. AE, Wroclaw. Prace Naukowe AE [Research Papers of the AE] no. 787, 1998 (in Polish)

[OLEA94] O'Leary D.E.: A Probability of Fuzzy Events Approach to Validating Expert Systems in a Multiple Agent Environment. Expert Systems With Applications, Vol.7, No.2, 1994

[OWOC98] Owoc M.L.: From Local to Global Validation of a Knowledge Base. AE, Wroclaw, Prace Naukowe AE [Research Papers of the AE] No. 772, 1998

[OWOC98a] Owoc M.L. Measuring Aspects of Knowledge Validation. AE, Wroclaw. Prace Naukowe AE [Research Papers of the AE] no. 787, 1998

[OWOC96] Owoc M.L., Ochmanska M.: Limits of Knowledge Base Validation. EXPERSYS-96. Artificial Intelligence Applications. IITT - International Paris, 1996

[OWGA98] Owoc, M. L. , Galant V.: Validation of Rule-Based Systems Generated by Classification Algorithms, in: Proceedings of the Information Systems Development Conference, Bled'98 – Slovenia, Kluwer Academic/Plenum Pub., 1999

[OWOC99] Owoc M.L., Ochmanska M.: Towards Knowledge Validation Theory. AE, Wroclaw, Prace Naukowe AE [Research Papers of the AE] no. 815, 1999

[SCGE88] Schultz R.D., Geissman J.R.: Bridging the Gap Between Static and Dynamic Verification. Proc. of AAAI-88 Workshop on Validation and Verification Expert Systems. AAAI, 1988

[SUMU94] Suh Y., Murray T. J.: A Tree-Based Approach for Verifying Completeness and Consistency in Rule-Based Systems. Expert Systems With Applications, Vol. 7, No. 2, 1994.

[TACO97] Talavera L., Cortes U.: Inductive hypothesis validation and bias selection in unsupervised learning. EUROVAV-97, 4th European Symposium on the Validation and Verification of Knowledge Based Systems, Leuven, 1997

[VADR93] Vanthienen J. Dries E.: Illustration of a Decision Table Tool for specifying and implementing Knowledge Based Systems. Proc. of the Fifth International Conf. On Tools with A.I., 1993

[ZLPR94] Zlatarewa N., Preece A.: State of the Art in Automated Validation of Knowledge-Based Systems. Expert Systems with Applications Vol. 7, No.2, 1994

Progressive Instantiation for the Logical Validation of Nonmonotonic KBs

Éric GRÉGOIRE
CRIL Université d'Artois

Key words: nonmonotonic logics, local search, inconsistency handling

Abstract: Checking the logical (in)consistency of knowledge-based systems and components (*KBs*) is an important but computationally hard issue. In this paper, an effective technique is proposed to perform this task in an incremental way for first-order nonmonotonic *KBs*. It is based on a depth-limited instantiation schema and a powerful heuristic about local search when this last one fails to prove consistency. It allows various forms of depth-limited (in)consistencies to be checked for very large *KBs*. Most notably, it allows conflicting rules and data to be discovered and reported to the knowledge engineer.

1.   INTRODUCTION

The validation of knowledge-based systems and components (*KBs*) encompasses various issues. In particular, ensuring that *KBs* do not contain contradictory knowledge and data is of prime importance. Although the involved information can be represented using various formalisms that are not explicitly based on logic, such a task is related to logical consistency checking. When a *KB* is provided with a standard logic deductive inference mechanism, this issue is even more serious since any conclusion and its contrary can be deduced from the smallest pieces of contradictory information.

37

Unfortunately, checking logical consistency is a computationally costly task. When the *KB* is based on a representation language that corresponds to clausal propositional logic, it is NP-complete [Cook 71], meaning that it is exponential in the worst case (unless P=NP, which is highly improbable). However, thanks to the recently discovered efficiency of local search techniques that remains currently unmatched, a really dramatic progress has been obtained with respect to the size of propositional *KBs* that can be checked for (in)consistency (e.g. [Selman et al. 92, 93] [Mazure et al. 97a, 98a]). When first-order logic (FOL) *KBs* are considered, (in)consistency checking is even more difficult in the worst case since FOL is semi-decidable. Fortunately, we can often end up considering the finite Herbrand's semantics of these *KBs* as this latter semantics often matches the intended one. More generally, we agree with an increasing number of authors (e.g. [Selman et al. 97]) who believe that it is now viable to tackle many finite FOL problems by considering their instantiated propositional equivalent counterparts. However, a direct and full instantiation often leads to a combinatorial size blow up of the corresponding instantiated *KB*. Accordingly, finding task-specific instantiation schemata that limit the size of the resulting propositional instance and that prove adequate with respect to the initial problem is currently a hot research issue.

In this respect, the specific problem that we address here concerns the incremental construction of nonmonotonic consistent first-order *KBs*. Each time a new piece of consistent information *knowledge* is introduced into a consistent *KB*, the augmented *KB* should be shown consistent. This incremental approach to the construction and logical validation of *KBs* permits us to propose and study a form of progressive instantiation that is restrained to the possible interaction of *knowledge* and the previous contents of *KB*, only. This proves often viable for very large FOL *KBs*. The progressive instantiation corresponds to a progressively increasing number of reasoning steps that are allowed in the (in)consistency checking process. The important point is that when a proof of inconsistency is extracted at one instantiation level, it applies for the whole FOL *KB*. On the other hand, if the available time-resources are limited, we can make do with a guarantee that inconsistency will not occur within a preset limited depth in the reasoning steps. The *KB* is based on declarative knowledge representation FOL languages that can be multi-sorted (although the single-sorted case will often be considered for simplicity of presentation). Moreover, these *KBs* will be nonmonotonic, allowing forms of defeasible reasoning and knowledge to be encoded. In this respect, this paper extends a previous work [Brisoux et al. 98] whose scope covered standard monotonic first-order logic, only. The nonmonotonic formalism that we select offers a good trade-off between expressiveness and computational efficiency constraints: it is based on a preference models semantics and makes use of abnormality propositions *à la* McCarthy [McCarthy 86] to represent default rules and faulty behaviors of modeled components. This formalism underlies several forms of logical (in)consistencies that we discuss and handle in a way that is computationally effective (most often).

Accordingly, we resort to the power of local search in the propositional setting to perform the successive (in)consistency checks. Powerful heuristics in the use of local search allow us to detect the various forms of inconsistencies when they occur. Most notably, it allows conflicting rules and data to be discovered and reported to the knowledge engineer.

The paper is organized as follows. First, the selected nonmonotonic framework is presented, together with its various forms of (in)consistencies. The incremental instantiation schema and a concept of depth-limited (in)consistency from [Brisoux et al. 98] are then extended to the nonmonotonic case. Heuristics in the use of local search techniques are then presented that allow the various forms of (in)consistencies to be detected. Before the limits and perspectives of this work are outlined, some typical experimentation results are reported.

2. A NONMONOTONIC FRAMEWORK AND FORMS OF (IN)CONSISTENCIES

In a standard first-order monotonic setting, the rule asserting that all cars have four wheels would be represented by the $KB = \{\forall x \quad car(x) \Rightarrow four\_wheels(x)\}$. If the additional pieces of information $car(my\_car)$ and $\neg four\_wheels(my\_car)$ are introduced into KB then this one becomes inconsistent. Many approaches have been proposed these last twenty years to allow defeasible knowledge and default rules to be represented in a logical setting, and thus to avoid these cases of inconsistency. Here, we select a simple formalism that we claim to be a good trade-off between expressiveness, simplicity and computational efficiency perspectives. We simply enrich first-order logic with a finite set of McCarthy's [McCarthy 86] abnormality unary predicates **AB'** $=\{Ab_i$ s.t. $i \in [1..n]\}$. These predicates allow exceptions to rules to exist without the need to represent them explicitly. In the above example, we could encode the rule asserting that cars have four wheels by default, using $KB = \{\forall x \quad car(x) \wedge \neg Ab_i(x) \Rightarrow four\_wheels(x)\}$. Such formulas are interpreted under a model-preference semantics *à la* Shoham (we do not use the heavy circumscription apparatus here). Roughly, we shall infer a conclusion from KB iff it is *true* in all *preferred* models of KB, i.e. the models where Ab_i are interpreted *false* as much as possible. Given a car, we shall infer by default that it has four wheels. If we learn that it does not have four wheels, we shall simply consistently conclude that it is abnormal.

In the following a *KB* is viewed as a finite set of first-order clauses that are function-free and multi-sorted. Moreover, a *KB* can include existential formulas of a specific form. As usual in the data and knowledge base fields, we restrict ourselves to Herbrand interpretations, only. We thus consider a finite set **P** of predicate symbols of finite arities, including a set of abnormality unary predicates **AB'**, an infinite set **V** of variables and a finite non-empty set **T** of constants (non-constant functional symbols are not allowed). In the propositional case, we just have a finite set of *0*-arity predicates, called propositional variables. The logic is multi-sorted in the following way. Each ith argument of any predicate P of **P** can be a variable or a constant. In this last case, the constant must belong to a specific subset T_{Pi} of **T**. A predicate P together with its arguments is called an atom. An atom or a negated atom is called a literal. An atom or a literal without any variable is called ground. We shall note **AB** the set of ground atoms built on **AB'**. For sake of generality, we shall assume that a total pre-order applies on **AB**, allowing priorities to be represented between ground default rules. As a shorthand, we shall write ground abnormality predicates Ab(*ground_term*) using the simpler Ab_j notation where j is a positive integer expressing the preorder on **AB'**, and call Ab_j an abnormality proposition. In the same vein, an atom formed from the predicate P and its arguments is noted $P(\ )$ when there is no need to represent these last ones explicitly.

A clause is a finite disjunction of literals, of the form $P_1(\ ) \lor ... \lor P_n(\ ) \lor \neg Q_1(\ ) \lor ... \lor \neg Q_m(\ )$ where all variables are supposed to be universally quantified over their domains. A clause containing exactly one literal is called a unit clause. A clause (or a set of clauses) is said to be ground when it does not contain any variable. In the following, a *KB* is defined as a finite set of clauses and existential formulas of the form $\exists\ x_1, ..., x_t\ P_1(\ ) \lor ... \lor P_n(\ ) \lor \neg Q_1(\ ) \lor ... \lor \neg Q_m(\ )$ (where $x_1, ..., x_t$ are the only variables in the formula). Let us stress that a more explicit notation should stress that $x_1, ..., x_t$ variables should belong to the intersection of the domains of the corresponding predicate arguments for which they occur. This framework and the results in this paper could be easily extended to include the equality predicate.

The semantical counterpart of the logic is defined as usual. In the propositional case, interpretations are sets of propositional variables. Propositional variables inside this set are assumed *true* while the others are assumed *false*. A model of a *KB* is an interpretation that interprets *KB* as *true*, using usual compositional rules. In the first order case, interpretations are defined in the usual compositional way, using domains of interpretations, valuation function for variables and interpretation function allowing clauses to be interpreted as *true* or *false*. However, Herbrand interpretations are considered, only. The intuitive idea is that the domain of interpretation of *KB* should be restricted to the constants that occur in it. Accordingly, a Herbrand interpretation takes the only constants mentioned in the *KB* (i.e. the Herbrand domain) as domain of interpretation for variables and constants. Actually, we enlarge this set to include the constants occurring in the additional knowledge that will be introduced in *KB*. As the logic is multi-sorted, we keep in this semantic counterpart of the logic the constraint asserting that each ith argument of any predicate P of **P** that is a constant must be selected from a specific subset $\mathbf{T}_{Pi}$ of **T**. The Herbrand base is defined, modulo this constraint, as the set of all the ground atoms of the language. It is finite since we do not allow non-constant functional symbols. Accordingly, a Herbrand interpretation of *KB* will be any subset of the Herbrand base (all members of the subset interpreted *true* and the other ones *false*). A Herbrand model of the *KB* will be any Herbrand interpretation that satisfies the *KB*, i.e. that interprets the *KB* as *true*. Accordingly, we say that a *KB* is consistent if and only if there exists at least one Herbrand interpretation that satisfies it.

While standard deduction is defined in the usual way: $KB \models f$ iff f is *true* in all (Herbrand) models of *KB*, nonmonotonic inference is defined as follows. $KB \hspace{2pt} \vert\sim f$ iff f is *true* in all *preferred* (Herbrand) models of *KB*. For sake of generality, as we just study here the consistency issue, we do not make precise the preference concept. We simply assume that ground abnormality propositions are minimized, i.e. set to *false* as often as possible, taking into account the priorities expressed by the pre-ordering on **AB**.

3. DEPTH-LIMITED CONSISTENCY AND INCONSISTENCY

Like [Brisoux et al. 98], we shall tackle the consistency issue of a first-order $KB+ =_{def} KB \cup \{knowledge\}$ using a progressive and guided expansion of $KB+$ inside a propositional setting. In order to avoid an unmanageable direct exponential increase of size of the represented knowledge, we develop a depth-limited inconsistency/consistency concept that corresponds to a partial instantiation or expansion schema that limits the number of reasoning steps, guided by the additional knowledge that can introduce inconsistency. From a practical point of view, we rely on the following assumptions about practical situations; on the one hand, inconsistency is often due to a limited number of rules and facts, limiting the reasoning steps that are necessary to prove it. On the other hand, if the available time-resources are limited, we can make do with a guarantee that inconsistency will not occur within a preset limited depth in the reasoning steps.

Let us consider a consistent KB and some extra consistent *knowledge* to be included into KB. Let us also assume that both KB and *knowledge* contain at least one constant. Let $KB+ =_{def} KB \cup \{knowledge\}$ and let T_0 be the set of constants occurring in *knowledge*. Let KB_0 contain all ground clauses from $KB+$, augmented with the ground formulas obtained by the exhaustive instantiation of all existential formulas from $KB+$.

DEFINITION 1. [Brisoux et al. 98]
Depth-*i* consistency/inconsistency is defined in the following constructive inductive way.

Base $(i = 1)$
Let C_1 be the set of clauses from $KB+$ containing at least one predicate occurring in *knowledge*. Let $T_1 =_{def} T_0 \cup \{constants\ occurring\ in\ C_1\}$. Let $KB_1 =_{def} KB_0 \cup \{$ground clauses obtained by instantiating clauses in C_1 using T_1 instead of T as instantiation domain$\}$. We say that:
KB is depth-1 consistent (resp. inconsistent) iff KB_1 is consistent (resp. inconsistent)

Induction $(i > 1)$
Let C_i be the set of clauses from $KB+$ containing at least one predicate from C_{i-1}. Let $T_i =_{def} T_{i-1} \cup \{constants\ occurring\ in\ C_i\}$. Let $KB_i =_{def} KB_{i-1} \cup \{$ground clauses that can be obtained by instantiating clauses in C_i using T_i instead of T as instantiation domain$\}$. We say that:
KB is depth-*i* consistent (resp. inconsistent) iff KB_i is consistent (resp. inconsistent)

Let us now recall that this concept converges on the standard definitions of consistency and inconsistency (at least, when the logic is one-sorted. For simplicity of presentation, we shall now assume that the logic is one-sorted, although the following results can be extended easily to the multiple-sorted case).

LEMMA 1. [Brisoux et al. 98]
$\exists\ n\ s.t.\ KB_n$ is *stable*, i.e. $KB_n = KB_{n+1}$. (Such a fixed-point KB_n is noted KB_{end}).

THEOREM 1. [Brisoux et al. 98]
$KB+$ is consistent (resp. inconsistent) iff KB_{end} is consistent (resp. inconsistent).

Since $KB_i \subseteq KB_{end}$ for any i, we know that whenever KB_i is inconsistent then KB_{end} is inconsistent. Accordingly, at each instantiation step, when an inconsistency is encountered, it can be reported to the knowledge engineer as no further instantiation step will allow consistency to be recovered. On the contrary, no definitive proof of consistency is obtained until KB_{end} is shown consistent. In the nonmonotonic case, it can prove useful to refine the depth-i (in)consistency concept to shed light on the various roles that abnormality propositions can play in this respect.

DEFINITION 2.
Let $\mathbf{AB}(KB_i) =_{def} \{Ab_j$ s.t. $Ab_j \in \mathbf{AB}$ and (Ab_j and/or $\neg Ab_j$ occurs in clauses of KB_i)}
Let $\mathbf{AB\_true}(KB_i) =_{def} \{Ab_j$ s.t. $Ab_j \in \mathbf{AB}(KB_i)$ and $KB_i \models Ab_j\}$
Let $\mathbf{AB\_false}(KB_i) =_{def} \{Ab_j$ s.t. $Ab_j \in \mathbf{AB}(KB_i)$ and $KB_i \models \neg Ab_j\}$
Let $\mathbf{AB\_unsettled}$ (KB_i) $=_{def}$ $\{Ab_j$ s.t. $Ab_j \in \mathbf{AB}(KB_i)$ and $Ab_j \notin$ $\mathbf{AB\_true}(KB_i)$ and $Ab_j \notin \mathbf{AB\_false}(KB_i)\}$

LEMMA 2.
Let $i \in [1..end]$. We have that
$\mathbf{AB}(KB_i) = \mathbf{AB\_true}(KB_i) \cup \mathbf{AB\_false}(KB_i) \cup \mathbf{AB\_unsettled}(KB_i)$

Intuitively, $\mathbf{AB\_true}(KB_i)$, $\mathbf{AB\_false}(KB_i)$ and $\mathbf{AB\_unsettled}(KB_i)$ are containing the abnormalities that are necessarily *true*, necessarily *false* and unsettled with respect to KB_i, respectively (the propositions from the third set could thus be *independently* assumed *false* by default with respect to this instantiation level). Since standard deduction is monotonic and since any instantiation step only increases the resulting ground knowledge base, we have that:

THEOREM 2.
Let $i \in [1..end]$. We have that
$KB_i \subseteq KB_{end}$
$\mathbf{AB\_true}(KB_i) \subseteq \mathbf{AB\_true}(KB_{end})$
$\mathbf{AB\_false}(KB_i) \subseteq \mathbf{AB\_false}(KB_{end})$
Let $i \in [1..(end-1)]$. We do not necessarily have that
$\mathbf{AB\_unsettled}(KB_i) \subseteq \mathbf{AB\_unsettled}(KB_{i+1})$

This theorem is of great practical importance in the sense that if at any instantiation step, we find an inconsistency due to a conflict of information between elements of the sets KB_i, $\mathbf{AB\_true}(KB_i)$ and $\{\neg Ab_j$ s.t. $Ab_j \in \mathbf{AB\_false}(KB_i)\}$, inconsistency will remain with respect to the fully instantiated KB_{end} and thus for the whole FOL $KB+$. Accordingly, it could be useful to inform the knowledge engineer about such conflicts with respect to KB_i before larger ground knowledge bases are considered. In the following, we shall elaborate on this from a computational perspective.

Assume that the current instantiation step has given rise to KB_i. Several cases must be distinguished.

First, KB_i can be consistent. In this case, it seems useful to distinguish between two possible situations. On the one hand, abnormality propositions can be used in a very general way; they allow exceptions to exist with respect to rules in KB. On the other hand, they can be given a more restricted role in some applications and be used in the spirit of consistency-based diagnosis (see e.g. [Reiter 87] [Hamscher et al. 92] [Console et al. 84]), where they are intended to detect exceptions that should normally not occur (for instance, these latter ones express a fault in a device component or a process failure). In this latter case, abnormality propositions must be interpreted *false* at the building stage of the knowledge base.

DEFINITION 3.
Assume $\mathbf{AB}(KB_i) \neq \varnothing$.
KB_i is *no-fault consistent* iff $\mathbf{AB\_true}(KB_i) = \varnothing$.

Under this specific use of abnormality propositions, when KB_i is consistent while $\mathbf{AB\_true}(KB_i) \neq \varnothing$, it seems necessary to inform the knowledge engineer of the contents of $\mathbf{AB\_true}(KB_i)$. On the other hand, when $\mathbf{AB}(KB_i) \neq \varnothing$, no-fault consistency entails the consistency of KB_i, while the converse does not necessary hold. An even stronger constraint would ensure that all abnormality propositions already mentioned in KB_i and whose truth value is not settled, i.e. all elements of $\mathbf{AB\_unsettled}(KB_i)$, can be *simultaneously* assumed *false*.

DEFINITION 4.
KB_i is *consistent under no future fault circumstances* with respect to $\mathbf{AB}(KB_i)$ iff $KB_i \cup \{\neg Ab_j \text{ s.t. } Ab_j \in \mathbf{AB\_unsettled}(KB_i)\}$ is consistent.

Clearly, when KB_i is consistent under no future fault then KB_i is consistent whereas the converse does not necessarily hold. At first glance, when KB_i is consistent while it is not consistent under no future fault circumstances, we could think that it should be useful to ask the knowledge engineer to correct the information so that consistency under no future fault circumstances is ensured. However, several solutions might exist and forcing one particular solution by the knowledge engineer (unless KB_{end} is reached) is not necessarily a good idea since at a further instantiation step, another (conflicting) solution can be required to preserve consistency. For instance, we could have only two models for KB_i. In the first one, we interpret Ab_7 to *true* and Ab_9 to *false*, while in the second one we interpret Ab_9 to *true* and Ab_7 to *false*. If we adopt in a definitive way the first model by asking the knowledge engineer to correct the information leading Ab_7 to be *true* in this model, in a further step of instantiation, we might encounter an additional inconsistency that translates the fact that the second model was in fact the only possible one with respect to a superset of KB_i, and thus the only acceptable one with respect to KB_i. Accordingly, unless KB_{end} is reached, in the general case it is not useful to refine the consistency concept, using the no future fault circumstances one. Thus, when KB_i is consistent and when an interpretation of abnormality propositions *à la* consistency-based diagnosis applies, it might just be useful to check for no-fault consistency, only.

Let us thus now consider that KB_i is inconsistent and the more general role for abnormality propositions. Several causes of inconsistency must be distinguished.

DEFINITION 5.
We say that a *conflict between abnormalities* occurs with respect to KB_i iff
$(\textbf{AB\_true}(KB_i) \cap KB_i) \cap (\{\neg Ab_j \text{ s.t. } Ab_j \in \textbf{AB\_false}(KB_i)\} \cap KB_i) \neq \varnothing$.

THEOREM 3.
If a *conflict between abnormalities* occurs with respect to KB_i then $KB+$ is inconsistent.

Indeed, in the presence of a conflict between abnormalities in KB_i, we know that KB_i is inconsistent, which is subset of KB_{end}. Accordingly, these conflicts can be reported to the knowledge engineer, who is in charge to correct them, as early as they are detected. Assume now that all possible conflicts between abnormalities with respect to KB_i have been resolved by the knowledge engineer.

DEFINITION 6.
KB_i is said to be *strictly inconsistent* iff KB_i is inconsistent and no conflict between abnormalities does occur with respect to KB_i

THEOREM 4.
If KB_i is *strictly inconsistent* then $KB+$ is inconsistent.

Accordingly, the knowledge engineer is asked at this level to restore consistency of KB_i and this cannot always be achieved by reconsidering a set of rules and data that necessarily includes Ab_i propositions. We also know that no further instantiation step will solve this inconsistency. In this respect, informing the engineer about which clauses do actually conflict is useful in this case.

To summarize, the dynamics of the progressive instantiation schema does not prevent us from detecting specific forms of inconsistencies that can be solved at the time they are discovered. Accordingly, at each intermediate step of instantiation, we need to check the consistency of KB_i. If it is consistent then we move to KB_{i+1} unless a diagnosis-like interpretation of abnormality is under consideration. In this latter case, it is useful to find **AB_true**(KB_i). In case of inconsistency, we check for conflicts between abnormalities. When all of them are solved by the knowledge engineer, we can turn to strict inconsistencies and ask the knowledge engineer to solve them, before we proceed to the next instantiation step. In the following sections, this strategy will be reconsidered in regard of the computational aspects of its sub-tasks.

4.   COMPLETE AND LOCAL SEARCH FOR INCONSISTENCY CHECKING

Currently, the most efficient techniques for propositional (in)consistency checking are based on experimentally optimized versions of the so-called and well-known Davis and Putnam like procedures [Davis et al. 62] (in short, DP) whose general skeleton is given in Figure 1.

On the other hand, local search methods often prove more efficient for showing the consistency of large consistent instances. Let us describe them briefly. Most of them (mainly, GSAT and its variants [Selman et al. 92, 93, 97] [McAllester et al. 97] [Mazure et al. 97a]) perform a greedy local search for a satisfying assignment of a set of propositional clauses. The algorithms generally start with a randomly generated truth assignment of the propositional variables (i.e. assigns *true* or *false* to each propositional variable). Most of them then change (« flips ») the assignment of the variable that leads to the largest increase in the total number of satisfied clauses. Such flips are repeated until either a model is found or a preset maximum number of flips is reached. This process is repeated as needed up to a preset maximum of times. To escape from local extrema, local search algorithms are provided with additional variant (e.g. random) moves. In the following, a procedure called TSAT is used [Mazure et al. 97a, 98b]. It makes use of a tabu list forbidding recurrent flips and appears competitive in most situations. Let us stress that all results in this paper are not just TSAT-related, but seem valid for most local search techniques. Let us also stress that the initial interpretation of the first try is not selected in a random way in our application when the consistency of KB_i $(i > 1)$ is checked; instead, we start from a model of KB_{i-1}. Also, the initial interpretations of the successive tries are selected in a way that attempts to get the best coverage of the space of interpretations.

Procedure DP(KB_i);
Input: a set KB_i of propositional clauses
Output: *true* if a model of KB_i exists, or a definitive statement that KB_i is inconsistent
Begin
   Unit_propagate(KB_i);
   if the empty clause is generated **then return**(*false*)
   else if all variables are assigned **then return**(*true*)
      else begin
         p := some unassigned literal selected by a branching rule;
         return (DP(KB_i ∧p) ∨ DP(KB_i ∧¬p));
         end;
  End;

Figure 1. DP basic skeleton

Clearly, local search procedures are logically incomplete in the sense that they do not cover the whole search space (made of all the possible interpretations of KB_i) and cannot thus directly prove that a formula is inconsistent. Recently, we have discovered that the trace of local search algorithms can allow one to approximate smallest inconsistent minimal subbases very often when these algorithms fail to prove consistency within a preset amount of computing time [Mazure et al. 97b, 98a]. More precisely, for each clause, taking each flip as a step of time, the number of times during which this clause is falsified is updated. A similar trace is also recorded for each literal occurring in KB_i, counting the number of times it has appeared in the falsified clauses. When the local search technique fails to prove consistency, it appears extremely often that the most often falsified clauses most probably belong to minimally inconsistent subbases of KB_i if KB_i is actually inconsistent. Likewise, literals that exhibit the highest scores belong to these subbases. In this respect, focusing DP on these clauses and literals is often extremely efficient for proving that KB_i is actually inconsistent [Mazure et al. 98a, 98b]. Let us stress that this last result is only valid when the ratio between the size of the minimal inconsistent subbases and the size of KB_i is small, which is often the case in actual applications, and in particular in our incremental construction of consistent nonmonotonic KBs, where inconsistency is often due to a limited number of conflicting rules and data.

Accordingly, a two-steps strategy can often prove efficient for checking (in)consistency. First, a local search procedure is run. If consistency is established, then the process is over. If no model is found after a preset computing time, a complete search based on DP that focuses on the trace delivered by the failed local search is run to settle the (in)consistency status of KB_i.

5.   COMPUTING THE NONMONOTONIC CASE

In [Brisoux et al. 98], we have shown how the above two-steps strategy can prove experimentally efficient with respect to the incremental consistency/inconsistency issue for very large *monotonic KBs*. Addressing the nonmonotonic case as described here could be done in the same way, with no loss of efficiency (the worst-case analysis and the experimental efficiency of this two-steps strategy have already been established in the specific context of belief revision in [Bessant et al. 98, 99] and monitoring systems [Grégoire 99], at least in the nonmonotonic *propositional* case).

However, it appears necessary to adapt it in regard of the specific strategy that we propose for detecting various kinds of (in)consistency, taking computational considerations in consideration and making it dependent on the exact epistemological role of abnormality propositions: i.e. either a diagnosis-like one or a more general one that permits them to be *true*.

Let us focus on the more general case first. In order to detect conflict between abnormalities, we first check if (**AB_true**$(KB_i) \cap KB_i) \cap (\{\neg Ab_j$ s.t. $Ab_j \in$ **AB_false**$(KB_i)\} \cap KB_i) \neq \varnothing$. This can be done in a time that is linear in the number of abnormality propositions in KB_i. In case of consistency of KB_i, we can "saturate" KB_i with respect to entailed abnormalities by computing **AB_true**(KB_i) and $\{\neg Ab_j$ s.t. $Ab_j \in$ **AB_false**$(KB_i)\}$ and then by inserting these sets inside KB_i. This can be done using a number of NP-oracles that is linear in the number of abnormality propositions that occur in **AB**(KB_i) \ (**AB_true**$(KB_{i-1}) \cup$ **AB_false**(KB_{i-1})). In case of inconsistency, when no conflict between abnormalities occurs, we can turn our attention to strict conflicts. When the number of abnormality propositions is too large for this approach to be followed, another strategy would simply consist in checking the inconsistency/ consistency of KB_i using our two-steps strategy described in the previous section; namely, use the local search approach; the trace of the failed search often gives a good indication of the clauses that make the knowledge base inconsistent. This can be checked formally using DP, and the result can be reported to the knowledge engineer.

In the more specific use of abnormality propositions *à la* diagnosis, which requires these propositions to be *false*, another strategy can be adopted. Assume that we are considering KB_i and that at the previous step, $\{\neg Ab_j$ s.t. $Ab_j \in$ **AB_false**$(KB_{i-1})\}$ has been *possibly* introduced inside KB_{i-1}. Obviously enough, no unit clause (and thus no negated clause formed from **AB_false**(KB_{i-1})) is allowed to flip during a further local search process. First, a local search process is run on KB_i, with all abnormality propositions occurring in **AB**(KB_i) fixed to *false*. If consistency is shown, we move to the KB_{i+1} case (we can even try to find $\{\neg Ab_j$ s.t. $Ab_j \in$ **AB_false**$(KB_i)\}$ and introduce it in KB_i, but this is not compulsory). If we fail to prove consistency after a preset amount of computing time, we are given a useful trace. If KB_i is actually consistent, at least one abnormality propositions that was assumed to be *false*, must actually be *true*. This can be checked efficiently most often, as they necessarily occur in the most often falsified clauses when these ones form the smallest inconsistent subbases of KB_i. When these latter clauses do not contain any such abnormality propositions, then KB_i can only be strictly inconsistent.

Experimental results concerning the monotonic case have already been reported in [Brisoux et al. 98], illustrating both the progressive expansion of FOL *KB*+ and the actual efficiency of the computational approach with respect to each KB_i. Let us just illustrate the nonmonotonic case here, using a test (run on a 166 Pentium) that is a good representative of the size of the tested benchmarks and of the obtained computational results, when large KB_i are considered. For instance, we merged 5 large consistent *KBs* that are related to VLSI circuits [DIMACS 93] (namely, ssa-7522-{156, 157, 158, 159, 160}) with a small inconsistent Dubois' SAT instance [DIMACS 93]. The resulting inconsistent propositional KB_i contains 15929 clauses that are not necessarily Horn, using 7041 variables and is intractable for standard improved Davis and Putnam techniques [Davis et al. 62]. We restored the consistency of KB_i by introducing 1593 different Ab_i propositions in a random way inside KB_i (however, making sure that KB_i becomes consistent and using at most one abnormality proposition per clause). KB_i remains intractable using standard DP procedures; using TSAT we show within 4.6 seconds CPU time that it is consistent.

Assume abnormality propositions have here a specific role: they should not be required to be *true* for KB_i to remain consistent unless the knowledge engineer is informed of this situation. The first step consists in checking whether there exists a model for KB_i with all Ab_i set to *false*. TSAT (with its weight option, a tabu length set to 10, 10 tries and 10000 flips) is run on KB_i during 1min01s30. It fails to deliver a model (indeed, no such model does exist). Running a Davis and Putnam optimized procedure [Mazure et al. 98b] on this trace allows us to prove that no such model does exist, using 0sec94 CPU time. We set to *true* the abnormality proposition that occurs in the most often falsified clause that contains an abnormality proposition. Less than 6 sec. are required by TSAT to show that KB_i becomes now consistent. In less than 1 min, using a combination of TSAT and DP, we show that no other combination of *true* abnormality propositions would make KB_i consistent. Accordingly, we have found **AB_true**(KB_i), which appears to be a singleton and can be reported to the knowledge engineer.

6.   PERSPECTIVES AND CONCLUSIONS

Let us discuss the assumptions allowing this approach to be effective very often for very large first-order finite *KBs*. First of all, we think that consistency checking that is performed in parallel with the incremental construction of the *KB* is clearly a better practice than any a posteriori global checking. Obviously enough, each consistency check will thus be guided by the knowledge that is introduced. The progressive expansion schema allows inconsistency to be detected as early as possible, and with respect to small instantiated subparts of the *KB*. If the available time-resources are limited, we can make do with a guarantee that inconsistency will not occur within a preset limited depth in the reasoning steps. From a computational perspective, the approach is viable only when the minimally inconsistent propositional subbases of the instantiated *KB* remain of a tractable size for the best complete satisfiability checking techniques. These subbases translate the smallest chains of reasoning that can lead to a proof of consistency. As this limit is currently around a few hundred clauses [Selman et al. 97], this should allow most realistic application-oriented problems to be addressed in an effective way, under the obvious requirement that the instantiated knowledge bases remain of a size that is manageable by current computers and operating systems.

We see two immediate possible improvements with respect to this current work. On the one hand, it is a straightforward task to partition the set of abnormality propositions according to their actual role (exception handling or fault-detection) and adapt the work in this respect. On the other hand, for clarity of presentation, we have focused on the single-sorted ones and do not allow for non-constant functional symbols. This last point could be easily relaxed, as far as a finite case is still considered. Adapting the results in this paper to the many sorted case does not yield any special additional conceptual difficult problem.

ACKNOWLEDGMENTS

This work was supported in part by a "Contrat d'objectifs" and the Ganymède II project of the Région Nord/Pas-de-Calais.

REFERENCES

Bessant B., Grégoire É., Marquis P. et Saïs L. (1998), « Combining nonmonotonic reasoning and belief revision: a practical approach », *Proc. 8ᵗʰ Int. Conf. on Artificial Intelligence – Methodology, Systems, Applications (AIMSA'98)*, F. Giunchiglia (ed.), Sozopol, Bulgaria, LNCS 1480, Springer, pp. 115-128.

Bessant B., Grégoire É., Marquis P. et Saïs L. (1999), « Computing a new form of iterated syntax-based belief revision in a nonmonotonic framework », in: M.-A. Williams (ed.), *Frontiers in Belief Revision*, Kluwer. (in press)

Brisoux, L., Saïs, L. and Grégoire, É. (1998), "Validation of knowledge-based systems by means of stochastic search", In: *Proc. DEXA workshop on verification, validation and integrity issues in expert and databases systems*, R.R. Wagner (ed.), Vienna, IEEE Computer Press, pp. 41-46. (extended version to appear in *Int. Journ. of Intelligent Systems*)

Console, L., Friedrich, G. and Golumbic, M.C. (1984), Special Issue on Model-Based Diagnosis, *Annals of Mathematics and Artificial Intelligence*, **11**.

Cook S.A. (1971), "The complexity of theorem-proving procedures", In: *Proc. of the 3ʳᵈ Annual ACM Symposium on Theory of Computing*, pp. 151-158.

Davis, M., Logemann, G. and Loveland, D. (1962), "A machine Program for Theorem Proving", *JACM*, **5**, pp. 394-397.

DIMACS (1993), Second Challenge on Satisfiability Testing organized by the Center for Discrete Mathematics and Computer Science of Rutgers University http://dimacs.rutgers.edu/Challenges/

Grégoire, É., Mazure, B. and Saïs, L. (1998), "Logically-complete local search for propositional nonmonotonic knowledge bases", In: *Proc. 7th Int. Workshop on Nonmonotonic Reasoning*, Niemelä I. and Schaub T. (eds.), Trento, pp. 37-45.

Grégoire, É. (1999), "A fast logically-complete preferential reasoner for the assessment of critical situations" (to appear)

Hamscher, W., Console, L. and De Kleer, J. (1992), *Readings in Model-Based Diagnosis*, Morgan Kaufmann.

Mazure, B., Saïs, L., Grégoire, É. (1997a), « Tabu Search for SAT », In: *Proc. of the 14th Nat. Conf. on Artificial Intelligence (AAAI-97)*, Rhode Island, pp. 281-285.

Mazure, B., Saïs, L. and Grégoire, É. (1997b), « An Efficient Technique to Ensure the Logical Consistency of Cooperative Agents », *Int. Journ. of Cooperative Information Systems*, World Scientific, **6**(1), pp. 27-36.

Mazure, B., Saïs, L. and Grégoire, É. (1998a), « Boosting Complete Technique Thanks to Local Search Methods », *Ann. of Math. and Artificial Intelligence*, **22**, pp. 319-322.

Mazure, B., Saïs, L. and Grégoire, É. (1998b), « System Description: CRIL Platform for SAT», In: *Proc. of the 15ᵗʰ Int. Conf. on Automated Deduction (CADE'15)*, Lecture Notes in Computer Science 1421, Kirchner C. and Kirchner H. (eds.), Springer, pp. 124-128.

McAllester, D., Selman, B. and Kautz, H. (1997), "Evidence for Invariants in Local Search", In: *Proc. of the 14th Nat. Conf. on Artificial Intelligence (AAAI-97)*, pp. 321-326.

McCarthy, J. (1986), « Applications of circumscription to formalizing common-sense knowledge », *Artificial Intelligence*, **28**, pp. 89-116.

Reiter, R. (1987), « A theory of diagnosis from first principles », *Artificial Intelligence*, **32**, pp. 57-95.

Selman, B., Levesque, H. and Mitchell. D. (1992), « A New Method for Solving Hard Satisfiability Problems », In: *Proc. of the 14th Nat. Conf. on Artificial Intelligence (AAAI-97)*, pp. 440-446.

Selman, B., Kautz, H. A. and Cohen, B. (1993), « Local Search Strategies for Satisfiability Testing », In: *Proc. 1993 DIMACS Workshop on Maximum Clique, Graph Coloring, and Satisfiability*.

Selman, B., Kautz, H. and McAllester, D. (1997), "Computational Challenges in Propositional Reasoning and Search", In: *Proc. of the 15th Int. Joint Conf. on Artificial Intelligence (IJCAI-97)*, Nagoya, Japan, pp. 50-54.

Computer Algebra based Verification and Knowledge Extraction in RBS. Application to Medical Fitness Criteria

Luis M. Laita [12]
Dept. AI, Universidad Politécnica de Madrid
laita@fi.upm.es

Eugenio Roanes-Lozano[1,2]
Dept. Algebra, Universidad Complutense de Madrid
eroanes@eucmos.sim.ucm.es

Víctor Maojo[2], **Luis de Ledesma**[1]
Dept. AI, Universidad Politécnica de Madrid
vmaojo@infomed.dia.fi.upm.es, ledesma@fi.upm.es

Abstract: This article deals with the application to automated extraction of knowledge and verification of consistency in Rule-Based Knowledge Systems (to be denoted as RBS), of a theoretical result that relates tautological consequence in many-valued logics to the ideal membership problem in Algebra. An implementation in a Computer Algebra System is described.

Keywords: Mutivalued propositional logics, consistency verification, Gröbner Bases.

1 INTRODUCTION

This article deals with the application to automated extraction of knowledge and verification of consistency in Rule-Based Knowledge Systems (to be denoted as RBS), of a theoretical result that relates tautological consequence in many-valued logics to the ideal membership problem in Algebra. An implementation in a Computer Algebra System is described. As illustration we study a particular decision procedure in Medicine.

---

[1]Supported by project DGES PB96-0098-C04 (Spain).
[2]Supported by project FIS 95/1952 (Spain).

The first proof of this result was published in [Alonso et al. 87], and was improved in [Chazarain et al. 91]. An Algebraic Geometry based approach appears in [Roanes et al. 98]. Our program runs on a standard 128 Megabytes Pentium based PC. It checks for consistency and automatically finds consequences in RBS containing about 200 propositional variables under bivalued logics and RBS containing about 150 variables under three-valued logics. It has also been applied to five and seven-valued logics.

2   BASIC CONCEPTS AND NOTATIONS

2.1   Basic Logical Notions

Let $X = \{X_1, X_2, ..., X_n\}$ and $C = \{c_1, c_2, ..., c_t\}$ be a set of propositional variables, and a set of connectives respectively. $P_C(X_1, X_2, ..., X_n)$ represents the set of well formed propositional formulae from X and C. The letter A (with or without subscripts) represents a generic element of $P_C(X_1, X_2, ..., X_n)$. s_j is a number to be interpreted as the "arity" of the connective c_j.

We use the following restricted concept of a "p-valued propositional logic", based on the idea of "tautological consequence". We only deal with the case when p is a prime number.

A p-valued propositional logic PL_p consists of:

— a set $P_C(X_1, X_2, ..., X_n)$ of well formed formulae (w.f.f.)

— a set $L = \{0, 1, ..., p-1\}$. The elements $0, 1, ..., p-1$ are considered as the truth values of the p-valued logic. $p-1$ represents the value "true", 0 represents "false", and the other elements represent intermediate truth values

— a set of truth tables defined by functions $H_j : L^{s_j} \longrightarrow L$ (for each connective $c_j \in C$)

— a function v, called "valuation" $v : X \longrightarrow L$

— for each v, another function $v' : P_C(X_1, X_2, ..., X_n) \longrightarrow L$, recursively defined as follows:

$v'(A) = v(A)$ if $A \in X$

$v'(A) = H_j(v'(A_1), ..., v'(A_{s_j}))$ if A is well formed from c_j and $A_1, ..., A_{s_j}$

— a relation named "tautological consequence" (defined in the next section). That A_0 is a tautological consequence of $A_1, A_2, ..., A_m$ is denoted as $\{A_1, A_2, ..., A_m\} \models A_0$.

Let us consider for example Lukasiewicz's three-valued logic with modal operators. The set of connectives is:

$$C = \{c_1 = \neg,\ c_2 = \Diamond,\ c_3 = \Box,\ c_4 = \vee,\ c_5 = \wedge,\ c_6 = \rightarrow,\ c_7 = \leftrightarrow\}.$$

$\Diamond$ and $\Box$ are modal logic connectives. $\Diamond$ means "it is possible that", and $\Box$ means "it is necessary that". The other connectives have the usual meaning. $Z_3 = \{0, 1, 2\}$ is the field of integers modulo 3, where 0 represents "false", 1 represents "indeterminate" and 2 represents "true". The truth value functions H are given by the following truth tables:

$H_\neg$	
0	2
1	1
2	0

$H_\Diamond$	
0	0
1	2
2	2

$H_\Box$	
0	0
1	0
2	2

$H_\vee$	0	1	2
0	0	1	2
1	1	1	2
2	2	2	2

$H_\wedge$	0	1	2
0	0	0	0
1	0	1	1
2	0	1	2

$H_\rightarrow$	0	1	2
0	2	2	2
1	1	2	2
2	0	1	2

2.2 The Concepts of Tautological Consequence and Contradictory Domain

A propositional formula A_0 is a tautological consequence of the propositional formulae $A_1, A_2, ..., A_m$, denoted $\{A_1, A_2, ..., A_m\} \models A_0$ iff for any valuation v such that if $v'(A_1) = v'(A_2) = ... = v'(A_m) = p - 1$, $v'(A_0) = p - 1$.

A formula A is a "logical contradiction" iff for any valuation v, $v'(A) = 0$.

$\{A_1, A_2, ..., A_m\}$ is a "contradictory domain" iff $\{A_1, A_2, ..., A_m\} \models A$, where A is any w.f.f. of the language in which A_1, A_2, ..., A_m are expressed. The name contradictory domain comes from the fact that, if all formulae follow from $\{A_1, A_2, ..., A_m\}$, in particular a "logical contradiction" can also be inferred.

2.3 Basic Algebraic Concepts and Notations

In order to manage the information contained in the RBS, we translate this information into polynomials.

$Z_p[x_1, x_2, ..., x_n]$ is the polynomial ring with coefficients in Z_p and the elements $x_1, x_2, ..., x_n$ as variables. These lower case letters correspond to the upper case letter in the set X. The letters q and r, possibly with subscripts, are variables that range over the elements (polynomials) of $Z_p[x_1, x_2, ..., x_n]$.

I is the ideal $< x_1^p - x_1, x_2^p - x_2, ..., x_n^p - x_n >$ generated by the set of polynomials $x_1^p - x_1, x_2^p - x_2, ..., x_n^p - x_n$.

A polynomial is assigned to each logical formula. This is achieved by defining a function

$$f_j : (Z_p[x_1, x_2, ..., x_n])^{s_j} \longrightarrow Z_p[x_1, x_2, ..., x_n]/I$$

for each connective c_j (see [Roanes et al. 98] for details).

For example, the translation into polynomials of Lukasiewicz's three-valued connectives is:

$$f_{\neg}(q) = (2 - q) + I$$
$$f_{\diamond}(q) = 2q^2 + I$$
$$f_{\square}(q) = (q^2 + 2q) + I$$
$$f_{\vee}(q, r) = (q^2r^2 + q^2r + qr^2 + 2qr + q + r) + I$$
$$f_{\wedge}(q, r) = (2q^2r^2 + 2q^2r + 2qr^2 + qr) + I$$
$$f_{\rightarrow}(q, r) = (2q^2r^2 + 2q^2r + 2qr^2 + qr + 2q + 2) + I$$
$$f_{\leftrightarrow}(q, r) = (q^2r^2 + q^2r + qr^2 + 2qr + 2q + 2r + 2) + I$$

For instance, the function that corresponds to "implies" in a Lukasiewicz's-style seven-valued logic is:

$$f_{\rightarrow}(q, r) = (3q^6r^2 + 6q^5r^3 + 4q^4r^4 + 6q^3r^5 + 3q^2r^6 + 3q^6r + 4q^5r^2 +$$
$$2q^4r^3 + 2q^3r^4 + 4q^2r^5 + 3qr^6 + 5q^5r + 6q^4r^2 + q^2r^3 + 6q^2r^4 + 5qr^5 +$$
$$q^4r + 2q^3r^2 + 2q^2r^3 + qr^4 + 4q^3r + q^2r^2 + 4qr^3 + 4q^2r + 4qr^2 + 5qr + 6q + 6) + I$$

These translations can be obtained with a Maple procedure.

The functions f_j translate the basic propositional formulae $\neg X_i$, $\diamond X_i$, $\square X_i$, ..., $X_i \wedge X_k$ into (classes of) polynomials. The next function θ, interacting with the functions f_j, translates any propositional formula into (classes of) polynomials

$$\theta : P_C(X_1, X_2, ..., X_n) \longrightarrow Z_p[x_1, x_2, ..., x_n]/I$$

recursively defined as follows

$\theta(X_i) = x_i + I$, for all i = 1,..., n.
$\theta(A) = f_j(\theta(A_1), ..., \theta(A_{s_j}))$ if A is $c_j(A_1, ..., A_{s_j})$.

2.4 Tautological Consequence and the Ideal Membership Problem

The main theoretical result [7] is that "*a formula A_0 is a tautological consequence of other formulae A_1,..., A_m, if and only if the polynomial translation of the negation of A_0 belongs to the ideal of $Z_p[x_1, x_2, ..., x_n]/I$ generated by the polynomial translations of the negations of A_1, ..., A_m, i.e.*

$$\{A_1, A_2, ..., A_m\} \models A_0 \Leftrightarrow f_{\neg}(\theta(A_0)) \in <f_{\neg}(\theta(A_1)), ..., f_{\neg}(\theta((A_m))> \quad .$$

3   KNOWLEDGE EXTRACTION AND CONSISTENCY IN RBS

3.1 Extraction of consequences from RBS

The set $P_C(X_1, X_2,...,X_n)$ defined above will hereafter be the set of all w.f.f. constructed using all the propositional variables X_1, X_2,..., X_n that appear in the rules of a RBS. Let $A_1, ..., A_m \in P_C(X_1, X_2, ..., X_n)$ be the formulae that represent the rules, facts, additional information (ADIs), and negations of integrity constraints (NICs) of that RBS. J will denote the ideal $< f_\neg(\theta(A_1)), ..., f_\neg(\theta(A_m)) >$.

Thus, a formula A_0 follows from the information contained in the RBS iff the polynomial translation of the negation of A_0 belongs to $J + I$.

It is possible to check whether a polynomial belongs to an ideal using Gröbner Bases (GB). It has to be ascertained whether the Normal Form (NF) of the polynomial, modulo the ideal, is $\mathbf{0}$ (see e.g. [Winkler 96] for details).

3.2 Application to the Study of RBS Consistency

We shall say that the RBS is inconsistent when one of the following two failures occur:

(i) $\{A_1, A_2, ..., A_m\}$ is a contradictory domain.

(ii) $\{A_1, A_2, ..., A_m\} \models A_0$, where A_0 is an integrity constraint IC.

As an IC is a formula of $P_C(X_1, X_2, ..., X_n)$, this second case is reduced to the first one if the RBS is augmented with the corresponding NIC.

Thus the RBS is inconsistent $\Leftrightarrow 1 \in J + I$ (because 1 belongs to the ideal iff the ideal is the whole ring, which means that all formulae are tautological consequences of the RBS) $\Leftrightarrow GB(I + J) = \{1\}$.

4 APPLICATION TO THE STUDY OF MEDICAL FITNESS CRITERIA

4.1 Table Description

A set of medical data: effort test proof, one, two, or three blood vessels diseased, LVEF (Left Ventricle Ejection Fraction) value, was presented to a panel of ten experts on coronary diseases. They were asked about the fitness of taking, as consequence, determined actions: revascularization, PTCA (Percutaneous Transluminal Coronary Angioplasty), CABG (Coronary Artery Bypass Grafting). Their opinions were set out in a table containing 800 information items: [Field et al. 92, Lazaro et al. 96].

Some of these items, are transcribed afterwards as illustration.

A Effort test positive
A.1 Left common trunk disease
A.1.1 Surgical risk low/moderate

% LVEF (F)	Revascularization	PTCA	CABG
$F > 50$	1:12345678^1 * ^{9} + A	2:12345678^1 * ^{9} − +A	
$50 \geq F > 30$	5:12345678 *^{10} +A	6:12345678^1 * ^{9} − +A	
$30 \geq F \geq 20$	9:12345678^1 *^{9} +A	10:1234567^{1}8^1 *^{8} − + A	

A.1.2 Surgical risk high

% LVEF (F)	Revascularization	PTCA CABG
$F > 50$	$3{:}12345678^4 *^6 +A$	$4{:}12345^1 67^1 8^1 *^7 - +A$
$50 \geq F > 30$	$7{:}12345678^3 *^7 +A$	$8{:}123456^1 7^1 8^2 *^6 - +A$
$30 \geq F \geq 20$	$11{:}1234567^1 8^2 *^7 +A$	$12{:}123456^2 78^2 *^6 - + A$

The experts are informed in the six cases **1, 2, 5, 6, 9, 10** that, for a certain patient, the data are: effort test positive, suffers from left common trunk disease, surgical risk is low/moderate and LVEF is in a given percentage bracket. In the cases **3, 4, 7, 8, 11, 12** the datum "surgical risk low/moderate" changes to "high", while the other data are unchanged.

A number (**1, 2, ..., 800**) is assigned to each row of digits, symbols $+, -$, $*$, and letters A, D, I of the table. The rules R1, R2,..., R800 of the RBS to which the table will be translated are numbered according to these numbers.

Once a set of data is given, the panelists are asked about the fitness of revascularization, PTCA, and CABG. The panelists' answer is transcribed, as shown above, as a row of digits with or without superscripts, symbols $+, -, ?$, $*$, and letters A, D, I.

The superscripts express the number of experts that assign a value from 1 to 9 to the appropriateness of an action. "$*$" stands for the median.

The symbols $+$, $-$ and ? (the later appears in other parts of the table) respectively mean that an action is fit, unfit and of indeterminate fitness. If the panelists refer to Revascularization, only one of these symbols is transcribed. PTCA and CABG are referred simultaneously by a couple of these symbols.

The letter A at the end of a row means "agreement" about fitness, unfitness or undecided fitness. D means "disagreement" and I (which appears in other parts of the table) means "undecided agreement". There exists disagreement D if the ratings of (at least) three panelists ranks between 1 and 3, and the ratings of another three (at least) ranks between 7 and 9 (i.e. big standard deviation). There is agreement when there are no more than two opinions reflected outside an interval of $[1,3]$, $[4,6]$ or $[7,9]$ that contains the median. In any other case, there is undecided agreement I.

4.2   A RBS Translation of the Table

The relation between the data and the corresponding list of digits and symbols in, for instance, **2**, can be reinterpreted as the statement: "*IF* the effort test of a patient is positive *AND* he suffers from left common trunk disease *AND* his surgical risk is low/moderate *AND* his LVEF is over 50%, *THEN* the experts have assessed that PTCA is unfit but CABG is fit"; moreover, "there is agreement (A) in this assessment". These "*IF-THEN*" assertions can be translated to rules of a RBS as follows.

Let us assign a propositional variable, denoted $X[i]$ ($i = 1,..,13$) (possibly preceded by $\neg$), to each datum and therapeutic action.

— Surgical Risk high: $\neg X[1]$, low/moderate: $X[1]$.

— Effort test positive: $X[2]$, negative: $\neg X[2]$, not done or not decisive: $\Diamond \neg X[2]$.

— LVEF $> 50\%$: $X[7]$, $50\% \geq$ LVEF $> 30\%$: $X[8]$, $30\% \geq$ LVEF $\geq 20\%$: $X[9]$.

— Left common trunk disease: $X[3]$, three blood vessels disease: $X[4]$, two blood vessels disease: $X[5]$, one blood vessel disease: $X[6]$, anterior proximal descendent affected: $X[13]$ and anterior proximal descendent not affected: $\neg X[13]$).

— Revascularization: $X[10]$, PTCA: $X[11]$, CABG: $X[12]$.

The relation between a given set of data and its corresponding experts' answer, can be reinterpreted as a RBS rule under the following conventions.

— The literals are either the propositional variables $X[i]$ ($i = 1, .., 13$) or these propositional variables preceded by $\neg$, $\Box$, $\Diamond$, or by any permissible combinations of these symbols.

— Rules have the form

$$\circ_1 X[1] \wedge \circ_2 X[2] \wedge ... \wedge \circ_n X[n] \rightarrow \circ_{n+1} X[n+1] \vee .... \vee \circ_s X[s].$$

The symbols "$\circ_i$" stand for $\neg$, $\Box$ or $\Diamond$, for any of the permissible combinations of these symbols, or for no symbol at all. In this article's case, the symbols $\Box$ and $\Diamond$ (and their combinations) precede nor the variables $X[i]$, $i = 1, ..., 13$ (with the exception of the case "effort test not done or not decisive", represented, as said above, as $\Diamond\neg X[2]$) neither the negations of variables that represent data (antecedents). As $\Box X[i] \models X[i]$, and $X[i] \models X[i]$, when the data are given with high or acceptable precision, the rules that contain them as antecedents can be fired. But if given with low precision (denoted $\Diamond X[i]$), as $\Diamond X[i] \not\models X[i]$, the rules cannot be fired.

— The expression of a NIC would be $\Box \neg \alpha$ if α is an IC. For instance, there is a medical restriction that states that PTCA and CABG cannot be simultaneously performed. $X[11] \wedge X[12]$ is an example of integrity constraint IC. The formula NIC: $\Box\neg(X[11] \wedge X[12])$ is thus added to the RBS as new information.

— We write the symbol $\wedge$ in the conclusion when at the end of the row of digits the couple of symbols made from $+,-$ and ? is: $-+$, $+-$, $--$, $-?$ or $?-$ (as in item **188** below). We write the symbol $\vee$ when that couple is: $++$ (as in item **20** below), $+?$, $?+$ or $??$.

— The different possibilities are translated as follows (note that they are listed in decreasing order of fitness):

$$x \quad + A \quad \rightarrow \quad \Box x$$
$$x \quad + I \quad \rightarrow \quad x$$

$$x \quad + D \quad \rightarrow \quad \Diamond x$$
$$x \; ? \text{ (the three cases)} \quad \rightarrow \quad tautology$$
$$x \quad - D \quad \rightarrow \quad \Diamond \neg x$$
$$x \quad - I \quad \rightarrow \quad \neg x$$
$$x \quad - A \quad \rightarrow \quad \Box \neg x$$

We translate the information items that contain "?" by a trivially true implication. This is to avoid including contradictions derived from the existence of different opinions in the cases "?". See [Laita et al. 98] for an alternative approach.

For example, information items **3** and **4** (detailed above) are translated to RBS rules as follows.

R3: $X[1] \wedge X[2] \wedge X[3] \wedge X[7] \rightarrow \Box X[10]$

R4: $X[1] \wedge X[2] \wedge X[3] \wedge X[7] \rightarrow \Box \neg X[11] \wedge \Box X[12])$.

An example of an item that expresses disagreement ($\Diamond$), is:

A.2 Three blood vessels disease
A.2.2 Surgical risk high

% LVEF (F)	Revascularization	PTCA	CABG
$50 \geq F > 30$	....	$20{:}123^3 4^2 5 * 78^2 9^3 + +D$	

that is translated as

R20: $\neg X[1] \wedge X[2] \wedge X[4] \wedge X[8] \rightarrow \Diamond X[11] \vee \Diamond X[12]$.

The translation of the table into an RBS allows two important processes to be carried through: verify if the table contains anomalies and, once these have been corrected, extract new knowledge.

5   IMPLEMENTATION IN CoCoA

The computer algebra language CoCoA[3] [Capani et al. 96] includes the commands GBasis(ideal) and NF(polynomial,ideal) that calculate the Gröbner Basis and the Normal Form, respectively.

It performs the translation of rules, facts, negations of integrity constraints... into polynomials. Then it can check whether or not the RBS is consistent and

---

[3]More information about CoCoA can be obtained from cocoa@dima.unige.it or directly at the web page: http://cocoa.dima.unige.it

whether or not a formula follows from a consistent subset (as explained above). Indeed, the contradiction below (and many others) were found this way.

CoCoA requires that logical formulae be written in prefix form. NEG, POS, NEC, OR1, AND1, IMP will denote $\neg$, $\Diamond$, $\Box$, $\vee$, $\wedge$, $\rightarrow$ respectively.

The polynomial ring A and the ideal I are declared first.

```
A::=Z/(3)[x[1..13]];
USE A;
I:=Ideal(x[1]^3-x[1],...., x[13]^3-x[13]);
```

The connectives are translated into polynomials of the quotient ring A/I as follows (functions f_j were defined above). NF means "Normal Form" (OR1 and AND1, respectively, are used instead of OR and AND, because the latter are reserved words in CoCoA).

```
NEG(M):=NF(2+2*M,I);
POS(M):=NF(2*M^2,I);
NEC(M):=NF(M^2+2*M,I);
OR1(M,N):=NF(M^2*N^2+M^%
2*N+M*N^2+2*M*N+M+N,I);
AND1(M,N):=NF(2*M^2*N^2+2*M^%
2*N+2*M*N^2+M*N,I);
IMP(M,N):=NF(2*M^2*N^2+2*M^%
2*N+2*M*N^2+M*N+2*M+2,I);
```

5.1 Detection of Inconsistency Directly Produced by the Rules and Facts

Let us consider, for instance, the rule that corresponds to item **40** of the table

A.4 Two blood vessels disease,
proximal anterior descendent not affected
A.4.2 Surgical risk high

% LVEF (F)	Revascularization	PTCA	CABG
$F > 50$	....	**40**:$1^5 * 2^1 3^3 45^1 6789$? $- A$	

R40: $X[1] \wedge X[2] \wedge X[5] \wedge \neg X[13] \wedge X[7] \rightarrow tautology \wedge \Box\neg X[12]$.

What would happen if a patient whose data are $X[1]$, $X[2]$ and $X[7]$, suffered at the same time from left common trunk disease $(X[3])$ and two vessels disease with anterior proximal descendent not affected $(X[5] \wedge \neg X[13])$?

In this situation, as both rules R4 and R40 can be fired, a simple visual logical examination of the consequents obtained shows a contradiction (rule **4** strongly rejects PTCA and strongly recommends CABG, whereas rule **40** is inconclusive about PTCA but strongly rejects CABG). Thus, there exists an anomaly in the table.

Let us analyze the different alternatives:

i) The patient does not suffer from both diseases or it is possible that he suffers from both but they are not going to be treated simultaneously. In such a case, the maximal consistent sets of facts must be carefully determined.

ii) The patient suffers from both diseases and they are going to be treated simultaneously.

    a) There exists the possibility of treating one of the two diseases with one technique and the other with the other technique.

    b) It has to be decided which technique to apply: it is not possible to apply one technique to one disease and a different technique to the other disease.

An interaction with the experts is necessary in order to search for the best representation of knowledge from the medical viewpoint. In particular, it seems that the case in which two diseases are to be simultaneously treated was not considered by the experts who produced the table.

Let us suppose that we have the case ii)b) (the most interesting case from the logical viewpoint).

In order to determine whether or not R4 and R40, together with the potential facts that appear in their antecedents (denoted F2, F3, F4, F6, F7, F10), are consistent, it is enough to calculate the Gröbner basis of the corresponding ideal (constant 2 represents the tautology):

```
R4:=IMP(AND1(AND1(AND1(x[1],x[2]),x[3]),x[7]) ,
    AND1(NEC(NEG(x[11])),NEC(x[12])));
R40:=IMP(AND1(AND1(AND1(AND1(x[1],x[2]),x[5]),NEG(x[13])),
    x[7]),AND1( 2 , NEC(NEG(x[12])))));
J4:=Ideal(NEG(F2),NEG(F3),NEG(F4),NEG(F6),NEG(F7),NEG(F10),
    NEG(R4),NEG(R40) );
GBasis(I+J4);
    [1]
```

and thus, there is inconsistency.

The process of RBS verification is more complex than it seems to be. Initially, many rules must be examined at the same time. If the program detects inconsistency, it is necessary to exactly locate the rules that produce it in order to debug the problem. For this purpose, we use a simple procedure which we have named CONSIST, that takes the set of facts and adds rules, NICs and ADIs one by one, checking the consistency of the system before adding the next one.

The example shown here presents the simplest case: a direct incompatibility between two rules has been detected and located (there are also other problems).

A solution to this conflict is to substitute R4 and R40 by NR4 and NR40 respectively.

```
NR4:=IMP(AND1(AND1(AND1(x[1],x[2]),x[3]),x[7]),
    AND1(NEC(NEG(x[11])),POS(x[12])));
NR40:=IMP(AND1(AND1(AND1(AND1(x[1],x[2]),x[5]),NEG(x[13])),
    x[7]), AND1( 2 , POS(NEG(x[12])))));
J5:=Ideal(NEG(F2),NEG(F3),NEG(F4),NEG(F6),NEG(F7),NEG(F10),
    NEG(NR4),NEG(NR40) );
GBasis(I+J5);
```

is not [1] and thus there is consistency.

5.2 Inconsistencies Produced by Additional Informations

Let us consider as illustration items 208 and 188, to which the following information (denoted as ADI: "additional information") is added

$$(X[11] \vee X[12]) \wedge \neg (X[11] \wedge X[12])$$

(revascularization can be performed by either, but not both simultaneously)
PTCA or CABG).

C Effort test not done or not decisive
C.6 One blood vessel diseased with proximal
anterior descendent not affected
C.6.2 Surgical risk high

% LVEF (F)	Revascularization	PTCA	CABG
$F > 50$	$- - - - - - - -$	208:$*^9 2^1 3456789 - -A$	

is translated as:

$$R208 : \Diamond \neg X[2] \wedge X[1] \wedge X[6] \wedge \neg X[13] \rightarrow \Box \neg X[11] \wedge \Box \neg X[12]$$

C Effort test not done or not decisive
C.4 Two vessel diseased with proximal anterior
descendent not affected
C.4.2 Surgical risk high

% LVEF (F)	Revascularization	PTCA	CABG
$50 \geq F > 30$	$- - - - - - - -$	188:$1^3 *^4 3^1 4^1 5^1 6789 ? - A$	

is translated as:

$$R188 : \Diamond \neg X[2] \wedge X[1] \wedge X[5] \wedge \neg X[13] \rightarrow tautology \wedge \Box \neg X[12]$$

If a patient suffers $X[5]$, then he suffers $X[6]$. So rules 208 and 188 can be fired simultaneously. Let us check for inconsistency with CoCoA. Let us consider the ideal generated by rules 208 and 188, all their potential facts, and ADI. Its GBasis is [1], which means there is inconsistency. CONSIST detects that the element that produces inconsistency is ADI.

5.3   Extraction of New Knowledge with CoCoA

If the RBS is consistent it makes sense to check if some formulae follow from the RBS. For example, let us determine whether

$$\Diamond \neg (\Box X[11] \vee \Box X[12])$$
$$\Diamond \neg X[11] \to \neg \Diamond X[12])$$
$$\Diamond \neg X[11] \wedge \neg X[12])$$

follow from the rules R3,NR4,R7,R8,R11,R12,R20,R39,NR40, the facts F2,F3, F4,F5,F6,F7,F10 and the NIC:

```
J6:=Ideal( NEG(F2),NEG(F3),NEG(F4),NEG(F5),NEG(F6),NEG(F7),
    NEG(F10),NEG(R3),NEG(NR4),NEG(R7),NEG(R8),NEG(R11),
    NEG(R12),NEG(R20),NEG(R39),NEG(NR40),NEG(NIC) );
GBasis(I+J6);
```

is not [1], thus there is no inconsistency. Therefore it makes sense to check if the above mentioned formulae follow from these rules, facts and the NIC (if there were inconsistency, they would trivially follow):

```
NF( POS(NEG(OR1(NEC(x[11]),POS(x[12])))) , I+J6);
  0
NF( POS(NEG(IMP(POS(NEG(x[11])),POS(NEG(x[12]))))) , I+J6);
  0
NF( AND1(POS(NEG(x[11])),POS(NEG(x[12]))) , I+J6);
```

is not 0 (thus the first and second formulae follow, but the third formula does not follow).

The complete process of verification and extraction of knowledge takes, in this case, around ten seconds on a Pentium-based PC with 128 Mb of RAM.

6   CONCLUSION

A Computer Algebra based method has been applied to the processes of verification and knowledge extraction in RBS.

As an example, we have studied a decision table describing fitness criteria in heart diseases. Such a study has been intended to be both an illustration of the method and an illustration of the usefulness of multivalued logic in knowledge representation, when imprecise knowledge is involved. Once anomalies are detected, they are presented to the experts for a possible remake of the table. Alternative rules that do not lead to anomalies are proposed. As a matter of course, these anomalies may be due to a lost of information when translating the table into a RBS, or even to the relatively arbitrary translation of the symbols $+$, $-$, $?$, A, D and I. Nevertheless our whole process of taking the information in the table into a RBS was judged interesting and accurate by the experts. Partly because of our suggestions, they have made a substantial remake of the table.

References

[1] Alonso, J.A., Briales, E., Riscos, A. (1987). *Preuve Automatique dans le Calcul Propositionnel et des Logiques Trivalentes*. In Proc. Congress on Computational Geometry and Topology and Computation. Univ. Sevilla.

[2] Capani, A., Niesi, G. (1996). *CoCoA User's Manual (v.3.0b)*. Dept. of Mathematics, University of Genova.

[3] Chazarain, J., Riscos, A., Alonso, J.A., Briales, E. (1991). *Multivalued Logic and Gröbner Bases with Applications to Modal Logic*. Journal of Symbolic Computation 11; pp181-194.

[4] Field, M., Lohr, M.K. (Eds.)(1992). *Guidelines for Clinical Practice. From Development to Use*. Washington D.C., National Academy Press.

[5] Laita, L.M., Roanes Lozano, E., Maojo, V. (1998). *Inference and verification in Medical Appropriateness Criteria*. In: Calmet, J., Plaza, J. (Eds.) Artificial Intelligence and Symbolic Computation, Proc. de AISC'98. (LNAI-1476), pp183-194. Berlín, Springer-Verlag.

[6] Lázaro, P., Fitch, K. (1996). *Criterios de uso apropiado para by-pass coronario*. Unpublished report.

[7] Roanes Lozano, E., Laita, L.M., Roanes Macías, E. (1998). *A Polynomial Model for Multivalued Logics with a Touch of Algebraic Geometry and Computer Algebra*. Mathematics and Computers in Simulation, 45(1); pp83-99.

[8] Winkler, F. (1996). *Polynomial Algorithms in Computer Algebra*. Wien, Springer-Verlag.

A Knowledge Based Tool to Validate and Verify an Aion Knowledge Base

Drs. Silvie Spreeuwenberg, Ing. Rik Gerrits
LibRT B.V.

Key words: validation, verification, knowledge based systems, tools, Aion, meta rules

Abstract: We present a tool for the validation and verification of a knowledge base (KB). Validation techniques become more and more important when knowledge based systems (KBS) are widely used to automate business critical processes. The tool can be used during and after the development of a KBS and focuses on a logical verification of the KBS. The techniques used to verify a knowledge base are meta rules, an inference engine to verify hypotheses posed by meta rules (saturation), and meta information (provided by the user). The tool is written in the same language as the knowledge bases that can be verified: Aion. Aion is a widely used commercial development environment for the development of knowledge bases and intelligent components.

1.   INTRODUCTION

I had a knowledge based system (KBS) to determine the type of a concept. The KBS was tested and correct until I added a new rule to determine a new type. The results were completely different than expected and it took some time to find that a form of circularity in the rules caused the problem. This is what I call the butterfly theory in a KBS. Thinking about solutions to avoid this problem resulted in this presentation about validation and verification techniques.

1.1   What's the need?

An iterative development cycle is preferred for developing knowledge based (KB) systems [1]. Decreasing the number of cycles between analysis, implementation and test decreases development time. Early detection of faults using V&V by detection of contradictions and inconsistencies can contribute to this reduction. Furthermore the issue of assuring the quality of a KBS is becoming an increasingly important challenge as KB components are more and more often embedded within safety critical or business critical applications [2].

During maintenance a change in one (1) knowledge rule may introduce contradictions, redundancy or incompleteness in a complex chain of knowledge rules. Especially when non-programmers/system analysts can define and maintain the knowledge in a KBS, they are helped to cope with the complexity when they are supported with V&V tools.

In all the main phases of the knowledge engineering life cycle, validation and verification is an important aspect to come to a high quality KBS. In the knowledge analysis phase you validate the knowledge rules with an expert. In the implementation phase the logical correctness of the implemented rules is checked and in the test phase you will use test cases to validate the knowledge base. Tools to support the validation and verification process can be used on each phase of this cycle. For example:

– Datamining can be used to support the knowledge elicitation process by automatic rule generation. This datamining technique uses the knowledge in databases to validate expert knowledge by searching for evidence based on available data [3].
– Automatically checking your knowledge base on inconsistent, redundant or incomplete knowledge during development of a KBS.
– Automatic generation of test cases for a KB.

These tools will increase the quality and reduce the time to market of a KBS. This will be an important factor in the consideration of using knowledge-based technologies for automating business critical processes.

In this article we focus on the automatic support of validation and verification in the implementation phase of the knowledge engineering process.

2.   DEFINITIONS OF CHECKS

When verifying the logical correctness of a knowledge base one checks whether the rules in the knowledge base are consistent, complete, not redundant and not obsolete. This check can cover all the rules in the knowledge base or a subset of the rules in a knowledge base. The control structure present in most real knowledge based systems can post rules or rule sets dynamically. If that is the case, these subsets have to be verified in isolation.

The following paragraphs discuss the techniques used to verify a knowledge base.

2.1   Consistency

To verify consistency, one must demonstrate that for all inputs, the knowledge base produces a consistent set of conclusions, i.e., that for each set of possible inputs, all the conclusions can be true at the same time.

2.2   Completeness

To verify completeness one must demonstrate that for all inputs, the knowledge base produces some conclusion.

2.3   Redundancy

A knowledge base is redundant when the same knowledge is represented in different places or there exists knowledge which does not contribute to the output of the system (but can in fact be true knowledge).

3.   AUTOMATIC VALIDATION AND VERIFICATION

The overview of validation and verification tools found in the literature can be divided into two schools. One is solely concerned with the validation of a (logical) knowledge base, the other integrates validation and verification in the knowledge engineering process. Our approach combines the techniques used in both schools and can be integrated in the knowledge engineering process by its flexible architecture.

3.1   Theoretical school

The theoretical approach to validate the rules in a knowledge base is based on predicate logic. The rules are written in conjunctive normal form and boolean logic is used to simplify and verify the formula [4].

Other approaches are based on decision table methods. Rules conditions and actions parameters are separated. Algorithms then examine the existence of relationships among rows and columns [5]. A variant of this method that can cope with anomalies across numerous rules (rather than between pairs of rules) constructs a graphic representation of the rule base and searches for cross-references [6].

3.2   Practical school

Some practical approaches construct tools which support the whole process of analysis, implementation and test of a knowledge base. During the definitions of the rules, these tools use all validation techniques and the tool forces a valid knowledge base to be generated. The construction process is divided into phases. Each phase is supported with an appropriate set of validation techniques where checks assure that each phase is still valid in next phase's [7].

Such tools can be based on constraint propagation techniques [7], [8]. It uses the integrity constraints to construct minimal and coherent initial fact bases and meta rules (for semantic validation). Then it saturates each of them (forward chaining) in order to detect conflicts in the rule base.

Another example of such a tool is based on formal specification language theory, which makes validation and verification independent from implementation specific properties and can be executed early in the development life cycle [9].

3.3   Our approach

Our tool can be used by a developer after or during construction of a knowledge base or can be integrated in a tool in which a user can write her own business rules.

The output of the tool is a document in which all invalid rules (combinations) detected are reported. Each fault is classified and explained. The report will also include a direction for repairing the fault. We explicitly didn't choose for automatic reparation of faults because domain knowledge will often be needed to find the right solution to an invalid rule.

We use a combination of the approaches we find in the theoretical and practical schools based on predicate logic [4] and constraint satisfaction [7].

3.3.1   Meta model

A meta model of the rule base is constructed. The meta model is object oriented and represents the rules found in a knowledge base. The rules are parsed and divided into conditions and conclusions. Conditions are divided into clauses.

An example of a knowledge rule in terms of the meta model is given in figure 1.

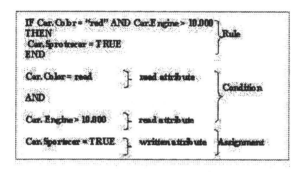

Figure 1. Example of meta model construction

Meta information is generated from the rules in the knowledge base and stored in the meta model. This meta information includes the defined input- and output of the knowledge base, the maximum and minimum values of variables and the values of an attribute.

```
IF Car.Color = "red" AND Car.Engine > 10.000
THEN
Rule
 Car.Sportscar = TRUE
END


Car.Engine

Attribute.ValueRange.StartValue = 10.000
Attribute.ValueRange.EndValue = null
Attribute.ValueRange.StartIncluded = false
Attribute.ValueRange.EndIncluded = null
```

Figure 2. Example of meta information generated from a rule

Information about attributes (meta information) is used to check completeness and redundancy.

3.3.2   Meta Rules

Meta rules work on this meta model and define the checks accomplished by the tool. We can distinguish two classes of meta rules in our approach:
1. Meta rules which select a thesis, which has to be proved to detect a fault.
2. Meta rules which define a fault directly in terms of the meta model.

The first class of meta rules is used to detect faults which can be hidden in a chain of logic. So these meta-rules are used to find all kind of contradictions and redundancy. The second class of meta rules are used to detect other faults in rules. For example: incomplete knowledge.

The conditions of the meta rules which detect faults in a chain of logic generally contain two parts:
1. the first part selects potential invalid rules, (this selection is implicitly defined in the condition of the meta rule)
2. this leads to a hypotheses which is tested in the second part of the rule with the use of the inference engine (see next paragraph).

When the hypothesis succeeds the conclusion that the rule is invalid will be reached.

Figure 3. Example of a meta rule

The first four clauses of the meta rule in figure 3 say that two rules, which assign a different value to the same attribute, are potentially invalid. The last clause of the meta rule calls a function which returns true if rule2 *succeeds* given the truth values for which rule1 succeeds. So the hypothesis is that rule2 succeeds, i.e. the condition of rule2 is true. Then we have to prove that rule1 succeeds under the same conditions. When we proved this thesis successfully the meta rule succeeds and a fault is detected.

3.3.3   Proof a thesis

By running the rules to be tested in a forward chaining mode, providing them with the right truth values (input), the thesis (potentially invalid rules) are proved. In the example meta rule of figure 3, this functionality is defined in the method succeeds(hypothesis, input, chain) which is sent to a potentially invalid rule (i.e. the class Rule).

The method "succeeds" collects the values of attributes under which the hypothesis rule succeeds. In most cases this truth-value can be determined by the system. For example: in an assignment this value comes after the '=' sign. However when methods are used in conditions of rules the system can not always find the truth-value. In that case the user is prompted to give a value for the attributes so that the condition succeeds. These collected truth-values are added as facts to the target knowledge base (the knowledge base, which is to be verified). Then the target knowledge base is started in a forward chaining mode. After the forward chaining process the results of the inference engine are analysed. If the thesis indeed succeeds, the chain of rules, which causes the rule to fire, is returned.

This process resembles the "saturation" process used by Nouira and Fouet [7].

4.   V&V IN AION

The validation and verification tool is made in and for Aion applications. Aion is a development environment for knowledge based systems. Some characteristics are:

– Inference engine
  The inference engine supports rule processing in a backward or forward chaining mode. Furthermore decision tables are supported.
– Object oriented
  The programming language is object oriented.
– Meta programming features
  These features allow a programmer to ask information about the state of the inference engine.
– Callable Object Building System (COBS)
  This feature allows you to automate all the functions a developer can use in Aion.

4.1   The tool

The validation and verification application consists of three components: a user interface, the verification engine and a reporting component.

The following steps are performed to verify a knowledge base:

1. Open and read an Aion8 application to create all the necessary objects in the meta model.
   1.1 Select knowledge base to be verified.
   1.2 Select rule sets in the knowledge base to be verified.
2. Start analysis process.
   2.1 Start forward chaining process and execute the meta rules.
      2.1.1 Select potential 'invalid' rules through meta rules.
      2.1.2 Prepare the KB to verify the selected rule(s).
      2.1.3 Run the KB and 'catch' the results.
   2.2 Analyse the results.
3. Report the results.

The user selects the knowledge base and rule sets in the knowledge base which have to be verified. The COBS functionality of Aion is used to open and read the Aion application. When the verification process is started and there are potential invalid rules detected, COBS is used again to start the

Aion application in a forward chaining mode to test the thesis. By using the meta programming features of Aion we capture the results of the inference engine to analyse whether the thesis is satisfied. These meta programming features give us also the possibility to catch the chain of logic which has caused the thesis to be satisfied. Invalid rules are reported in a HTML document.

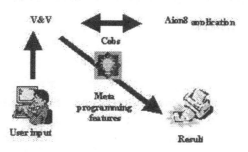

Figure 4. Context diagram of V&V tool

The tool can be integrated in the development environment. A developer will use the tool after the main part of the programming effort is finished or during maintenance of a knowledge base.

The COBS functionality of Aion allows you to make end-user interfaces for experts who want to define and maintain the knowledge in a knowledge base. The validation and verification tool can be easily integrated in such domain specific knowledge editor.

4.2   Abstractions

A few abstractions are taken in the first version of the verification tool that we will mention in this paragraph.

Rules and rule sets can be conditionally posted. In the first version of the tool we do not analyse the control of the application. To cope with rule sets that will never be used at the same time, the user has to select the rule sets, which have to be taken into account simultaneously. This approach will also capture the fact that some (generic) rule sets are used in more than one infer method in combination with different rule sets.

Attribute names don't have to be unique in an Aion application when they belong to a different class. Because the class name doesn't have to be referred to when you reason about the current class, you should find the owner (class) of each attribute to identify attributes uniquely. In the first version of the tool we abstracted from this fact and assume that all attribute-names are unique.

Attributes can get their value from a database. Database access is not explicitly captured in the application. To gather information from the database and the queries we have to initialise the database and verify the database model and queries on the database. We think some specialised tools will be more suitable for this task.

4.3 Future directions

In the near future we like to extend this tool to include a form of semantic validation by using domain specific meta-rules. These domain specific meta-rules can be seen as constraints or business rules. To avoid confusion with the meta-rules used to define potential conflicts we will call this kind of rules 'business-rules'. These business-rules will be specified and defined by a business analyst or domain expert. The defined business-rules can be stored and edited from within the V&V tool. An example of such a rule is given in figure 5. This rule states that men can't be pregnant.

```
IF patient.gender = 'man'
   AND patient.pregnant = TRUE
THEN
   ConstraintViolation
END
```

Figure 5. Example of a domain specific meta rule

The business-rules are included in the application. The tool will then search for rules which conflict with the business rule in the same way as we detect contradictions (see paragraph 3.3). To execute the meta rules the application will be started in a forward chaining mode. If a constraint is satisfied the corresponding (forward chaining) business-rule will fire immediately. All fired meta-rules will be printed in a report, which includes the context information necessary to understand the problem encountered.

Besides the extension from logical to semantic validation the user has to be better supported when solving the detected problems. The tool will be extended with active support during the problem solving process by suggesting solutions to the problem. These solutions can be automatically applied by a push on a button. We distinguish that the end-user has to be in charge in this problem solving process.

5.   COMPARISON WITH SIMILAR SYSTEMS

Most systems, which verify a knowledge base, cope with a restricted language, for example first order predicate logic [10], [11] or formal specification language [9] as opposed to the rich language of a programming environment like Aion.

Other systems support the entire analysis process and do not focus on the development and maintenance stage of an application. As mentioned in paragraph 3.3, the tool that we develop is a validation and verification component. We focus on the development and maintenance stage of an application but its use is not restricted to this stage because the tool is developed as a component.

A programmer can integrate this component in a development environment for use during the development and maintenance of an application. But the component can also be integrated in a domain specific knowledge editor tool and used early in the analysis stage. One can also think of integration in a test-tool, however, we recommend to start with validation and verification techniques early in the development life cycle.

6.   DISCUSSION AND CONCLUSION

We have presented a tool developed in and for Aion applications that supports the verification and validation of rules. The tool can be used during development and maintenance of the knowledge based system. Another application is the integration of our technique in a domain specific editor to support the definition of knowledge rules by a domain expert or business analyst.

The tool uses meta rules, meta information and the inference engine of Aion to accomplish this task. By using the same inference engine in the verification process as the inference engine used to evaluate and fire the knowledge rules to be verified, there can be no discrepancy between the run time logic and the logic used in the validation process.

We think this tool can reduce the time to market for knowledge based systems, improve their quality and has added value during maintenance of applications by developers, which are not very familiar with the functionality of the application. The tool is a "must-have" when domain experts, who lack the knowledge about logic a developer should have, define their own knowledge rules.

REFERENCES

[1] Boehm, B.W., 1986, A spiral Model of Software Development and Enhancement. Computer, 21, 61-72

[2] Ed P. Andert Jr., 1992, Automated knowledge base validation, AAAI Workshop on Verification and validation of Expert Systems (July 1992)

[3] Vijay S. Mookerjee and Michale V. Mannino, 1997, Sequential Decision Models for Expert System Optimization, IEEE, 9, 675 – 687

[4] James A Wentworth and Rodger Knaus and Hamid Aougab, Verification, validation, and evaluation of expert systems, FHWA Handbook Volume 1

[5] Cragen and Steudel, 1987, A decision table based processor for checking completeness and consistency in rule based expert systems, International journal of Man Machine studies. Vol 26, 633-638

[6] Prece, Shingal, 1994, Foundation and application of knowledge base verification, International journal of intelligent Systems, 9, 683 – 701

[7] Rym Nouira, Jean-Marc Fouet, 1996, A knowledge based tool for the incremental construction, validation and refinement of large knowledge bases, Workshop proceedings ECAI96

[8] R. Nouira, J.M. Fouet, 1996, A meta-knowledge based tool for detecting invalid, conflictual and redundant rules, AAAI-96, Proc. Ninth national conference on artificial intelligence

[9] F.v.Harmelen, 1995, Structure preserving specification languages for knowledge based systems, International journal of human computer studies, vol 44, 187-212

[10] Alon Y. Levy and Marie-Christine Rousset, 1996, Verification of Knowledge bases on containment checking, Workshop proceedings ECAI96

[11] Z. Bendou and M. Ayel, 1996, Validation of rule bases containing constraints, Workshop proceedings ECAI96

Constraints for Validation of Conceptual Graphs

Juliette Dibie-Barthélemy[1,2]
[1]LAMSADE, Université Paris IX - Dauphine, Place du Maréchal de Lattre de Tassigny, Paris, France
Juliette.Dibie@inapg.inra.fr

Ollivier Haemmerlé[2]
[2] INA-PG, Département OMIP, 16, rue Claude Bernard, Paris, France
Ollivier.Haemmerle@inapg.inra.fr

Stéphane Loiseau[3]
[3] LERIA, Univ. d'Angers, UFR Sciences, 2, Bd Lavoisier, Angers, France
loiseau@info.univ-angers.fr

Abstract: The works on validation propose solutions to ensure the quality of knowledge based systems. We are interested in the validation of a specific model of knowledge representation: the conceptual graph model. We present a semantic validation of conceptual graphs based on constraints given by an expert. The semantic validation of a knowledge base composed of conceptual graphs consists in checking its quality according to two kinds of constraints. The existential constraints allow one to express knowledge which must be deduced or which must absolutely not be deduced from the knowledge base. The descriptive constraints characterize the properties a conceptual graph must verify in the knowledge base. Descriptive constraints can be minimal or maximal to express the notions of "at least" and "at most". We introduce the notion of specification which is a combination of constraints linked by logical operators. The validation of a knowledge base is made according to these specifications, by means of a conceptual graph operation: the projection.

Keywords: Semantic validation, conceptual graphs, constraints

1   INTRODUCTION

One of the main reasons for the limited use of KBS (Knowledge Based System) is that managers lack confidence in them. They are not willing to let computer systems whose quality is not ensured take decisions in important areas in which the KBSs are suitable. The works on validation propose solutions to ensure the quality of KBSs. Many works deal with the validation of RBS (Rule Base Systems) [11, 12]. A few works have recently studied how to validate knowledge models, and how to use validation to build KBS better [7]. Few works have been done on how to validate semantic networks; [13] [8] study how to check the global coherency of a terminological KB, i.e. a KB based on terminological logic. As far as we know, no works have been done on how to validate conceptual graphs (CGs). The CG model is a model of knowledge representation based on labelled graphs. We propose solutions to validate CGs. We have been working on CG validation in three directions. The first one is a syntactical validation which consists in checking if the knowledge base is a "well formed" knowledge base respectively to the syntactic rules of the model. The second one is a logical validation, which allows us to avoid some ambiguities induced by the CG model (we want to ensure that the knowledge scanned by the user corresponds to what he wants to scan). These works were presented into [3, 4], and resulted from the model of the CGs itself. In this paper we present a third kind of validation, based on constraints given by an expert to check the quality of an existing KB composed of CGs. This validation is clearly different from the other two since it is domain dependent.

Using constraints for validation has commonly been done for RBS. Constraints are complementary knowledge given for validation, so it provides a semantic way to guarantee the KB quality. First, we propose to check the KB on existential constraints. They are test CGs which must be deduced from the base, and are called positive existential constraints, or which must absolutely not be deduced, and are called negative existential constraints. Second, we provide a way to express and check descriptive constraints on the KB. They express a set of properties that each occurrence of a CG G_{In} must respect. A descriptive constraint (G_{In}, G_{Out}) characterizes the properties G_{Out} that G_{In} must verify in the knowledge base. A minimal (resp. maximal) descriptive constraint expresses that if there exist specializations of G_{In} in the KB, then these specializations must at least (resp. at most) respect some conditions. We propose a language that enables one to express a specification that is a set of constraints connected by logical operators; for instance, we can specify that the KB must respect a positive existential constraint, or, a minimal descriptive constraint and a maximal descriptive constraint. Checking a specification is possible using compositions of projections; projection is the basic operation in the CG model.

This paper is organized as follows. The second section summarizes the model of CGs [14] as formalized by [10] in which our KBs are expressed. The third section presents existential constraints. Section four provides the definition of descriptive constraints and how to check them. The fifth section presents specifications that combine existential and descriptive constraints to better validate.

2 THE CONCEPTUAL GRAPH MODEL

In the CG model, knowledge is divided into two parts: the terminological part which is called the *support* and the assertional part which is called the *conceptual graphs*.

2.1 The Support

The support is composed of sets of elementary knowledge: concepts, instances and relations. It provides the ground vocabulary, its hierarchical organization, and other information specifying the way it can be used.

Definition 1 *A support is defined as a quintuplet* $S = (T_c, T_r, M, \tau, \sigma)$:

— T_c *is the set of concept types, which is partially ordered by a "kind of" relation noted* $\leq$. *This set possesses a greatest common element* $\top$ *and a smallest one* $\bot$;

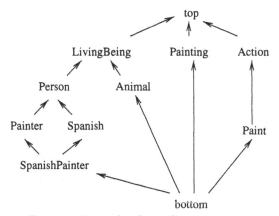

Figure 1. Example of set of concept types.

— T_r *is the set of relation types. This set is partitioned into sets* T_{ri} *of relation types of same arity* i $(i \geq 1)$. *Each one of these sets is partially ordered by a relation noted* $\leq$;

Figure 2. Example of set of relation types.

— M *is the set of individual markers. Each individual marker represents an instance of a concept. The generic marker* $*$ *is a particular marker referring to an unspecified instance of a concept;*

Example: $M = \{Braque, Dali, Ernst, Miró, BlueI, BlueII\}$ *is a set of individual markers (the instances of concepts we use).*

— τ *is an application of M into $T_c \setminus \{\bot\}$. $t \in T_c$ is associated with each $m \in M$, specifying "m is an instance of t";*

Example: $\tau_{Braque} = Painter, \tau_{Dali} = SpanishPainter, \tau_{Ernst} = Painter,$ $\tau_{Miró} = SpanishPainter, \tau_{BlueI} = Painting, \tau_{BlueII} = Painting$ *specifies the concept type of each of the instances.*

— σ *is an application of T_{ri} into $(T_c)^i$. For each $t_r \in T_{ri}$ is associated a uplet $\sigma(t_r) \in (T_c)^i$. This application allows one to specify the maximum concept type allowed as the ith neighbour for each relation type.*

Example: $\sigma_{agt} = (Action, LivingBeing), \sigma_{poss} = (LivingBeing, Painting),$ $\sigma_{obj} = (Action, Painting)$ *specifies for example that the relation agt links necessarily a LivingBeing and an Action (or one of their sub-types).*

2.2   The Conceptual Graphs

The CGs which are built upon the support express the factual knowledge. The CGs are composed of two kinds of vertices: the concept vertices represent entities, attributes, states, events, and the relation vertices express the nature of the relations between concepts.

Definition 2 *A conceptual graph G defined on a support S is a non-oriented, bipartite, multigraph $G = (R, C, U, lab)$. R and C denote the two classes of relation and concept vertices, with $C \neq \emptyset$. U is the set of edges; the edges adjacent to a relation vertex r are totally ordered. These edges are labelled $i, 1 \leq i \leq degree(r)$. Every vertex has a label defined by the labelling function lab : (1) the relation type in the case of a relation vertex ; (2) a couple (concept type, marker) in the case of a concept vertex (marker must satisfy τ and the neighbour constraints σ must be respected).*

The specialization relation (noted $\leq$) partially orders the set of CGs. The projection operation (a graph morphism allowing a restriction of the vertex labels) is a way of defining the specialization relation: G' $\leq$ G if and only if there exists a projection of G into G'.

Definition 3 *A projection of a CG $G = (R, C, U, lab)$ into a CG $G' = (R', C', U', lab')$ is a pair of mappings $\Pi = (f, g)$, f from R to R', g from C to C' such that:*

— *for every edge $(r, c) \in U$ labelled i, $(f(r), g(c))$ is an edge of U' labelled i;*

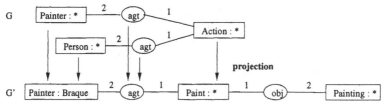

Figure 3. There is a projection from G into G', G' ≤ G (G' is more specific than G)

— $\forall r \in R,\ lab(f(r)) \leq lab(r)\ and\ \forall c \in C,\ lab(g(c)) \leq lab(c).$

Definition 4 *A CG G is said* under normal form *if each individual marker belonging to G appears exactly once.*

It is possible to compute the normal form corresponding to a given CG by joining all its concept vertices labelled by the same individual marker.

As mentioned before the specialization relation is a pre-order, thus there exist equivalence classes of CGs for ≤. Two CGs *G* and *H* are said *equivalent* if $G \leq H$ and $H \leq G$. The notion of irredundance was defined in [2] to study the equivalence relation associated with the pre-order of the specialization relation. Each equivalence class for ≤ contains a unique irredundant CG.

Definition 5 *A CG G is* irredundant *if there is no projection from G into one of its strict subgraphs.*

2.3 The Logical Interpretation

[14] proposed a logical interpretation of CGs (the Φ function), in which a unique correspondence between CGs and first order logic is defined. $\Phi(G)$ is a well formed formula of the first order predicate calculus associated with every CG *G*. $\Phi(S)$ is a set of logical formulae associated with the support *S*.

Example 1 :
Let G' be the CG of figure 2.2. Its logical interpretation is: $\Phi(G') = \exists x, y$
$Painter(Braque) \wedge Paint(x) \wedge Painting(y) \wedge agt(x, Braque) \wedge obj(x, y).$

The logical semantics are sound and complete: a correspondence exists between the specialization relation and the logical deduction.

Property 1 (Soundness [14] and completeness [2] of Φ). *Let $\Phi(S)$ be the set of formulae associated with the support, G and H two CGs* **under normal form**. *$G \leq H$ if and only if $\Phi(S), \Phi(G) \vdash \Phi(H)$.*

We consider that all the CGs we use are under normal form to be coherent with the property 1. Moreover, due to the ambiguities induced by the redundancy [3], we suppose that the CGs are irredundant.

3 EXISTENTIAL CONSTRAINTS

The existential constraints allow a validation by checking whether or not a CG must be deduced from the base. An existential constraint is an input CG noted G_{In}. It can be respectively positive or negative according to whether we want to deduce its knowledge from the knowledge base or not.

Definition 6 *Let $\mathcal{KB}$ be a knowledge base composed of a support S and an irredundant CG under normal form Γ (in the following, we note such a knowledge base (S, Γ)). $\mathcal{KB}$ satisfies a positive existential constraint G_{In}^+ if there exists a projection of G_{In}^+ into $\mathcal{KB}$.*

For example, if we want to check that there are painters in the knowledge base, we define an existential constraint $G_{In}^+ = $ [Painter : *]. The knowledge base composed of the CG G' of figure 2.2 satisfies the constraint G_{In}^+ because there exists a projection from G_{In}^+ into G'.

The logical interpretation of the satisfaction of a positive existential constraint is the following.

Property 2 *A knowledge base $\mathcal{KB} = (S, \Gamma)$ satisfies an existential constraint G_{In}^+ if and only if $\Phi(S), \Phi(\Gamma) \vdash \Phi(G_{In}^+)$*

Definition 7 *Let $\mathcal{KB}$ be a knowledge base (S, Γ). $\mathcal{KB}$ satisfies a negative existential constraint G_{In}^- if there is no projection of G_{In}^- into $\mathcal{KB}$.*

The logical interpretation of the satisfaction of a negative existential constraint is the following.

Property 3 *A knowledge base $\mathcal{KB} = (S, \Gamma)$ satisfies an existential constraint G_{In}^- if and only if $\Phi(S) \wedge \Phi(\Gamma) \wedge \neg\Phi(G_{In}^-)$ is satisfiable.*

4 DESCRIPTIVE CONSTRAINTS

The descriptive constraints allow a validation by ensuring a set of properties for each occurrence of a given subgraph in the knowledge base. Intuitively, a descriptive constraint associated with a CG G allows one to specify that if there exists a specialization of G in the knowledge base, then this specialization must respect some conditions. It restricts the possible specializations of G in the base to specific specializations. For instance a descriptive constraint allows one to specify that "if a painter paints, then he must paint a painting".

4.1 Definition of The Descriptive Constraints

Let c_1 and c_2 be two concept vertices and G_1 and G_2 two CGs respectively composed of the only vertex c_1 and c_2. We say that c_1 and c_2 are *comparable* if there exists a projection of G_1 into G_2 or a projection of G_2 into G_1. In order to define the notion of descriptive constraint, we need to link concept vertices belonging to different CGs: we propose to use *coreference links* [14] which are graphically represented by a dotted line between these concept vertices.

Definition 8 *Let G_1 and G_2 be two CGs, C_1 and C_2 being their respective classes of concept vertices. A coreference link between two comparable concept vertices of $C = C_1 \times C_2$ is an equivalence relation on C.*

We use coreference links in the definition of descriptive constraints. The conditions that must be respected by all the specializations of G in the base are characterized by descriptions, the concept vertices of G being linked by coreference links to some concept vertices of each description.

Definition 9 *A description G' of a CG G is a specialization of G, such that each concept vertex of G is linked by a coreference link to one of the concept vertices of G'. We call* head *of the description (noted* head(G')) *the subgraph composed of the concept vertices linked by a coreference link to the concept vertices of G and of the relation vertices linking these concept vertices together. The head of a description G' is unique.*

Definition 10 *A descriptive constraint is a couple (G_{In}, G_{Out}) where G_{In} is an irredundant input CG and G_{Out} is an irredundant output CG which must be a description of G_{In}. A descriptive constraint can be either minimal or maximal and respectively noted $(G_{In}, G_{Out})_{min}$ and $(G_{In}, G_{Out})_{max}$*

Example 2 (followed throughout the paper):
Let G_{In} and G_{Out} be the following CGs:

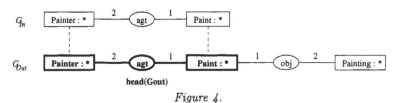

Figure 4.

Intuitively, the descriptive constraint $(G_{In}, G_{Out})_{min}$ means that if a painter paints then he must paint at least one painting, and the descriptive constraint $(G_{In}, G_{Out})_{max}$ means that if a painter paints then he must paint at most one painting .

4.2 Satisfaction of Descriptive Constraints

A knowledge base satisfies a descriptive constraint (G_{In}, G_{Out}) if the specializations of G_{In} in the knowledge base conform to the expected output CG G_{Out}. We introduce the notion of *image graph*, used in the definitions of the satisfaction of minimal and maximal descriptive constraints.

Definition 11 *Let* H *and* G *be CGs. We say that there exists a projection from* G *into* H *with* h *the* image graph *of* G *if* h *is a subgraph of* H *and there exists a surjective projection from* G *into* h.

4.2.1 Satisfaction of Minimal Descriptive Constraints

Let $\mathcal{KB}$ be a knowledge base (S, Γ). Let $(G_{In}, G_{Out})_{min}$ be a *minimal descriptive constraint*. The minimal descriptive constraint is *satisfied* by $\mathcal{KB}$ if and only if for each projection from G_{In} into Γ such that γ is the image graph of G_{In}, there exists at least one projection of the description G_{Out} into Γ with γ the image graph of the head of G_{Out}.

Example 3 :

Let $\mathcal{KB}$ *be the knowledge base composed of* $\Gamma = \{\gamma_1, \gamma_2, \gamma_3\}$, *a juxtaposition of the connected CGs* γ_1, γ_2 *and* γ_3:

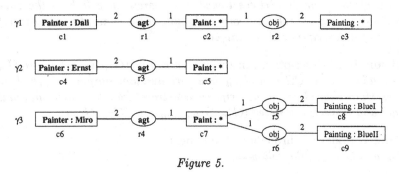

Figure 5.

Let us consider the CG G_{In} *and its description* G_{Out} *presented in example 2 and the CGs* γ_1 *and* γ_2.
Let $\mathcal{KB}'$ *be a knowledge base composed of* $\Gamma' = \{\gamma_1, \gamma_2\}$. *We check if* $\mathcal{KB}'$ *satisfies the minimal descriptive constraint DC.*

(1) *There is a projection from* G_{In} *into* γ_1 *with* γ_1' *the CG limited to the vertices* c_1, r_1 *and* c_2 *and the image graph of* G_{In}; *there is a projection from* G_{Out} *into* γ_1 *with* γ_1' *the image graph of* head(G_{Out});

(2) *there is a projection from* G_{In} *into* γ_2 *but there doesn't exist a projection from* G_{Out} *into* γ_2.

$\mathcal{KB}'$ *doesn't satisfy the minimal descriptive constraint DC: the painter Dali paints and he paints a painting, but the painter Ernst paints and he paints nothing.*

The logical interpretation of the satisfaction of a minimal descriptive constraint relies on the notion of S-substitution. A *S-substitution* is an application of a logical formula φ associated with a CG into another one ψ such that with each term or atom of φ a term or an atom of ψ is associated [2].

Property 4 Let $\mathcal{KB}$ be a knowledge base (S, Γ). Let $(G_{In}, G_{Out})_{min}$ be a minimal descriptive constraint. The minimal descriptive constraint is satisfied by $\mathcal{KB}$ if and only if:

for each S-substitution ρ from $\Phi(G_{In})$ into $\Phi(\Gamma)$,
$\exists$ a S-substitution ρ' from $\Phi(G_{Out})$ into $\Phi(\Gamma)$ with
$\rho'(\Phi(head(G_{Out}))) = \rho(\Phi(G_{In}))$.

Example 4 :
Let us consider example 3, with knowledge base $\mathcal{KB}'$ composed of the factual knowledge $\Gamma' = \{\gamma_1, \gamma_2\}$. The logical interpretation [14, 2] of CGs G_{In}, G_{Out} and Γ' are:

$\Phi(G_{In}) = \exists x, y \; Painter(x) \wedge Paint(y) \wedge agt(y, x)$
$\Phi(G_{Out}) = \exists u, v, w \; Painter(u) \wedge Paint(v) \wedge Painting(w) \wedge agt(v, u) \wedge obj(v, w)$
$\Phi(\Gamma') = \exists l, m, n \; Painter(Dali) \wedge Paint(l) \wedge Painting(m) \wedge agt(l, Dali) \wedge obj(l, m) \wedge Painter(Ernst) \wedge Paint(n) \wedge agt(n, Ernst)$

We obtain the same result from a logical point of view as from a graphic one.

(1) Let ρ_1 be a S-substitution from $\Phi(G_{In})$ into $\Phi(\Gamma')$, $\rho_1 = \{(Painter, Painter), (x, Dali), (Paint, Paint), (y, l), (agt, agt)\}$, there exists a S-substitution ρ' from $\Phi(G_{Out})$ into $\Phi(\Gamma')$, $\rho' = \{(Painter, Painter), (u, Dali), (Paint, Paint), (v, l), (Painting, Painting), (w, m), (agt, agt), (obj, obj)\}$ and $\rho'(\Phi(head(G_{Out}))) = \rho_1(\Phi(G_{In}))$.

(2) Let ρ_2 be a S-substitution from $\Phi(G_{In})$ into $\Phi(\Gamma')$, $\rho_2 = \{(Painter, Painter), (x, Ernst), (Paint, Paint), (y, n), (agt, agt)\}$, there doesn't exist a S-substitution ρ' from $\Phi(G_{Out})$ into $\Phi(\Gamma')$ with $\rho'(\Phi(head(G_{Out}))) = \rho_2 (\Phi(G_{In}))$.

$\mathcal{KB}'$ doesn't satisfy the minimal descriptive constraint DC because of case (2).

4.2.2 Satisfaction of Maximal Descriptive Constraints

Let $\mathcal{KB}$ be a knowledge base (S, Γ). Let $(G_{In}, G_{Out})_{max}$ be a maximal descriptive constraint. The *maximal descriptive constraint* is *satisfied* by $\mathcal{KB}$ if and only if for each projection from G_{In} into Γ such that γ is the image graph of G_{In}, there is at most one projection of G_{Out} into Γ with γ the image graph of the head of G_{Out}.

Example 5 :
Let us consider the CG G_{In}, its description G_{Out} and the CGs γ_2 and γ_3 presented in example 2. Let $\mathcal{KB}'$ be a knowledge base composed of the factual knowledge $\Gamma' = \{\gamma_2, \gamma_3\}$. We check if $\mathcal{KB}'$ satisfies the maximal descriptive constraint DC.

(1) There is a projection from G_{In} into γ_2 and there does not exist a projection from G_{Out} into Γ with γ_2 the image graph of $head(G_{Out})$;

(2) there is a projection from G_{In} into γ_3 and there are two projections from G_{Out} into Γ' with γ'_3 the CG limited to vertices c_6, r_4 and c_7 and the image graph of $head(G_{Out})$.

$\mathcal{KB}'$ doesn't satisfy the maximal descriptive constraint DC, because of the two projections from G_{Out} into Γ' in case (2): Ernst paints and he paints nothing, but Miró paints more than one painting.

The logical interpretation of the satisfaction of a maximal descriptive constraint is as follows.

Property 5 Let $\mathcal{KB}$ be a knowledge base (S, Γ). Let $(G_{In}, G_{Out})_{max}$ be a maximal descriptive constraint. $\mathcal{KB}$ satisfies the maximal descriptive constraint if and only if:

$$\text{for each S-substitution } \rho \text{ from } \Phi(G_{In}) \text{ into } \Phi(\Gamma),$$
$$\nexists \text{ S-substitution } \rho' \text{ from } \Phi(G_{Out}) \text{ into } \Phi(\Gamma) \text{ with}$$
$$\rho'(\Phi(head(G_{Out}))) = \rho(\Phi(G_{In}))$$
$$\text{or } \exists ! \text{ S-substitution } \rho' \text{ from } \Phi(G_{Out}) \text{ into } \Phi(\Gamma) \text{ with}$$
$$\rho'(\Phi(head(G_{Out}))) = \rho(\Phi(G_{In})).$$

Example 6 :
Let us consider example 5, with knowledge base $\mathcal{KB}'$ composed of the factual knowledge $\Gamma' = \{\gamma_2, \gamma_3\}$. The logical interpretations of the CGs G_{In}, G_{Out} and Γ' are:
$\Phi(G_{In}) = \exists x, y \; Painter(x) \wedge Paint(y) \wedge agt(y, x)$
$\Phi(G_{Out}) = \exists u, v, w \; Painter(u) \wedge Paint(v) \wedge Painting(w) \wedge agt(v, u) \wedge obj(v, w)$
$\Phi(\Gamma') = \exists l, m \; Painter(Ernst) \wedge Paint(l) \wedge agt(l, Ernst) \wedge Painter(Miró)$
$\wedge Paint(m) \wedge Painting(BlueI) \wedge Painting(BlueII) \wedge agt(m, Miró) \wedge$
$obj(m, BlueI) \wedge obj(m, BlueII)$
We obtain the same result both from a logical and a graphic point of view.

(1) Let ρ_1 be a S-substitution from $\Phi(G_{In})$ into $\Phi(\Gamma')$, $\rho_1 = \{(Painter, Painter), (x, Ernst), (Paint, Paint), (y, l), (agt, agt)\}$, there doesn't exist a S-substitution ρ' from $\Phi(G_{Out})$ into $\Phi(\Gamma')$ with $\rho'(\Phi(head(G_{Out}))) = \rho_1(\Phi(G_{In}))$.

(2) Let ρ_2 be a S-substitution from $\Phi(G_{In})$ into $\Phi(\Gamma')$, $\rho_2 = \{(Painter, Painter), (x, Miró), (Paint, Paint), (y, m), (agt, agt)\}$, there exist two S-substitutions ρ' and ρ'' from $\Phi(G_{Out})$ into $\Phi(\Gamma')$:
$\rho' = \{(Painter, Painter), (u, Miró), (Paint, Paint), (v, m), (Painting, Painting), (w, BlueI), (agt, agt), (obj, obj)\}$ and $\rho'(\Phi(head(G_{Out}))) = \rho_2(\Phi(G_{In}))$;
$\rho'' = \{(Painter, Painter), (u, Miró), (Paint, Paint), (v, m), (Painting, Painting), (w, BlueII), (agt, agt), (obj, obj)\}$ and $\rho''(\Phi(head(G_{Out}))) = \rho_2(\Phi(G_{In}))$.

$\mathcal{KB}'$ doesn't satisfy the maximal descriptive constraint DC because of case (2).

5 SPECIFICATIONS FOR VALIDATION

The semantic validation aims at ensuring that the coherence of the factual knowledge is checked with respect to specifications, which are built by combining constraints, and represent expert knowledge given for validation purpose.

Definition 12 *A knowledge base KB is semantically valid if and only if KB satisfies each specification of the knowledge based system.*

The semantic validation of a knowledge base consists in defining the specifications of the knowledge based system and then studying their satisfaction. A specification is defined by means of constraints combined with disjunction and conjunction operators.

Definition 13 *A specification can be built following these three construction rules.*

1. *A constraint (existential or descriptive) is a specification.*

2. *If s_1 and s_2 are specifications, then $(s_1 \vee s_2)$ and $(s_1 \wedge s_2)$ are specifications.*

3. *Only specifications built by means of rules 1 and 2 are constraints.*

In 3 and 4.2, we saw how to check if a constraint (existential or descriptive) is satisfied or not by a given knowledge base. We can introduce the satisfaction domain $\{S, N\}$, S for "satisfied" or N for "not satisfied".

Checking the satisfaction of a specification consists in associating a "satisfaction value" S or N with it. The satisfaction value of a specification depends on the satisfaction values of its components and of its structure. The following table gives the satisfaction values of the disjunction and the conjunction of two specifications s_1 and s_2, based on their respective satisfaction values:

s_1	s_2	$s_1 \vee s_2$	$s_1 \wedge s_2$
S	S	S	S
S	N	S	N
N	S	S	N
N	N	N	N

The combination of existential and descriptive constraints by means of disjunction and conjunction operators allows one to express specifications, which are complex constraints with a powerful expressiveness.

6 CONCLUSION

In this paper, we proposed solutions to semantically validate CGs. We introduced the notion of specifications, which are expert knowledge given for validation purpose. A knowledge base is semantically valid if it satisfies all the given specifications. The satisfaction of specifications by a knowledge base relies on the projection operation, which is the ground operation of the CG model. The CoGITo platform [6], a tool designed for the implementation of applications based on CGs [9, 1] provides different algorithms of the projection operation. Our validation techniques have been implemented on that platform and tested on a real application in accidentology [5] which concerns modelling knowledge of multiple experts and was developed by the ACACIA team of the INRIA research institute. We have been working on several knowledge bases. The syntactic validation was tested for instance on a support composed of about four hundred concept types and two hundred and fifty relation types and revealed thirty errors. The logical validation was made on a syntactically valid knowledge base composed of approximatively one hundred concept types and fourteen relation types, and of seven CGs; among these graphs, two were logically invalid. On this last base, five specifications were defined according to typical conditions presented in the report [5]. These specifications showed that the knowledge base was not semantically valid. In this paper, we consider the validation of a given knowledge base by means of expert specifications. Another point of view on our work is to consider that the specifications are given before the building of the knowledge base. In that case, the validation is done during the knowledge acquisition stage. Such an incremental validation would allow us to reject immediately invalid knowledge, and thus to ensure that the knowledge base is valid as soon as it is built.

We are currently working on the restoration of an invalid knowledge base in order to correct the base and to obtain a valid knowledge base. The ideal solution would be to provide an automatic restoration, but it is a very difficult problem. The solution we are working on is a combination of automatic and interactive parts of restoration.

References

[1] Bos, C., Botella, B., and Vanheeghe, P. (1997). *Modelling and simulating human behaviours with conceptual graphs.* In Proceedings of the 5th Int. Conference on Conceptual Structures, Lecture Notes in Artificial Intelligence 1257, pp275–289, Seattle, U.S.A. Springer Verlag.

[2] Chein, M. and Mugnier, M.L. (1992). *Conceptual graphs: fundamental notions.* Revue d'Intelligence Artificielle, 6(4), pp365–406.

[3] Dibie, J. (1997). *Validation des graphes conceptuels.* Rapport de stage de DEA, Université Paris IX, Dauphine, Paris, Septembre.

[4] JDibie, J. (1997). *Une validation logique des graphes conceptuels.* 4th Rencontres Nationales des Jeunes Chercheurs en Intelligence Artificielle, pp85–88.

[5] Dieng, R. (1997). *Comparison of conceptual graphs for modelling knowledge of multiple experts: application to traffic accident analysis.* Rapport de recherche 3161, INRIA, Sophia Antipolis.

[6] Haemmerlé, O. (1995). CoGITo: *une plate-forme de développement de logiciels sur les graphes conceptuels.* PhD thesis, Université Montpellier II.

[7] Haouche, C. and Charlet, J. (1996). *KBS validation : a knowledge acquisition perspective. ECAI*, pp433–437.

[8] Hors P. and Rousset, M.V. (1996) *Modeling and verifying complex objects: A declarative approach based on description logics.* ECAI'96.

[9] Martin, P. and Alpay, L. (1996). *Conceptual structures and structured documents.* In Proceedings of the 4th Int. Conference on Conceptual Structures, Lecture Notes in Artificial Intelligence 1115, Springer-Verlag, Sydney, Australia, pp145–159.

[10] Mugnier, M.L. and Chein, M. (1996). *Représenter des connaissances et raisonner avec des graphes.* Revue d'Intelligence Artificielle, 10(1):7–56.

[11] Palmer, G.J. and Craw, S. (1995). *Utilising explanation to assist the refinment of knowledge-based systems.* Proceedings of the 3rd European Symposium on the Validation and Verification of Knowledge Based Systems (EUROVAV'95), Chambery, France, pp201–211.

[12] Preece, A. and Zlaterava, N. (1994). *A state of the art in automated validation of knowledge-based systems.* Expert Systems with Applications, 7(2):151–167.

[13] Rousset, M-C. (1994). *Knowledge formal specifications for formal verification: a proposal based on the integration of different logical formalism.* European Conference on Artificial Intelligence, pp739–743.

[14] Sowa, J.F. (1984). *Conceptual structures: information processing in mind and machine.* Addison Wesley Publishing Company.

PRONTO - Ontology-based Evaluation of Knowledge Based Systems

Trevor J.M. BENCH-CAPON, Dean M. JONES
Department of Computer Science, The University of Liverpool, Liverpool, England, L69 7ZF

Key words: ontology, rule base, conceptualisation, verification, validation

Abstract: In this paper we examine some of the ways in which an ontology can be used to assist in the evaluation of knowledge-based systems. Key elements of the support provided by the ontology relate to attempting to give coherence to the domain conceptualisation; making the role of experts in evaluation more structured and less at the mercy of interpretation; constraining the number of test cases required to give good coverage of the possible cases; and structuring the testing to give better assurance of its efficacy, and provide for a possible basis for greater automation of the testing process. The discussion is focussed on the development of a prototype software tool to support the approach and this is illustrated using a simple, well known, example relating to the identification of animals.

1.   INTRODUCTION

In recent years ontologies have received an increasing amount of attention as a means of supporting the design, development and documentation of knowledge based systems (KBSs). An ontology can be seen as an "explicit specification of the conceptualisation of a domain" (Gruber 1995). Interest in them arises from the growing realisation that the clean separation of knowledge about the domain from task and control knowledge, on which many of the original hopes and expectations for KBSs were founded, is really very difficult to achieve in practice. Invariably the knowledge base will be distorted by considerations arising from the task to be performed on the knowledge, the problem solving method used, the form of representation, and

93

the ways in which and the sources from which the knowledge was acquired. See Visser (1995) for a discussion of these problems.

Ontologies can trace their development from domain models. The idea here is that an ontology can provide a description of the domain which is - as far as possible - independent of the way in which the domain knowledge is to be used, and the task it will be used for. Hitherto, ontologies have been used mainly for knowledge base development, knowledge sharing and knowledge reuse. They do, however, also have considerable potential for use in the verification and validation of KBSs as well. Some preliminary remarks on the role of ontologies in verification and validation were made in Bench-Capon (1998); this paper builds on those remarks and elaborates this role into an implemented prototype.

Throughout the paper we will use as an illustrative example a very simple rule base described in a well known text book on AI (Winston 1992). This rule base, called *ZOOKEEPER*, is concerned with the identification of animals. It is a useful example since everyone has a reasonable familiarity with the domain, and the example is small enough to be presented in a complete form (it is recapitulated in Appendix A). Moreover, since it appears in a text book it represents the sort of rule base which many people see as their first encounter with a KBS, and thus is responsible for many of the ideas people have about such systems.

In section 2, we describe the possibilities that an explicit specification of the conceptualisation of a domain allows for in the evaluation of a KBS. Section 3 describes in more specific terms the way in which we use ontologies for this purpose. In section 4 we outline how we go about developing an ontology for a given rule base and in section 5 we show what this allows. Section 6 is a discussion of ontology-based evaluation in relation to traditional notions of verification and validation and we give some concluding remarks in section 7.

2.   USING ONTOLOGIES IN THE EVALUATION OF KNOWLEDGE-BASED SYSTEMS

In the evaluation of KBSs, a clear distinction can be made between evaluation of the internal and external consistency of a rule base. A rule base is internally consistent if it is structurally sound, which can be determined by ensuring that it free of subsumed rules, contradictions, dead end rules and the like. Internal consistency does not guarantee that a rule base will give the correct answer for any valid query, only that the rules are logically coherent. Determining whether or not the identifications produced by the rule-base are correct is the goal of the evaluation of its external consistency. This typically involves supplying sets of typical observations to the system and evaluating the results produced by the system in relation to some external yardstick (commonly the knowledge of a domain expert.) Additionally, we might present the rules to an expert and ask for confirmation of their correctness.

Given that we have a rule base which is both internally and externally consistent, can we say that the rule base is entirely satisfactory? The answer we give here is no, particularly if we are going to take seriously the possibility of extending the system with additional rules to cater for a wider range of cases. What we are suggesting is that evaluation of a rule base should encompass more than ensuring the absence of structural defects and that the correct answer is always given for the current set of cases, i.e. more than ensuring the internal and external consistency as these were defined above. What we want, in addition, is for the representation to have some kind of conceptual coherence, for it to be expressed within some well defined conceptualisation of the domain, which will promote extensibility and robustness.

Firstly, the distinctions that are made in a rule base should be based on a single, consistent conceptualisation of the domain. In our *ZOOKEEPER* example, distinctions were proliferated as and when they were needed in order to discriminate amongst the seven particular animals, and without much regard for distinctions that had already been made. If a system is to be built correctly, it should make principled distinctions, and make them in a justifiable manner. For example, spots are "dark" and stripes are "black". Do we want a distinction between "dark" and "black"? What other varieties of spots and stripes might there be? Is there really a good difference between being white in colour with black stripes, black in colour with white stripes and whiteandblack in colour? Without a clear conceptualisation to serve as a reference point, it is futile to ask an expert to say whether rules are correct or not. For example, it might be that certain markings resemble rosettes. While one might be prepared to call them "spots" in the absence of an option to call them "rosettes", assent to a rule using "spots" depends on an assumption as to whether the finer grain distinction is available or not.

We also need the required observations to be relatively easy to obtain, if the system is to be able to come up with answers consistently. For example, some of those required by the *ZOOKEEPER* rule base need judgement to be applied - in particular, the requirement be that an albatross flies "well". This might well raise differences of opinion and interpretation. Others are rather hard to obtain: "lays eggs" is an occasional thing which might be hard to observe (and not observable at all in the case of a male of the species). At the very least we need to be aware of what information is likely to be available so that we resort to the information which is harder to obtain only when it is essential. In the ZOOKEEPER rule base it is essential that an giraffe or a zebra be first classed as an ungulate. Both of the observations required to classify an animal as an ungulate are, however, not always available. If the designer is unaware of this practical problems may arise in that giraffes and zebras may not be identified even though sufficient information is available, whereas if the designer is aware of this problem, rules identifying zebras and giraffes in terms of more readily available observations can be supplied.

Much of the problem derives from the initial failure to conceptualise the domain in a coherent fashion. The strategy is first to classify an animal as a mammal or a bird, then sub-divide mammals into carnivores and ungulates, and then to discriminate members of these categories in terms of some observable features which are indicative of the particular animals in the collection. The higher level distinctions are theory driven, and the rules are determined by theory: for example Z4 is justified on the grounds that "some mammals fly and some reptiles lay eggs, but no mammal or reptile does both" (Winston, p122). But in the context of use of the system, Z4 is applicable only to the albatross, since the other two birds are flightless, and if it can fly it is an albatross, so its oviparity is neither here nor there. On the other hand, if we were to take the notion of extensibility seriously Z9 would be inadequate since it describes leopards and jaguars as well as cheetahs. As it stands here the rules are defective, with respect to the standards of a well constructed system, because they derive from conflicting conceptualisations of the domain, and conflicting ideas of how the system will be used. Separation of the animals into mammals and birds, and mammals into carnivores and ungulates, is obviously useful for a zoological taxonomy, but is of little practical importance in performing the identifications the system is supposed to supply.

The problems above derive in part from the lack of a clear specification of what the system will be used for as a starting point. Viewed simply from the standpoint of its real use, as an example rule base to illustrate forward and backward chaining, it is adequate. It is only when we project it into standing as a real application that we would need to specify whether it was supposed to identify only seven or an indefinite range of animals; whether it is meant to incorporate a known theory about animal classification, or to restrict itself to what can be seen; what kind of judgements the user of the system can be expected to make, and the like. As they stand the rules represent more the unstructured outpouring of information about the animals, rather than a well thought out plan for identification.

One major problem that has always existed in checking the external consistency of rule bases of a substantial size (and in this context even *ZOOKEEPER* can be considered substantial), is the combinatorial explosion that combining the predicates in test cases gives rise to. In the original *ZOOKEEPER* there were 20 predicates each of which appeared capable of being true or false independently, giving more than a million possible combinations. On this basis exhaustive testing can be considered impossible, and so test data must be selected by using some selected plausible combinations. There is, however, no systematic way of generating these and so coverage of the important cases is not only not ensured, but there is not even any reliable way of estimating the coverage provided by the test data. In section 4, we will show how this can be improved through constructing an ontology for the rule base. First, we will illustrate how we construct the ontology for the rule base, continuing to base our on discussion on *ZOOKEEPER*.

3.   THE DEVELOPMENT OF AN ONTOLOGY FOR RULE BASE EVALUATION

The question we address in this section is how we go about developing an ontology for the evaluation of a specific rule base. A recent survey of ontology development methodologies (Jones *et al.*, 1998) showed that there are two general strategies that are pursued in the construction of a new ontology, the stage-based approach and the evolving prototype approach. It was suggested that where a clear task can be identified and the purpose and requirements of the ontology are evident at the outset, the stage-based approach is most appropriate since this allows the ontology to be assessed in relation to the given requirements at the completion of each stage. In common with this, and since we have a well defined task, we adopted a stage-based strategy in the development of an ontology for the *ZOOKEEPER* rule base. We will now describe each of the phases in turn.

It was also suggested in Jones *et al.* (1998) that the initial phase of the development of a new ontology is commonly concerned with defining the minimal necessary scope of the ontology, as this allows us to ensure that the ontology at least satisfies the requirements of the task. The minimal requirement for our ontology of *ZOOKEEPER* is that it should permit the expression of all the facts and rules about the animals found in the original rules. Consequently, the first scoping exercise is to list the classes in the ontology, the hierarchical relationships between them (shown in Fig. 1) and the attributes that can be identified from the rules that are used to describe the classes. For *ZOOKEEPER*, the user is expected to be able to answer questions about the following predicates (note that the predicates relating to whether the animal is a mammal, bird, carnivore and ungulate are internal to the system; the user is neither asked questions about these predicates, nor sees any information about them.)

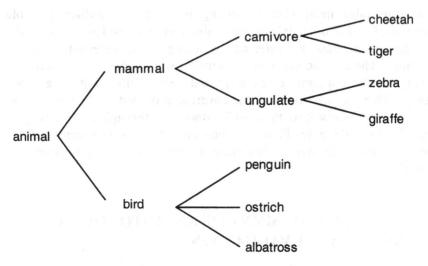

Figure 1. Class Hierarchy for ZOOKEEPER

a) has hair
b) gives milk
c) has feathers
d) flies
e) lays eggs
f) eats meat
g) long legs
h) long neck
i) tawny colour
j) dark spots

k) white colour
l) black stripes
m) black and white colour
n) swims
o) flies well
p) pointed teeth
q) claws
r) eyes point forward
s) hoofs
t) chews cud

One problem that can immediately be identified with this list is that, although some of the predicates seem to imply alternatives, only one option is used in the rule base because the alternatives are not needed by the current set of rules. For example, although it is possible to express the observation that an animal has eyes that point forward, the equally valid observation that an animal's eyes point sideways cannot be expressed. As outlined in section 2, the above predicates are not, as they stand, conceptually coherent. The second phase of the development of our ontology must be to organise the predicates into a principled set based on a coherent conceptualisation of the domain. Those predicates that allow for the addition of alternatives are grouped below with suitable values:

Coat :
  Material {hair,feathers}
  Colour {white, tawny, black}

Markings :
  Pattern {spots,stripes,irregular,none}
  Shade {light,dark, n/a}

Facial Features
  Eyes {forward,sideways}
  Teeth {pointed,rounded,none}

Feet {claws,hoofs}
Flies {no, poorly, well}
Eats {meat, plants, both}

Size :
  Neck {long, normal}
  Legs {long, normal}

Gives Milk {true, false}
Lays Eggs {true, false}
Chews Cud {true, false}
Swims {true, false}

Table 1. Attributes and Values for *ZOOKEEPER*

teeth{pointed, rounded} [p]
eats{meat, plants, everything}[f]
legs{long, normal} [g]
neck{long, normal} [h]

stripes{black, white} [l]
spots{dark, light} [j]
flies{well,poorly, no} [d,o]
eyes{forward, sideways} [r]

Some of the predicates specify alternative values for the same attribute and these can also be grouped together:
    skin covering {hair,feathers} [a,c]
    markings{spots,stripes} [j,l]
    movesBy{swims,flies} [n,o]
In other cases the only values for the predicate are true or false:
    gives milk [b]
    lays eggs [e]
    chews cud [t]
We can retain the remaining predicates (renamed where appropriate):
    colour{white, tawny,black and white} [i,k,m]
    feet{hoofs,claws} [q,s]
At the end of the second stage, we have a representation in which no two predicates describe the same attribute in the conceptualisation. However, the predicates do not yet form a collectively coherent set. Some of our predicates, *e.g.* flying and swimming, are not mutually exclusive (consider ducks and swans), so they must be separated. Moreover, flying appears to be a qualitative thing rather than a simple boolean: we could ask whether the same should apply to swimming as well, and indeed whether we want to include some kind of land motion such as running. We can also make the markings and colour situation more coherent by saying that an animal has a basic colour, and markings, which may be lighter or darker than the basic colour.

Predicate	Cheetah	Tiger	Zebra	Giraffe	Ostrich	Penguin	Albatross
Material	hair	hair	hair	hair	feathers	feathers	feathers
Colour	tawny	tawny	white	tawny	black	black	white
Pattern	spots	stripes	stripes	spots	irregular	irregular	none
Shade	dark	dark	dark	dark	light	light	n/a
Eyes	forward	forward	sideways	sideways	sideways	forward	sideways
Teeth	pointed	pointed	rounded	rounded	none	none	none
Feet	claws	claws	hoofs	hoofs	toes	toes	toes
Neck	normal	normal	normal	normal	long	normal	normal
Legs	normal	normal	normal	long	long	normal	normal
Gives Milk	true	true	true	true	false	false	false
Flies	no	no	no	no	no	no	well
Eats	meat	meat	plants	plants	both	meat	meat
Lays Eggs	false	false	false	false	true	true	true

Table 2. Attributes of Animals in *ZOOKEEPER*

Where we have gaps, because the options do not occur explicitly, these need to be filled. The problem of making the predicates mutually coherent is addressed in the third stage of development of the ontology. The rationalisations that occur during this phase are largely dependent upon the details of the conceptualisation being considered and are consequently difficult to generalise. However, the tasks carried out during this stage include (but are not limited to):

1. separation of predicates that are not mutually exclusive;
2. inclusion of additional alternatives to predicates separated during 1.;
3. decide whether values are boolean, qualitative, etc.;
4. decide which predicates have values that are mutually exclusive

At the completion of the third stage, we arrive at the situation where we can identify a set of attributes, and the possible values they can take. This will provide us with a well defined vocabulary with which to construct a set of rules. The set of conceptually coherent attributes for the *ZOOKEEPER* example is shown in Table 1.

The fourth phase is concerned with ascribing the relevant attribute-value pairs to each of the classes in our ontology, which provides us with a definition for the classes, under the current conceptualisation. Firstly, we construct a table listing each of the bottom-level classes and the relevant values for each of the attributes, such as that given in Table 2 (Note that some of the answers are conjectural - we are not experts, and are unsure what ostriches in fact eat, for example.) This process is likely to identify additional possibilities for some of the attributes (for example birds do not have teeth, and penguins eat fish), which will force us to extend the ontology accordingly. These attribute-pairs can be generalised to higher-level classes where it is both possible and plausible to do so. Some generalisations are logically possible given the current set of animals but are not realistic, e.g. all carnivores have tawny coats.

Next, we need to add some axioms, stating combinations which are impossible. Some of these combinations will have been identified during the third stage, especially in task (iv) from the list above. Examples include:

A1 Not (eats meat and chews cud)

A2 Not (Material feathers and chews cud)

A3 Not (Pattern none and shade not n/a)

In fact we could supply many more such axioms, but at this stage we need not attempt to be exhaustive. The addition of some axioms allows us to remove attribute values from the definitions of some of the classes, *e.g.* given A1 we do not need to include a value for the predicate `chews_cud/2` for each of the carnivores.

We now have an ontology which we can use to verify and validate a knowledge base built on it. First, however, we need to check the quality of the ontology itself. This is where the expert comes in: the expert should not be shown the encoded rules, but rather the ontology. This changes the role of the expert significantly. The expert no longer examines rules, but instead the vocabulary. With respect to the vocabulary the expert should check:

1. that the attributes represent sensible distinctions
2. that the values are exclusive
3. that the values are exhaustive

The point about values can be addressed from two standpoints: either from the point of view of the existing collection, or from the point of view of a potentially extended collection. The first will indicate what is needed to test the rule base against its current operation, and the other will provide an indication of its extensibility. Also, to facilitate testing the expert should indicate whether observations are always available, or only sometimes available. Following this process we might modify Table 1 to give Table 3.

Here always observable *attributes* are indicated in bold, as are *values* required by the current seven animals. The expert should also examine the table of attributes (Table 2), to confirm that these entries are correct. The table can be further verified by ensuring that it does not conflict with any of the axioms. By concentrating on the ontology rather than the rules, the role of the expert becomes much more well defined, and more systematic so that there is less possibility of interpretation allowing errors to go unnoticed.

Coat :
  Material {hair,feathers,scales}
  Colour {white, tawny, black, grey, russet}

Markings :
  Pattern {spots,stripes,irregular,none}
  Shade {light,dark, n/a}

Facial Features
  Eyes {forward,sideways}
  Teeth {pointed,rounded,none}

Feet {claws,hoofs,toes}
*[Comment: feet are hard to observe
(Winston)]*

Flies {no, poorly, well}

Eats {meat, plants, both}
[Comment: meat includes fish]

Size :
  Neck {long, normal}
  Legs {long, normal}

Gives Milk {true, false}
Lays Eggs {true, false}
Chews Cud {true, false}
Swims {true, false}

Table 3. Validated Attributes and values for *ZOOKEEPER*

4. PRONTO - A TOOL FOR ONTOLOGY-BASED EVALUATION OF RULE BASES

Once we are satisfied with the ontology we can proceed to evaluate the rule base. The ontology allows a substantial improvement on the number of test cases that were originally identified as necessary in section 2. The grouping together of attributes in the ontology identifies predicates that are not independent. If we allow for 5 colours, coverage of these as booleans would require 64 cases. By considering them as they are in the ontology, however, there are only five cases. If we confine ourselves to testing only the attributes which the expert has identified as always available as observations, and only the values actually used by our current collection, we have only 1152 combinations. The useful test data moreover, contains only those cases which conform to the constraints imposed by the axioms. This enables a substantial further pruning. If we are able to identify a good set of axioms, then exhaustive testing becomes a possibility. We can now rigorously specify the minimal set of test cases that are required to exhaustively test the rule base. The ontology provides the essential input for our automated test harness, a prototype of which - called PRONTO - has been implemented in Prolog.

Once the minimal set of test cases for a given rule base has been identified, testing can begin with the evaluation of the results being provided by an expert. Incorrect output falls into one of the three possibilities that are outlined below with the potential causes of each type:

1. no answer; this can arise in several situations:
a) the case represents an impossible combination, so an axiom should be added to the ontology to exclude such cases;
b) the case is possible but these animals are not in the collection. The rule base is correct, and the combination should not be observed in practice. We can therefore either add a new rule, extending the coverage to animals outside the current collection, or simply disregard it; or
c) the case is possible, but identification is reliant on some not always available feature.
2. a single incorrect answer. This indicates either:
a) the case is possible and an offending rule requires amendment, or
b) the case is impossible and an axiom should be added to the ontology is in order to exclude it;
3. multiple answers; here there are further possibilities;
a) if no answers are correct, we have a similar situation to 2., *i.e.* either
    i) the case is possible and more than one rule requires amendment, or
    ii) the case is impossible and an axiom should be added to exclude it.
b) if the solution contains a single correct answer with at least one incorrect result, the ontology is sufficient to discriminate the correct result but at least one rule needs to be made more specific (possibly using not always available features).
c) if there is more than one correct solution the current ontology is inadequate and requires another predicate to discriminate the cases. The rule base should then be amended to include this new predicate. Additional modifications to the rule base may be required if the solution also includes erroneous results.

We should be careful in modifying the rule base not to introduce new problems. For example, a test case that produces a solution of type (1c) may encourage us to remove the antecedent that relies on the hard to observe feature. This, in turn, may result in the same case producing solutions of type (2) or (3). If so, we may have to reconcile ourselves to a certain incompleteness, or find some always available discriminating observation. Results of type (2) might lead us to introduce antecedents relating to intermittently observable features, whereas case (3) may motivate us to remove them.

This classification of the types of erroneous results leads us to the development of the testing process as represented diagrammatically in Fig. 2. Note that process 1, *generate case*, uses the ontology; the decision *violates axioms?*, uses the output from process 1 together with the axioms from the ontology; process 2, *execute cases*, uses the rule base and the mappings from the ontology predicates into the rule base predicates; *answer correct?* and *animal in collection?* requires an extensional description of actual animals

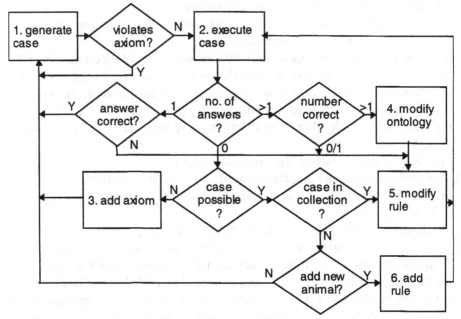

Figure 2. Schematic of Testing Process

such as is provided by Table 2; processes 3 and 4, *add axiom* and *modify ontology* modify the ontology; processes 5 and 6, *modify rules* and *add rule*, modify the rule base; and *case possible?* and requires input from the expert. Adding axioms will prune the cases subsequently generated and additional and modified rules are tested before a new case is generated.

The ontology cannot, of course, work magic: the testing effort required even with this test harness is substantial and non-trivial, requiring as it does considerable expert input. It does, however, supply the discipline and structure necessary for testing a system, and in any event testing is always for any system an important and lengthy task, typically consuming anything between 25% and 30% of the development time of a software project. Moreover, the time spent in getting the initial ontology right, particularly with respect to a complete specification of the necessary axioms, is handsomely repaid by savings in testing required. In addition to these possibilities for evaluation against the ontology, normal structural checks should, of course, be applied. The quasi-random testing is, however, unnecessary given the more structured approach permitted by the ontology.

```
M01: hair(X) :- coat_material(X,hair).
M02: gives_milk(X) :- gives_milk(X,true).
M03: feathers(X) :- coat_material(X,feathers).
M04: flies(X) :- flies(X,true).
M05: flies(X,well) :- flies(X,true).
M06: lays_eggs(X) :- lays_eggs(X,true).
M07: has(X,Y) :- feet(X,Y).
M08: spots(X,dark) :- markings_pattern(X,spots),
                      markings_shade(X,dark).
M09: spots(X,white) :- markings_pattern(X,spots),
                       markings_shade(X,light).
M10: stripes(X,black) :- markings_pattern(X,stripes),
                         markings_shade(X,dark).
M11: stripes(X,white) :- markings_pattern(X,stripes),
                         markings_shade(X,light).
```

Table 4. Mappings between *ZOOKEEPER* Rule base and Ontology

5.   DEMONSTRATION OF PRONTO

Once we have defined the ontology for a rule base, we need to map the predicates found in the rule base onto the terms in the ontology. We can do this as a set of Prolog rules. A possible set of mappings is given in Table 4. Note that no mapping rules are given for teeth/2, eats/2, eyes/2, colour/2, legs/2 or neck/2 since those appear both in the rule base and the ontology. Note also that not always observable attributes are randomly included in test cases to reflect that they are sometimes available.

Our first example of the use of PRONTO illustrated in Appendix B1, the rule base identifies the test case of a swimming animal as a giraffe. Although this case could be eliminated from the evaluation process by adding an axiom, this would be the wrong option since the conditions are not impossible. It is simply a matter of fact that giraffes cannot swim, although some other long necked, spotted, tawny ungulate might be able to. In the classification given in section 4, this result is of type (2a) - a single incorrect result which is theoretically plausible. The correct option in this scenario is to add the condition swims(X,false) to rule Z11 to indicate that giraffes cannot swim. In our second example, given in Appendix B2, however an animal with claws is identified as a giraffe. If we look at the original rule base, all of the conditions in Z11 are satisfied. Since, according to our ontology, all ungulates have toes, we know that the case is impossible and we have a scenario of type (2b). The solution here, as can be observed from the example, is to add an axiom to rules out cases where we have both chews_cud(X,true) and feet(X,claws).

For our third example, consider rules Z13 and Z14. On the basis of the guaranteed observable predicates, which, recall, do not include swimming and flying, cases will allow both these rules to fire, identifying the animal as both a penguin and an ostrich. Such a situation is shown in Appendix B3. Examination of this case reveals that ostrich is the right answer, since the cases contain `legs(X,long)` and `neck(X,long)`. This situation is classified as type (3b) - our ontology is sufficient to discriminate the animal that the case should be identified as but an additional erroneous solution is also included. We could rectify this situation without recourse to the intermittently observable predicates by adding `legs(X,normal)` as an extra condition to Z14. Discriminating between a cheetah and a leopard would, however, require an extension to the ontology, since in terms of what is currently in the ontology the two are identical. We would need to extend the ontology to allow for a condition such as having the ability to climb trees, or having retractable claws.

6.　　DISCUSSION

Here we begin with Boehm's well known distinction between verification and validation (Boehm 1981):

verification: are we building the product right?

validation: are we building the right product?

The purpose of verification is to determine whether or not the implemented system correctly fulfils its design while the process of validation aims to ensure that the functionality embodied in the design meets the user's actual requirements. Verification is usually performed in one of two ways:

1. domain-independent analysis of relationships between the rules (this correlates to what we termed the assessment of internal consistency in section 2);

2. comparison of the behaviour of the system to a (more or less) formal design specification.

Validation, according to Boehm's definition, should be performed by comparing the requirements specification (which makes the user's requirements explicit) with the formal design specification. However, for KBSs formal requirements specification and design specification documents are rarely available. In theory, validation of a KBS should only be based on the results of test cases if the system has already been verified. For this reason, in the evaluation of KBS systems verification and valuation are often not distinguished and we find descriptions of V&V techniques, rather than separate discussions of methods of verification or of validation. When

	1a	1b	1c	2a	2b	3a(i)	3a(ii)	3b	3c
verification			✔	✔		✔		✔	
validation	✔	✔			✔		✔		✔

Table 5. Case Types as Verification or Validation

Boehm's definitions are applied to the evaluation KBSs, the clear distinction becomes somewhat blurred.

The ontology used in PRONTO specifies the conceptualisation underlying the rule base rather than the domain and can be taken to form part of the design specification. Now, whether erroneous results require us to change the rule base or the ontology indicates whether we are performing verification or validation. When the ontology is used to determine that the rule base should be changed, the system is being verified since it does not match the design as embodied by the ontology. On the other hand, when we are required to modify the ontology we are performing validation as (this part of) the specification does not fulfil the requirements of the user. Recall the different types of erroneous results that were distinguished in section 4; where the rule base requires modification (types 2a, 3a(i) and 3b) the system does not satisfy the ontology and we can say that making these types of changes is verification of the system. However, where the ontology needs refinement (types 1a, 1b, 1c, 2b, 3a(ii) and 3c) we can say that the specification does not match users requirements and modifying the ontology is validation of the system.

The situation is slightly more complex, however, because if we actually revisit the descriptions given in section 4, we see that in case 1b the ontology and the rule base are in fact correct and should only be modified if we want to extend the coverage of the rule base (thereby extending the user's requirements. This is, therefore, neither verification nor validation. Also, results of type (3c) require that we modify both the ontology and the rule base. However, as the initial rule base matches the specification in the form of the ontology, here we are performing validation only. This is summarised in Table 5.

The question is, do we need to worry about maintaining the distinction? That is, does our ability to assess whether a particular evaluation technique is verification or validation help in producing better KBSs? We would say that the answer is no, since the purpose of the distinction was originally to help determine whether the problem lies with the implementation or the design. If knowing whether we are involved in verification or validation requires us to know whether a test case indicates a problem with the rule base or with the ontology, we have already addressed the original problem and provided we recognise that there are two separate forms of difficulty, the terminology used is not important

7.   CONCLUSIONS

In this paper we have shown how an ontology can be used to aid verification and validation, illustrated by a simple example, and a discussion of an implemented prototype system. The main conclusions are:
- having an ontology provides an objective point of reference for verification and validation activities;
- much of the interaction with the expert can be done in terms of the ontology. This means that the role of the expert is better defined, and it is not necessary to judge rules which may depend for their meaning on implicit assumptions, and the context within which they will be used. Essentially the expert can focus on the conceptualisation, free from implementation details;
- testing can be structured by the ontology;
- when test fails, the failures can be classified so as to determine the appropriate response;
- some test results will result in a modification of the program and others in a modification of the ontology. As was discussed in section 6 this provides a useful distinction between failures resulting from the way the conceptualisation has been implemented to the program and failures resulting from inadequacies in the conceptualisation itself.

For future work we would like to extend the Pronto system to incorporate existing work in the evaluation of KBSs. In particular, we aim to incorporate a facility that will assist in the identification the rules which need modification (Coenen and Bench-Capon, 1993).

REFERENCES

Bench-Capon, T.J.M. (1998) "The Role of Ontologies in the Verification and Validation of Knowledge Based Systems", *Proceedings of the Ninth International Workshop on Database and Expert Systems*, IEEE Press, Los Alamitos, pp64-69.

Coenen, F.P. and T.J.M. Bench-Capon (1993) *Maintenance of Knowledge Based Systems: Theory, Tools and Techniques*, Academic Press, London.

Boehm, B.W. (1981) *Software Engineering Economics*, Prentice Hall.

Gruber, T.R. (1995) "Towards Principles for the Design of Ontologies Used for Knowledge Sharing", *Int. J. Human-Computer Interaction*, 43, 907-928.

Jones, D.M., T.J.M. Bench-Capon, and P.R.S. Visser (1998) "Methodologies for Ontology Development", *Proc. IT&KNOWS Conference of the 15th IFIP World Computer Congress*, Budapest, Chapman-Hall.

Visser, P.R.S. (1995) "Knowledge Specification for Multiple Legal Tasks", Kluwer.
Winston, P.H. (1992) *Artificial Intelligence*, Third Edition. Addison Wesley, Reading, Mass.

APPENDIX A - THE *ZOOKEEPER* RULE BASE

The rulebase for *ZOOKEEPER* is given in Winston (1992), page 121-4. It is explicitly limited to the identification of seven animals: a cheetah, tiger, zebra, giraffe, ostrich, penguin and an albatross. It has 15 rules, enabling identification of these seven animals, often in several ways, to allow for some observations being unobtainable. The rules (expressed here in Prolog form) are:

```
Z1:  mammal(X)    :- hair(X).
Z2:  mammal(X)    :- givesMilk(X).
Z3:  bird(X)      :- feathers(X).
Z4:  bird(X)      :- flies(X),
                     laysEggs(X).
Z5:  carnivore(X) :- mammal(X),
                     eats(X,meat).
Z6:  carnivore(X) :- mammal(X),
                     teeth(X,pointed),
                     has(X,claws),
                     eyes(X,forwardPointing).
Z7:  ungulate(X)  :- mammal(X),
                     has(X,hoofs).
Z8:  ungulate(X)  :- mammal(X),
                     chewsCud(X).
Z9:  cheetah(X)   :- carnivore(X),
                     colour(X,tawny),
                     spots(X,dark).
Z10: tiger(X)     :- carnivore(X),
                     colour(X,tawny),
                     stripes(X,black).
Z11: giraffe(X)   :- ungulate(X),
                     legs(X,long),
                     neck(X,long),
                     colour(X,tawny),
                     spots(X,dark).
Z12: zebra(X)     :- ungulate(X),
                     colour(X,white),
                     stripes(X,black).
Z13: ostrich(X)   :- bird(X),
                     not flies(X),
                     legs(X,long),
                     neck(X,long),
                     colour(X,blackandwhite).
Z14: penguin(X)   :- bird(X),
                     swims(X),
                     not flies(X),
                     colour(X,blackandwhite).
Z15: albatross(X) :- bird(X),
                     flies(X,well).
```

APPENDIX B1

Testing case:
  swims: true
  lays_eggs: false
  gives_milk: true
  legs: long
  neck: long
  feet: hoofs
  teeth: rounded
  eyes: forward
  markings_pattern: spots
  markings_shade: dark
  coat_colour: tawny
  coat_material: hair
One result: giraffe.
Is the answer correct (y/n/q)?
|: n.
You need to modify a rule.
Enter head of rule to modify.
|: animalis.
Enter arity of rule to modify.
|: 2.
Current listing for rule is:
Clause 1:
animalis(A, cheetah) :-
        carnivore(A),
        colour(A, tawny),
        spots(A, dark).
Clause 2:
animalis(A, tiger) :-
        carnivore(A),
        colour(A, tawny),
        stripes(A, black).
Clause 3:
animalis(A, giraffe) :-
        ungulate(A),
        legs(A, long),
        neck(A, long),
        colour(A, tawny),
        spots(A, dark).
Clause 4:
animalis(A, zebra) :-
        ungulate(A),
        colour(A, white),
        stripes(A, black).
Clause 5:
animalis(A, ostrich) :-
        bird(A),
        not flies(A),
        legs(A, long),
        neck(A, long),
        colour(A, black),
        spots(A, white).

Clause 6:
animalis(A, penguin) :-
        bird(A),
        swims(A),
        not flies(A),
        colour(A, black),
        spots(A, white).
Clause 7:
animalis(A, albatross) :-
        bird(A),
        flies(A, well).
Select option:
1. Add clause.
2. Add condition to clause.
3. Remove clause.
4. Remove condition from clause.
|: 2.
Enter clause number to add condition
for animalis/2.
|: 3.
Current clause.
animalis(A, giraffe) :-
        ungulate(A),
        legs(A, long),
        neck(A, long),
        colour(A, tawny),
        spots(A, dark).
Enter new condition.
|: swims(A,false).
New clause.
animalis(A, giraffe) :-
        ungulate(A),
        legs(A, long),
        neck(A, long),
        colour(A, tawny),
        spots(A, dark),
        swims(A, false).
Re-testing case:
  swims: true
  lays_eggs: false
  gives_milk: true
  legs: long
  neck: long
  feet: hoofs
  teeth: rounded
  eyes: forward
  markings_pattern: spots
  markings_shade: dark
  coat_colour: tawny
  coat_material: hair
No answers.

APPENDIX B2

```
Testing case :
   lays_eggs: false
   gives_milk: true
   chews_cud: true
   legs: long
   neck: long
   feet: claws
   teeth: rounded
   eyes: forward
   markings_pattern: spots
   markings_shade: dark
   coat_colour: tawny
   coat_material: hair
One result: giraffe.
Is the answer correct (y/n/q)?
|: n.
Is the case possible (y/n)?
|: n.
You need to add an axiom.
Enter attribute and value pairs
for
new axiom.
Enter attribute.
Possibilities:
[coat_material,coat_colour,
markings_pattern,
```

```
markings_shade,  eyes,  teeth,
feet, flies, eats, neck, legs,
gives_milk,lays_eggs,
chews_cud, swims].
|: chews_cud.
Enter value for attribute
'chews_cud'.
Possibilities: [true, false].
|: true.
Enter attribute.
Possibilities: [coat_material,
coat_colour, markings_pattern,
markings_shade,  eyes,  teeth,
feet,
flies, eats, neck, legs,
gives_milk,lays_eggs,
chews_cud,
swims].
|: feet.
Enter  value  for  attribute
'feet'.
Possibilities: [claws, hoofs,
toes].
|: claws.
```

APPENDIX B3

Testing case:
   swims: true
   gives_milk: false
   legs: long
   neck: long
   flies: false
   feet: claws
   teeth: pointed
   eyes: forward
   markings_shade: light
   markings_pattern: spots
   coat_colour: black
   coat_material: feathers
More than one result: [penguin,
ostrich].
Can you modify a rule (y/n/q)?
|: y.
Enter head of rule to modify.
|: animalis.
Enter arity of rule animalis to
modify.
|: 2.
Current   listing   for   rule
animalis/2
is:
Clause 1:
animalis(A, cheetah) :-
     carnivore(A),
     colour(A, tawny),
     spots(A, dark).
Clause 2:
animalis(A, tiger) :-
     carnivore(A),
     colour(A, tawny),
     stripes(A, black).
Clause 3:
animalis(A, giraffe) :-
     ungulate(A),
     legs(A, long),
     neck(A, long),
     colour(A, tawny),
       spots(A, dark).
Clause 4:
animalis(A, zebra) :-
     ungulate(A),
     colour(A, white),
     stripes(A, black).

Clause 5:
animalis(A, ostrich) :-
     bird(A),
     not flies(A),
     legs(A, long),

     neck(A, long),
     colour(A, black),
     spots(A, white).
Clause 6:
animalis(A, penguin) :-
     bird(A),
     swims(A),
     not flies(A),
     colour(A, black),
     spots(A, white).
Clause 7:
animalis(A, albatross) :-
     bird(A),
     flies(A, well).
Select option:
1. Add clause.
2. Add condition to clause.
3. Remove clause.
4.   Remove   condition   from
clause.
|: 2.
Enter clause number to add
condition for animalis/2.
|: 6.
Enter new condition.
|: legs(A,normal).
Re-testing case:
   swims: true
   gives_milk: false
   legs: long
   neck: long
   flies: false
   feet: claws
   teeth: pointed
   eyes: forward
   markings_shade: light
   markings_pattern: spots
   coat_colour: black
   coat_material: feathers
One result: ostrich.

Formal Methods for the engineering and certification of safety-critical Knowledge Based Systems

Giovanna Dondossola

ENEL-SRI, Distribution Area, Department of Electronic Systems and Automation
Via Volta 1, Cologno Monzese 20093 Milan, Italy E-mail: dondossola@pea.enel.it

Key words: functional and non functional requirements, safety requirements, software criticality and integrity levels, embedded computer-based control systems, knowledge based systems, knowledge engineering and certification, combining formal and informal methods, formal specification methods, formal verification and validation techniques, certification techniques, dynamic testing

Abstract: The main aim of this work is positioning formal methods in the context of knowledge based software. Peculiar aspects of formal methods for knowledge-based systems and their role in knowledge engineering are summarised. Particular attention is posed on the verification and validation capabilities of formal methods as the actual added value substantiating the onerous effort required by their development and exploitation. This paper constitutes a result of the Safe-KBS Project[1] whose basic aim was defining development and certification methodologies specifically oriented to the production of knowledge-based software embedded into safety critical systems.

[1] The Safe-KBS project was partially funded by the ESPRIT Programme of the Commission of the European Communities as project n° 22360. The partners in the Safe-KBS project were Sextant-Avionique, Det Norske Veritas, Enel-Sri, Tecnatom, Computas Expert Systems, Uninfo, Qualience. This paper has been written after the termination of the project and represents an effort performed by ENEL alone.

113

1.   INTRODUCTION

This paper presents basic ideas concerning the use of formal methods in the knowledge-based software development, also highlighting the effective impact that formal methods adoption produces on the certification of safety-critical software embedding KB components.

A knowledge-based system (KBS) is a software system that includes a knowledge base, containing an explicit representation of the knowledge relevant to some specific competence domain, and a reasoning mechanism that can exploit such knowledge in order to provide high-level problem-solving performance. KBS are developed in the so-called knowledge representation languages (KRL) which all have a logical foundation. The first and still widely used paradigm in knowledge representation is based on rules. From a formal point of view rule-based representations provide subsets of first order logic augmented with meta-level capabilities. Another paradigm adopted in knowledge representation is based on objects, whose examples are all the languages based on Description Logic and Frame Logic, which are suitable to capture domain ontology. More recent representation languages are based on hybrid paradigms integrating rules and objects.

A *safety-critical* KBS is a KB software system which implements a function or component characterised by the highest *Software Integrity Level (SIL)* [2], while a *safety-related* KBS refers to KB software used to implement functions or components of any software integrity level.

Formal methods (FM) refer to the use of techniques from formal logic and discrete mathematics in the specification, design, construction and verification of computer systems and software. Therefore a formal method is often equipped with a logical calculus which may be checked systematically by an automatic tool.

The advantages of FM in software development, widely recognised by the traditional software community, are beginning to be recognised by the Knowledge Engineering (KE) research community. Recent works are moving towards two directions, namely the development of new KB-specific FM (see [Fensel 95b], [Fensel 96], [Fensel 98a], [van Harmelen 92]) and the application of existing methods provided by the traditional Software Engineering. Comparative analyses of FM for KB-specific versus generic

---

[2] According to the standard ISO/IEC DIS 15026 the Software Integrity Level (SIL) is the *assigned* level to which risk associated with a software product or item is to be contained when used in a system for a specific application.

software can be found in [Fensel 94], [Fensel 95a], [Aben 95], [van Harmelen 95], [Meseguer 96].

A primary aim in using FM in KBS is to improve the quality of KB software development processes and products. In this respect people working on FM from the KE community purse the objective to increase the level of precision currently available in KE practise, both in terms of the methodologies, or control tools, adopted for structuring development processes into interacting work items and of the development tools used to perform those work items.

The basic role that FM have in KE is to provide specification languages that have a mathematical foundation. The major benefit here derives from a double application of FM both to the KBS formal specification and the formal validation/verification of KBS specification. Discrete mathematical models allow to obtain precise and unambiguous specifications and provide the means for defining and developing automatic tools for formally validating the specification, globally increasing the quality of the software documentation and implementation, therefore reducing the effort required by software maintainability. Being oriented to a specific class of software systems, specification languages recently developed by the KE community (such as those based on Dynamic Logic, i.e. KARL [Fensel 95b] and $(ML)^2$ [van Harmelen 92]) make a major emphasis on the ability to describe the *dynamic* aspects of the reasoning process, which is usually modelled as procedural control knowledge on elementary inference steps defined in a declarative way. A combination of declarative and procedural capabilities is required in order to express the peculiarities of KBS. This is the reason why specification languages from KE were conceived as means formalising the (informal) *conceptual model* of the KBS, which represents a refinement of the requirements including high level design aspects (by using the traditional software terminology).

Furthermore formal specification supports system verification by allowing to compare two different level descriptions of the system, namely the specification and the implementation levels, according to specified criteria (such as structural, behavioural). By generalising this capability, it can be said that FM support a step-wise approach to system verification where a following description of the system is compared with the preceding one.

A second important role of FM is in the verification of implemented systems against their informal specification (aka conformance testing). Here is a low-level system description that is formalised and formally checked for adherence to system specification. Most of the practise and research[3] in the

---

[3]See the World Wide Web online Proceedings of the Workshop on "Validation & Verification of Knowledge-Based Systems" at URL http://www.cs.vu.nl/~frankh/VVKR98-schedule.html.

KBS V&V techniques refers to systems implemented by using rule-based KRL. KBS V&V tools realise algorithms able to detect anomalies in a knowledge base expressed as a set of rules. Anomalies are expressed in terms of the syntactic form of single rules, rule pairs and rule chains and anomaly detection consists of search procedures in the rule space. Therefore KBS V&V practise focuses on the verification of the internal structure of the knowledge base. Extensions of the anomaly definitions considering the hierarchical relationships among objects of hybrid representations have been provided, but no V&V tool supporting anomaly detection in hybrid knowledge bases has been developed yet. The anomaly definition approach has been also applied at the level of conceptual model. Inference steps of the reasoning process are expressed by sorted predicates and anomalies are caused by subsumption relationships among sorts. Moving the anomaly detection V&V technique towards the conceptual level reduces the gap between KBS formal specification languages together with their validation techniques on one side, and KRL together with their verification techniques on the other side.

A final role of FM is in the automatic generation of test cases from specification to be used in the final system testing. Manual test case generation is a tedious, repetitive and costly work that can greatly benefit from the availability of automatic tools. Deductive techniques provided by FM can be exploited to automate well-founded test design strategies.

The use of FM in KBS development is presented in the following section structure:

- Section 1 introduces the FM requirements for the KBS specification
- Section 2 is about the formal verification and validation of KBS
- Section 3 concerns the impact of the use of FM on the KBS life cycle model
- Section 4 deals with the support to the KBS certification provided by FM.

2.   THE KBS FORMAL SPECIFICATION

In his recommendations for the certification of safety critical systems, Rushby suggests that the use of formal methods should be limited to "those aspects of design that are least well covered by present techniques. These arise in redundancy management, partitioning, and the synchronisation and co-ordination of distributed components, and primarily concern fault tolerance, timing, concurrency, and nondeterminism." ([Rushby 95], pg. 43).

The RTCA document [RTCA 92] in its Section 12.3.1 recommends that "Formal methods may be applied to software requirements that:

- are safety-related,
- can be defined by discrete mathematics,
- involve complex behaviour, such as concurrence, distributed processing, redundancy management, and synchronisation."

By restricting the scope of our considerations to the KB software technology, it could be observed that KB software exhibits several of the complex design aspects cited by Rushby. In particular KBS contribute to the complexity of a system with their decision procedures. Currently available KBS V&V techniques [Meseguer 96] do not satisfactorily dominate KBS complexity.

In order to characterise the safety related KB software requirements the results of the Functional Failure Analysis performed within the Safe-KBS project on different KBS have been considered. Thus KBS requirements relevant for formal methods have been obtained by generalising the contents of Safety Parameters.

Formal methods application is particularly suitable to provide the following specification and/or V&V requests:

- analysis of the control knowledge for checking, for instance, the correctness of the logic, of the extrapolation of data and of the algorithm used to perform particular sub-tasks
- demonstration of KBS desired (critical) properties, i.e. the correctness of the intended function of a component
- demonstration of KBS undesired properties concerning what should not happen or what is not to be done, i.e. malfunctions or possible unintended functions of a component that have critical implications
- time constraints and boundaries of the KBS reasoning process (time-outs, periodicity constraints, sporadic constraints, timing exceptions)
- data flow integrity constraints
- functional independence and partitioning
- fault tolerance requirements such as degraded modes of the KBS
- functional requirements of KBS critical tasks.

The needs of KBS expressed above ask for formal methods being able to support deep analyses of KBS behaviours, which in turn can be fulfilled by powerful specification and execution capabilities. In the following of this section specification requirements for KBS formal methods are considered, whilst formal V&V techniques applicable to KBS are treated in the next section.

It is generally hard to specify in advance a KBS completely because of the incremental nature of the requirements elicitation process. Actually specification is a typical incremental activity both in conventional and KB software. A complete and correct specification, both formal and informal, can never be given in advance but it is surely the result of an iterative process of adjusting, completing and improving of some intermediate specification whose number of iterations depends on the complexity of the system.

A formal specification is a description of the behaviour and properties of a system written in a mathematically based language, specifying what a system is supposed to do at the right level of abstraction. Mathematical notations have always to be enriched by natural language text introducing and explaining formal concepts and sentences.

Usual requirements of formal methods for generic software which remain particularly important for KBS as well are:

– the possibility (sometimes the need) of describing the system at different abstraction levels without loosing the clarity and precision essential to the critical aspects
– the independence from (low level) design and implementation details
– the independence from efficiency issues
– the incremental style of the specification activity
– the provision of structuring mechanisms
– the explicit treatment of time
– the availability of formal semantics
– the provision of formal proof techniques
– the flexibility and exhaustivity of the analysis methods.

KBS often require complex reasoning capabilities. Formalisation of real complex reasoning systems can be achieved in practice by structuring and decomposing the reasoning process into different reasoning components. Therefore FM for the KBS development share two main requirements with frameworks developed within the research field on formalising complex reasoning [Traverso 96], namely

– the formalisation of local and global reasoning. Local reasoning formalisation requires the capability of formally describing basic reasoning steps that are local to a reasoning module, while global reasoning formalisation requires formal descriptions of basic reasoning steps allowing formalising interactions among modules. Local (global) reasoning processes should be described formally by composition of local (global) reasoning steps
– the formalisation of multi-level reasoning, i.e. the capability of structuring formal specifications at different levels (mainly the application domain level and the problem solving level).

As stated in [Fensel 95a], specific aspects of KBS which result in specific requirements for KBS formal methods are:

– the separation of knowledge and control
– the generic specification of the dynamic of the reasoning

- object-meta relationship between domain knowledge and inference processes
- the combination of non-functional and functional specification techniques.

The appropriateness of a semantic framework for the formalisation of the dynamic of the KBS reasoning can be evaluated in terms of five characterising aspects of reasoning processes, introduced by [Fensel 98b]:

1. the *state*: three choices concern the representation of a state of a reasoning process, namely
    1.1. whether its characterisation is necessary at all
    1.2. whether it is syntactic or semantic
    1.3. whether it should be local or global
2. the *history*: two questions concern the representation of the history of the reasoning process, namely
    2.1. whether it has to be part of the state description or not
    2.2. whether two states achieved through different paths have to be considered different or equal
3. the *elementary state transitions*: the description of state transitions must be easily and intuitively related to state changes
4. the connection between states and state transitions
5. the composed state transitions.

Fensel's evaluation emphases the need that with KBS specification methods must be possible to only characterise complex sub-steps functionally (without making commitments to their algorithmic realisation) and to express algorithmic control over the execution of sub-steps.

Due to the wide spectrum of purposes underlying FM development, no FM exists which fulfils the entire set of stated requirements for KBS formal methods. Each FM development has concentrated on a subset of them. Frameworks based on dynamic logic, temporal logic and algebra better capture procedural and dynamic control of KBS reasoning.

Many FM that originated in traditional software engineering area provide a functional and/or behavioural specification of the entire system, which is not based on any pre-identified informal conceptual model. In Safe-KBS an experiment has been performed where the TRIO formal method [Bertani 96], [Ciapessoni 95], developed for conventional software, has been used to formalise some critical parts of a KBS in the avionics. That experiment has shown that control knowledge of the conceptual model can be specified in TRIO by combining its basic logical, temporal and process-oriented operators [Dondossola 98].

A lesson learned from FM developed within the KE area is that the association of an informal conceptual model to a FM, in such a way that there exist a structural correspondence between the two, allows to improve the methodological and automatic support provided by the FM to the software development process. The identification of the informal model corresponding to the FM allows deriving a large set of guidelines for the construction of the initial formal model [Aben 95]. Guidelines to build a formal specification which corresponds to (parts of) a given informal model represent a very useful FM technological support, especially because the use of formal languages requires specialised skills and mathematical background. To clarify which is the informal conceptual model underlying a given FM represents an improvement step toward the aim of reducing the gap between informal (oriented to application-specialists) and formal (oriented to technology-specialists) methods. In fact this enforces FM to adopt an approach to the specification process which integrates informal and formal techniques. From the automatic support side, FM endowed with an informal conceptual model enforce a tight integration of their support tools with tools supporting the informal model, thus promoting the development of broad-spectrum full CASE environments.

3.   THE FORMAL V&V OF KBS

A big step further in exploiting FM peculiarities in KBS development is represented by their application for V&V purposes. Formal validations and verifications should supplement informal V&V activities by supporting specification validation and design (system) verification with formal techniques.

All FM considering the specifications formalisation as their primary concern have devoted their effort for defining highly expressive languages endowed with fully formal semantics, thus making the basis for developing fully formal V&V techniques. Highly expressive methods have to face with efficiency issues arisen by the automatic proofs on real-sized specifications. On the other hand, FM with high expressive power are able to provide V&V techniques which are semantically powerful. In the selection of the appropriate FM one should be aware of the impact of the method expressive power on its V&V capabilities. Therefore a generally applicable criterion in the selection of the appropriate FM could be "Be as much expressive as required by the needs of semantic analysis".

FM oriented toward specifications operationalisation are less expressive, support prototyping as their major validation approach, thus providing better execution performance.

3.1   Formal Validation Techniques

Formal Validation Techniques apply to any (life cycle product of the type) formal specification at the aim to assess them against the needs for which the KBS is developed. Specific validation techniques can be enforced on formal specifications whose effectiveness is primary related to the expressive adequacy of the underlying formal specification method. The ability of a FSM to capture the complexity aspects of a KBS is a pre-requisite for the development of powerful (often computationally complex) V&V techniques.

Specifications structured over different abstraction levels simplify the validation task. Even Rushby [Rushby 93] recommends a wide use of abstraction and focus on particular properties rather than general ones. The idea is that complete analysis of selected properties of a highly simplified version of a design can be more effective at detecting errors than partial coverage of more general properties, or a more realistic design. In general formal validation is internal to a single specification at a given abstraction level, and desired properties and/or behaviours to be validated are expressed in the same format as specifications.

Most effective types of formal validation techniques applicable to KBS[4] have been identified and their description is given below.

- *Syntactical analysis*: checks specifications at the aim to ensure that all their expressions are well-formed
- *Type checking*: checks specifications at the aim to ensure that entities are always used in ways compatible with their types. It can be seen as a specialised kind of formal deduction attempting to prove the theorem "the specification is type-correct". If the Type Checker (the tool implementing the technique of type checking) is allowed to use general-purpose theorem proving, rather than just perform algorithmic checks like a programming-language compiler, then the type system can become very sophisticated, and type checking becomes a very powerful way to detect errors in a specification[5]
- *Model generation*: supports:
  - *consistency analysis* by means of *satisfiability proofs* which establish whether the specification has at least a model, i.e. if it doesn't contain contradictions

---

[4] Applicable to KBS does not mean KBS-specific. Indeed the identified techniques are completely general and can be used for traditional software as well.

[5] In Rushby's opinion, strong type checking (the stronger the better) should always be required for formal specifications offered in support of certification for safety-critical systems.

– *adequacy analysis* by means of several kind of proofs:
  – *truth proof*: to research models which verify the specification. In one sense also the formulae represent models for the specifications, but it is not easy to understand the possible behaviours of specified systems looking at them. The Model Generator (the tool implementing the technique of model generation) produces interpretations of formulae which are all, or a subset of, the possible models of the specification, i.e. it generates possible behaviours of the system
  – *falsehood proof*: to research the models which get false the specification
  – *unsatisfiability proof*: to prove that a specification does not have any model
  – *validity proof*: to verify if the specification is a tautology, i.e. it admits the empty model (if the specification admits the empty model, then every model is a model for it; for instance 'A | ~A' admits the empty model because 'true A' is a model and 'false A' is a model too)
  – *completion proof*: to establish if a formula is in contradiction with a partial model and to find the possible completions of the model w.r.t the formula. This functionality can also be used to verify that a given partial behaviour corresponds to an interpretation where the specification formula is evaluated to true
  – *property proof*: to establish (by refutation) if a given property is a logical consequence of the specification
– *Theorem proving and Proof checking*: establishes if a given property (the theorem) is logically derivable by the specification (the axioms of the logical theory) by applying sound inference rules. A Theorem Prover (the tool implementing the technique of theorem proving) is a computer program that automates formal deductions through a combination of heuristics and brute-force search. A Proof Checker (the tool implementing the technique of proof checking) is a program that leaves the selection of the proof steps to an insightful human and simply checks that each one is carried out correctly. Effective automatic reasoning tools for FM generally combine theorem proving with proof checking techniques, thus providing semi-automatic or partially interactive Theorem Provers. Therefore the term "Theorem Prover" is generally used to cover all forms of (partially) automated deduction
– *Symbolic execution or Simulation*: executes the specification directly, using highly efficient forms of deduction, so that test cases can be run directly against the specification. Therefore simulation allows the specification and its underlying model to be debugged and system

behaviour to be observed and explored in the same formally rigorous context as that of the specification

- *Animation or Prototyping*: examines a specification (to evaluate its model) by constructing an executable program (rapid prototype) for testing purposes. Specification Animators (the tools implementing the technique of prototyping) reinterpret a formal specification into a high-level dynamically executable form. Specification animations are not formal in a strict sense, but support the validation task by providing analysts with an early view of the high-level dynamic behaviour of the KBS formal conceptual model.

Simulation and animation are not alternative to "total" formal validation techniques such as model generation and theorem proving, but rather they have complementary roles. As suggested in [NASA 97], during requirements specification and (or) high-level design phases simulation can be used to probe in an efficient way the behaviour of a system on selected test cases, and the more expensive theorem proving technique can be used to establish its general behaviours and properties.

3.2   Formal Verification Techniques

From a methodological point of view formal verification assumes that there are two system descriptions to be compared for mutual adequacy and/or correspondence. It could be also be called formal cross-validation. Formal verification techniques apply between (any life cycle product of the type) formal specifications at different levels of detail, or between specifications and implementations.

A set of formal verification techniques applicable to KBS[4] has been identified and their description is given below.

- *Formal inspection:* refers to the comparative analysis between formal specification and implementation
- *Model checking:* the basic ingredients of model checking are:
  - a propositional temporal logic used to write specifications
  - a language for describing the system to be verified as a finite state automaton
  - a model checking procedure which efficiently and automatically determines whether the specifications are satisfied by the state-transition graph generated by the system automaton *(correspondence proofs)*.

Model checking is an efficient technique that has been applied very successfully in the design and verification of finite state concurrent reactive processes, and recently lifted to be applicable to multi-agent systems [Benerecetti 98]. It is applicable to KBS generating state spaces with limited dimensions and it does not allow to prove universal properties

- *History checking*: compares a given system behaviour, called *history*, with the specification for compatibility. In a typical application of this technique the designers describe a set of expected behaviours of the system along with some illegal behaviours and checks whether the former are compatible with the specification while the latter are not. History checking could be considered as a special case of the model checking technique, where state automata are replaced by histories and propositional temporal logic by a more complex temporal logic
- *Hierarchical verification or Proof refinement:* is applicable to specifications described by using different hierarchical layers. Typically hierarchical verification ensures that each layer does at least what is required to support the layer above. The application of this technique is greatly simplified if the FM is endowed with a refinement calculus. As observed by [Rushby 93], great caution must be exercised when formal treatments of negative properties are combined with those for hierarchical verification as such technique does not guarantee that negative properties proved at a higher specification layer will be preserved in a lower layer. Therefore negative properties must be verified at the lowest specification layer
- *Structural testing*: exploits the correspondence between syntactic structure and semantic meaning typical of models expressed in a formal way for defining specific form-dependent system properties. Consistency and completeness testing techniques, which detect anomalies in rule bases on the base of rule form, is an example of this technique
- *Symbolic execution*: executes the specification in order to allow the specification to serve as a "test oracle" in the conformance testing of the KBS implementation. For example outputs from specification execution can be compared with outputs from implementation execution, or outputs from implementation execution can be run against the specification for checking their consistency
- *Test case generation*: FM support the KBS conformance testing by allowing the automatic test case generation from the specification. In fact the most critical point in conformance testing is to select the input data to be used to test the KBS functionality in an appropriate way. Since a correct formal specification is also a description of the intended I/O behaviour of the system, it can be used to select the input data to be used as test cases.

4.   THE KBS LIFE CYCLE MODEL

A life cycle model including FM has been defined within the Safe-KBS project as a refinement of a FM-free life cycle version oriented to the development of KBS in safety critical context [Safe-KBS R3.4-a/b]. In the present section the FM impact on a generic KBS life cycle is summarily reported[6] in terms of life cycle prescriptions, generic structure and detailed activities. The application of these concepts on the Safe-KBS life cycle model can be found in [Dondossola 98].

First of all I will introduce a set of prescriptions to be used in tailoring the KBS life cycle to the case at hand.

1. Given a safety-critical KBS its safety analysis reveals that in general only part of its software is actually safety-critical, the others being only safety-related (but non safety-critical) or neither that. The use of a FM is *mandatory required* for the development of truly safety-critical KB software. FM are *only recommended* for safety-related (non safety-critical) KB software

2. The most appropriate FM for a specific KBS shall be selected among a set of reliable FM among those available

3. The *highest degree of rigour* in the application of the selected FM is proposed for safety-critical KB software, i.e. the maximum potentiality of the FM shall be used. Specification, validation and verification activities shall make use of the FM and its supporting tools. Lower levels of rigour in the application of the selected FM shall be used for safety-related (but non safety-critical) KB software. A more sophisticated scheme for selecting the appropriate level of rigour in dependence of the analysis needs, complexity and SIL of the specific KBS is presented in [Dondossola 99]

4. Formal specification and V&V techniques shall be integrated with correspondent informal KBS techniques

5. As the degree of confidence in achieving high software integrity levels can not be measured in practise, others more sound techniques, based on different technologies providing robust forms of diversity, should be applied in conjunction with FM to obtain more certain probabilities [Rushby 95].

From the whole process side the use of FM requires a formal specification process which alternates formulisation and formal V&V steps and spans over several development stages. From the product point of view the use of FM requires the development of a formal specification which is a high

---

[6] Several commonly used life cycle concepts will be used in this section by assuming the life cycle ontology developed within the Safe-KBS project.

quality product. The formal specification of the KBS can eventually be used as the explicit, precise model against which to verify and test its implementation. FM-related life cycle processes and their activities are detailed below.

- Development: development plan definition, requirements specification, (high level) design, final verification and refinement
- Verification and Validation: V&V plan definition, V&V activities of all intermediate products of the life cycle
- Safety Management: activities for controlling the safety of the KBS requirements, (high level) design, and implementation.

As far as the Development process is concerned, formal methods use implies life cycle tasks such as:

- definition of the scope of formal methods for the case at hand
- collection of informal specification to be formalised
- definition of the relationships between functional and critical requirements
- selection of suitable formal methods
- formalisation
- integration of informal and formal specifications
- extraction of test data from formal specifications.

The Verification and Validation should include life cycle tasks such as:

- definition of the requirements to be formally validated
- selection of suitable formal V&V techniques
- integration of formal and informal V&V techniques[7]
- formal validation of requirements specification
- formal verification of (high level) design
- requirements traceability into intermediate life cycle products
- generation of test data for the KBS conformance testing
- verification of the implemented system against its formal requirements (high level design).

An evaluation of the FM contribution in fulfilling the Safe-KBS life cycle requirements has been performed. The evaluation is based on a requirement coverage metrics, i.e. the rate between the number of requirements whose fulfilment benefits from the adoption of FM and the total amount of stated requirements. The numerical estimates showed that FM provide a good

---

[7] The application of different V&V techniques on the same software product is a sound quality assurance strategy, especially in critical contexts. It can be adopted only after that the integrated role of the selected techniques has been defined and their complementary/overlapping purposes identified. Often this is a non-trivial task, especially in cases where heterogeneous techniques, such as formal V&V techniques and traditional functional testing, have to be integrated.

coverage of safety and quality issues, followed by integrability and certification ones.

5.   CERTIFICATION

Certification is the process of issuing a certificate to indicate conformance with a standard, a set of guidelines or some similar document. Commonly the software (third party) certification gives some form of confidence, generally of quality and dependability, of the software process and/or product. A certification methodology puts the basis of the certification process from the party of the Certification Authority, providing guidelines on the methods and techniques used to approach the evidence produced by the developer. It also provides the necessary technological support packages, intended to help certifiers during the independent certification activities but also in the liaison related work with the developer. FM support a certification process spanning over the entire software life cycle, that is FM increase the possibility that even intermediate products, as well as the final product, may be certified.
The use of FM during KBS development supports certification by increasing, on one hand processes and products quality, on the other hand the degree of confidence in achieving failure rates on the order required by high integrity levels.
Aimed at supporting the relationships with the Certification Authority during development, the Safe-KBS life cycle contains a specific certification process representing the point of view of a certification team from the party of the software developer. The certification team is in charge of
- verifying, both against the certification model and with the Certification Authority the life cycle plans (i.e., actually what the development groups intends to do), according to a process certification perspective
- preparing the data for product certification by the Certification Authority.
In [Dondossola 99] a technological support to FM is proposed which includes guidelines for tailoring FM exploitation to the needs of the specific project, and an assessment scheme for FM. Such technological support, aimed at facilitating the integration of FM in industrially practiced development/certification processes, represents an attempt to assess methods and techniques to be used as common means by both certification bodies and teams in reaching an agreement on the application plan of formal methods.
Finally FM could be part of the certification methodology itself at the aim to complement the capabilities of practised certification methods (based on

static and dynamic testing [Vermesan 97], [Vermesan 98]) with those of formal V&V techniques.

6.   CONCLUSIONS

In the present work FM roles in developing safety-critical KB software have been presented. Specification and V&V requirements of FM have been derived from the safety and KB software dimensions, and peculiar aspects of a KBS life cycle model based on FM have been described.
A leading principle of this work is that a disciplined and scalable use of formal methods during KBS development increases the quality of the software produced and the degree of confidence in achieving failure rates on the order required by high (catastrophic and hazardous) safety criticality levels.
In traditional software engineering much experience has been consolidated about formal methods and their use is especially encouraged in those domains in which the software application is embedded in a system which is "critical" from some point of view (safety, resources, money). The advantages of FM are widely recognised by tool developers/users and standard organisations (see [RTCA 92], [IEC 1508] and [MOD 91]). Therefore the use of formal methods in KBS development also represents a good chance to have the KB technology accepted both by designers/developers of critical software and by Certification Authorities in charge of approving critical software systems embedding KB components.
The author hopes that this work will be able to help at integrating FM in practised KBS development/certification processes and at prescribing their use in coming proposals of standards for KBS development.

REFERENCES

[Aben 95] M. Aben, *Formal Methods in Knowledge Engineering*, PhD dissertation, University of Amsterdam, February 1995
[Benerecetti 98] M. Benerecetti, F. Giunchiglia, L. Serafini, *Multiagent Systems Verification via Model Checking*, Workshop on Validation & Verification of Knowledge-Based Systems, Trento (Italy), June 1998
[Bertani 96] A. Bertani, E. Ciapessoni, *TRIO Model Generator: User Manual*, Deliverable D3.1 of ARTS Trial Application of the ESPRIT project n. 20695, 1996
[Ciapessoni 95] E. Ciapessoni, D. Mandrioli, A. Morzenti, P. San Pietro, *Manuale di TRIO+*, ENEL Research Report, (in Italian) November 1995
[Dondossola 98] G. Dondossola, *Formal Methods in the development of safety critical knowledge-based components*, in Failure & Lessons Learnt in Information Technology Management, Vol. 2 No. 4: 183-200, 1998

[Dondossola 99] G. Dondossola, A. Vermesan, *A scheme for Formal Methods Assessment in the context of developing Certifiable Control Systems*, submitted to FM99 Conference, Toulouse (FR) September 1999.

[Fensel 94] D. Fensel, F. van Harmelen, *A comparison of languages which operazionalise and formalise KADS model of expertise*, Knowledge Engineering Review, Vol. 9 , 105-146, 1994

[Fensel 95a] D. Fensel, *Formal Specification Languages in Knowledge and Software Engineering*, Knowledge Engineering Review, Vol. 10, No. 4, December 1995

[Fensel 95b] D. Fensel, *The Knowledge Acquisition and Representation Language KARL*, Kluwer Academic Publ., Boston, 1995

[Fensel 96] D. Fensel, R. Groenboom, *MLPM:Defining a Semantics and Axiomatization for Specifyng the Reasoning Process of Knowledge-based Systems*, Machine Learning and Knowledge Acquisition, 1996

[Fensel 98a] D. Fensel, R. Groenboom, G.R. Renardel de Lavalette, *Modal Change Logic (MCL): Specifying the Reasoning of Knowledge-based Systems*, Data and Knowledge Engineering, Vol. 26, No. 3: 243-269, 1998

[Fensel 98b] D. Fensel, F. van Harmelen, W. Reif, A. ten Teije, *Formal support for Development of Knowledge-Based Systems*, in Failure & Lessons Learnt in Information Technology Management, Vol. 2 No. 4: 173-182, 1998

[IEC 1508] IEC 1508 95 IEC, International Electrotechnical Commission, Draft International Standard 1508: *Functional Safety: Safety-Related Systems*, Geneva, Switzerland, 1995

[Meseguer 96] P. Meseguer, A.D. Preece, *Assessing the Role of Formal Specifications in Verification and Validation of Knowledge-Based Systems*, Proc 3rd IFIP International Conference on "Achieving Quality in Software" (AQuIS'96), pg. 317-328, Chapman and Hall, 1996

[MOD 91] UK Ministry of Defence: *Interim Defence Standard 00-55: The procurement of safety critical software in defence equipment*, Part 1, Issue 1: Requirements; Part 2, Issue 1: Guidance, April 1991

[NASA 97] *Formal Methods Specification and Analysis Guidebook for the Verification of Software and Computer Systems*, Volume II: A Practitioner's Companion, NASA-GB-001-97

[RTCA 92] RTCA/Eurocae DO178-B/ED-12B: *Software considerations in airborne systems and equipment certification*, Requirements and Technical Concepts for Aviation, Washington, DC, December 1992. This document is known as EUROCAE ED-12B in Europe

[Rushby 93] J. Rushby, *Formal Methods and the Certification of Critical Systems*, SRI Technical Report CSL-93-7, December 1993 (300 pages)

[Rushby 95] J. Rushby, *Formal Methods and their Role in the Certification of Critical Systems*, SRI Technical Report CSL-95-1, March 1995. This is a shorter (50 pages) and less technical treatment of the material [Rushby 93]. It will become a chapter in the FAA Digital Systems Validation Handbook (a guide to assist FAA Certification Specialists with advanced technology issues)

[Safe-KBS R3.4-a/b] Safe-KBS, Esprit Programme Project No. 22360, Task 3.4 report: *The Safe-KBS life cycle: final technical/management report*, 1998

[Traverso 96] P. Traverso, *Formalising Complex Reasoning*, IRST Technical Report # 9610-01, 1996

[van Harmelen 95] F. van Harmelen, D. Fensel, *Formal Methods in Knowledge Engineering*, Knowledge Engineering Review, Vol. 10, No. 4, December 1995

[Vermesan 97] Vermesan, A.I., *Quality Assessment of Knowledge-Based Software: Certification Considerations*, Proceedings of Third IEEE International Software Engineering Standards Symposium (ISESS '97) Walnut Creek, CA

[Vermesan 98] Vermesan, A.I., *Software Certification for Industry – Verification and Validation Issues in Expert Systems*, Proceedings of the Ninth IEEE International Workshop on Database and Expert Systems Applications (DEXA'98), Vienna, Austria, August 1998

Design pattern for safety-critical knowledge-based systems

Rune Steinberg, Roar Fjellheim, Ståle A.Olsen
Computas AS, Vollsveien 9, 1327 Lysaker, Norway

Key words: Decision-support systems, Knowledge-based systems, Safety-critical systems, Design patterns, Knowledge-level modelling

Abstract: The fact that a human decision-maker acts as an intermediary between a computer system and it's environment suggests that decision-support systems may be a promising application of knowledge-based technology in safety-critical systems. This creates a need for guaranteeing the quality of knowledge-based components embedded in safety-critical systems. In order to achieve this end the ESPRIT project named Safe-KBS has developed a life-cycle for embedded safety-critical knowledge-based systems. While most of this work has been concentrated on process properties, the work described here focuses on design issues, i.e. product properties. It is argued that, despite the fact that a well-designed life cycle will contribute substantially to the confidence in such a system, there is also a particular need to concentrate on design issues. The life cycle has therefore been supported by a catalogue of so-called design patterns for safety-critical knowledge-based systems. The design patterns describes design solutions that seek to increase the confidence of using knowledge-based technology in safety-critical systems.

1.   INTRODUCTION

Decision support systems (DSS) are computer-based systems designed to help a human decision-maker in making decisions in a partially structured domain. The system is not intended to replace or replicate a human expert but to provide the decision-maker with good decisions about sub-problems that are relevant for the task at hand. This enables the decision-maker to

131

control and direct the decision-making process and to decide whether to use or reject advice provided by the computer. A considerable amount of work has been done in this field and several successful applications have been developed [1] [2]. Almost all of these applications concern non-critical systems leaving an opportunity to study the application of DSS for safety-critical systems. The fact that a decision-maker acts as an intermediary between the DSS and its environment suggests that a DSS may be a promising application of knowledge-based (KB) technology in safety-critical systems. This idea is not new and several papers [3] [4] [5] may be found, but few provide any suggestions on how to exploit the industrial potential in this opportunity.

The ESPRIT project named Safe-KBS1 goes several steps further, aiming at extending the market of knowledge-based systems (KBSs) to safety-critical systems. Due to the different characteristics of traditional software and KBSs, the methods used to develop traditional safety-critical software can not be applied to develop safety-critical KBSs without major changes. However, significant achievements have been reached in several relevant research fields (KBS development [6] [7] [8] [9], verification and validation for KBS [10] [11] [12] [13], software development standards [14] [15] [16], quality assurance and certification for traditional safety-critical systems [17] [18]). Despite the fact that these fields may be considered as mature, there is a lack of a complete methodology that provides means for guaranteeing the quality of KB components embedded in a safety-critical system. Safe-KBS has answered to this challenge by developing a life-cycle for embedded safety-critical KBSs.

While most of the work has been concentrated on the process aspect of the task [19], the results described here focus on design issues, i.e. the product properties of safety-critical KBSs [20]. Our motivation for pursuing this approach is mainly driven by the particular characteristics of KBSs. It seems to be a fair amount of agreement that the most feasible approach to ensure the safety in safety-critical systems is to concentrate on process aspects. Putting a significant part of the available development effort into product oriented activities such as verification and validation is not deemed to be the most feasible approach due to the high costs, the demanding mathematical skills that are needed, and the limitation of current theories. Thus, the effort is concentrated on process aspects and the claim that we may succeed by providing the right development methodology. This hypothesis

1 Safe-KBS is partially funded by the ESPRIT, the EU information technologies program, as project number 22 360. The participants are: Computas (N), Det Norske Veritas (N), Enel (IT), Qualiance (FR), Sextant Avionique (FR), Tecnatom (SP), UNINFO (IT).

may hold for traditional safety-critical systems, but seems far more doubtful when we turn our attention to safety-critical KBSs. The reason is that KB technology brings up a large set of problems that we cannot avoid without discarding the most interesting parts of this technology. These problems stem from the inherently complexity of the algorithms we want to use to build our systems and concern a wide range of different problem types depending on the requirements at hand.

The objective of this paper is to suggest how embedding problems may be solved and how the solutions can be described. Few assumptions are taken regarding concrete algorithms or KB technologies. Consequently, the solutions take the form of abstract principles for solving these types of problems. A secondary objective has been to find a way to describe these solutions so that we are able to effectively use and discuss them in system design. The problem of describing a solution may at first seem to be of minor importance, but the solutions are useless if we are not able to meet this objective.

The approach to meet the objectives has been to collect a set of design solutions from the literature and from own company experience. A considerable amount of papers describes design solutions for traditional safety-critical software [23] [24] [25] [26]. Furthermore there exists a lot of papers describing design of KBSs, mostly by examples from prototypes or working systems [27] [28] [29] [30] [31] [32]. Few papers agree on how to present such issues. Design issues are considered from a rather informal position and one lacks deliberate means to discuss and compare them. A major problem that we had to face was that all design solutions looked different. Our aim was to mine out the very essence of this considerable amount of experience.

An important mean used to meet our objectives was to codify design solutions in terms of design patterns. The reason for this is that design patterns seem to be the most promising way to describe design solutions in such a way that we are able to meet our objectives. Design patterns enable us to focus on the most interesting problems to be solved and to provide design solutions that may be instantiated and tailored in order to solve the problem at hand.

2. DESIGN PATTERNS AND OBJECT-ORIENTED DESIGN

Design patterns are a concept (re-) invented by a group of researchers in object-oriented design in the beginning of the 90ths-[33] [34] [35]. The main idea behind this concept is to document the experience obtained through several iterations of solving a set of related problems. By extracting common properties between all these problems we are able to provide a solution description that are sufficiently general to be used in solving new problems. This enables us to capture experience, distribute it and reuse the essence of the solution. There are no single definition on what a pattern is, but to quote James Coplien [36], a good pattern will contribute to the following: solve a problem, the solution is a proven concept, the solution isn't obvious, it describes a relationship between structures and mechanisms, and it has a significant human component. The expected benefit of using patterns is that we are able to build on experience resulting in improved quality and decreased development effort.

A design pattern describes a particular level of abstraction often in terms of architecture such as a blackboard or a client/server or a micro architecture usually involving a few classes and the relationships between them. Patterns are documented using a uniform format including a set of essential sections. A collection of patterns is often woven together into a catalogue of patterns serving to solve problems of a particular kind. A catalogue of patterns is characterised by the format selected to describe the problem and solutions. A pattern format usually includes a *name*, a *problem* description, i. e. a context where the pattern applies, a *solution* and the *consequences*. The name is the mean to create a vocabulary that enables us to talk about the pattern (or the solution). The problem part describes a recurring problem (an abstraction of all the problems that contributed to the pattern). The solution describes the elements that make up the solution in terms of a conceptual model of the solution. A broad range of illustrations is believed to be an essential part of the solution. In object-oriented patterns, these illustrations are provided in terms of object diagrams. The object diagrams usually describe a particular example of the solution. The consequences discuss the possible trade-offs that should be considered when applying the pattern.

Putting all the buzzwords away, the best way to understand the pattern concept is to study a concrete example. Buschmann et. al. ([33]) describes a catalogue of architectural patterns including a blackboard architecture that will be described below

The name of pattern is Blackboard, a well-known architectural model where several specialised subsystems assemble their knowledge to build a possibly partial or approximate solution.

The problem addressed by the pattern is situations where there are no feasible deterministic solutions for the transformation of raw data into high-level data structures. Typically characterised by a problem that, when decomposed into sub-problems spans several fields of expertise. The solutions to partial problems may require different representations and paradigms. There is possibly no predetermined strategy for combining partial solutions.

The solution includes a collection of independent programs or knowledge sources that work in co-operation on a common data set (a blackboard). Each knowledge source is specialised in solving a particular part of the overall task. A central control-component co-ordinate the independent knowledge sources according to the current state of progress. There is no pre-determined activation of each knowledge source. During the problem solving process the system works with partial solutions, that in the end are intended to be modified, rejected or combined into a final solution. The structure of such a system may be composed of a blackboard component, a collection of supporting programs or knowledge sources, and a control component as depicted in the diagram below.

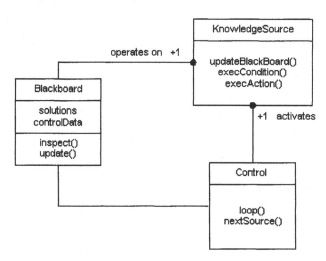

Figure 1. Blackboard architectural pattern

3. PATTERNS IN KNOWLEDGE MODELLING

Menzies ([37]) describes the striking similarity between design patterns and inference structures in knowledge-level modelling such as in KADS [38] [39] [40] [41] [42]. KADS provides a library of inference structures covering basic inferences that may appear in a KBS involved in monitoring, diagnosis, planning, etc. The inference structures emerged from domain-specific inferences by removing the domain specific elements. The result is a domain independent inference structure presented as a reusable component for knowledge-level modelling.

An inference structure is a network of atomic inference steps and abstract domain roles which explicitly describes which inferences can be made, and implicitly describes which cannot. The KADS notation use rectangles to depict domain roles (data structures), ovals to depict inference steps (functions) and lines to depict relationships between domain roles and inference steps (dataflow). Consider an example of medical diagnosis where we apply an inference structure for heuristic classification as depicted in figure 2.

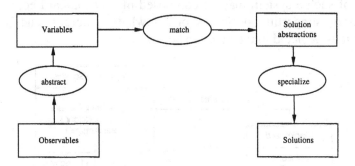

Figure 2. Heuristic classification

We may *observe* that a patient has a body temperature of 38 Celsius degrees. This *Observable* is abstracted in the sense that irrelevant attributes are removed in order to fit a set of matching *Variables*. Thus we may for instance abstract our observation to state that the patient has fever. These variables must then be matched with a set of *Solutions Abstractions* describing possible causes for having a fever. In real life we would (hopefully) have a significantly larger set of observables all matched to an appropriate set of solution abstractions. If we were lucky, these solution abstractions are good enough to be further specialised into a set of *Solutions*.

4.   CODIFYING KNOWLEDGE INTO PATTERNS FOR SAFETY-CRITICAL KBSS

In order to discover and describe patterns for designing safety-critical KBSs we need a source of design problems and their solutions. In addition, we must define an appropriate format used to describe the patterns. Not surprisingly few real safety-critical KBSs exists. Thus, it is most unlikely that we could succeed in discovering a single source of experience to build our patterns. A fact that has forced us to approach the task rather differently than what is done to discover object-oriented design patterns, or KADS inference structures. Instead we were forced to pick and compose pieces of experience from both the design of traditional safety-critical systems, as well as from non-safety-critical KBSs.

As mentioned above we concentrate on conceptual problems regarding embedding KBSs in safety-critical systems. One subject that strikes people's mind when discussing such systems is the problem of controlling time- and memory behaviour. It is well known that most of the interesting algorithms we may want to implement in a KBS have exponential time complexity functions, or no guarantee of termination. Thus we need some mechanisms in order to ensure that we are able to make the most of the available technology and at the same time keep sufficient control in order to satisfy strict requirements on the behaviour of the system.

The main problem we have to solve before embedding a KBS in a safety-critical application is to ensure that decisions provided by the KBS are guaranteed to be correct. Whether an incorrect decision will lead to a hazard or not depends on the context of the problem the KBS are about to solve i. e. the problem domain, the status of the system, etc.

We have concentrated our work on three problem areas: (i) safety, (ii) reliability and (iii) real-time (see [21] [3] [22] for a discussion of the interpretation of these terms). Concerning safety, (i) we have considered the problem of detecting incorrect decisions. Since we are dealing with an embedded KBS we may accept occurrences of incorrect decisions provided that some particular additional components (which are introduced in our patterns) together with the embedding system can produce an alternative solution. In order to face the problem of reliability (ii) we have focused on well-known techniques that add a certain level of redundancy to the KBS. The reason for focusing on real-time problems (iii) as a third problem area is that real-time considerations are essential in modelling real-world systems. A large part of safety-critical applications model real-world systems. This is a factor that significantly contributes to the problems related to safety and reliability. Rodd et al. ([31]) come to the conclusion that what defines a real-time system is the system's ability to guarantee a response after a fixed time has elapsed. Musliner et al. ([22]) mention several challenges that real-time AI systems may face including: continues operation, interfacing an external environment, dealing with missing or uncertain data, focusing resources on the most critical events, etc. We consider several of these problems from an architectural perspective, i.e. how one can design (micro) architectures that solve or handle such problems.

The Safe-KBS pattern format emphasis four keywords or sections: *name*, *overview*, *problem*, and *solution*. The description of the solution does not go very deep into details, and it gives limited advice concerning implementation details. It includes a *diagram* section providing the static and dynamic structures of the solution.

One notable discrepancy with object-oriented design pattern formats and the format of the Safe-KBS patterns is our lack of a section discussing the *consequence* of applying a specific pattern. We still believe that such a part is a most important part of a pattern. However, as discussed earlier, the lack of available systems in the domain of safety-critical KBSs forced us to leave out this discussion from the patterns.

In order to describe a set of patterns it is useful to select an appropriate level of abstractions. We decided to consider two different levels: an architectural level and a component level.

At the architectural level we view the knowledge-based software used in a system as a black-box subsystem termed *KBS*. The software that uses conventional, non-KB techniques and are not part of the KBS or other specified components/systems, is viewed as a black-box subsystem termed *Non-KBS*. The KBS and Non-KBS, together with any additional components make up the software application.

At the component level we are mostly interested in the inner workings of the components and how we might go about realising a particular functionality. The notation we have used to explain the inner workings of a component is adapted from the inference structure diagrams used in KADS (see the example below). As with the notation used in the architectural patterns the notation is not formally defined.

Comparing architectural- and component patterns, the architectural design patterns attack the problem of embedding KBSs in a safety-critical system from a rather obvious angle. KB and non-KB components are considered as black boxes providing an approach to deal with the embedding problem without going into details about how the KB or the non-KB components are designed. The essence of an architectural pattern will to great extent rely on how a non-KBS and one or more KB components may be combined with additional components in order to solve a particular problem. The component patterns will complete the picture by providing details about how to design the KB part of the system.

5.   ARCHITECTURAL DESIGN PATTERNS

Our catalogue of architectural patterns consists of twelve different patterns as listed below:

1. KBS with stand-in
2. KBS with filter
3. Safety guaranteed by KBS
4. Open-loop KBS
5. Transactional KBS
6. Blackboard KBS

7. Multi-agent KBS
8. KBS with communication manager
9. KBS with timeout
10. Any-time KBS
11. Performance guaranteed by KBS
12. Scheduled KBS

Most of the pattern names provide a rough indication on what the pattern is about. It is difficult to provide a very precise categorisation, but if we use the origins of the patterns we can categorise them as follows: Pattern number 1 to 4 deals with safety related problems, pattern number 5 to 8 concerns reliability problems and the rest deals with real-time problems.

KBS with stand-in provides a non-KBS solution to the problem where the KBS are not able to handle the given request. It is intended to be used in order to avoid the system reaching an unsafe state. This pattern may be combined with several of the other patterns

KBS with filter describes means to check the result produced by the KBS. This is a mechanism that aims at preventing the KBS from providing an incorrect answer. A rule-based implementation of this pattern may for instance contain a rule base with negative rules or rules defining thresholds for certain output- or input values. The point is that the KBS should be able to generate a warning if the input is outside the KBSs range of experience or the output violates one or more (correctness) rules, see [43].

Safety guaranteed by KBS utilises the results from the safety analysis in order to monitor the system in operation. This is again an example of a design that seeks to detect a potential transition from a safe state to an unsafe state.

Open-loop KBS describes the situation where a human operator provides the link between the KBS and the environment.

Transactional KBS employ techniques used in traditional database management systems to increase the reliability of a KBS. Requests to the KBS should be made in the form of transactions that are; *atomic*, preserve *consistency*, are *isolated* from other requests, and which effects are *durable* when successfully completed. A separate transaction manager is introduced to administer the transactions.

Blackboard KBS and *Multi-agent KBS* are well-known architectural patterns that are referred to as promising architectures for building diverse redundancy and similar design techniques into a KBS, hence increasing the reliability of the KBS.

KBS with communication manager describes an approach to de-couple the KBS and other software components in order to keep a clean interface between the KBS and the embedding system and its environment. This will contribute to increased reliability in terms of modularization and de-coupling.

KBS with timeout will be described in detail below, so it suffices to say that it seeks to solve the problem of guaranteed response time.

In *Performance guaranteed by KBS* the KBS is used to plan and control the performance of a conventional system. In this way the conventional system can be made deterministic for a limited set of states. This may prevent the system from entering an unsafe state by ensuring that the deterministic system only will be operated within the states it is proven for.

Any-time KBS describes an application of any-time algorithms to solve problems in an incremental manner. This is a pattern that aims at providing a solution to the problem of guaranteed response time but where the deadline (response time) may vary by depending on the state of the system and the type of input. Thus, the KBS are able to utilise relaxed deadlines to make improved solutions.

Scheduled KBS analyses incoming tasks and routes them to the most promising problem-solver. The pattern addresses a typical real-time problem that concerns the problem of focus resources on the most critical events and to use the most appropriate component to handle it.

5.1   KBS with time-out

Problem

In general the properties of Knowledge Based Systems are such that the response time of requests can not be determined beforehand. The reasoning algorithms used tend to be unbounded or have very high upper bounds. Furthermore the execution time depends heavily on the current state of the system – e.g. number of rules in the knowledge base, size of the applicable search space, and so on.

Introducing some kind of functionality to cope with this problem is not straightforward. Careful considerations must be taken in order to minimise complexity, maintain a high degree of maintainability and testability, all while ensuring that the tasks processed by the KBS can be stopped at any time.

Solution

If the KBS is not able to produce a solution within a given time limit it must be stopped in order to ensure that some other alternative actions are initiated, and possibly free up the resources used by the KBS. The need is mainly expected to arise due to some unexpected behaviour and as such guarantee that the system will provide a response even if the KBS is not able to produce a solution.

A Timer, see figure 3, is used to keep track the progress of the KBS reasoning. When a new problem is given to the KBS, the client should also specify the deadline for the solution to the Timer. In normal operation the KBS will be able to provide a solution before the deadline occurs, so in this case the Timer will remain idle. In the other case that the KBS fails to solve the problem before the specified deadline, the Timer activates and responds by sending a timeout signal that notifies the client that deadline has been violated. Note that no solutions are provided at the deadline, only a warning that the deadline could not be met.

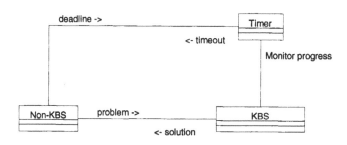

Figure 3. KBS with time-out

6. COMPONENT DESIGN PATTERNS

The catalogue of component design patterns includes five different patterns concerning the inner workings of components in a KBS. These patterns were picked according to a model of the three applications that was included in the project as case studies and include: *Monitoring, Model-based diagnosis, Assessment, Scheduling,* and *Planning.* The component design patterns are quite different from the architectural patterns in particular due to the use of inference diagrams. In order to demonstrate the idea, a more detailed description of the monitor pattern is provided below.

6.1 Monitoring

Problem
Monitoring concerns taking measurements of some aspect of an operational system, and comparing those values with a reference model of the system.
Solution
Monitoring concerns taking measurements of some aspect of an operational

system and comparing those values with a reference model of the system. Looking at the diagram in figure 4 we will use this simplified view of a monitor component to identify three main tasks of monitoring, where each task may range from a simple computational task to a knowledge-based task

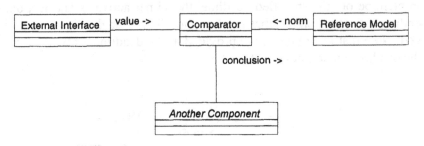

Figure 4. Monitoring component view

The essential task in monitoring is performed by the *comparator* that compares a measured value to its reference norm. The comparator may in its simplest form compare a numerical value with a numerical norm generated by the *reference model.* However, it may also be necessary to use knowledge-based methods for example to compare complex sets of values, or to handle uncertain or noisy measurements.

The reference model performs the second task. This component computes the reference norm, which the measured value is compared with. In its simplest form, this may be a constant value, on the other hand it may be a KB-component simulating the behaviour of a complex system.

It should also be said that the value and norm to be compared have to match. That is, the correct norm must be selected and the values must be comparable. For instance, imagine comparing an integer value to a norm that has the value set {low, medium, high}. This gives rise to some kind of pre-processing, that is not naturally placed in any specific component. These issues concern concrete design that guide one to implement this functionality centrally in the comparator, or closer to the sources.

The third task concerns how and when a value-norm pair are selected for monitoring. In a simple data-driven approach, the appearance of a measurement from a sensor is used to trigger the monitoring. Nevertheless, there are many examples where this approach is less than good. For example when acquiring a measurement, incurs a cost is incurred that the system should try to minimise. Alternatively, say in a surveillance system with a large number of sensors that continuously senses the environment, such an approach might not be able to deliver the required performance with respect to response time, dynamic priorities, etc. In this case, a model driven approach should be used, in which a pair is selected based on some reasoning about how to achieve high utility from the current selection.

Figure 5 looks in more detail on how monitoring might be implemented using a model driven approach. The *system model*, or rather the part of the system model that is relevant here, is an abstract description of the system that we want to monitor. This model describes which aspects of the system that may be measured, the norms used to express these aspects and also holds the current values of the model parameters (norms). The other important model is the *measurement reference model* that contains the knowledge on how to calculate expected values, these values are then compared with the real environment values.

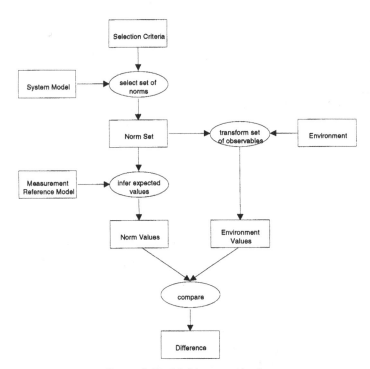

Figure 5. Model driven monitoring

In the model driven approach, the relevant set of norms is selected first using some kind of *selection criteria*. The criteria used may be seen as input to the monitoring component. A concrete implementation should consider what amount of computing is done outside the monitoring component vs. inside the component. For instance, the criteria input might be specific enough to make the selection function rather trivial, or on the other hand the criteria supplied might only be used to focus the selection.

When a *norm set* has been chosen, the set is used to guide the process of collection measurements from the environment and transforming the measured values to values that are comparable to the *norm values*. Of course some aspects of matching the values may be delayed until the *compare function*.

7.   CONCLUSION

It remains to be seen whether the pattern concept contributes to increased quality of software. Although we think it does, very little empirical research has been done in order to support this hypothesis, see for example [37]). The reason to believe that the hypothesis of increased quality is correct is based on reports from the object-oriented community and the argument that patterns intend to capture well-proven design solutions. What is noteworthy about this is not the argument in itself but how the task is carried out. The following factors contribute to this statement:

Patterns focus on practicability by describing proven solutions of recurring problems rather than scientific solutions.

Patterns create a vocabulary for understanding and communicating knowledge about design. This contributes to unified terminology of design that expands the developer communication bandwidth.

Patterns narrows the design space faced by the developer when designing a system. This will also help people understand a system more quickly when it is documented with the patterns its uses.

Even if these assumptions is carried over from object-oriented design, they seem equally or even more valid when dealing with safety-critical KBSs where safety and reliability may depend more on architectural than algorithmic considerations.

Patterns may be introduced in several of the phases in software development. Until now, the design phase has been a natural choice. In addition to this, the implementation of patterns in a particular application could be included in activities for quality assurance such as walkthroughs and inspections. Even more interesting is the emerging efforts of specifying object-oriented patterns formally, see [44][45][46]. This will remove much of the unclear and subtle parts of the patterns, and as such also the ambiguities that may occur when implementing the patterns. Depending on the language used to specify the patterns we may also be able to formally prove some of the properties we expect these patterns to satisfy, and hence increase the confidence that they behave as intended. However, before we dive into these matters there is a need for understanding how patterns for safety-critical KBSs may look like and what problems they should address, which is what our work is about.

There are probably many ways to build an inventory of patterns for KBSs or safety-critical KBS. Our patterns could be written in several ways, emphasising other levels of abstraction and formats. Compared with other patterns, some of our patterns may seem naively simple. We do however consider simplicity as a very important property that enables us to communicate powerful ideas without being too general. We believe our patterns cover some of the fundamental design principles that deal with important problems one may encounter when designing a safety-critical KBS.

The effort needed to discover and refine our patterns has been dominated by a comprehensive study of current literature. Besides writing two catalogues of design patterns we discovered that the literature almost without exception emphasises functionality and algorithms. Concrete design issues are sometimes neglected or poorly described. In addition there are no uniform way of describing such issues. Therefore it is quite hard to pick up the good solutions and leave out the rest. We think design patterns may contribute to solve this problem and provide an effective mean to describe and communicate well-proven design solutions for KBSs. The loose connection between the architectural- and component patterns indicates the need for further work on elaborating a theory on how patterns can be put together to form a more complete design that contains more than the sum of its constituent parts.

Only the future will show whether KB-technology is or will be sufficiently mature to be used in a broader scale of safety-critical systems than what is the done today. We will be forced to face a lot of problems if we want to unleash and utilise the power of this technology. We believe that our patterns contribute to increase the confidence of KB-technology in such a way that we some time in the future may reach a level where we are able to safely embed KB technology into safety-critical systems.

ACKNOWLEDGEMENTS

We thank Anca Vermesan for all support regarding the publication of this paper and all other contributors from the Safe-KBS project and in particular Christian Arnaudo, Encarna Mesa, Antoine Mensch, and Jean-Marc Meslin.

REFERENCES

[1] Power, D.J. *A Brief History of Decision Support Systems*. DSS Resources, World Wide Web, http://dss.cba.uni.edu/dss/dsshistory.html, 1999.

[2] V. Dahr, R. Stein, *Intelligent Decision Support Methods*, Prentice Hall, USA, 1997.

[3] M.G. Rodd, *Safe AI – Is it Possible*, Engineering Applications of Artificial Intelligence, 8(3), June 1985.

[4] John Fox, et. al. *Decision making and planning by autonomous agents; a generic architecture for safety-critical applications*, in Research and Development in Expert Systems XII, pp.159-169, SGES Publ. 1995.

[5] E. Hollnagel, *The reliability of expert systems*, John Wiley and sons, UK, 1989.

[6] G. Guida and C. Tasso. *Design and development of knowledge-based systems*, Wiley, 1994.

[7] F. Barber, V. Botti and E. Onaindia, *Temporal Reasoning in REAKT: An Environment for real-time knowledge-based systems*, AICOM, 7(3/4), Sept./Dec. 1994.

[8] R. A. Fjellheim et. al. *REAKT Application Methodology Handbook*, D2.1.3, EP705: REAKT, 1994.

[9] A. Mensch et. al. *REAKT: An architecture for real-time knowledge-based systems*, Esprit project no. 5146 and 7805.

[10] G. Dondossola, *Formal Methods in the development of safety critical knowledge-based components*, Proceedings of the European workshop on V&V of KBS at KR'98.

[11] J. R. Geissman and R. D. Schultz, *Verification and Validation of expert systems*, AI Expert 3[2], 1988, 26-33.

[12] A. I. Vermesan and T. Bench-Capon, *Techniques for the Verification and Validation of Knowledge-Based Systems: A Survey Based on the Symbol/Knowledge Level Distinction*, Software Testing, Verification and Reliability, Vol. 5, 233-271 (1995) John Wiley & Sons, Inc.

[13] F. van Harmelen, D. Fensel, *Formal Methods in Knowledge Engineering*, Knowledge Engineering Review, Vol. 10, No. 4, December 1995.

[14] IEC 1508 95 IEC, International Electrotechnical Commission, *Draft International Standard 1508: Functional Safety: Safety-Related Systems*, Geneva, Switzerland, 1995.

[15] International Standard, *Information technology – Software life cycle processes*, ISO/IEC 12207, 1995.

[16] The Institute of Electrical and Electronics Engineers, Inc., *IEEE Standards Collection Software Engineering*, 1994 edition. USA.

[17] N. G. Leveson: *Safeware: system safety and computers*, Addison-Wesley, 1995.

[18] N. Storey: *Safety-critical computer systems*, Addison-Wesley, 1996.

[19] Safe-KBS, ESPRIT program project no. 22360, *Task reports 1.x-3.x, 5.x*, 1996 - 1998.

[20] Safe-KBS, ESPRIT program project no. 22360, *Task report 4: Design patterns for safety-critical KBS*, 1998.

[21] S. Parthasarathy. *A framework for knowledge representation in safety-critical systems*, Engng Applic. Artif. intell. Vol. 7, No. 1, pp. 59-65, Elsvier Science, 1994.

[23] Victor L. Winter, John M. Covan, Larry J. Dalton, Leon Alkalai, Ann T. Tai, Rick Harper, Barry Flahive, Wei-Tek Tsai, Ramin Mojdehbakhsh, Sanjai Rayadurgam, Kinji Mori, and Michael R. Lowry, *Key Applications for High-Assurance Systems*, pp. 35-45 , Communications of the ACM, 40(1) pp. 67-93, Jan. 1997.

[24] B. Krämer and N. Völker, *Safety-Critical Real-Time Systems*, Kluwer Academic Publ. 1997.

[25] Theme issue - *Reliable Systems*, IEEE Software, Vol. 12, No. 3, May 1995.

[26] Theme issue – *Safety Critical Systems*, IEEE Software, Jan. 1994.

[27] A. Bykat, *Intelligent Monitoring and Diagnosis Systems: A Survey*, Applied Artificial Intelligence, 5(4):339-352, 1991.

[28] Jon D. Holt, *Practical Issues in the Design of AI Software*, Engineering Applications of Artificial Intelligence, 9(4):429-437, 1996.

[29] D. A. Linkens and M. Chen, *Expert Control Systems-II. Design Principles and Methods*, Engineering Applications of Artificial Intelligence, 8(5):527-537, 1995.

[30] D. Hong et. al. *An Implementation Architecture of Knowledge-Based System for Engine Diagnosis*, Applied Artificial Intelligence, 7(4):397-417, 1993.

[31] M. G. Rodd, H.B. Verbruggen and A. J. Krijgsman, *Artificial Intelligence in Real-time Control*, Engineering Applications of Artificial Intelligence, 5(5):385-399, 1992.

[32] T.J. Laffey et. al. *Real-Time Knowledge-Based Systems*, AI Magazine, 9(1), Spring 1988.

[33] F. Buschmann et. al. *Pattern – oriented software architecture; A system of patterns*, Wiley, 1996.

[34] E. Gamma et al: *Design patterns – Elements of reusable object-oriented software*, Addison-Wesley, 1995.

[35] J. Vlissides, Patterns: The Top Ten Misconceptions, *Object Magazine* 7(1):31-33, March 1997.

[36] J. Coplien, Software Design Patterns: Common Questions and Answers, ftp://st.cs.uiuc.edu/pub/patterns/papers/PatQandA.ps

[37] T. Menzies: *Object-oriented patterns: Lessons from expert systems*, Software practice and experience, Vol. 1(1), December1997.

[38] A. Aamodt et. al., *The CommonKADS Library*, KADS-II/T1.3/VUB/TR/005/1.0, 1992.

[39] M. Aben, *CommonKADS Inferences*, KADS-II/M2/TR/UvA/041/1.0, 1993.

[40] J. Breuker, *Reusable Components for Artifical Problem Solvers: the Common KADS library experience*, Dept. of Social Science Informatics, University of Amsterdam, 1994.

[41] J. Kingston, *Designing knowledge based systems: The CommonKADS design model*. University of Edinburgh, 1997.

[42] D. S. W. Tansley and C. C. Heyball, *Knowledge-based systems analysis and design, A KADS developer's handbook*. Prentice Hall, 1993.

[22] D. J. Musliner et. al., *The challenges of real-time AI*, IEEE Computer, January 1995.

[43] P. Compton, P. Preston. Knowledge based systems that have some idea of their limits. Tenth Knowledge Acquisition for Knowledge-Based Systems Workshop, Banff, Canada, SRDG Publications, University of Calgary, Calgary, Canada.

[44] A. H. Eden, J. Gil, Y. Hirshfeld, A. Yehudai. *Towards a mathematical foundation for design patterns*, http://www.math.tau.ac.il/~eden/bibliography.html, 1998.

[45] R. Helm, I. M. Holland, D. Gangopadhyay. *Contracts: Specifying Compositions in Object Oriented Systems*. OOPSLA 90, SIGPLAN Notices, vol. 25 no. 10.

[46] A. Lauder, Kent S. *Precise Visual Specification of Design Patterns*, http://www.cs.ukc.ac.uk/people/staff/sjhk/detail/publications/ECOOP98.html Procs. ECOOP98, Springer Verlag 1998.

Organising Knowledge Refinement Operators

Robin Boswell and Susan Craw
School of Computer and Mathematical Sciences The Robert Gordon University
Aberdeen, AB25 1HG, UK
rab,s.craw@scms.rgu.ac.uk

Abstract: Knowledge refinement tools seek to correct faulty knowledge based systems (KBSs). The goal of the KRUSTWorks project is to provide a source of refinement components from which specialised refinement tools tailored to the needs of a range of KBSs can be built. Central to the toolkit is a set of generic refinement operators and a representation language for KBS rules. The language abstracts those properties of rule elements which determine whether they can take part in rule chaining, and how they can be refined. It is used to organise the refinement operators so that each can be applied to similar rule elements found in different KBSs. This organisation facilitates the re-use of refinement operators when new KBSs are encountered, and the development of new ones. The toolkit was evaluated by applying it to a KBS shell significantly different from the ones previously encountered. The rule elements from this shell could be represented within the existing hierarchy, but it was necessary to add some new refinement operators. A KRUSTTool was then able to fix bugs actually occurring in the application, which confirms the usefulness of the refinement operators, and of our approach to organising and applying them.

Keywords: Knowledge Refinement, Knowledge Management, Refinement Operators

1 INTRODUCTION

Knowledge refinement is the process of changing the knowledge in a knowledge-based system (KBS) in reaction to evidence that the KBS is not producing correct solutions. The KBS is evaluated on tasks for which the correct solution has been provided by an expert. Those where the KBS and expert solutions differ provide evidence that the KBS is faulty.

Knowledge refinement tools each perform the same general steps. The tool is presented with a faulty KBS and some evidence of faulty behaviour; often this evidence consists of examples that the KBS fails to solve correctly, together with the correct solutions. The refinement tool reacts to a piece of evidence by undertaking the following three tasks: *blame allocation* determines which rules or parts of rules might be responsible for the faulty behaviour; *refinement creation* suggests rule modifications that may correct the faulty behaviour; and *refinement selection* picks the best of the possible refinements. The goal of refinement is that the refined KBS correctly solves as many of the examples as possible, with the expectation that novel examples will also have an improved success rate.

Most knowledge refinement systems are designed to work with KBSs developed in a single language ([Ourston and Mooney, 1994, Richards and Mooney, 1995, Murphy and Pazzani,1994]), or a particular shell ([?]). However, it is wasteful to develop refinement tools for individual languages and shells. Instead, we are developing re-usable refinement components that can be applied to a variety of KBS environments. These include refinement operators, refinement filters, and evaluation functions. In this paper we concentrate on a central component: the set of refinement operators. Our aim is to organise a small set of refinement operators so that they can exploit similarities in behaviour between rules in a range of KBS shells. As a result, it should be possible to re-use these operators when a new KBS is encountered, and to develop new operators relatively easily by amending existing ones.

In section 2, we describe the particular approach taken by our refinement tools. Section 2.1 explains how the knowledge required to carry out the various refinement tasks can be represented in a generic form, so that the tools can be written in a KBS-independent way, thus widening their applicabilty and facilitating their re-use. The core of the paper is section 3 which concentrates on the particular task of refinement implementation. It develops a hierarchical knowledge representation which abstracts the relevant properties of rule elements, and shows how this hierarchy is used to organise our toolkit of refinement operators. Section 4 demonstrates the power of our approach by showing how the refinement operators were successfully applied to a new and significantly different type of KBS. The remaining sections describe related work and conclusions.

2   THE KRUSTTool APPROACH TO REFINEMENT

This paper is based on our experience with the KRUST refinement system ([?]). We now refer to refinement tools that apply the basic mechanism of the original KRUST system as KRUSTTools. We are developing a KRUSTWorks framework from which an individual KRUSTTool for a particular KBS will be assembled; i.e. there is not one unique KRUSTTool. Figure 2 shows a KRUSTTool performing the operations highlighted above for a single refinement example. The KBS's problem-solving is analysed, and blame is allocated to the knowledge that has taken part in the faulty solution, or which failed to contribute to the solution as intended.

In the KRUSTTool approach, the next step, refinement creation, is divided into two stages: the generation of abstract refinements, and the implementation of these refinements as actual rule changes. These abstract refinements specify that a rule or condition be specialised or generalised, or that its priority be increased or decreased. At the implementation stage, knowledge specific refinement operators implement the abstract refinements by making actual repairs to the rules.

KRUSTTools are unusual in proposing many faults and generating many repairs initially, and so a KRUSTTool applies filters to remove unlikely refinements before any refined KBSs are implemented. It then evaluates the performance of these refined KBSs on the training example itself and other examples that are available.

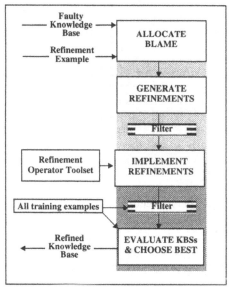

*Figure 1.*The Operation of a KRUSTTool

2.1 A Generic Toolkit

We seek to create a generic refinement toolkit, providing tools to perform the various refinement steps shown in figure 2. These tools should be able to exploit common features shared between different KBS, and thus avoid duplicating effort. We can exploit these commonalities by building common representations for

1. the knowledge content of rules, and

2. the reasoning process.

The relevant aspects of the knowledge content of rules are two-fold: the ways in which conditions and conclusions can be refined, and the ways in which they can match, causing rule-chaining. These features determine the design of our knowledge representation language for rules, or *knowledge hierarchy.* KRUSTTools use this language to build an internal representation of the static knowledge contained in rules which we call the *knowledge skeleton.*

Secondly, the aspects of the reasoning of a KBS which are relevant to refinement are the ways in which the rules *actually* fired, leading to an incorrect conclusion, and the alternative ways in which they *might* have fired to lead to a correct conclusion. We represent this firing behaviour in an extension of a proof-tree which we call a *problem graph*, the details of which appear in ([?]). Here we simply note that, to provide the knowledge needed in the construction of the problem graph, the knowledge hierarchy must take account of the matching behaviour for rule elements as well as their refinement operators.

Figure 2.1 relates the knowledge skeleton and problem graph to the refinement steps of a KRUSTTool. The tool performs the following steps.

1. The tool translates the KBS's rules into its internal representation language, forming the knowledge skeleton.

2. The tool is given a training example, for which the KBS gives an incorrect solution, together with information about how the KBS reaches its conclusions, normally in the form of an execution trace. The tool uses the information to build a problem graph.

3. The tool proceeds with refinement generation, implementation and testing using as input the problem graph, knowledge skeleton, and (at the evaluation phase) other training examples. The diagram shows how the knowledge skeleton organises both the matching functions that are used to create the problem graph, and also the refinement operators that are used for refinement implementation.

3   ORGANISING THE OPERATORS

The output of the refinement generator is one of a fixed set of abstract refinements, which must then be implemented. We seek to do this in a generic way, using a set of non KBS-specific refinement operators. We must therefore devise a knowledge representation for KBS rules whose structure is based on those aspects of the rule's behaviour which are relevant to refinement. We can then create a set of refinement operators designed to apply to the various terms in the structure, so that the organisation of the operators will mirror that of the knowledge hierarchy.

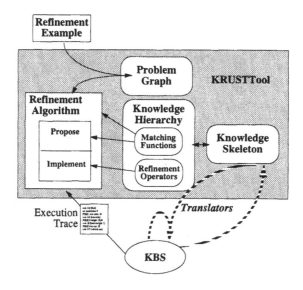

Figure 2. The KRUSTTool and KBS Processes

3.1 Developing The Hierarchy

The aim of refinement is to cause certain rules which previously succeeded to fail, and *vice versa*. This can be achieved by modifying individual *conditions* within rules so that they fail rather than succeed, and so on. However, we note that certain kinds of conditions, such as assignments, can never fail. This property will naturally be represented within our hierarchy. We call conditions which can succeed or fail, or, to put it another way, can be true or false, *tests*.

The second important property of rule elements, the capacity to be involved in rule chaining, must also be represented within our hierarchy. We call rule elements which can be involved in chaining, *goals*. We are solely concerned with the matching behaviour between the condition of one rule and the conclusion of another, so our definition of goals is independent of the direction of rule chaining.

The organisational requirements of refinement operators have thus led us to create an initial knowledge hierarchy as shown in figure 3.1. Note that a goal can be true or false, so appears as a sub-class of test.

We now proceed to develop the knowledge hierarchy further, and define refinement operators for the different classes in the hierarchy. In general, we continue to partition the classes until each leaf node represents a class of rule element with a well-defined set of associated refinement operators, and, where applicable, matching functions.

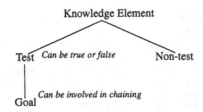

Figure 3. Initial subdivision of knowledge elements

3.2   Refining Tests

The function of a refinement operator is to take an abstract refinement, of the form "specialise condition" or "generalise condition", and implement it as an actual change. The purpose of the refinement is to change the behaviour of the condition *for a particular refinement case.* Moreover KRUSTTools agree with other refinement programs in preferring conservative refinements. Consequently, "specialise condition" actually means "implement the minimal specialisation to the condition so that it fails when the KBS is run on the refinement case", and similarly for generalisation. We therefore need to define refinement operators which perform such specialisations and generalisations for the various types of test we encounter in KBSs.

We have already defined one kind of test: the goal, whose truth value in a rule is determined by the firing of other rules. There are also tests whose truth is determined locally, such as comparisons. We consider refinement operators for non-goals first, as these are simpler.

3.2.1   Refining Non-goals

The only test we have so far needed to define which is not a goal is the comparison. Comparisons are defined to be equations or inequalities. The adjust_value operator refines a comparison in a minimal way by "balancing" it so that in the case of generalisation it just succeeds, and in the case of specialisation, it just fails.

3.2.2   Refining Goals

We first show that it is possible to implement refinement operators for the goal class itself, then go on to define sub-classes of goal, with more specialised operators. To do so, we have to consider the distinguishing feature of goals: their chaining behaviour. All types of goal succeed if their arguments match the arguments of facts in working memory, the details of the matching process depending on goal type. For example, the condition (enlist ?Student ?Org) matches the fact (enlist student42 army). The matching procedure for this type of goal states that two goals match if they have the same key-word, and the corresponding arguments unify. Matching variables with constants is triv-

ial in this instance, but becomes more interesting if we add meta-knowledge to describe the type of the variable. The following example shows how meta-knowledge about an ordered attribute can be used in refining a goal condition.

```
military_deferment(Student) :-
    enlisted(Student, army, [medium,long]).
```

This rule states that a student obtains military deferment if he enlists in the army for a period lying in the range `medium` to `long`. An expert may suggest this rule should fire for a case where the period of enlistment is `short`. To generalise the condition, we make use of meta-knowledge which states that the enlistment period is an ordered attribute with values `short`, `medium`, `long`. The above rule's condition can therefore be generalised to `enlisted(Student, army, [short, long])`.

This refinement operator was applied to a particular goal type, but it was based purely on the way meta-knowledge constrains the matching of goals, not on any property of the particular goal type. It will therefore be inherited by the sub-classes of goal defined in the next section.

3.2.3 Sub-classes of Goal

There are a variety of goal types which may be found in different KBSs. We identify four sub-classes of goal, distinguished by their chaining behaviour. However, these sub-classes also differ in the way in which they can be refined, so the partitioning allows us to introduce and organise further refinement operators.

Ordered Terms consist of a keyword followed by arguments; e.g. the PROLOG literal `colour(sky, blue, light)`.

These do not offer any further opportunity for refinement, unless they contain additional terms as sub-expressions. Such nested terms are discussed below in section 3.3.

OAV Triples are a sub-class of Ordered Term where the keyword is the attribute and the object and value form the remaining two arguments; e.g., `colour(sky, blue)`.

AV Tuples consist of a keyword followed by a series of attribute-value pairs, e.g. `weather(sky, blue, temperature, 40, humidity 5%)`. An AV Tuple contrasts with an Ordered Term in that the significance of each value item is determined not by its position, but by the preceding attribute name. For each keyword, a fixed set of attributes must be defined, though not all the attributes need be used in a rule condition. The variable number of conditions in an AV Tuple allows us to create additional refinement operators associated with this goal type. AV Tuples can be generalised by removing attribute-value pairs, and specialised by adding them.

Negations take any other goal as an argument; e.g., not(colour(sky, blue)). Negations can be refined by applying any operator applicable to their argument, but reversing its "direction". In other words, a negation is specialised by generalising the goal within it, and *vice versa*.

3.3   Nested Terms

Many rule elements, including those described so far, consist of a single element from the hierarchy, but a rule element can consist of an arbitrarily deep structure. For example, the negation mentioned above takes a goal as an argument. These recursive style rule elements have also proved useful for more complex knowledge formats found in some KBS languages. For example, the following CLIPS and POWERMODEL conditions both select students whose debt is less than £1000.

> CLIPS **version**   (student ?name &: (< ?debt 1000))
> POWERMODEL **version**   ?student.debt < 1000;

The CLIPS condition above will be represented as an Ordered Term with a keyword and two arguments, where the second argument is itself a comparison: (student ?name (< ?debt 1000)). The POWERMODEL condition will be represented as an OAV Triple, where the value argument is a comparison. When a KRUSTTool implements refinements to such nested terms, the Ordered Term and OAV Triple operators will be applied to the terms as a whole, and comparison operators will be applied to the comparisons.

4   EVALUATION

One criterion for evaluating the effectiveness of our organisation of refinement operators is the ease with which they can be applied to new KBS shells. One such shell which we were able to use for evaluation is the product formulation expert system (PFES). This differs from CLIPS, POWERMODEL and PROLOG, the models for our approach, in that it is intended for solving design or formulation problems, whereas the expert systems to which we have applied KRUSTTools have typically solved classification problems. Because of its purpose, PFES has a number of features distinguishing it from some or all of the other shells.

— The result is not a single class value, but a set of data called a *formulation*, or in more familiar terms, a recipe.

— The shell is forward-chaining.

— The shell makes use of a data structure called an agenda. This is an ordered untyped list which items may be added to or read from. It is used to communicate data between rules, where for example, one rule may

generate data, a second may filter it, and a third may use the data that remain.

The complex nature of the result was not a problem, since [Palmer and Craw, 1995], have already shown that KRUSTTools can make use of multiple results from a KBS. The forward-chaining has a bearing on the construction of the problem-graph, but we have seen in section 3.1 that it is irrelevant to the organisation and application of refinement operators. The third factor proved more interesting. We show below how we were able to represent PFES agendas within KRUSTTools. A further feature of the particular PFES application which we used was the availability of large numbers of examples. This permitted us to create new inductive refinement operators, which are described below.

The PFES KBS we used for our evaluation was Zeneca Pharmaceuticals' tablet formulation system (TFS). Tablet formulation is a complex synthesis task, and TFS is one of the few knowledge based formulation systems in regular commercial use. To create a KRUSTTool for PFES, as for any other new KBS, we had to perform two tasks: associate KBS rule elements with existing elements in the knowledge hierarchy, adding new elements to the hierarchy if required; and add further refinement operators if required.

Many of the rule elements in PFES could be immediately identified with standard rule elements already found in KRUST's knowledge hierarchy. For example, the PFES condition `attribute-has-value specification budget ?budget` can be represented as an OAV Triple, and the PFES condition is `?value greater-than 0` can be represented as a comparison. We next consider agendas, for which the representation was less obvious.

4.1 The Representation of Agendas

Agendas did not initially appear to correspond to any term in the hierarchy. However, it is possible to consider the role of the agenda in a declarative rather than a procedural way; in other words, we can regard the command to add an item to an agenda as an assertion that the item is on the agenda. From this viewpoint, PFES agendas can be seen as a mechanism for storing attribute-value data, so that they can be represented within the existing hierarchy as Ordered Terms, as the following examples demonstrate. Not all agendas have the same semantics, but the number of different possibilities actually employed within PFES applications is fairly limited. Figure ?? shows an example based on the student loan domain (we use this domain rather than the pharmaceutical one for reasons of commercial confidentiality and ease of understanding). Here, **student-enrollment-agenda** is a list of students, where each student is followed by his or her period of enrollment. The figure shows the contents of an agenda at some point during the running of PFES, together with the PFES rule elements that write to and read from the agenda, and the KRUSTTool representation of these elements as Ordered Terms. Note that a conclusion that writes to the agenda, and the corresponding condition that reads from it, have the same KRUSTTool representation, though the two appear different in PFES. This ensures that the existing matching functions for Ordered Terms provide the correct chaining behaviour for agenda-related conditions and conclusions.

Snapshot of student-enrollment-agenda

```
student10 2 student18 4 student20 3
```

PFES Read/Write Operations on student-enrollment-agenda

Conclusions:	1) add ?student to-bottom-of student-enrollment-agenda
	2) add ?years to-bottom-of student-enrollment-agenda
Conditions:	1) ?student is-on student-enrollment-agenda
	2) ?years is-after ?student on student-enrollment-agenda

KRUSTTool representation of each operation

```
1) on-agenda(student-enrollment-agenda, ?student)
2) agenda-unlabelled-attribute(student-enrollment-agenda,
                              ?student, ?years)
```

Figure 4. An agenda and its associated operations

4.2   New Refinement Operators

We have shown that the existing hierarchy was able to accommodate all the rule elements used in PFES. However, we found that the set of refinement operators needed extending. Since PFES rule elements could be represented in the hierarchy, we were able to apply the existing refinement operators. However, for some tasks, we found that these were insufficient, and we needed to create new inductive operators. Our original design assumed that few training cases would be available, so our initial operators drew their evidence from a single refinement example. However, in the case of PFES, many examples were available, so we investigated the contribution that could be made by operators which learned from many examples at one time. The approach may be summarised as follows ([?]).

1. Select as positive examples those examples that exhibit a particular fault, and as negative examples those that do not.

2. Identify features distinguishing these two groups.

3. Use these features to guide refinement implementation.

It proved necessary to add four inductive operators Each operator is applicable to a different existing rule element type, thus illustrating how our structuring of the refinement operators made it simple to add and apply new operators as required. The first operator is described in detail, the rest more briefly.

inductive_adjust_value refines comparisons in a similar way to `adjust_value`, but it learns from all available examples, not just from the refinement example. The operator examines the traces for all examples where the comparison had the same behaviour (success or failure) as for the refinement case. It then contrasts those where the system conclusion was correct from those where the comparison was blamed for an incorrect system conclusion. From these two classes of traces, it induces a new threshold value for the comparison which will correct the behaviour of all the faulty examples, while not interfering with the correct examples.

inductive_add_fact applies to failed OAV Triples, where the attribute has numeric type. The operator creates a new fact to match the failed goal, taking into consideration any subsequent comparisons applied to the Value element.

inductive_change_formula uses a least squares approximation to correct a faulty arithmetic expression.

inductive_split_rule is a specialised operator, applicable to rules which fire multiple times, thus adding a sequence of items to an agenda. The operator makes multiple copies of the original rule, adding extra conditions to each copy. The effect is that the new rules put the same items on the agenda as the original rule, but in a different order.

Since the extra trace information required by these operators is represented in a KBS-independent form, as a problem graph, the operators are applicable to other KBSs, not just to PFES.

5 RELATED WORK

Our knowledge hierarchy describes the rule-elements within a KBS, and so it may be regarded as an ontology for rule-elements which tells a KRUSTTool which refinement operators may be applied to each element. Our aim is therefore similar to that of [?]. In their work on problem-solving methods (PSMs), they devise ontologies for both tasks and methods. These ontologies state the abilities of each PSM, and the requirements of each task, thus allowing an *adapter* to select a method appropriate for a given task. This approach allows PSMs to be written in a task-independent way, and so to be applied to a range of tasks. KRUSTWorks' refinement operators therefore correspond to the PSMs, and the knowledge hierarchy forms a PSM ontology. It indicates the requirements of each operator by stating the rule element types to which the operator may be applied. This allows the refinement operators to be written in a KBS-independent way, and so applied to a range of KBSs. However, KRUSTWorks differs from the work of Fensel *et al* in that it is devoted to the single task of refinement, so there is no need to create a task ontology.

KRUSTTools are distinguished from other refinement tools by their ability to refine KBSs written in a variety of shells. KRUSTTools' organisation of refinement operators according to abstract properties of knowledge elements is simply not relevant to tools such as CLIPS-R ([?]) whose target is CLIPS knowledge bases, or EITHER ([?]) and FORTE ([?]) whose target is PROLOG KBSs. However, a comparison can be made between the refinement operators offered by these tools. They all use operators which delete rules and conditions, and which specialise and generalise comparisons. In addition, all the tools possess inductive operators for condition addition. EITHER uses ID3 to induces new rule conditions from example properties. CLIPS-R creates new rule conditions by copying existing CLIPS patterns from elsewhere in the KBS and generalising them. FORTE uses a path-finding algorithm to learn new rules which expresss complex relationships in terms of simpler ones. What all these inductive operators have in common is that they operate at the level of rules. In contrast, all but one of the KRUSTTools' inductive refinement operators are linked to particular rule element types, reflecting the importance within KRUSTTools of identifying the significant properties of rule element types.

6   CONCLUSIONS

Most refinement tools apply to a single KBS environment. We have presented an alternative approach to refinement which uses generic representations for the knowledge contained in rules, and for the reasoning process of a KBS. This has enabled us to build a set of KBS-independent tools, applicable to a variety of KBS environments. In this paper, we have concentrated on the refinement operators within the KRUSTWorks tool-kit. Our generic forms of knowledge representation allow us to organise these operators so that they may be applied to a variety of KBSs, exploiting similarities of behaviour in syntactically-differing rule elements. This facilitates operator re-use, and the development of new operators.

This toolkit was based on our experience developing KRUSTTools for CLIPS, POWERMODEL and PROLOG KBSs. We have validated our approach by applying KRUSTWorks to a significantly different KBS shell, PFES. Our experience with PFES has shown that it was relatively straightforward to develop a KRUSTTool for this new KBS, and to add and apply new operators when required. Moreover, the tool was then able to perform successfully in debugging and maintaining this KBS. For the simpler bugs, the refinements corresponded exactly to those made by the developers; for more complex changes, the KRUSTTool found alternatives that were judged acceptable by the domain expert.

ACKNOWLEDGMENTS

The work described in this paper is supported by EPSRC grant GR/L38387, awarded to Susan Craw. We also thank IntelliCorp Ltd. and Zeneca Pharmaceuticals for their contributions to the project.

References

[Boswell, 1998] Boswell, R. (1998). *Knowledge Refinement for a Formulation System*. PhD thesis, School of Computer and Mathematical Sciences, The Robert Gordon University.

[Craw, 1996] Craw, S. (1996). Refinement complements verification and validation. *International Journal of Human-Computer Studies*, 44(2):245–256.

[Craw and Boswell, 1999] Craw, S. and Boswell, R. (1999). Representing problem-solving for knowledge refinement. In *Proceedings of the Sixteenth National Conference on Artificial Intelligence*. In press.

[Fensel et al., 1997] Fensel, D., Motta, E., Decker, S., and Zdrahal, Z. (1997). Using ontologies for defining tasks, problem-solving methods and their mappings. In Plaza, E. and Benjamins, R., editors, *Knowledge Acquisition, Modeling and Management, Proceedings of the 10th European Workshop (EKAW97)*, pages 113–128, Sant Feliu de Guixols, Spain. Springer.

[Ginsberg, 1988] Ginsberg, A. (1988). *Automatic Refinement of Expert System Knowledge Bases*. Research Notes in Artificial Intelligence. Pitman, London.

[Murphy and Pazzani, 1994a] Murphy, P. M. and Pazzani, M. J. (1994a). Revision of production system rule-bases. In Cohen, W. W. and Hirsh, H., editors, *Proceedings of the Eleventh International Conference on Machine Learning*, pages 199–207, New Brunswick, NJ. Morgan Kaufmann.

[Murphy and Pazzani, 1994b] Murphy, P. M. and Pazzani, M. J. (1994b). Revision of production system rule-bases. In Cohen, W. W. and Hirsh, H., editors, *Proceedings of the Eleventh International Conference on Machine Learning*, pages 199–207, New Brunswick, NJ. Morgan Kaufmann.

[Ourston and Mooney, 1994] Ourston, D. and Mooney, R. (1994). Theory refinement combining analytical and empirical methods. *Artificial Intelligence*, 66:273–309.

[Palmer and Craw, 1995] Palmer, G. J. and Craw, S. (1995). Utilising explanation to assist the refinement of knowledge-based systems. In *Proceedings of the 3rd European Symposium on the Validation and Verification of Knowledge Based Systems (EUROVAV-95)*, pages 201–211.

[Richards and Mooney, 1995] Richards, B. L. and Mooney, R. J. (1995). Refinement of first-order horn-clause domain theories. *Machine Learning*, 19(2):95–131.

Validation and refinement versus revision

F. Dupin de Saint-Cyr   S. Loiseau
bannay@info.univ-angers.fr   *loiseau@info.univ-angers.fr*
LERIA, Université d'Angers, 2 bd Lavoisier, 49045 ANGERS Cedex 01 France

Keywords: validation, refinement, coherency, diagnosis, revision, consistency handling, non monotonic inference relation

Abstract: This paper is a first work on the link between two fields: validation and refinement in knowledge base systems and revision in knowledge representation. The validation evaluates knowledge base quality; among the criterion which can define this quality an interesting one is coherency. The coherency of a set of rules can be viewed as the potential consistency of this set of rules with respect to every possible input. Refinement is a way to modify an incoherent knowledge base in order to restore its coherency. A revision operation is an inference relation, which is defined in order to reason under inconsistency, it provides a way to select rules to delete in order to restore the consistency. In the two fields, usually the initial knowledge base is consistent and the inconsistency can only come from some input on which a deduction must be done. This paper underlines the link between refinement and revision by comparing consistency to coherency and then by defining an inference relation for refinement.

1. INTRODUCTION

Numerous works have been done to propose criteria to measure the quality of a knowledge base (KB for short), and algorithms to evaluate those criteria. This kind of works can be grouped under the term *validation*. The validation process leads to proving either the respect of a given criterion, this provides an assessment about the KB quality, or the inadequacy of the KB with respect to this criterion. In this last case, the developer has to localise the cause(s) of this inadequacy, in order either to modify the rules of the KB such that it respects the criterion, or to assess that the causes of the inadequacy are not really revealing a bad quality in the KB but only a lack of integrity constraints. This process of localising causes of inadequacy, and finding potential modification can be called *refinement* process on a KBS. Validation and refinement have been specially studied in conjunction with real KBs, in order to provide tools to help KB developers. Many articles have been made on these topics in preceding EUROVAV conferences [Ayel95, VanHarmelen-VanVelde97]. In the validation field, information is divided into two parts: inputs and rules. In this paper, a KB is a set of rules. These rules give the meaning of the KB. A set of inputs is a set of facts. When the rules are applied to a set of inputs they leads to an output. For validation purpose, constraints are provided: they represent additional information, the constraints are settled to determine what inputs should never be dealt with or what output must be obtain from a given input. A particular constraint is a test constraint which is a mapping from an input to an output. Different criteria to measure the quality of a KB can be considered [Nguyen&al85]: *iredundancy, completeness, coherency.* Most research in validation has focused on KB coherence problems. A KB is coherent if and only if with any valid input, contradictory results cannot be inferred. The KB coherency can be defined as the consistency of the set of rules and constraints taken with each possible set of inputs. In other words, incoherency can be taken for potential inconsistency of the rules depending on inputs. The most difficult stage in this research is to transform this informal definition into formal and computationable (provable) criteria.

Apart from the validation field, a lot of researchers have studied inconsistency handling in KBs. Generally, the KB considered is a set of propositional logic formulas. Among all possible formulas, two particular cases can be distinguished: atomic formulas which represent ponctual facts, implicative formulas which represent general rules. Unlike in the validation field, in this kind of approach, facts and rules can be found together in the same KB. The KB available is then used in order to deduce new information about the system that it describes. The difficulty is to reason with an inconsistent KB, because the possible deductions become trivial, if we do not want to throw away the whole KB we have to deal with inconsistency. A particular problem is the insertion of a new fact (this fact being a new piece of information about the system represented) in an initially consistent KB; reasoning with the KB after the arrival of this new fact is called *revision* [Alchourrón&al85, Winslett88, Katsuno-Mendelzon91]. So, the problem of revision is to find which formula ψ can be deduced from a formula φ which has been added to the KB, in other words, to verify if φ added to the KB allows to infers ψ, but here the inference must not be the classical inference since φ can bring inconsistency to the KB and classical inference will allow to deduce anything and its contrary from an inconsistent KB. This is why, many researchers have proposed, so called, *non monotonic inference relations* which are able to deal with inconsistency.

This paper is a preliminary work to compare the two fields of research (validation versus revision) in order to see what techniques and theories may be exported from one to the other. This paper is organised as follows. In a first part, we are concerned with revision. Some examples of non monotonic inference relations are presented (this approaches are defined in [Benferhat&al93, DupindeSaintCyr&all94a,b]). In the second part, we present an approach to validate and refine rule bases. This approach was presented in [Bouali&al97], the validation is based on a rule base coherency criteria [Rousset88, Ginsberg-Williamson93], and the refinement uses the notion of diagnosis [Reiter87, Console&al93]. In the third part, we propose to compare the two approaches: (i) we compare consistency to coherency, then (ii) we show how to define an inference relation for refinement, this helps us to situate refinement with respect to revision.

2. KB REVISION

In the rest of this paper, we denote by Λ a finite propositional language. Elements of Λ, or *formulas*, are denoted by Greek letters $\alpha, \beta, \ldots$ An *interpretation* in Λ is an assignment of a truth value in $\{T, F\}$ to each formula of Λ in accordance with the classical rules of propositional calculus; we denote by Ω the set of all such interpretations. An interpretation ω is a *model* of a formula α ($\omega \spadesuit \alpha$) iff $\omega(\alpha)=T$. A formula β is called a logical consequence of α ($\alpha \spadesuit \beta$) iff each model of α is a model of β. A formula α which is satisfied by every interpretation is called a *tautology* (denoted by $\spadesuit \alpha$). A formula α is said to be consistent iff it has at least one model. Any inconsistent formula is denoted by $\bot$. Non monotonic inference relation will be denoted by $\sqcap$. The problem of revision is to decide if given a knowledge base Δ and a new information φ, we can deduce ψ, denoted by $\varphi \sqcap_\Delta \sqcap \psi$. We recall that classical logic is *monotonic* in the sense that an inferred result is never questioned. In plausible reasoning such property is not always desirable since when we reason with general information we need to revise our conclusions in the light of new information. This is why we need to define non monotonic inference relations to reason with general information.

1.1   General definitions

In order to revise a knowledge base Δ by φ, many approaches have been proposed. The basic idea developed in the syntactical approaches (they are called syntactic because the way the formulas are written can influence the inferences: {p,q, ¬p ¬q} will not behave like {pq , ¬p¬q }) is to select some consistent subsets of $\Delta \cup \varphi$, called preferred sub-theories, and to use the classical inference on these subsets.

Definition 1
If f is a preference relation on subsets of formulas the non monotonic inference relation based on f is defined by: $\varphi\square_{f,\Delta}\psi \Leftrightarrow$ for all preferred (w.r.t. f) sub-theory S of Δ consistent with φ, $S \cup \varphi \spadesuit \psi$

The point is to define a preference relation which is able to select the most interesting preferred sub-theories. In order to discriminate between the consistent subsets of KB, the selection criterion generally makes use of uncertainty considerations by using explicitly uncertainty measures [Wilson93, Benferhat&al95] or by using measures expressing priorities [Rescher64, Brewka89, Nebel91, Benferhat&al93, Lehmann92] (for a more detailed description of this kind of approach see [Cayrol-Lagasquie95]). These approaches consist in ranking the KB into priority levels (these levels are often supposed given by an expert (except in Pearl's system Z [Pearl90] where an automatic technique to rank the formulas is proposed, the algorithm is dedicated for KB in which formulas are default rules and the ranking is based on the specificity of the defaults) and maximising the set or the number of formulas satisfied at each level starting from the highest priority level. An important aspect of this kind of approach is that violating however many formulas at a given level is always more acceptable than violating only one formula at a strictly higher level: thus, these approaches are non-compensatory, i.e., levels never interact.

An alternative approach [Pinkas91, Dupin&all94a,b] is to weight the formulas of the KB with positive numbers called penalties. Intuitively, the penalty associated to a formula represents the importance of the formula, the higher it is, the more important is the formula and the more difficult it will be to reject this formula. Inviolable formulas are given an infinite penalty. Contrarily to priorities, penalties are compensatory since they are additive: the cost associated to a subset of formulas of a KB is the sum of the penalties of the rejected formulas, i.e., which are in the KB but not is this subset. The subset having a minimum cost are the preferred subset of KB. The penalties are supposed given by an expert.

1.2   Some examples of non monotonic inference relations

The first idea proposed in order to select among the possible sub-bases of an inconsistent KB, is to select sub-bases X1, ..., Xn which are consistent and maximal - either maximal for inclusion (X is a consistent sub-base maximal for inclusion if it does not exist a consistent sub-base Y such that X is included into Y) or maximal by its cardinality.

Example 1

Consider a domain where we want to determine if people can spent time as voluntary helpers. The variables WageEarner, Manager, Priest, HouseWife, are input variables which distinguish between different kinds of people. The variable SportHours denotes if the person can spent time (more than 2 hours) doing sport. FreeTime describes whether people have free time or not. HelpHours denotes if the person can spent time (more than 8 hours) as a volunteer helper. The following rules base RB describes our domain:

r1: WageEarner $\wedge$ Manager $\rightarrow$ ¬FreeTime
r2: ¬FreeTime $\rightarrow$ ¬HelpHours
r3: Priest $\rightarrow$ HelpHours
r4: HouseWife $\rightarrow$ HelpHours
r5: ¬FreeTime $\rightarrow$ ¬SportHours
r6: HouseWife $\wedge$ WageEarner $\rightarrow$ $\perp$

A question can be: what can we deduce from RB when we learn the facts WageEarner and Manager and Priest? It means that we look for the formulas ψ such that: WageEarner$\wedge$Manager$\wedge$Priest$\Box_{f, RB}\psi$. By definition of $\Box_{f, RB}$ it means that:

S, S being a preferred (w.r.t. f) sub-theory of RB consistent with WageEarner $\wedge$ Manager $\wedge$ Priest, S $\cup$ { WageEarner $\wedge$ Manager $\wedge$ Priest} $\spadesuit\psi$

If we use $\Box_{\subseteq, RB}$: the preferred sub-bases of RB consistent with the formula WageEarner $\wedge$ Manager $\wedge$ Priest are: A={r1, r2, r4, r5, r6}, B={r1, r3, r4, r5, r6}, C={r2, r3, r4, r5, r6} (they are also preferred w.r.t. a cardinality ordering). The set of propositional variables that can be deduce from all the three bases is: {¬HouseWife}. It means that WageEarner$\wedge$Manager $\wedge$Priest $\Box_{\subseteq, RB}$¬HouseWife. But we cannot decide if HelpHours is true or not with this inference relation.

Now, if the selection of the sub-bases is not strong enough, complementary information is needed about the KB, for so, the formulas of the KB can be weighted in order to represent a confidence degree which can be assessed to them by an expert. In this case, the KB can be stratified into priority levels (either directly by the expert or by an algorithm based on the syntax of the formulas like in Pearl's system Z).

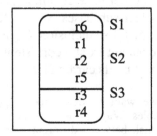

Figure 1. Example of RB stratification into 3 priority levels

Now, the selection can take into account these levels, let S1, S2 , ... Sn be these levels ranked by decreasing priority. Let us present the lexicographic ordering (it is not the only way to order the sub-bases: you can also consider the best-out ordering proposed by [Dubois&all92] or the discrimin ordering proposed by [Brewka89], but it has been proved [Benferhat&al93] that A bo-preferred to B $\Rightarrow$ A discrimin-preferred to B $\Rightarrow$ A lex-preferred to B)

Definition 2 ([Benferhat&al93])

Let A and B be two consistent sub-sets of KB, A is *lexicographically-preferred* to B iff $\exists\ S_i$ such that $|B_i| < |A_i|$ and $j\ < i,\ |A_j| = |B_j|$ (where $X_i = X \cap S_i$)

Example (followed)

A={r1,r2,r4,r5,r6}is the lexicographically-preferred sub-base consistente with WageEarner∧Manager∧Priest. It means that: WageEarner∧Manager ∧Priest $\square$ lex,RB¬HouseWife∧ ¬FreeTime∧ ¬HelpHours∧ ¬SportHours (since A ∪{WageEarner∧Manager∧Priest} ♠¬HouseWife∧¬FreeTime∧¬HelpHours∧¬Sport Hours .)

Instead of using priority levels, the formulas can be weighted with positive numbers called penalties. For any formula φ_i of the KB, there is an associated penalty α_i which represents a degree of confidence into φ_i, it will be understood as the cost that the user must pay in order to discard the formula φ_i. An infinite penalty is associated to unviolable formulas. The inference relation associated to a penalty KB use the following preference relation:

Definition 3 ([Dupin&all94a])

The cost C(A) of a sub-base A of KB is the sum of the penalties of the formulas in KB \ A. A sub-theory A of KB is *k-preferred* to a sub-theory B   iff $C(A) \le C(B)$.

Example 1

Let us consider the following penalty KB:

r1: WageEarner ∧ Manager → ¬FreeTime $\alpha_1 = 20$
r2: ¬FreeTime → ¬HelpHours $\alpha_2 = 20$
r3: Priest → HelpHours $\alpha_3 = 5$
r4: HouseWife → HelpHours $\alpha_4 = 5$

r5: ¬FreeTime → ¬SportHours $\alpha_5 = 20$
r6: HouseWife ∧ WageEarner → ⊥ $\alpha_6 = +\infty$

The k-preferred sub-base of RB consistent with WageEarner∧Manager∧Priest is A (C(A)=5, C(B)=20, C(C)=20). So, WageEarner∧Manager∧Priest□ $_{k,RB}$¬HouseWife ∧¬FreeTime∧¬HelpHours∧¬SportHours.

Among the non monotonic inference relations which can be defined, some can be more appealing since they seem more "rational". Kraus, Lehmann and Magidor [Kraus&al90] have proposed a set of properties for a non monotonic consequence relation. These properties are defined in order to capture the intended meaning of a "rational " non monotonic relation. This set of properties is called System P and has been refined by adding a "rational monotony property" in [Alchourrón&al85].

2.   KB VALIDATION-REFINEMENT

The validation approach is a bottom-up approach that attempts to measure the KB quality so that, if necessary, it can suggest to the expert to improve it. The KB refinement is supported by such a quality measurement. It aims to help the user to modify the KB in order to improve its quality. In rules base systems, many works [Rousset88, Beauvieux&Dagues90, Loiseau 92, Ginsberg-Williamson93, Bouali&al97] have been made on coherency.

In this part, rules are not exactly formulas of classical logic, a rule has the following form: "Ri: *If* L1 ∧ ... ∧ Ln *Then* Lm". Ri is the name of the rule. Li are literals or "⊥", we distinguish the subset, denoted by *R*, of rules of RB which have been stated as reliable by the designer and which cannot be modified. These rules are called *constraints*. Among these rules, those having the symbol "⊥" as a consequent are called *integrity constraints*. The other rules, denoted by *r* (RB = r ∪ R), are called *expert rules*. In the example, the name of the rules that belong to R begin with a capital letter. A fact is a literal (represented by a propositional variable or its negation). A fact base, denoted by *F*, is a set of facts. The *input facts* are the facts that can be given by a user during a session. An input fact is an instance of an *input literal*. The set of input propositional variables is determined once for all by the designer. We introduce the symbol ◆$_{MΠ}$ such that Δ ◆$_{MΠ}$ φ if φ can be deduced by modus ponens from a set of facts and rules Δ (to a rule "*If* L1 ∧ ... ∧ Ln *Then* Lm" is associated the classical formula L1 ∧ ... ∧ Ln → Lm). The designer provides the rules base to validate as well as the input propositional variables set. To apply a rules base RB to a fact base F consists in computing the set of facts which can be deduced by modus ponens on F and RB.

In part 3.1, we present the RB VT_coherency property [Bouali&al97] which provides a measure to evaluate the quality of RBs. In part 3.2, we present a way to restore the VT_coherency of a RB, i.e., to refine the RB.

2.1   Validation

The VT_coherency property uses a set of test cases given by the designer. Formally, a test case is a pair $<F_{test}, O>$ where F_{test} is an input fact base, and O (for Output) is a fact. Each test case is supposed to be certified as being reliable by the designer, it means that: $F_{test} \cup O \cup R \circledR_{MII} \perp$. In consequence, each test case can be represented by a logical association which is known to be held in the domain, between the input fact base F_{test} and the output fact O. This logical association is a constraint that can be associated with the test case.

A rules base is coherent if and only if with any valid input, contradictory results can not be inferred. Two main problems have to be solved. First, we have to know how to characterize a valid input. Second, we have to find a way to infer results from any valid input. In this approach, a valid input is an input fact base satisfying a set of constraints. These constraints are obtained from the rules base and the test cases.

Definition 4
Let $<\{f1, ..., fn\}, O>$ be a test case, where $\{f1, ..., fn\}$ is an input fact base, and O is a non input fact, "*If* f1 $\wedge$ ... $\wedge$ fn *Then* O" is the *associated constraint* to the test case, denoted by R_T.
Let T_{test} be a set of test cases, we call R_{test} the set of constraints associated with each test case of T_{test}.

Definition 5([Loiseau92])
An input fact base F_i *satisfies the constraints* R if $F_i \cup R \circledR_{MII} \perp$.

Example
r1: *If* WageEarner $\wedge$ Manager *Then* ¬FreeTime
r2: *If* ¬FreeTime *Then* ¬HelpHours
r3: *If* Priest *Then* HelpHours
r4: *If* HouseWife *Then* HelpHours
r5: *If* ¬FreeTime *Then* ¬SportHours
R6: *If* HouseWife $\wedge$ WageEarner *Then* $\perp$
Here, the last rule R6 is a constraint, the other rules are expert rules. The input literals set is {WageEarner, Manager, Priest, HouseWife, ManyChildren, ManyWorkHours}. Consider that we have the following set of test cases:
T1:<{WageEarner, Manager, ManyWorkHours}, ¬HelpHours>
T2:<{HouseWife, ManyChildren}, ¬HelpHours>
T3:<{Priest}, HelpHours>
T4:<{WageEarner, Manager, ¬ManyWorkHours}, SportHours>
T5:<{WageEarner, Manager, ManyWorkHours}, ¬SportHours>
R_{test} is composed of 5 constraints associated to T1,...,T5. For example, the constraint associated with T2 is: "*If* HouseWifeM anyChildren *Then* ¬HelpHours". F={House

Wife,ManyChildren,Priest} does not satisfy the constraints $R \cup R_{test}$ (since $F \cup \{R_{T2}, R_{T3}\} \blacklozenge_{M\Pi} \perp$)

Definition 6 ([Bouali&al97])

A rules base RB is *VT_coherent* with respect to a set of test cases T_{test} if

1. For each input fact base F_i satisfying the constraints $R \cup R_{test}$, $F_i \cup RB \ \circledR_{M\Pi} \perp$
2. For each test case $<F_{test}, O> \in T_{test}$, $F_{test} \cup O \cup RB \ \circledR_{M\Pi} \perp$.

The VT_coherency property generalizes and improves the properties given in the following works: [Rousset88] [Ginsberg88b] [Beauvieux-Dagues90] [Loiseau92] [Ginsberg-Williamson93] and [Levy-Rousset96].

Example

The KB presented above is VT_incoherent. On one hand, {WageEarner, Manager, Priest} is an input fact base satisfying $R \cup R_{test}$ ({WageEarner, Manager, Priest} $\cup$ R6 $\cup$ R_{test} $\circledR_{M\Pi} \perp$), and on the other hand, it enables the firing of r1, r2 and r3 leading to the contradiction: HelpHours and H elpHours. Hence, the VT_incoherency.

We can remark that with T2 a contradiction can be obtained, because the condition part of T2 {HouseWife, ManyChildren} provides a way to fire r4 whose conclusion is "HelpHours" which is contradictory with the conclusion of the test case T2: " HelpHours ". This is an other way to show the VT_incoherency. In some cases, it is only the test cases that bring incoherencies.

2.2 Refinement

Once a rule base is VT_incoherent, we have to refine it to restore the coherency. On one way, we can define a minimal proof of an incoherency as a conflict composed of an input and a set of rules. On the other way, many conflicts can exist, so we define a cause of all the incoherences as a diagnosis which is composed of inputs and rules such that if those inputs and those rules are forbidden then the rest of the rule base is VT_coherent. This process to compute diagnoses is called the refinement process because it provides a way to restore the coherency by modifying the rules base. We do not present conflicts in this paper, cf. [Bouali&al97] for more details.

By analogy with the debugging of a classical program, providing a conflict should be equivalent to providing an input along with the appropriate part of the program leading to the possible invalidity. It should be more efficient to provide the designer with a possible cause of the VT_incoherency (a diagnosis) of the rules base rather than a proof of the VT_incoherency (a conflict). Continuing the analogy with the debugging of a classical program, a cause should be one or a few lines of code whose incorrectness could be sufficient to explain the invalidity of the program (all the conflicts).

The VT_incoherency of a rules base can be explained (i) by the lack of constraints which could exclude the input fact bases leading to a contradiction because they are not valid in the domain, and/or (ii) by bad rules that lead to a contradiction with valid input fact bases. A possible cause of the VT_incoherency is called diagnosis. A rules base diagnosis is composed by a set of input fact bases and a set of expert rules. To each input fact base $F_i = \{f_{i,1}, ..., f_{i,n}\}$ of a diagnosis can be associated an integrity constraint "*If* $\wedge_j f_{i,j}$ *Then* $\perp$". Note that the more numerous the facts are in the integrity constraint and the less restrictive is this constraint, this is why, all the facts of F_i are taken in the conjunction of the integrity constraint.

Definition 7

Let us consider a pair $D=< E_D, r_D>$, E_D being a set of input fact bases $E_D = \{\{f_{1,1}; ..., f_{1,n}\}; ...; \{f_{p,1}; ...; f_{p,m}\}\}$ and r_D beeing a subset of r (the expert rules). Let us call R_{ED} the set of the p integrity constraints "*If* $\wedge_j f_{i,j}$ *Then* $\perp$" associated to E_D. Let D(RB) be the rules base repaired by the pair $< E_D, r_D>$, it corresponds to RB from which the rules r_D has been deleted and the p integrity constraints of R_{ED} are added: D(RB) = $(R \cup r \setminus\{r_D\}) \cup R_{ED}$.

$< E_D, r_D>$ is a *diagnosis* of an incoherent rules base RB, with respect to a set of test cases T_{test}, if D(RB) is VT_coherent with respect to T_{test}.

A VT_incoherent rules base becomes VT_coherent if some integrity constraints associated to the fact bases of the diagnosis are added and if the rules of the same diagnosis are deleted.

Definition 8

A diagnosis $<E_D, r_D>$ is *minimal* if there does not exist another diagnosis $<E_D', r_D'>$ verifying: $r_D' \subseteq r_D$, and ($E_D' \subseteq E_D$, or $\forall F'$ in E_D', $\exists F$ in E_D such that $F \subseteq F'$).

Examples

- Considering the two diagnosis E1= $<\{\{a,b\},\{a, c\}\}, \{r1\}>$ and E2=$<\{\{a,b\}\}, \{r1\}>$, E2 is minimal, since it is sufficient to forbid the conjunction of the litterals a and b and to suppress the rule r1 in order to apply the diagnosis E2, meanwile two conjunctions are forbidden in E1.
- Considering the diagnosis E3=$<\{\{a\}\}, \{r1\}>$, E1 is minimal in the set of diagnosis {E1,E3} since having a constraint which forbids a is more restrictive that having two constraints forbidding a $\wedge$ b and a $\wedge$ c.

Our approach considers only minimal diagnoses that contain a set of bad rules and missing constraints sufficient to restore the VT_coherency. Of course, several minimal diagnoses often exist. The choice of the right diagnosis to repair the rules base can be done using heuristics and/or with the help of the designer of the rules base. Here we propose to select the diagnosis which are not only consistent with the set of test cases but also do not block the derivation of the expected output from an input which is given in a test case, see [Bouali&al97] for more details.

Definition 9

$D=<E_D,r_D>$ is a *prefered* diagnosis of a rules base RB with respect to a set of test cases T_{test}, if D is a minimal diagnosis and for each test case $<F_{test}, O>$ in T_{test} s.t. $F_{test} \cup RB$ ♦$_{M\Pi}$ O, the rules base repaired by D, D(RB), verifies $F_{test} \cup D(RB)$ ♦$_{M\Pi}$ O.

The algorithm to compute the "diagnoses" of a physical system [Reiter87] in terms of "conflicts" proving the incoherency of the system can be extended to compute the minimal diagnoses of a rules base when the conflicts of the rules base are known [Bouali&al97].

3.   DISCUSSION

Two main differences can be underlined between validation-refinement and revision. First, validation uses a coherency property that is not used by revision which uses only classical consistency. Second, revision proposes many formal ways to modify a KB, meanwhile refinement proposes more informal solutions to modify a KB.

First, let us compare consistency and coherency. To each rule of a rules base a logical implication can be naturally associated. Under our assumptions, the functioning of an inference engine can be assimilated to that of a logical demonstrator based on modus ponens. It seams natural to evaluate the rules base coherency by testing the consistency of the logical formulae associated with the rules base. Numerous algorithms have been studied for this and could be used to evaluate the logical consistency of the set of rules. However, the existence of a model of the set of logical implications associated to the rules is a condition too weak to evaluate the coherency of the rules base.

Example 1

Let us come back again to our example expressed in classical logic:

r1: WageEarner ∧ Manager → ¬FreeTime
r2: ¬FreeTime → ¬HelpHours
r3: Priest → HelpHours
r4: HouseWife → HelpHours
r5: ¬FreeTime → ¬SportHours
r6: HouseWife ∧ WageEarner → ⊥

This base is consistent; for instance, the interpretation {WageEarner, Manager, ¬FreeTime, ¬HelpHours, ¬Priest, ¬HouseWife, ¬SportHours} satisfies it. But if we consider that {WageEarner, Manager, Priest} is a valid input in the domain, we would like to say that RB is not "coherent " according to our coherency property. {WageEarner, Manager, Priest} provides (with r1, r2, r3) {¬HelpHours} and {HelpHours} which are contradictory literals.

In the validation field, the coherency of a rules base depends on the input fact bases that a user could give during the utilisation phase: we call such inputs *valid inputs*. Each valid input can be translated into the conjunction of its facts. What coherency requires is that each formula associated to a valid input taken with the set of formulas associated with the rules base can not infer the contradiction by modus ponens.

Some difficulties appear. First, the cost of such an approach is proportional to the number of valid inputs. Second, the number of valid inputs can be infinite. Third, the way to obtain such valid inputs or a modelisation of them must be found: as soon as we do not consider given test cases as the only valid inputs, the difficulties arise, there is no efficient and simple solution. So, even if works on classical logic can provide some results to researchers who are studying the problem of the evaluation of the coherency of a rules base, they are not sufficient to provide a correct and complete solution to the coherency problem as we have presented it. This is why we introduce (VT) coherency definitions.

Second, is refinement by diagnosis a kind of revision? As we said before, computing the potential consistency of a rule base cannot be done reasonably because the potential inputs of the rules base can be very numerous and even infinite. So, for consistency detection the revision field can not bring any help to the validation field. Let us see if the refinement proposed above can be viewed as a revision operator.

Definition 10

Given a rules base RB and a set of test cases T, let us define the relation $\boxempty_{\text{diag}}$ as:

$\varphi \ \boxempty_{\text{diag, RB, T}} \ \psi \ \Leftrightarrow \ \varphi$ is a conjunction of input facts, and ψ is a conjunction of output facts s.t.: $\varphi \cup R \cup R_{\text{test}} \ \circledR_{\text{MΠ}}$ (R_{test} being the set of constraints associated to T) and

a) if RB is VT-coherent then $\varphi \cup R \cup r \ \blacklozenge_{\text{MΠ}} \ \psi$

b) else for each prefered diagnosis $<E_D, r_D>$:

$\varphi \cup R \cup R_{\text{test}} \cup R_{\text{ED}} \circledR_{\text{MΠ}}$ and $\varphi \cup R \cup r \backslash \{r_D\} \ \blacklozenge_{\text{MΠ}} \ \psi$.

In other words, if RB is VT-coherent with T, from φ we infer ψ, if and only if φ is a valid input and taken with the RB, it allows to infer ψ by modus ponens. In the other case, i.e., if RB is VT-incoherent, for any prefered diagnosis $<E_D, r_D>$, φ must be valid with respect to the diagnosis E_D (i.e., with R_{ED}) and taken with RB from which the rules r_D are removed it should infer ψ by modus ponens.

Here, the inference relation is defined under particular formulas, the formulas φ and ψ must be under the form of a conjunction of facts, it is impossible to infer an implication for instance, or to put a rule as an input. Moreover, the inference can only take into account valid inputs.

Besides, the computation of diagnoses can be done once for all and then the inference relation uses an inference by modus ponens based upon a new rules base. This computation does not depend upon the input.

The inference relation defined is a very particular revision operator, since the KB can be modified once for all with respect to the set of test cases and then from any valid input an output can be computed. In general, a classical revision operator must take into account each input in order to update the knowledge contained into the KB and then the inference can be done.

In conclusion, though *revision* can not bring any help in the field of *validation* because there is no algorithms allowing to compute potential inconsistancies or, as we call them, incoherencies, revision can be linked with *refinement*. We have seen that an inference relation can be defined from a rules base RB and a set of test cases T by the computation of diagnoses. A diagnosis consists in a set of rules to delete and a set of conjunctions of facts to forbid. The inference relation we propose is an inference by modus ponens which takes into account a new rules base RB' computed once for all from RB and T (if RB is VT-coherent with T, RB'=RB else RB' is RB from which some rules are deleted and some integrity constraints are added following a choosen diagnosis). In fact, in case of VT-incoherency, there are many ways to choose a diagnosis which can repair RB into an RB'. In this paper a preference relation on diagnosis is proposed. The inference relation must then examin every possible rules base RB' corresponding to each preferred diagnosis.

An interesting perspective of this article, is to use revision techniques in order to refine the selection of preferred diagnoses: this selection could take into account some preferences on the rules as it is shown in the first part of this paper.

REFERENCES

[Alchourrón&al85] Alchourrón, Gärdenfors and Makinson. On the logic of theory change: partial meet contraction and revision functions. Jl of Symbolic Logic, vol 50, 510-530, 85.

[Ayel95] EUROVAV (European Symposium on the Validation and Verification of Knowledge Based-Systems), Chambéry, 1995.

[Beauvieux-Dagues90] Beauvieux, A., Dague, P. A general consistency (checking and restoring) engine for Knowledge Bases. ECAI, p.77-82 (1990).

[Benferhat&al93] Benferhat, Cayrol, Dubois, Lang, Prade. Inconsistency management and prioritized syntax-based entailment. IJCAI, vol 3, 640-645. 1993.

[Benferhat&all95] Benferhat and Smets. Belief functions for logical problems: representing default rules in ε-beliefs logics. In Abstract of the Dagstuhl Seminar, 1993.

[Bouali&al97] Bouali, Loiseau, Rousset, M.C. Revision of Rule Bases. EUROVAV 1997.

[Brewka89] G. Brewka. Preferred subtheories: an extended logical framework for default reasoning. IJCAI, 1043-1048. 1989.

[Cayrol-Lagasquie95]. Cayrol, Lagasquie-Schiex. Non-monotonic syntax-based entailment: a classification of consequence relations. Lecture notes in AI, 946, p. 107-114.1995.

[Console&al 93] Console L., Friedrich G., Dupré D.T. Model-Based Diagnosis Meets Error Diagnosis in Logic Programs, IJCAI, p.1494-1499 (1993).

[Dubois&al92] Dubois, Lang, Prade. Inconsistency in possibilistic knowledge bases -To live or not live with it. Fuzzy Logic for the Management of Uncertainty, Wiley, 335-351.1992.

[Dupin de Saint-Cyr&all94a] Dupin de Saint-Cyr, Lang and Schiex. Gestion de l'inconsistance dans les BC: une approche syntaxique basée sur la logique des pénalités.RFIA,94.

[Dupin de Saint-Cyr&all94b] Dupin de Saint-Cyr, Lang and Schiex. Penalty logic and its link with Dempster-Shafer theory. In Proc. of the 10th Uncertainty in AI, p. 204-211. 1994.

[Ginsberg-Williamson93] Ginsberg, Williamson, Inconsistency and Redundancy Checking for Quasi-First-Order-Logic Knowledge Bases. International Journal of Expert Systems, vol.6(3), p.321-340 (1993).

[Katsuno-Mendelzon91] Katsuno, Mendelzon. On the difference between updating a knowledge base and revising it. Proc. of the 2nd Inter. Conf. on Principles of Knowledge Representation and Reasoning, p. 387-394, Cambridge, MA, 1991.

[Kraus&al90], Kraus S., Lehmann D., Magidor M. 1990. Nonmonotonic reasoning, preferential models and cumulative logics. Artificial Intelligence, 44, 167-207.

[Lehmann92] D. Lehmann. 1992. Another perspective on default reasoning. Tec. Report.

[Levy-Rousset96] Levy, A. Rousset, M.C. Verification of knowledge bases based on containment checking. AAAI, p.585-591 (1996).

[Loiseau92] Loiseau. Refinement of Knowledge Bases Based on Consistency. ECAI, p. 845-849 (1992).

[Nebel91] B. Nebel. Belief revision and default reasoning: syntax-based approaches. In Proc. of the 2nd KR, p. 417-428. Cambridge, MA, 1991.

[Nguyen&al85] Nguyen, T.A., Perkins, W.A., Laffey, T.J., Pecora, D. Checking an expert systems knowledge base for consistency and completeness. IJCAI, p.375-379 (1985).

[Pearl90] J. Pearl. System Z: A natural ordering of defaults with tractable applications to default reasoning. Proc. of Theoretical Aspects of Reasoning about Knowledge, pages 121-135. Morgan Kaufman, San Mateo. 1990

[Pinkas91] G. Pinkas. Propositional nonmonotonic reasoning and inconsistency in symmetric neural networks. In Prof. of the 12th IJCAI. p. 525-530. Sydney, Australia, 1991.

[Reiter87] Reiter, R. A theory of diagnosis from first priciples. AI, vol 32, p. 57-95 (1987).

[Rescher64] N. Rescher. Hypothetical Reasoning. North-Holland, 1964.

[Rousset88] Rousset, M.C. On the consistency of knowledge bases: the COVADIS system. ECAI, p.79-84 (1988).

[VanHarmelen-VanVelde97] EUROVAV (European Symposium on the Validation and Verification of Knowledge Based-Systems) 1995, Leuven.

[Wilson93] N. Wilson. Default logic and Dempster-Shafer theory. ECSQARU, p. 372-379, Granada, Spain 1993.

[Winslett88] M. Winslett. Reasoning about action using a possible models approach. Proc of the 7th National Conference on Artificial Intelligence, p. 89-93, St. Paul, 1988.

Illustrating Knowledge Base Restructuring and Verification in a Real World Application

VANTHIENEN, Jan and MORENO GARCÍA, Ana María

Katholieke Universiteit Leuven. Department of Applied Economic Sciences. Naamsestraat 69, 3000 Leuven. Belgium. (Jan.Vanthienen@econ.kuleuven.ac.be)
Dep. Economía Financiera y Dirección de Operaciones. University of Seville. Avda. Ramón y Cajal, nº 1. 41018 Seville. Spain. (anafi@ibm.net)

Key words: knowledge base restructuring, verification & validation, maintenance

Abstract: This paper discusses the restructuring of a knowledge-based system as a particular use of a decision table modeling tool. The aim of this exposition is to apply the approach in a real world application, SEAR (an Enterprise Human Resources Advisory System). All problems in restructuring the Knowledge-Based System (KBS) will be analyzed. It will be shown how a decision table tool is an interesting alternative in this process that facilitates the maintenance. First, the real world application is given and its current structure is shown. Next, the restructuring process is applied to the application. A summary that contains the obtained results and a brief evaluation conclude this paper.

1.   INTRODUCTION

This article discusses the restructuring of a KBS as a particular use of a decision table modeling tool.

The past few years' investigations in methodologies for Knowledge Based System (KBS) development have demonstrated the utility for this proposal of employing decision tables, a technique originally used to support programming [Vanthienen, 1991]. Especially in the Verification and Validation (V&V) phase, the interest in decision tables has developed progressively [Suwa, Scott and Shortliffe, 1982; Vanthienen, 1986; Puuronen, 1987]. In short, this phase can substantially be improved through the use of decision tables.

Problems of validation and verification have led to the occasional use of schemes, tables or similar techniques in knowledge representation. It has been reported earlier, e.g. in [Cragun and Steudel, 1987] and [Vanthienen and Dries, 1994], that the decision table technique is able to provide for extensive validation and verification assistance. Most of the common validation problems can easily be solved using decision tables, as described in [Vanthienen, Aerts, Mues and Wets, 1995]. Furthermore, these authors show that the integration of decision tables in the modeling environment might reduce V&V problems.

Decision table techniques could support designers in reducing the risk of introducing anomalies. This approach will be illustrated by means of a real world case, SEAR [Moreno, 1998], viz. a human resources decision case. It will be described how the decision table technique is used to restructure the SEAR KBS.

This paper is structured as follows. Firstly, a real world application is given and its original structure is shown. Next, the restructuring process is applied to the real application. A summary that contains the obtained results and a brief evaluation conclude this paper.

2.   A REAL WORLD APPLICATION: SEAR

This section firstly presents the explanatory information and circumstances, viz. the background in which the application takes place. Afterwards the SEAR application will be presented.

2.1   Background

In its aim to optimize its human resources management, a company is often confronted with the problem of having to displace some of its workforce in the best possible economic and human way. This situation is especially delicate because the management has to take into account the interests of the company and its future objectives, as well as the employees' particular situation.

The number of a company's workforce is likely to change dramatically in a phase of transformation. It will be necessary to establish the ideal staff structure, in order to define, later on, the actions that lead to it and the costs that are implied. The re-engineering processes will be applied to the workforce including the relocation of some employees, and the adaptation of their formation to the new necessities of the work place. For example, a company of seven hundred employees represents a staff consisting of individuals in very different situations. In this case the expert has to study the characteristics of each employee to propose the pertinent changes.

The application that is exposed here, SEAR (an Enterprises Human Resources Advisory System), helps the user in this laborious, decisional process. Based on real data, the system was built on the factual relationships between the conclusion-decisions, whereby a group of historic examples were stored in a database. These data present some value attributes such as age or current salary.

SEAR is an application used in a social and juridical consultantship context. The software is operational since one year and was constructed in the VP-Expert shell. It consists of providing an advice of legal rules and regulations, and needs continuous maintenance. It allows the user to take decisions based on the Spanish Social Security General Regime Law and is described below.

2.2   SEAR

This section presents what is the original structure of SEAR and the way how this structure was obtained. SEAR was constructed, where possible, by modules, which are compounded in the system.

SEAR will be presented in three steps. First, the main solutions of the problem will be shown, second the predicates will be displayed and third the main rules in which the problem was designed will be presented.

2.2.1   The application

In accordance with the advice of the domain expert, the SEAR application starts from the analysis of the employee's profile. Based on the alternative profiles, different solutions are compounded in the system, as is shown in figure 1, some of which will be exposed below without going into detail. In this figure the main results of the system are shown but not the way to resolve it. Below will be presented some of the typical profiles or situations through which employees can be characterized. The user who has to take decisions based on the system will be a human expert.

The employee's data include information such as name and surname, age, time worked in the company, annual gross wage (sueldo bruto anual, SBA), family load, and some other related information.

Depending on the user's answers, the system is tracing its way towards the most appropriate solution. For instance, one common case is related to employees older than 60. In this case the system makes a valuation of the possibility of proposing them a favorable premature retirement. The expert indicates that the enterprise has to keep the employee's income in a proportion of 90% of the Annual Gross Wage amount. This amount will be obtained through two sources: a part comes from the public administration, another from private agreements. The public part comes from the National Unemployment Institute (Instituto Nacional de Empleo, INEM) or from the Social Security Institute (Instituto de la Seguridad Social, INSS), depending on the specific situation of the employee. The rest arises from the establishment of a contract between the enterprise and private insurance companies, by means of an agreement.

❖ *Complete Permanent Disability (IPT)*
❖ *To keep the contract of employment*
❖ *To change the contract of employment*
❖ *Unemployment allowance*
❖ *Family assistance*
❖ *Unemployment assistance*
❖ *Older than 52 allowance*
❖ *Wrongful dismissal*
❖ *To carry out the contract of employment*

Figure 1. Solutions of the SEAR KBS

A new problem arises when the employee is between 60 and 65, as the expert proposes to maintain the Social Security rates payments till the age of 65. At that age a normal retirement situation is put in place, whereby the employee receives a complete retirement pension. If the employee does not contribute for these five years, a part of his pension is off.

Another employee profile defined by the system, but not so common, is related to the request of a Complete Permanent Disability allowance (Invalidez Permanente Total, IPT). This is only possible in very specific cases.

In the Spanish Social Security System there are two levels of aid: *contributive* and non-contributive or *assistance*. As the contributive aid is only temporary, the assistance aid will serve as a complementary aid.

The contributive level contains the *unemployment allowance* that will be obtained through some calculations based on the Retirement Regulation Base (Base de Reguladora de Desempleo, BRD), with some minimum limits.

There is assistance help for workers who have finished a contributive help and which have family responsibilities, it is called *family assistance*. It will be demanded before the unemployment assistance, which it is exposed below.

Another type of assistance aid is called the *unemployment assistance*. Depending on the age and family load of the employee the *unemployment assistance* will be calculated. The amount that is received is a percentage of the minimum wage established by Government.

These actions give more flexibility to the company to plan an adequate and well distributed workforce. However, they have to be well designed and agreed between the company, the syndicate and the worker individually. Sometimes, it is advisable not to change anything in case it produces high costs or deteriorates the company's image. For all this, the expert should be advised by marketing and human resources departments.

2.2.2   The predicates

For SEAR, the user is expected to be able to answer questions about the current and past situation of the employee. These questions are related with the predicates, which are the following:

- NAME : " EMPLOYEES' NAME AND SURNAME?
- YEARSOLD : "HOW OLD IS THE EMPLOYEE (IN YEARS)?
- MONTHSOLD : "AND HOW MANY MONTHS MORE?
- CURRENTMONTH : "WHAT IS THE CURRENT MONTH?
- IPT : "- IS IT POSSIBLE TO CONSIDER THE EMPLOYEE A COMPLETE PERMANENT DISABILITY?
- ENTERPRISEYEARS : "- HOW LONG HAS THE EMPLOYEE WORKED FOR THE COMPANY?
- ENTERPRISEMONTHS : "- AND HOW MANY MONTHS MORE?
- SBA: "- WHAT IS HIS ANNUAL GROSS WAGE (WITHOUT PRIMES)?
- BCD1 : "HOW MUCH MONEY WAS PAYED IN THE LAST MONTH UNEMPLOYMENT ASSESSMENT BASE (FOR TAX)?
- BCD2..6 : " AND TWO..SIX MONTHS AGO?
- CHILDREN : "HOW MANY CHILDREN HAS THE EMPLOYEE?
- FAMILYLOAD : "WHAT IS THE EMPLOYEE'S FAMILY LOAD? (- THAT IS: CHILDREN, SPOUSE, RELATIVES UP TO THE SECOND DEGREE WHO DON'T RECEIVE ANOTHER PENSIONS KIND).

2.2.3   The main rules

Following are the main rules applied in this application. These are used to define the employee's profile. Only the main knowledge base is displayed because its transformation of decision rules will be presented. Other knowledge bases are herewith connected via the "chain" command (corresponding with a chain X.kbs). They mainly contain the calculations, the type of aid, amounts and periods. In this paper, they remain invariable.

The SEAR rules

```
Rule 1.....              RULE 1
IF IPT=YES
THEN
(IF YOUNGER_THAN_55=YES THEN INV55 =
(0.55*209686)
ELSE INV75 = (0.75*209686))
        CHAIN R1.KBS (*)
Rule 2.....              RULE 2A
IF AGE>35 AND AGE<45.5 AND
FAMILYLOAD<>0
THEN CHAIN R2A.KBS
Rule 3.....              RULE 2B
IF AGE>35 AND AGE<47.5 AND
FAMILYLOAD=0
THEN CHAIN R2B.KBS
Rule 4.....              RULE 3
IF AGE<=35
THEN CHAIN R3.KBS
Rule 5.....              RULE 4A
IF AGE>=45.5 AND AGE<48 AND
FAMILYLOAD<>0
THEN FIND FACTS
FIND AF, AGREEMENT, DES70, DES60, SUB52,
LD, MONTHSD
CHAIN R4A.KBS
Rule 6.....              RULE 4B
IF AGE>=47.5 AND AGE<48 AND
FAMILYLOAD=0
THEN FIND FACTS
FIND AF, AGREEMENT, DES70, DES60, SUB52,
LD, MONTHSD
CHAIN R4B.KBS
Rule 7.....              RULE 5
IF AGE>=48 AND AGE<50
THEN FIND FACTS
FIND AF, AGREEMENT, DES70, DES60, SUB52
(**)
CHAIN R5.KBS
Rule 8.....              RULE 6
IF AGE >= 50
THEN FIND FACTS
FIND AGREEMENT, DES70, DES60, SUB52, LD,
MONTHSD
CHAIN R6.KBS
Rule 9.....              RULE MAXIMUM
IF ANT45 <= (3.5*SBA)
THEN MAXIMUM = (ANT45)
ELSE MAXIMUM = (3.5*SBA)
        CHAIN R7.KBS
```

```
Rule 10.....             RULE MINIMUM
IF ANT20 <= (SBA)
THEN MINIMUM = (ANT20)
ELSE MINIMUM = (SBA)
        CHAIN R8.KBS
Rule 11.....             RULE LML1
IF CHILDREN = 0
THEN LEGAL_MAX_LIMIT = (SMI*0.170)
Rule 12.....             RULE LML2
IF CHILDREN = 1
THEN LEGAL_MAX_LIMIT = (SMI*0.195)
Rule 13.....             RULE LML3
IF CHILDREN > 1
THEN LEGAL_MAX_LIMIT = (SMI*0.220)
Rule 14.....             RULE DES1
IF BRD07 < (LEGAL_MAX_LIMIT)
THEN DES70 = (BRD07)
ELSE DES70 = (LEGAL_MAX_LIMIT)
Rule 15.....             RULE DES2
IF BRD06 < (LEGAL_MAX_LIMIT)
THEN DES60 = (BRD06)
ELSE DES60 = (LEGAL_MAX_LIMIT)
Rule 16.....             RULE SD1
IF FAMILYLOAD = 0 OR FAMILYLOAD = 1
THEN SD = (SMI*0.75)
Rule 17.....             RULE SD2
IF FAMILYLOAD = 2
THEN SD = (SMI*1.00)
Rule 18.....             RULE SD3
IF FAMILYLOAD = (MORE)
THEN SD = (SMI*1.25)
Rule 19.....             RULE SD4
IF FAMILYLOAD = 0
THEN MONTHSD = 6
Rule 20.....             RULE SD5
IF FAMILYLOAD <> 0
THEN MONTHSD = 30
Rule 21.....             RULE S52-1
IF FAMILYLOAD = 0
THEN SUB52 = (SMI*0.75)
Rule 22.....             RULE S52-2
IF FAMILYLOAD = 1
THEN SUB52 = (SMI*1.00)
Rule 23.....             RULE S52-3
IF FAMILYLOAD = 2 OR FAMILYLOAD =
(MORE)
THEN SUB52 = (SMI*1.20)
```

(*) It chains with another knowledge base, called R1.

(**) It will generally put on each variable with a different FIND, but here it is a simplification.

2.3   The Validation of the current SEAR application

The validation was made in SEAR before its implementation. In short, it consisted of studying the convenience of the process and the possible discrepancies with its objectives. The protocol test to check the application was designed. Possible errors, such as errors within the knowledge, of knowledge interpretation or in the implementation, were checked. Besides, this phase contained the necessary historical empirical data, needed in order to examine whether the system results were correct.

The data given by the human expert were subjected to a treatment to obtain patterns of the behavior of certain variables in these historical data.

The objective of this study was that other simulated databases had similar behavior to the real database of the files processed by the human expert.

The process described previously had as only purpose to get a new database of resolved files which fitted most to reality and showed the human expert the results to be evaluated.

That is also due to the fact that the social and juridical knowledge is not the formal knowledge classically defined and algoritmizable, but in form of natural language, of easy handling so much that the human operator maintains a central function in the whole process of the investigation.

Now we are confronted with the situation of having to maintain the system to the new conditions of the real world. However, before the maintenance is done we think that the conversion into decision tables is a useful way to easily access the knowledge and do the verification. Moreover the decision table tool takes care of the optimization and the conversion to the rules form again. In most cases rule base maintenance will consist of modifying or replacing existing rules as a result of new conditions or relationships being created, removed or modified [Coenen and Bench-Capon, 1993]. In fact the modification of a rule can be viewed as the process of replacing it, and it is supposed to be easier in a decision table because its advantages in mainly visualization and verification. Decision tables have a very simple structure and can be checked easily for anomalies.

3.   THE RESTRUCTURING OF A KBS

The process of restructuring a KBS might be understood as establishing of a right modularization. Following [Vanthienen and Wijsen, 1996] KBS development can benefit from modularization for a number of reasons:

The concern for *KBS maintenance* is one of the factors that will have an impact on modularization decisions. Particularly, it is desirable to pack components that deal with the same subtopic into the same module or table. This will reduce the risk of incompleteness and of creating inconsistencies when changing the knowledge base in respect to that subtopic. Modularization also avoids redundant specification of knowledge, thereby eliminating the risk of creating inconsistencies. In [Debenham, 1996] the application of various simplification forms are illustrated that can help to avoid some of these problems.

With respect to *verification and validation*, modularization can be considered a very important concept. Since verification algorithms, and extension checks in particular, face a combinatorial explosion as the size of the knowledge base increases, attempts to overcome this problem include partitioning the knowledge base. The problems could be anomaly detection, aimed at detecting abuse or unusual use of the knowledge representation scheme used, among others. Although the decision tables approach dramatically reduces the time needed to check each individual module, the possibility of inter-modular anomalies that arise due to dependencies between (components of) different modules is nevertheless not ruled out. Therefore, it can be easily understood that modularization theory can be of assistance in selecting a partitioning that minimizes the presence of inter-modular dependencies, thereby reducing the need for time-expensive inter-modular checks.

Not only in verification, but also in validation, modularization theory can play an important role, providing a basis for generating an ensemble of test cases with respect to a specific subtopic. In addition, visualization of each of these modules will facilitate direct examination of the knowledge by the expert.

Execution speed may become a critical factor in real world problem solving, due to the growth in inferencing process time as the knowledge base becomes larger. Thereby, modularizing the knowledge base or transforming it into other representations such as decision tables can enhance efficiency, in a number of cases.

4.   ILLUSTRATION OF THE SYSTEM RESTRUCTURING

In this section it will be presented how the restructuring process is applied to the real application and how the anomalies are avoided in the new system.

Decision tables are chosen to restructuring SEAR because this technique is very intuitive and helps the user to avoid errors, being considered a powerful tool that easily visualizes the existing contradictions. It is interesting to the knowledge engineer as well as to human expert.

When designing or generating an application for an existing knowledge base, condition subjects, condition entries, conclusions and table references have to be transformed into the modeling facilities. Then, the SEAR project will be presented and a number of tables will be constructed to give solutions to the restructuring. This transition and its difficulties will be considered here. To know the new structure obtained through the decision tables, every table will be analyzed separately and later a graph with their relationships will be shown, and their verification will be given.

4.1   Sear table

Figure 2 presents the table *Sear* that contains knowledge concerning the IPT (or Complete Permanent Disability). The options to calculate the amount (55% or 75% of BRP) and the period of time (120 months of after) depend on the employee's profile. Besides, there are two links towards table *Limits* and *Des_6m*.

The construction of decision tables is a creative activity, but some routine actions are really time-consuming. This and the need to assure the quality of knowledge embedded in a KBS, have led to the construction of different tools for its verification. Developed at K.U.Leuven, Prologa (Procedural Logic Analyzer, [Vanthienen, 1986]) is one of them. It is an interactive design tool that helps the user in these routine tasks in constructing and manipulating the decision tables. This integrated system and related concepts are studied in the context of their utility as a base for working on decision table engineering.

Prologa constructs a contracted table with only the relevant conditions entries. Owing to its simplification this is a useful way to verify the system.

Sear			
1. IPT	Yes		No
2. Younger_than_55	Yes	No	-
1. ^Limits	.	.	x
2. ^DES_6m	x	x	.
3. 75% BRP_120m	x	.	.
4. 55% BRP_after	.	x	.
	1	2	3

Figure 2. Sear table

The user essentially provides the system with a list of *condition subjects* (in *Sear*, these are IPT and Younger_than_55) with their entries (in this case: yes and no), *action subjects* (in *Sear*, these are *Limits*, *Des_6m*, 75%BRP_120m and 55%BRP_after) and the rules that link it.

4.2   Limits table

Limits is a subtable of Sear. The Limits table includes arguments to evaluate the maximum and minimum limits (see figure 3) and is used to determine the levels that the enterprise has fixed to re-evaluate the employee situation. The system compares the annual gross wage (SBA) that the user introduced with the lower limit and upper limit. In both cases, the SBA is less than the lower limits and SBA*3.5 is also less than the upper limit, then the system continues and it will be necessary to negotiate with the employee. For instance if the annual gross wage is 3.000.000 Pta., the lower limits corresponding to 20 days of wage for year of service is 2.013.698 Pta. and the upper limit corresponding to 45 days is 4.530.822 Pta.

Limit			
1. Does it overcome MAX because	ant45 <= (SBA*3.5)		ant45 > (SBA*3.5)
2. Does it overcome MIN because	ant20 <= (SBA)	ant20 > (SBA)	.
1. 3.5 * SBA (Sol. R7)	.	.	x
2. SBA (Sol. R8)	.	x	.
3. ^NEGOT	x	.	.
	1	2	3

Figure 3. Limits table

4.3   Negot table

The *Negot* table (shown in figure 4) contains knowledge concerning variables that help us to calculate the different payments, such as unemployment allowance, family assistance, unemployment assistance or older than 52 allowance.

Negot							
1. Age group	[<=35]	[>35 and <45.5]	[>=45.5 and <47.5]	[>=47.5 and <48]	[>=48 and <50]	[>=50]	
2. Family load	.	.	0	1 or 2 or more	.	.	.
1. (Sol R2)	.	x	x	.	.	.	.
2. (Sol R3)	x	.	.	.	.	.	.
3. ^DES_6m	.	.	.	x	x	x	x
4. ^DES70	.	.	.	x	x	x	x
5. ^DES60	.	.	.	x	x	x	x
6. AF(75%SMI)	.	.	.	x	x	x	.
7. ^SD_MonthSD	.	.	.	x	x	.	.
8. SUB52	.	.	.	x	x	x	x
9. Agreement	.	.	.	x	x	x	x
	1	2	3	4	5	6	7

Figure 4. Negot table

4.4   Des_6m table

The *Des_6m* table contains the way to establish the legal maximum limits leading to the unemployment assistance quantity (see figure 5).

DES_6m			
1. Children	0	1	>1
1. LegaL_Max_Limit=170% SMI	x	.	.
2. Legal_Max_Limit=195% SMI	.	x	.
3. Legal_Max_Limit=220% SMI	.	.	x
	1	2	3

Figure 5. Des_6m table

4.5   Des60 and Des70 tables

The unemployment assistance quantity has to be calculated in the *Des60* and *Des70* (see figure 6 and 7).

Des60		
1. BRD*0.6<Legal_Max_Limit	yes	no
1. DES60=BRD*0.6	x	.
2. DES60=Legal_Max_Limit	.	x
	1	2

Figure 6. Des60 table

Des70		
1. BRD*0.7<Legal_Max_Limit	yes	no
1. DES70=BRD*0.7	x	.
2. DES70=Legal_Max_Limit	.	x
	1	2

Figure 7. Des70 table

4.6   SD_monthSD table

SD_monthSD table contains knowledge about the way of calculating the amount of Family assistance and the period of time in which the employee might receive this non-contributive pension (see figure 8).

SD_monthSD				
1. Family load	0	1	2	more
1. SD= 75% SMI	x	x	.	.
2. SD= 100% SMI	.	.	x	.
3. SD= 120%SMI	.	.	.	x
4. monthSD= 6m	x	.	.	.
5. monthSD= 30m	.	x	x	x
	1	2	3	4

Figure 8. SD_monthSD table

4.7   The whole system: the project

After an analysis of the rules inside the original system, a number of tables were constructed. The proposed system has seven tables: *Sear, Limits, Negot, Des_6m, Des70, Des60* and *Sd_monthSd* (see figure 9*)*. It was formalized using the method of decomposition of large decision tables into smaller components. For a thorough discussion on criteria to guide the decomposition decision, see [Vanthienen and Wijsen, 1996].

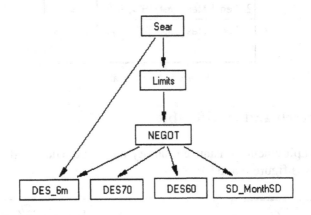

Figure 9. Table Structure

The evolution towards the final project implied the appearance of new tables and the omission of others. Some steps - each one corresponding to a project - were necessary to reach the final SEAR decision table system. Sometimes it was useful to integrate a table into another table. For instance there were two tables called *Max* and *Min*, which presented very similar structures. Subsequently, they merged into a new table, *Limits*.

In the opposite way, separate tables were created out of an existing one when some of the action subjects are related only with a specific group of condition subjects. For instance, *Des60* and *Des70* were separated from the original *Des_6m*.

The benefit of a particular decomposition may depend upon the intended use, like validation, consultation, rule generation, etc.

5.   VERIFICATION

The verification is done automatically with Prologa, which has an intra-tabular and an inter-tabular checking module. The first one signals anomalies inside tables at the moment that they appear.   The second one checks anomalies between the tables on demand, as is shown in figure 10. For a thorough discussion on intra-tabular anomalies, please refer to [Vanthienen, Aerts, Mues and Wets, 1995], and for inter-tabular anomalies to [Vanthienen, Mues and Aerts, 1998].

Prologa provides options to verify the decision tables offering *automatic reports* of the inter-tabular and intra-tabular situations. For instance, when an new rule is introduced a contradiction can appear (inconsistent entries). If the new rule is contradictory with a previous one, the *contradicting rules* are displayed. That helps the constructor to avoid errors in the system, but also facilitates the communication between the knowledge engineer and the human expert. No intra-tabular problems were found in the system.

Once intra-tabular verification is done, inter-tabular relations can be examined. Within this option the user can choose the kind of verification which may be the subject of the checking. Typical anomalies that can be examined are: redundancy, circularity, unfirable columns, etc. Then, an automatic report of the Inter-tabular verification is offered. No inter-tabular problems were found in the system.

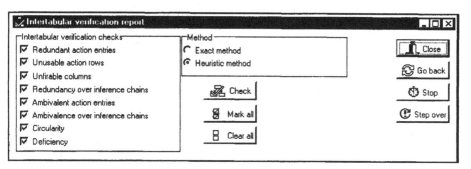

Figure 10. Screen of options for Inter-tabular verification

The main advantage of a tabular decision model is the presence of very *simple structures*. As such, they can be executed very fast and errors can be found and resolved quickly. Moreover, Prologa constructs a contracted table only with the relevant conditions. Owing to its simplification this is a useful way to validate if the system is right and thereby if the new structure is right too.

Once the system is restructured and verified it can be transformed into rules form (or other structures) to be used in a shell. Following we present the knowledge in rules form:

The SEAR rules

- **Table SEAR**

^DES_6m <-- IPT = Yes

75% BRP_120m (Sol. R1) <-- IPT = Yes and Younger_than_55 = Yes

55% BRP_after (Sol. R1) <-- IPT = Yes and Younger_than_55 = No

^Limits <-- IPT = No

- **Table Negot**

(Sol. R2) <-- (Age group = [>35 and <45.5]) or (Age group = [>=45.5 and <47.5] and Family load = 0)

(Sol. R3) <-- Age group = [<=35]

^DES_6m <-- (Age group = [>=45.5 and <47.5] and Family load = 1 or Family load = 2 or Family load = more) or Age group = [>=47.5 and <48] or Age group = [>=48 and <50] or Age group = [>=50]

^DES70 <-- (Age group = [>=45.5 and <47.5] and (Family load = 1 or Family load = 2 or Family load = more)) or Age group = [>=47.5 and <48] or Age group = [>=48 and <50] or Age group = [>=50]

^DES60 <-- (Age group = [>=45.5 and <47.5] and (Family load = 1 or)) or Age group = [>=47.5 and <48] or Age group = [>=48 and <50] or Age group = [>=50]

AF(75%SMI)<-- (Age group = [>=45.5 and <47.5] and Family load = 1 or Family load = 2 or Family load = more) or Age group = [>=47.5 and <48] or Age group = [>=48 and <50]

^SD_MonthSD <-- (Age group = [>=45.5 and <47.5] and Family load = 1 or Family load = 2 or Family load = more) or Age group = [>=47.5 and <48]

SUB52<-- (Age group = [>=45.5 and <47.5] and Family load = 1 or Family load = 2 or Family load = more) or Age group = [>=47.5 and <48]

or Age group = [>=48 and <50] or Age group = [>=50]

Agreement<-- (Age group = [>=45.5 and <47.5] and Family load = 1 or Family load = 2 or Family load = more) or Age group = [>=47.5 and <48] or Age group = [>=48 and <50] or Age group = [>=50]

- **Table Limits**

3.5 * SBA (Sol. R7) <-- It overcome MAX because = ant45 > (SBA*3.5)

SBA (Sol. R8) <-- It overcome MAX because = ant45 <= (SBA*3.5) and It overcome MIN because = ant20 > (SBA)

^NEGOT <-- It overcome MAX because = ant45 <= (SBA*3.5) and It overcome MIN because = ant20 <= (SBA)

- **Table Des_6m**

Legal_Max_Limit=170% SMI <-- Children = 0

Legal_Max_Limit=195% SMI <-- Children = 1

Legal_Max_Limit=220% SMI <-- Children = >1

- **Table Des60**

DES60=BRD*0.6 <--

BRD*0.6<Legal_Max_Limit = yes

DES60=Legal_Max_Limit<--

BRD*0.6<Legal_Max_Limit=no

- **Table Des70**

DES70=BRD*0.7 <--

BRD*0.7<Legal_Max_Limit = yes

DES70=Legal_Max_Limit<--

BRD*0.7<Legal_Max_Limit=no

- **Table Sd_monthSD**

SD= 75% SMI <-- Family load = 0 or Family load = 1

SD= 100% SMI <-- Family load = 2

SD= 120%SMI <-- Family load = more

monthSD= 6m <-- Family load = 0

monthSD= 30m <-- Family load = 1 or Family load = 2 or Family load = more

6.   CONCLUSION

In this paper, decision tables are chosen to restructure the real world application SEAR. This technique is very intuitive and helps the user to avoid errors. It is being considered a powerful tool that easily visualizes possible existing contradictions.

A new structure of the KBS was implemented. The rules were transformed into decision tables. They were restructured using the method of decomposition of large decision tables into smaller components.

Verification and validation have been done and the possible anomalies were presented and checked in each table separately as well as in the whole system. No problems were found in the V&V process. Intra-tabular anomalies were avoided in the process of the creation of the decision tables. Inter-tabular anomalies were checked at the end of this process. Verifying the KBS can be considered a trustworthy process for constructors and also a guarantee for users.

We advocate decision tables have incontestable qualities to improve the V&V and to maintain and implement the KBS. Particularly, Prologa has a lot of advantages in the creation of tables, visualization of the relation between tables, their modification, their transformation to other systems, etc.

REFERENCES

[Coenen and Bench-Capon, 1993] Coenen, F. and Bench-Capon, T., *Maintenance of Knowledge-Based Systems*, The Apic Series, Academic Press, London 1993, p. 78.

[Cragun and Steudel, 1987] Cragun B. and Steudel H., A Decision-Table Based processor for Checking Completeness and Consistency in Rule-Based Expert Systems, *Int. Journal of Man-Machine Studies*, Vol. 5, 1987, pp. 633-648.

[Debenham, 1996] Debenham, J.K., Knowledge Simplification, in proceedings 9th *International Symposium on Methodologies for Intelligent Systems ISMIS'96*, Zakopane, Poland, june 1996, pp. 305-314.

[Moreno, 1998] Moreno Garcia, A.M., *Los Sistemas Expertos y su aplicación a la gestión empresarial*, Doctoral Dissertation, University of Seville, Dept. Economía Financiera y Dirección de Operaciones, 1998, 389 pp.

[Puuronen,1987] Puuronen S., A Tabular Rule Checking Method, Proc. *Avignon87*, Vol. 1, 1987, 257-268.

[Suwa, Scott and Shortliffe, 1982] Suwa, M., Scott, A. and Shortliffe, E., *An approach to verifying completeness and consistency in a rule-based expert system*, AI Magazine 3, 1982, pp. 16-21

[Vanthienen, 1986] Vanthienen, J., *Automatiseringaspecten van de Specificatie, Constructie en Manipulatie van Beslissingstabellen*, Doctoral Dissertation, K.U.Leuven, Dept. of Applied Economic Sciences, 1986, 378 pp.

[Vanthienen, 1991] Vanthienen, J., Knowledge Acquisition and Validation Using a Decision Table Engineering Workbench, Proceedings of the *World Congress on Expert Systems*, Pergamon Press, Orlando (Florida), Dec. 16-19, 1991, pp. 1861-1868.

[Vanthienen and Dries, 1994] Vanthienen, J. and Dries, E., Illustration of a Decision Table Tool for Specifying and Implementing Knowledge Based Systems, *International Journal on Artificial Intelligence Tools*, Vol. 3, No. 2, 1994, pp. 267-288.

[Vanthienen, Aerts, Mues and Wets, 1995] Vanthienen, J., Aerts, M., Mues, C. and Wets, G., A modeling approach to KBS verification. In Proceedings of the *Third European Symposium on Validation and Verification of KBS*, 1995, pp. 155-171.

[Vanthienen and Wijsen, 1996] Vanthienen, J. and Wijsen, J. On the Decomposition of Tabular Knowledge Systems. *New Review of Applied Expert Systems*, 1996.

[Vanthienen, Mues and Aerts, 1998] Vanthienen, J., Mues, C. and Aerts, M., An illustration of verification and validation in the modelling phase of KBS development, *Data and Knowledge Engineering*, 27, pp. 337-352, 1998.

[Vanthienen, Mues, Wets and Delaere, 1997] Vanthienen, J., Mues, C., Wets, G. and Delaere, K., A tool-supported approach to inter-tabular verification. *Expert Systems with Applications*, 15, Pergamon, pp. 277-285.

Incorporating Backtracking in Knowledge Refinement

Nirmalie Wiratunga and Susan Craw
School of Computer and Mathematical Sciences The Robert Gordon University
Aberdeen, AB25 1HG, UK
nw,smc@scms.rgu.ac.uk

Abstract: Refinement tools seek to correct faulty rule-based systems by identifying and repairing faults that are indicated by training examples that provide some evidence of faults. Refinement tools typically use a hillclimbing search to identify suitable repairs. In this paper, the goal is to incorporate an effective backtracking mechanism with a refinement algorithm so that the search for repairs does not get caught by local maxima. However the repair cycle for each potential fault is expensive, so exhaustive backtracking is prohibitive for large knowledge bases. This paper investigates more guided backtracking algorithms developed for constraint satisfaction problems and adapts them for refinement problems. Experiments with these backtracking algorithms reveal that high accuracy refined knowledge bases are achievable, often at the expense of extra iterations, but an informed re-ordering of training examples reduces the number of iterations without increasing the error-rate. A test-bed is developed by corrupting a rule base with interacting faults, thereby allowing pairs of conflicting training examples to be identified. The algorithms are evaluated on training sets containing increasing numbers of these conflicting examples. One separate observation is that conflicting examples help to achieve refined knowledge bases with high accuracy.

Keywords: Knowledge Refinement, Informed Backtracking, Example Re-ordering

1 INTRODUCTION

Refinement tools support the knowledge acquisition and development of knowledge based systems (KBSs) by assisting the debugging of incorrect systems and the adaptive maintenance of KBSs whose problem-solving environment changes [Craw, 1996, Boswell et al., 1997]. Refinement tools are commonly presented with examples of problem-solving where the expert's solution is inconsistent

193

with the KBS's, and from these, the tool identifies potential faults in the KBS and suggests possible repairs. It also benefits from knowing some correctly solved examples as well, so that repairs are not too closely fitted to wrongly-solved examples only, to the detriment of the KBS's more general problem solving. Therefore the training set for the refinement tool's learning contains a selection of wrongly and correctly solved examples, each consisting of the facts that describe the problem-solving task, together with the expert's solution for this task.

Refinement tools adopt an incremental approach where each application of the algorithm attempts to fix one or more, but typically not all, of the wrongly-solved examples in the training set, and to improve the accuracy on the training set with a view to improving the accuracy more generally. The refinement task is sufficiently complex that the space of possible repairs demands a heuristic search, typically hill-climbing. EITHER [Ourston and Mooney, 1994] and FORTE [Richards and Mooney, 1995] try to repair the outstanding fault that is indicated by the *largest* number of examples, and choose the repair with the *fewest* changes to rules which are *nearest* the observables. KRUSTTools are KBS specific refinement tools, assembled from our KRUSTWorks generic refinement toolkit. The refinement algorithm central to this family also applies a hill-climbing search. Although it generates many refined KBSs designed to fix each incorrect example, it then chooses the refined KBS with the *highest* accuracy on the training examples as the input KBS for the next iteration of the algorithm. The result is that refinement tools are dogged by the standard hill-climbing problem of getting caught in local maxima, so the accuracy or performance of the KBS must be reduced before an overall improvement can be gained.

In this paper we explore different ways KRUSTTools may exploit previously abandoned repairs or refined KBSs to restart the refinement process when it gets stuck. First, we illustrate situations when KRUSTTools fail to generate refined KBSs and indicate how backtracking is applied. More selective backtracking algorithms, developed to solve constraint satisfaction problems (CSPs), are presented next, and these are then adapted to fit the KRUSTTool refinement cycle. Experimental results suggest the need for refinement-specific improvements to the basic backjumping algorithms and these changes are presented and evaluated. Finally we conclude with a few general observations and directions for future work.

2   REFINEMENT WITH KrustTools

A KRUSTTool incrementally refines a KBS by processing the training examples $\{e_1, \ldots, e_n\}$ one at a time, Figure 2. The input KBS is the best refined KBS from the previous iteration, or the original faulty KBS for the first iteration. In each iteration the next training example, called the *refinement example* for this iteration, is used to generate refined KBSs. If the expert's solution for the refinement example already coincides with the input KBS's solution then no refinement is necessary in this cycle. Otherwise, the refinement example's evidence allocates blame to possible faults in the KBS and generates potential repairs that are implemented as the refined KBSs proposed during this cycle. Two data structures of examples provide a selection mechanism for the best refined KBS. The *constraint examples buffer* contains the previous refinement examples that have already been corrected, and refined KBSs are rejected if they wrongly answer any constraint example in this buffer. The *training examples buffer* contains the training examples still to be processed, and the remaining refined KBSs are ranked by their accuracy on the training examples buffer; the previous filter guarantees 100% accuracy on the constraint examples buffer. During each cycle, the current refinement example is transferred from the training examples buffer into the constraint examples buffer.

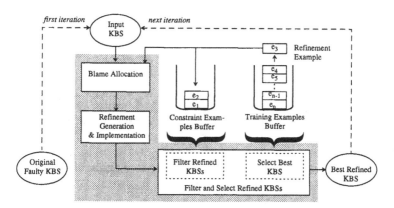

Figure 1. The KRUSTTool Process.

Our refinement algorithm is unusual in generating many refined KBSs in each iteration, and the hill-climbing selection of the *one* best refined KBS for the next iteration occurs at the *end* of each cycle. This offers the possibility of backtracking to alternative refined KBSs thereby achieving a best-first search. Figure 2 illustrates the start of a potential backtracking scenario; the updates to the constraint examples buffer (cebuf) and the training examples buffer (tebuf) are shown on the right. Refinement example e_2 generates 3 refined KBSs and R_{21} is selected as best. Refinement examples e_3 and e_4 generate several refined KBSs and again the best is selected. But now suppose R_{41} cannot be refined by e_5 because although 4 refinements are generated, all are rejected by the constraint examples; this is shown by a darkly shaded node for e_5. The *refinement path* in the diagram is ... $e_2.R_{21} \rightarrow e_3.R_{31} \rightarrow e_4.R_{41} \rightarrow e_5.\emptyset$ where $\emptyset$ indicates the absence of a selected refined KBS. Strictly, it is this refinement path that labels the nodes in the diagram and so the node labelled R_{51} is really named $R_{...21314151}$.

So what should the refinement algorithm do now: continue with e_6 and

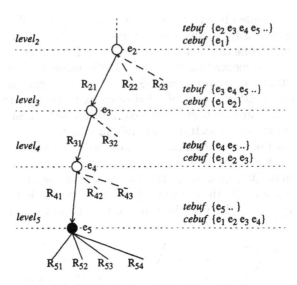

Figure 2. A Backtracking KRUSTTool.

ignore the fact that e_5 is not corrected, and is unlikely to be by future re-finements? A better alternative is to backtrack through the solution space of refined KBSs and restart the refinement process from an earlier node. Simple backtracking undoes each step one at a time, and so refinement is restarted with R_{42} and e_5. In this paper we investigate more guided backtracking that may restart refinement from earlier points, say R_{22} with e_3. These algorithms originated as search methods for solving constraint satisfaction problems and are introduced next.

3   HEURISTIC SEARCH SOLVES CSP

Constraint satisfaction problems (CSPs) consist of a set of ordered variables $\{v_1, \ldots, v_n\}$, a specified domain D_i for each variable v_i and a set of constraints $\{C_1, \ldots, C_m\}$. A CSP solution is an instantiation of each variable with a value from its respective domain such that none of the constraints is violated [Tsang, 1993]. Various backtracking searches have been proposed that partially undo the instantiation and resume the constructive process from a previous variable instantiation.

BackTracking (BT) [Bitner and Reingold, 1975] steps back to the previous variable v_{i-1}, and continues the search by finding a new instantiation for v_{i-1} consistent with the constraints and v_k, $k < i - 1$. BT recursively backtracks to previous variables until it has tried all values in the domain for each.

BackJumping (BJ) [Gaschnig, 1979] does not step back to the previous variable v_{i-1} but instead jumps back to the latest variable v_j whose instantiation conflicts with any of the instantiations for v_i. If there are no new instantiations available for v_j then BJ reverts to backtracking from v_j.

Conflict-directed BackJumping (CBJ) [Prosser, 1993] extends the notion of backjumping by replacing the backtracking after a backjump in BJ with backjumping.

BT is an exhaustive depth first search of the tree of variable instantiations; siblings are different instantiations of a particular variable and a parent instantiates the preceding variable in the given ordering. BJ explores a subset of the BT nodes and so our motivation for investigating backjumping is to reduce the number of refinement iterations.

BJ and CBJ are no longer exhaustive. However, for binary CSPs, where all constraints contain at most 2 variables, BJ and CBJ still find all solutions [Kondrak and van Beek, 1997]; any instantiations they fail to check for variables between v_i and the backjumped to v_j are guaranteed to result in the same inconsistency between the instantiation for v_j and the possible values for v_i. Therefore, for binary CSPs, BJ and CBJ have proved effective in reducing search.

4 CSP ALGORITHMS AID REFINEMENT

We wish to adapt the CSP algorithms to search the space of incrementally refined KBSs created by KRUSTTools, so that the KRUSTTool, when necessary, may revisit refined KBSs that have previously been abandoned by the refinement algorithm. We propose an analogy between CSPs and refinement problems so that the concepts applied in the CSP algorithms can be imitated in the refinement domain.

In refinement problems we incrementally refine the KBS to correctly answer the current and previous refinement examples. So, the most natural analogy between CSPs and refinement links variables with training examples, the current variable with the refinement example, and instantiated variables with correctly solved training examples in the constraint examples buffer. CSP constraints correspond to refined KBSs, and consistency is achieved when the refined KBS correctly answers the constraint examples. Finally the domain for a variable corresponds to the repairs that are proposed by a refinement example.

To complete the analogy we must describe when backtracking is triggered and how backjumps are determined. The KRUSTTool algorithm fails when the refinement example e_i and the input KBS R fail to create any refined KBSs (i.e. the generated KBSs *Generated*$_{Ri}$ is empty) or those generated are rejected by the constraint examples (i.e. *Filtered*$_{Ri}$ is empty). The *conflict set* for e_i, *confset*(e_i), will contain the potential backtracking points from e_i. If *Filtered*$_{Ri} = \{\}$ then we know which constraint examples caused the removal of each generated KBS, and these form the confset for the CBJ algorithm. BJ's confset is similar but also contains refinement examples prior to the conflicting ones. If $Generated_{Ri} = \{\}$ then backtracking is the only option; no conflicting constraint examples can be identified since there are no KBSs to test!

Let us revisit Figure 2's scenario. Refinement must backtrack because $Filtered_{R_{41}5} = \{\}$, although $Generated_{R_{41}5} = \{R_{51}, R_{52}, R_{53}, R_{54}\}$. Thus for each KBS in $Generated_{R_{41}5}$, some of the constraint examples in cebuf must be wrongly answered; suppose R_{51}, R_{52} wrongly solve e_2, and R_{53}, R_{54} wrongly solve e_3. For BT, e_5's conflict set is the previous refinement example $\{e_4\}$ and refinement proceeds by backtracking to e_4 on the refinement path and choosing the next branch; in this case R_{42} with e_5. For BJ and CBJ, e_5's conflict set contains the failed constraint examples e_2, e_3. So refinement continues from e_3, the most recent on the path, selecting the next available refined KBS R_{32} with e_4 as the refinement example; e_5 is moved back into tebuf as a future refinement example. If no more KBSs are available from e_3 then BJ backtracks to the e_2 node and CBJ backjumps according to e_3's and e_5's conflict sets.

4.1   Refinement Differs from CSP

We have drawn an analogy between CSPs and knowledge refinement that allows us to apply backtracking and backjumping algorithms with the KRUSTTool algorithm. However, there are two obvious differences between CSPs and refinement: the domain of potential repairs is not known in advance, instead it is constructed incrementally during refinement generation and filtering; and the behaviour of constraint examples can change – they can become uncorrected and so they provide new fault evidence. The first is dealt with by associating refined KBSs with the refinement examples that generate them, and reasoning about backtracking using constraint examples rather than KBSs.

Figure 4.1 illustrates a problem that can arise from the second point. In this scenario, R_{21} already answers e_3 correctly and so the output from the e_3 cycle is the input KBS R_{21}; this has been highlighted by light shading. It does not affect the search when it is advancing, but backtracking or backjumping to this point raises problems. In Figure 4.1, backtracking starts because $Filtered_{R_{41}5} = \{\}$. Suppose we are using BJ and $confset(e_5)$ is $\{e_2, e_3\}$, so we backjump to e_3. But the input KBS R_{21} already correctly answers e_3 and so no refined KBSs are available. We could simply backtrack further, but the refinement tool has just discovered a relationship: the changes to correct e_5 have interacted with the way that e_3 was previously proved. Thus if we backtrack beyond e_3 then it is possible that the same interaction will occur again.

Instead, we note these special examples and treat them differently. We call e_3 a *latent* example since it did not contribute any fault evidence as a refinement example. The other refinement examples are active. Given the conflicting relationship between the latent example e_3 and its activating refinement example e_5, we choose to solve their conflict at this point by re-instating e_3 in to tebuf and advancing the search from R_{51} with e_3 as the next refinement example.

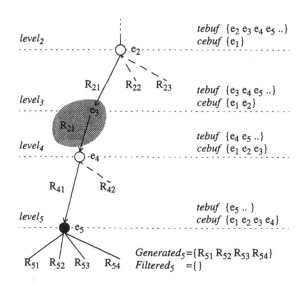

Figure 3. The Changing Behaviour of Constraint Examples.

4.2 Prioritising Latent Over Active

Latent examples provide no impact on the refinement initially since it is already answered correctly. But when it appears in the conflict set, not only does it provide fault evidence, but it has the added conflicting relationship with the current refinement example. We have amended the backjumping algorithms to take further account of latent examples in conflict sets. If in Figure 4.1, *confset*(e_5) is $\{e_3, e_4\}$, then backjumping will resume with e_4 and the fault evidence now presented by the latent example $e3$ will be lost. Instead, we prioritise latent examples that appear in conflict sets, and, rather than backjumping to the most recent conflicting example, we reinstate all conflicting latent examples into the tebuf. In Figure 4.1 the search proceeds with e_3 and R_{51}, the refined KBS in *Generated*$_{R_{41}5}$ with the highest accuracy, despite e_4 being in the conflict set. If the intervening active conflict examples (here e_4) remain a problem, backjumping offers the opportunity to investigate there later.

4.3 BT and BJ: A Comparison for Refinement

Backtracking one refinement cycle at a time (BT) is likely to lead to many iterations, so our goal in introducing backjumping (BJ and CBJ) was to reduce refinement cycles. Our first comparison counts the number of refinement iterations with BT, BJ and CBJ. Our experiments apply a Prolog KRUSTTool to a corrupted version of the student loans KBS [Pazzani, 1993]. The faulty KBS was created by introducing 5 corruptions to the 20 rules in the original student loans KBS: an extra rule, a changed comparison operator and an extra condition in 3 rules.

The training examples had to be carefully selected to ensure that back-tracking was exercised, since it is only prompted when conflicting repairs are attempted with interacting faults. Most training sets do not require such con-flicting repairs, and so we had to ensure our training sets did indeed contain some conflicts. We identified 9 conflicting pairs in a carefully chosen set of 8 examples from the complete student dataset, where repairs for one example in the pair conflicted with repairs for the other. Finding conflicting examples was relatively easy given the density of corruption of the KBS. Our selected dataset contained a further 22 "normal", unconflicting examples. Training sets of a given conflict level N were created from the selected dataset of 30 exam-ples by randomly choosing N conflict pairs, removing duplicate examples when they occurred, and randomly selecting from the "normal" examples until the training set contained 15 examples. KRUSTTools incorporating the BT, BJ and CBJ algorithms were applied to each training set and the corrupted KBS. Each test was repeated 10 times and the results averaged.

Figure 4.3 shows the number of iterations for each of the algorithms as the number of conflict pairs in the training set increases. The results were surprising. We had expected BT to have the most iterations, BJ to have fewer, and CBJ to have the fewest, reflecting the increased targeting of the search. With binary CSPs, BT is guaranteed to have at least as many iterations as BJ or CBJ. However, in the more dynamic space of refined KBSs this is not the case; backjumping searched a different part of the space that involved more iterations.

So has there been any gain from BJ's additional searching? Figure 4.3 shows the error rates of the final KBS produced by the 3 algorithms on the complete set of 30 examples; the error-rate of the original corrupted KBS is the horizontal dashed line on all error-rate graphs. BJ, the most greedy in refinement cycles, has indeed gained the lowest error rate. This behaviour is explained by noticing that, although BJ and CBJ are guaranteed to find all binary CSP solutions, this is not the case with refinement, since repairs in different cycles can interact: an earlier repair can provide part of a later repair or conflict with the later repair. Therefore the repairs that are proposed depend on the input KBS and thus the refinement path.

5   CONFLICT-BASED RE-ORDERING

Figure 4.3 shows another interesting trend: the error rate of the refined KBS decreases as the number of conflict pairs in the training set increases. This confirms the experimental results in [Palmer and Craw, 1996], that the more demanding the examples in the training set the higher accuracy achieved by refinement. It also suggested that we explore re-ordering the training examples to exploit conflict knowledge as soon as it is recognised. Minimal Bandwidth Ordering heuristic for static ordering of variables attempts to reduce the back-

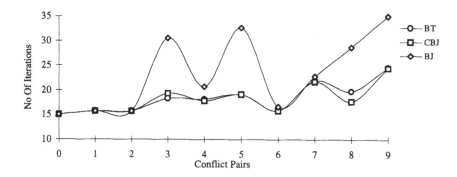

Figure 4. Number of Iterations (Basic Algorithms).

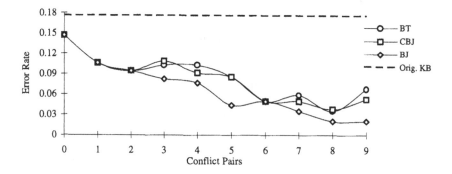

Figure 5. Error Rate of Final Refined KBS (Basic Algorithms).

tracking distance for CSP algorithms by placing mutually constrained variables close together in the search [Tsang, 1993]. The previous section recognised that the refinement example and the conflicting examples are mutually constraining since the repairs for the later one has affected the correctness of the earlier latent example. We try to use this idea of mutually constraining examples to associate the refinement example and the deepest conflicting constraint example in the sequence of training examples in an attempt to reduce the number of iterations of the backjumping algorithms without compromising the error-rate of the final refined KBS.

Figure 5 illustrates a hypothetical backjumping situation. The refinement search space contains three main refinement paths, of which two have been discarded: $e_2.R_{21} \rightarrow e_3.R_{31} \rightarrow e_4.R_{41} \rightarrow e_5.\emptyset$ and $e_2.R_{22} \rightarrow e_3.R_{31} \rightarrow e_4.R_{41} \rightarrow e_5.\emptyset$. Suppose in each case $confset(e_5) = \{e_2\}$ and so backjumping to e_2 produces the search as illustrated. But this also means that e_2 and e_5 are mutually constraining since the repairs to e_5 has affected the solution to e_2.

The Minimal-BJ (MBJ) and Minimal-CBJ (MCBJ) algorithms contain a

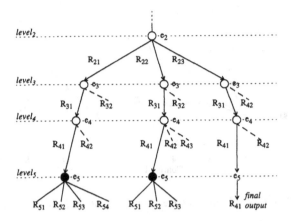

Figure 6. Searching without Conflict-Based Re-Ordering.

further amendment to the backjumping algorithms, so that backjumping to a node e_j that conflicts with the current refinement example e_i causes the algorithm to try to fix this pair of mutually constraining examples next. It re-sorts tebuf so that e_i is re-used immediately with the next refined KBS from e_j. Thus the pair of conflicting examples identified in backjumping become adjacent on the new branch of the refinement path. Figure 5 illustrates a possible outcome of re-ordering the tebuf examples so that e_5 is used as the next refinement example after backjumping to e_2, and indicates the potential saving in iterations over Figure 5.

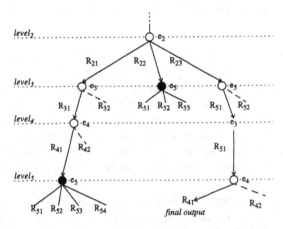

Figure 7. Searching with Conflict-Based Re-Ordering.

Although this re-ordering is not guaranteed to reduce iterations, the relationship between an example and its conflict set gives some justification for re-ordering the otherwise random order of the training examples. It is possible that successive re-ordering of nodes in this manner may at times lead to the original sequence. Even so, this will not result in cycling because BJ and CBJ will resort to backtracking once all branches of a node are explored.

We included the MBJ and MCBJ algorithms in our earlier experiments. Figure 5 superimposes the barchart for MBJ iterations on the line graphs for the basic algorithms; the results for MCBJ are similar to CBJ's so are not shown on the graph. Our goal of reducing the number of iterations in BJ has been achieved in general and MBJ's iterations are closer to BT and CBJ. There were 3 test runs where BJ performed fewer iterations than MBJ, and a closer examination of one indicated that re-ordering resulted in an increased search space when two examples e_i and e_j are affected by the same repair, where the fault evidence provided by e_j cannot be fixed before the fault evidence from e_i is fixed. Dependencies of this nature suggest the existence of a new type of constraint, and we intend to investigate ways to identify these in the future.

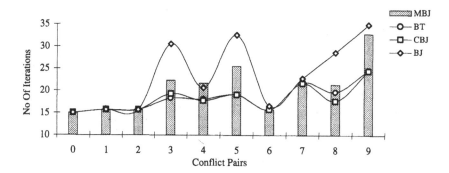

Figure 8. Number of Iterations (Conflict-Based Re-Ordering).

Figure 5 confirms that the refined KBS error rates with MBJ, and CMBJ, are unaffected by the dynamic re-ordering. So MBJ has achieved fewer iterations without increasing the error-rate of the final KBS.

6 CONCLUSIONS

We have transformed the natural hill-climbing of the KRUSTTool refinement algorithm into a best first search that reconsiders previously filtered out refined KBSs. It is the KRUSTTool's ability to generate many potential refined KBSs in response to fault evidence that enables CSP search strategies to be applied with the central refinement algorithm. The authors of other refinement algorithms [Ourston and Mooney, 1994, Richards and Mooney, 1995] have argued that the choice of repairs available to their tool is sufficiently flexible that hill-climbing problems occur rarely, and so make no attempt to deal with it. However dealing with mutually conflicting examples in a single refinement iteration is difficult,

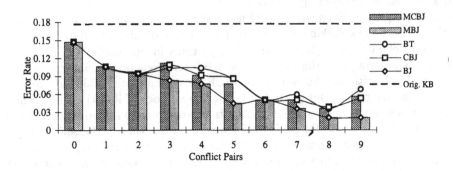

Figure 9. Error Rate of Final Refined KBS (Conflict-Based Re-Ordering).

and otherwise hill-climbing problems arise. Our testbed has shown that it is relatively easy to find mutually conflicting training examples for refinement tools if the KBS contains interacting faults.

Moreover, conflicting examples are good at suggesting high quality refinements, and training sets with more pairs of conflicting examples produce refined KBSs with lower error-rates. This confirms earlier work indicating the importance of difficult examples, where improved refinement was achieved by rejecting individual refined KBSs if the training set did not contain sufficiently difficult examples to test them thoroughly [Palmer and Craw, 1996]. With backjumping, refinement retreats to earlier refinement cycles and rejects refinement paths that should not have been explored.

Introducing backjumping to reduce the search in standard chronological backtracking reveals an interesting refinement phenomenon. The more selective backjumping may actually increase the search. However, we discovered the extra iterations are used profitably and provide a refined KBS with a lower error-rate. Amendments to the backjumping algorithms to reduce the iterations, whilst maintaining the low error-rate, concentrate on re-ordering the training examples by recognising the information gain offered by both latent and active examples in the conflict set, when backjumping is initiated. We are currently investigating the knowledge available in problem graphs, the data structure that represents the problem-solving activity for refinement examples. We hope to use these to identify one-way dependencies between constraint examples to prevent re-ordering problems such as we found in the previous section. They may also identify mutually constraining sets of examples, whose problem graphs have a large overlap, but which have dissimilar observable values; these could be scheduled in consecutive refinement cycles.

This work highlights the variety of refinement paths and re-ordering mechanisms open to refinement tools and has drawn our attention to relationships between training examples that may allow us to direct the refinement process towards staged goals in the identification and repair of KBS faults.

ACKNOWLEDGMENTS

The KRUSTWorks project is supported by EPSRC grant GR/L38387 awarded to Susan Craw and ORS grant 98131005 awarded to Nirmalie Wiratunga. We also thank IntelliCorp Ltd for its contribution to this project.

References

[Bitner and Reingold, 1975] Bitner, J. R. and Reingold, E. (1975). Backtrack programming techniques. *Communications of the ACM*, 18:651–656.

[Blake et al., 1998] Blake, C., Keogh, E., and Merz, C. (1998). UCI repository of machine learning databases. www.ics.uci.edu/~mlearn/MLRepository.html.

[Boswell et al., 1997] Boswell, R., Craw, S., and Rowe, R. (1997). Knowledge refinement for a design system. *Proceedings of the Tenth European Knowledge Acquisition Workshop*, pages 49–64, Sant Feliu de Guixols, Spain. Springer.

[Craw, 1996] Craw, S. (1996). Refinement complements verification and validation. In *Int. Journal of Human-Computer Studies*, 44:245–256.

[Gaschnig, 1979] Gaschnig, J. (1979). Performance measurements and analysis of certain search algorithms. Technical Report CMU-CS-79-124, Carnegie-Mellon University, PA.

[Kondrak and van Beek, 1997] Kondrak, G. and van Beek, P. (1997). A theoretical evaluation of selected backtracking algorithms. *Artificial Intelligence*, 89:365–387.

[Ourston and Mooney, 1994] Ourston, D. and Mooney, R. (1994). Theory refinement combining analytical and empirical methods. *Artificial Intelligence*, 66:273–309.

[Palmer and Craw, 1996] Palmer, G. J. and Craw, S. (1996). The role of test cases in automated knowledge refinement. In *Proceedings ESs 96, Annual Conference of the BCSG on ESs*, pages 75–90, Cambridge, UK. SGES Publications.

[Pazzani, 1993] Pazzani, M. J. (1993). Student loan relational domain. In UCI Repository of Machine Learning Databases [Blake et al., 1998].

[Prosser, 1993] Prosser, P. (1993). Domain filtering can degrade intelligent backtracking search. In *Proceedings of the Thirteenth IJCAI Conference*, pages 262–267, Chambery, France.

[Richards and Mooney, 1995] Richards, B. and Mooney, R. (1995). Automated refinement of first-order horn-clause domain theories. *Machine Learning*, 19:95–131.

[Tsang, 1993] Tsang, E. (1993). *Foundations of Constraint Satisfaction*. Academic Press, San Diego.

Verification and validation of a multistrategy knowledge-based system

Francisco Loforte RIBEIRO

Instituto Superior Técnico, Departamento de Engenharia Civil, Secção de Estruturas e Construção, Av. Rovisco Pais 1, 1049-001 Lisboa , Portugal.

Key words: knowledge-based expert systems, case-based reasoning, verification and validation

Abstract: This research is concerned with the verification and validation of a knowledge-based expert system for supporting human experts in assessing applications for the house renovation grant system. The development of the system followed the task structure analysis and the client centered approach. The task structure analysis describes the system at knowledge level in terms of tasks, problem solving methods and knowledge types. The implementation of the system followed the client centered approach method. The resulting system implements a framework integrating case-based reasoning, abductive assembly, decomposition and associative methods. In addition, the framework combines different types of knowledge which are required by the problem solving methods. The implementation was carried out together with the verification and validation allowing having the system more valid after each stage of the client centered approach. A total of nine different methods were employed for the verification and validation. Each method focused on different aspects of the system's validity and utility. The objectives of this paper are to establish a framework for verifying and validating a multistrategy system and to report de findings of verification and validation of the implemented system.

1.   INTRODUCTION

This paper describes the Verification and Validation (V&V) of a knowledge-based expert system (KBES) integrating case-based reasoning (CBR) with other problem solving methods. This system is aimed at supporting human experts in assessing applications for the house renovation grant system (HRGS).

The characterisation of the house renovation domain has shown that the assessment of applications for the HRGS is a complex activity mainly for the following reasons: it is comprised of several interrelated tasks processed in the majority of cases, in a staged fashion; a number of problem solving strategies are used to accomplish the tasks, each one requiring knowledge from different sources; it is data driven; and different goals can be established for each task, depending on the type of grant sought, the type of household, the characteristics of the property and local circumstances. The resulting system implements a framework which integrates case-based reasoning, abductive assembly, decomposition and associative methods. In addition, the framework combines different types of knowledge which are required by the problem solving methods.

There are a number of difficulties in verifying and validating KBESs during the development life cycle. This was recognised by several researchers working in the field. The difficulties in verifying and validating KBSs according to several authors include (O'Keefe R. et al., 1987; Green C. and Keyes M., 1987; Nasser J., 1988; Gupta U., 1991; and Cervera E., 1993). Most of the existing methods are designed for the V&V of rule-based systems where the knowledge-base is functionality static. A CBR system after each problem solving session can add a new case to its case library, and therefore inherently change the functionality of the overall system. To deal with these functional changes requires different methods from those available for the rule-based systems (Hennessy D. and Hinkle D., 1992). In addition, how to validate a case library storing past cases which have been used before and they are assumed to be useful in future for similar conditions?

2.   DEVELOPMENT OF THE SYSTEM

The development of the system followed the Task Structure Analysis and the Client Centred Approach. The Task Structure Analysis describes the system at knowledge level in terms of tasks, problem solving methods and knowledge types. The implementation of the system followed the Client Centred Approach method. The V&V was incorporated into the system implementation cycle. The system was verified and validated at every implementation stage of the CCA method. Marcot (Marcot B., 1987) stressed that the V&V of KBS should be integrated into the system development life cycle. Each validation step of the system with a set of test cases was followed by the refinement and updating of the system guided by detected errors and malfunctions found at that step. Therefore, each case added to the case library was verified and validated. The goal was that after a validation step an improvement of the system should be obtained through a refinement. Meseguer (Meseguer P., 1993) pointed out that KBS validation supported by knowledge-base refinement should increase the system's validity with respect to a task for which it was built.

3.   TASK STRUCTURE ANALYSIS

In order to carry out the task analysis of the assessment of applications for the HRGS, the task structure analysis method proposed by Chandrasekaran, Johnson and Smith (Chandrasekaran B. et al., 1992; Smith and Johnson 1993) was adopted in this research. The task analysis shown that the assessment of grant application tasks can be accomplished by a number of alternative problem solving methods. Five possible types of problem solving methods were identified by the task analysis for accomplishing the different tasks of the assessment of application for the HRGS. They include: i) CBR; ii) decomposition method; iii) associative method; iv) abductive assembly method; and v) algorithms. At the lowest level of the task structure one method is used to perform a sub-task corresponding to another method. According to Goel (Goel A., 1989), this use of one method for performing a sub-task in another method enables a *task-directed integration of methods*. Therefore, this provides a basis for designing the control of the processing. Figure 1 presents a partial view of task structure for the assessment of application for renovation grants and describes how the abductive assembly method accomplishes the assessment of the fitness of a property. Rectangles represent methods and circles represent tasks. As shown in figure 1, the abductive assembly method decomposes the fitness assessment task into four sub-tasks: i) *to find evidence of failures*; ii) *to generate hypotheses of the grounds of unfitness;* iii) *to select ground of unfitness; and* iv) *to calculate the level of fitness.* Each one of these tasks has a problem space that is smaller than the initial task and can be solved by a number of alternative methods.

4.   ARCHITECTURE OF THE SYSTEM

The task structure analysis carried out provided a basis for designing an architecture for the system. This architecture consists of six main components: case library; case-base reasoner; rule-base reasoner; domain models; user interface; and control of the processing. The control of processing knowledge allows the system to know which task and method to take at each step of the problem solving. To achieve this, the system incorporates three different mechanisms for control of processing: i) the top level control; ii) the intermediate level control; and iii) the local level control.

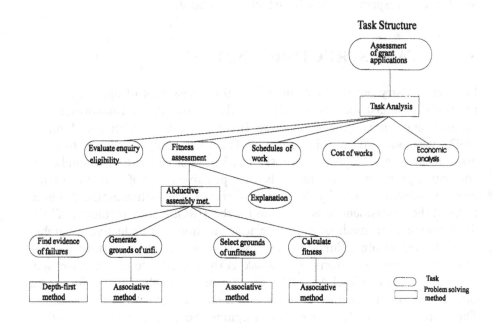

Figure 1. Part of task structure for the assessment of applications for renovation grants

5.   APPROACHES TO THE V&V OF CBR SYSTEMS

Let us System verification involves the checking of consistency, completeness, and adequacy of the system (Nasser J., 1988; Gupta, 1991). Several guidelines on verification of CBR systems have been proposed by CBR researchers. They include:

- The aspects affecting the consistency of a CBR system include the consistency of cases and the features used to represent the cases (Kriesgman and Barlleta, 1993).
- A CBR system becomes more competent by increasing the number of previous cases in its case base. Insufficient cases in the case base often results in an inability to solve a problem (Kolodner, 1993). The number

of cases required is an aspect to be examined during the system verification (Ng and Smith, 1998). Therefore, the number and consistency of cases should be checked during system verification process.

- The verification of CBR systems involves measuring the acceptance ratio of the retrieved cases (Golding and Rosenbloom, 1991). The verification of the content and representation of cases can be carried out by checking the solution of the recalled cases (Kolodner, 1993).
- Novel problems can be used to verify the retrieval and indexing mechanisms (Kolodner, 1993).

System validation involves checking the sensitivity, accuracy, usability, adaptability, depth, usefulness, and efficiency of the system during the development cycle (Marcot, 1987). Although the lack of a methodology, a number of CBR researchers have proposed several guidelines on CBR system validation. They include:

- Checking system sensitivity involves testing the appropriateness of indices for a CBR system (Kolodner, 1993).
- Accuracy has been described as a fundamental assessment issue during system validation (Kolodner, 1993). Therefore appropriateness of the retrieved cases should be a subject of validation (Koton, 1989). The accuracy of the CBR system can be assessed subjectively by experts and semi-experts of the domain (Bareiss, 1989)
- The accuracy of the adapted solution should be checked even if there is no exact case existing the case base (Ng and Smith, 1998).
- The query process and the way the results are interpreted should be assessed during system validation (Ng and Smith, 1998).
- The system's efficiency can be assessed by checking the running time of the system. Quantity validation can be used to test system efficiency. The search time for a number of cases can be measured against the expert's time, previous records, or standard recommendations (Ng and Smith, 1998)
- Questionnaires can be used for checking the usefulness of the system.
- Quantitative techniques can be used to assess the retrieval algorithm and the matching procedure (Simoudis, 1992). A recall rate can be used as a measure.
- To increase KBS validity, knowledge-base refinement should be guided by error importance with respect to the KBS task. Most serious errors should be solved at first, possibly causing some errors of lower importance, but always assuring a net validity gain (Meseguer, 1993).

6.   DIFFICULTIES AND ADVANTAGES IN THE V&V OF THE SYSTEM

There are several practical constraints that are unique to the system developed during the research. They include the following limitations: i) Since the general aim of the research was to investigate and explore the viability and suitability of using CBR in the domain of the assessment of applications for the HRGS, a great part of the time available for the research was committed to the knowledge modelling, case acquisition and programming tasks. As a result, the time available for the V&V was limited. ii) Evaluating the system required a number of representative real application cases stored in its case library and a number of real test cases to validate against. This required the commitment of the Client. To get the Client's involvement in the project required spending considerable time in obtaining contacts and holding meetings. iii) Past grant applications are stored in files. These files contain confidential documents with very restricted circulation. This specific limitation resulted in additional time spent in handling such files. iv) Because of the confidentiality and property pertaining to the knowledge stored in the system's case library, it was not possible to invite more experts from outside the Client to participate in the validation process. v) The system is the only one of its kind in the HRGS domain. Although the author does not rule out the possibility that some similar system may have been developed or may be still under development. Little research work has been published on the domain. This lack of similar research or systems, eliminated the possibility of validating the system against existing comparable systems.

Although there are a number of limitations in the V&V of the system, there are also a number of advantages. These supporting issues pertain to two types of reasons: i) the specific nature of the domain; ii) the modelling work carried out in the context of the research. Due to the specific nature of the domain includes: the number of test cases available for validation purposes was large; and the test cases are organised in different standard formats according to the type of grant sought making easy the validation of the system both as a whole and by its components. Due to the modelling work: Carrying out the task analysis helped to overcome the limitation of the lack of testable requirements and specifications. The task structure for the assessment of grant applications provided a good specification for the system. This specification allowed to evaluate the system not just in terms of its tasks and goals, but also in terms of its inferences. Yen and Lee (Yen J. and Lee J., 1993) stressed that by organising a specification of a KBS around the task structure supports and makes easy its V&V.

7.   THE FRAMEWORK FOR THE V&V OF THE SYSTEM

Taking into account to the limitations and guidelines described above the V&V of the system consisted of three main objectives: i) to assess the utility and the viability of the system's framework; ii) to assess the overall effectiveness of the system, as a whole and by its sub-components, in addressing the assessment of applications for the HRGS; and iii) to assess the qualities and benefits of the system in addressing the Client's needs. On the basis of these objectives, a concise V&V framework was designed and incorporated into the system's implementation cycle. A total of nine different methods were employed for the V&V: i) three for the verification; and ii) six for the validation. Each method focused on different aspects of the system's validity and utility. They are listed in tables 1 and 2 respectively. As listed in table 1, the verification of system consisted of checking: (i) checking correctness of the programme; (ii) checking consistency of the knowledge structures represented in the system, including cases, rules and objects; and (iii) checking completeness of the CBR knowledge-base. According to Preece (1990), the consistency and completeness checking are both methods usually used to determine the self-consistency and completeness of rule-based systems where the rule is assumed to be a logic expression. The system has no rules represented as independent knowledge structures. Instead it uses functions and methods, some of them incorporating if then expressions. Thus the consistency and completeness methods were applied to verify the logic expressions defined in functions and methods.

Validation of system was undertaken during all stages of its implementation cycle, which are: i) *the system skeleton*; ii) *the demo system*; and iii) *the working system*. The aims set at the beginning for validating system were: to determine the overall performance and effectiveness of the system in addressing the task of the assessment of grant applications with respect to the task structure; to determine the utility and validity of the research hypothesis; and to determine the Client's acceptance of the system. To achieve the above aims, and taking into account the difficulties and advantages outlined above, the validation of system was based on the following requirements: i) to use of past successful grant applications to test the validity of the system against known results; ii) to use of new applications to test the performance and effectiveness of the system in addressing the task; iii) to use of Client's experts and external experts for testing the system with new grant applications; and iv) to use of hypothetical test cases to reflect extreme conditions under which the system can be operated.

8.   VALIDATION DURING SYSTEM'S IMPLEMENTATION

Validation during the systems implementation was the first step in the validation process. the validation during the system's implementation of both case library and case-base retrieval mechanisms consisted of: Firstly, validating the 60 seed application cases stored in the case library, treating each one as a new application case. Thus, each of the seed application cases was validated one by one as a new problem and the results were compared to the information contained in each corresponding grant application. Secondly, during the validation of the 60 seed application cases the performance of the case-base retriever component and indexing scheme was tested in terms of: i) the precision of the case retrieval; and ii) the percentage of recall of application cases. Thirdly, activities 1 and 2 were repeated until 100% precision was found and 100% recall for the 60 seed application cases.

Table 1: Summary of methods used for the verification

Method	Techniques
Correctness checking	Check for spelling, syntactic and semantic errors.
Consistency checking	Checking the representativeness of cases;
	Checking for redundant or contradictory cases;
	Checking for illegal case features values;
	Checking for inconsistent matching;
	Checking for inconsistent solutions of the recalled cases;
	Checking for inconsistent case features;
	Checking for inconsistent *if then* expressions;
	Checking for redundant *if then* expressions;
	Checking for conflicting *if then* expressions;
	Checking for subsumed *if then* expressions.
Completeness checking	Checking the completeness of case library; Checking for missing objects and object attributes;
	Checking for missing links; Checking for un-referenced attribute values;
	Checking for illegal attribute values; and Checking for missing *if then* expressions;

Fourthly, the activities mentioned in 1 and 2 were repeated for each case added to the case library either manually or by the system after each successful running. This approach was revealed to be time consuming but effective. Initially, the performance was poor (100% precision for 25 of the 60 cases and 100% recall for 42 of 60 cases), but it improved over time until 100% precision was found and 100% recall was established for all of the 60 cases. Modifications were introduced as a consequence of errors detected in the process. Figure 2 illustrates the process followed.

9.   PREDICTIVE VALIDATION

Predictive validation was carried out after the validation of the initial 60 seed application cases and the case-base retriever. The predictive validation of the system of: i) comparing, in a very detailed way, solutions generated by the experts and other systems contained in each past grant application file with those provided by the system for the same grant application; ii) measuring the performance and functional features of the system; validating against criteria.

Table 2: Summary of methods used for the validation of the system

Method	Techniques
Validation as process of system implementation	Validation of the case library; and Validation of case-base retrieval.
Predictive validation	Performance and functional features; Validation against criteria; Sub-system validation; and Intermediate and final results.
Field tests	System effectiveness; and User effectiveness.
Face validation	User/Client acceptance; Test of innovative features; and Test ergonomic factors.
Robustness test	With hypothetical application cases reflecting extreme conditions.
Knowledge-base refinement	Integrates validation with refinement.

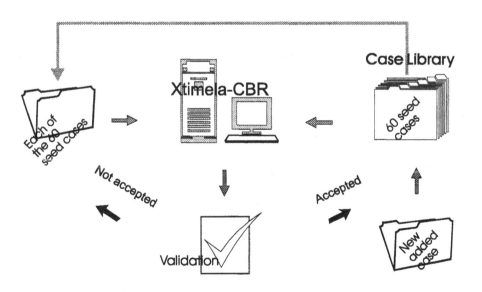

Figure 2. Illustration of the process followed for the validation of the seed cases

Twenty five past grant applications were employed for predictive validation, all of them different from the 60 seed application cases. These 25 test grant applications were selected from a sample of 100 applications provided by the Client which were successfully processed and implemented. To guide the predictive validation and assess results a standard form was created. The form groups thirty nine variables employed for carrying out the predictive validation, so that the reasons behind any discrepancies between the system's and the experts' results could be traced. Not all of the variables could be considered in every test case, because of the changes that occurred in the legal framework during the period of time covered by the test cases. As shown in table 3, the system suggested the same decision on the grant as the one provided by the human expert for all of the test cases. The grant eligibility suggested by the system supports the decision achieved for each grant application. Table 3, also indicates the time taken to run the system.

10.   FIELD VALIDATION

The predictive validation carried out with the knowledge-base refinement has demonstrated that the system is suitable for field validation because it can be used experimentally in supporting the assessment of new grant applications without causing problems for the users. To guide the field validation, a standard form was designed and implemented for the field tests. This form embodies the variables used to evaluate the system in addressing the task for which it was built. The variables were grouped into two main headings: i) system's effectiveness and ii) user's effectiveness. Five different grant applications, were randomly selected for field validation.

11.   FACE VALIDATION

Despite the difficulty of involving experts not linked to the Client to undertake a face validation, three experts in information technology were invited to give an independent judgement on the performance of the system and particularly on the model employed. The experts were generally impressed with the system, and they gave very encouraging opinions. Face validation was carried out into two phases by using a questionnaire designed by the author to guide the tests. The first phase, involved a briefing about the system and a detailed demonstration of its performance. The second phase, consisted of running the system using several application grants in order to allow the invited experts to test the performance of the system in detail. In broad terms, both experts agreed with the model employed to implement the system. They highlighted the potential benefits of CBR in the application area. As in the field validation, both experts also suggested improvements to the system's functionality, particularly related to the man-machine interface. These suggestions were implemented in a later stage.

Table 3: Comparison of the application eligibility and grant decision

Aplication Code	application eligibility		grant decision		time min-utes	criteria		
	expert	system	expert	system		Accu-racy	qua-lity	use-ful-ness
15302351	-	High	Approve grant	Approve grant	25	Equal	Equi-valent	Use-ful
1008527	-	High	Approve grant	Approve grant	30	Equal	Equi-valent	Use-ful
18535553	-	High	Approve grant	Approve grant	30	Equal	Equi-valent	Use-ful
6387317	-	High	Approve grant	Approve grant	25	Equal	Equi-valent	Use-ful
14184168	-	High	Approve grant	Approve grant	30	Equal	Equi-valent	Use-ful
13103949	-	High	Approve grant	Approve grant	25	Equal	Equi-valent	Use-ful
174499276	-	High	Approve grant	Approve grant	35	Equal	Equi-valent	Use-ful
13097338	-	High	Approve grant	Approve grant	40	Equal	Equi-valent	Use-ful
6380799	-	High	Approve grant	Approve grant	35	Equal	Equi-valent	Use-ful
163417	-	High	Approve grant	Approve grant	30	Equal	Equi-valent	Usef ul
21011276	-	High	Approve grant	Approve grant	40	Equal	Equi-valent	Use-ful
103257	-	High	Approve grant	Approve grant	35	Equal	Equi-valent	Use-ful
14216552	-	High	Approve grant	Approve grant	30	Equal	Equi-valent	Use-ful
13136911	-	Very High	Approve grant	Approve grant	50	Equal	Equi-valent	Usef ul
13163922	-	Very High	Approve grant	Approve grant	35	Equal	Equi-valent	Use-ful
1075116	-	Very High	Approve grant	Approve grant	35	Equal	Equi-valent	Use-ful
53537	-	Very High	Approve grant	Approve grant	30	Equal	Equi-valent	Usef ul
131405	-	High	Approve grant	Approve grant	40	Equal	Equi-valent	Use-ful

13144134	-	Very High	Approve grant	Approve grant	30	Equal	Equi-valent	Use-ful
2068312	-	Very High	Approve grant	Approve grant	35	Equal	Equi-valent	Use-ful
532853	-	High	Approve grant	Approve grant	25	Equal	Equi-valent	Use-ful
5343522	-	High	Approve grant	Approve grant	30	Equal	Equi-valent	Usef ul
15287315	-	Very High	Approve grant	Approve grant	35	Equal	Equi-valent	Use-ful
53429101	-	Very High	Approve grant	Approve grant	35	Equal	Equi-valent	Use-ful
19660526	-	Very High	Approve grant	Approve grant	25	Equal	Equi-valent	Use-ful

12.   ROBUSTNESS TEST

The robustness test was undertaken to test the behaviour of the system under extreme grant application conditions, regarding the households and dwelling-houses. Only the most important components of the system were tested. These components included: i) the application case database (case library and access procedures); ii) the new case indexer and iii) the case-base reasoner. These components were selected because much of the system's performance depends upon them. All robustness tests were carried by the author. A set of hypothetical grant applications was created, each case focusing on testing a particular aspect of the above mentioned system's components.

13.   CONCLUSIONS AND FINDINGS

The V&V of the system were an essential activity within system implementation cycle. It was carried out with certain pragmatism essentially due to existing constraints. The V&V of the system were carried out using different methods. Each method focused on different aspects of the system's validity and utility. The V&V have shown that these methods tend to complement each other. The integration of the V&V within the system implementation and refinement was a very useful procedure, because it enabled the author to keep track of the system performance at every stage of the CCA method. The validation of the initial seed cases, treating them as new applications and validating each case added to the case library, has contributed to the successful predictive validation of the system. Predictive validation was regarded as a structured extension of the system's knowledge-base. Because of the large number of test cases, predictive validation was easy to carry out. The field and face validations have highlighted the limitations of the system's user interface. Filed validation was useful for keeping track of the Client's specific needs and ultimately for the Client's acceptance of the research project. The Client was in a position to see what the project could deliver and what it could expect from the potentialities highlighted during the validation of the system. The face validation was useful for capturing the views of independent experts on the system performance and the model that supports the system. They provided useful contributions to the research.

REFERENCES

Bareiss, R. (1989) The experimental evaluation of case-based learning apprentice, Proc. Case-Based Reasoning Workshop, Morgan Kaufmann Publisher Inc., San Mateo, California, 162-167.

Chandrasekaran B., Johnson T. and Smith J. (1992), Task-Structure Analysis for Knowledge Modelling, Communications of the ACM, 39 (9), 124-138.

Cervera E. (1993), KBS Validation: From Tools to Methodology, Guest Editor's Introduction, IEEE Expert, 8 (3), 45-47.

Goel A. (1989), Integration Of Case-Based Reasoning And Model-Based Reasoning For Adaptive Design Problem Solving, PhD Dissertation, Ohio Sate University 1989.

Golding, A. R. and Rosenbloom, P.S. (1991) Improving rule-based systems through case-based reasoning, Proc. 9th Nat. Conf. On Artificial Intelligence, Vol. 1, AAAI Press/MIT Press, Menlo Park, California, 264-269.

Green C. and Keyes M. (1987), Verification And Validation Of Expert Systems, Proc. Western Conference on Expert Systems (WESTEX-87), IEEE Computer Society 1987, 38-43.

Gupta U. (1991), Validating and Verifying Knowledge-Based Systems, The IEEE, Computer Society Press 1991,176-187, Los Alamitos California.

Hennessy D. and Hinkle D. (1992), Applying Case-Based Reasoning to Autoclave Loading, IEEE Expert, 7 (5), 21-26.

Kolodner J. (1993), Case-Based Reasoning, Morgan Kaufmann Publishers, Inc., San Mateo, California.

Koton, P. (1989) Evaluating case-based problem solving, Proc. Case-Based Reasoning Workshop, Morgan Kaufmann Publisher Inc., San Mateo, California, 173-175.

Kriegsman, M. and Barletta, R. (1993) Building a case-based help desk application, IEEE Expert, 8(6), 18-26.

Marcot B. (1987), Testing Your Knowledge Base, AI Expert, 2 (8), August 1987, 42-47, Miller Freeman Publications.

Meseguer P. (1993), Expert System Validation Through Knowledge Base Refinement, Proc. 13th International Joint Conference on Artificial Intelligence IJCAI 93, Aug./Sep., Vol. 1, 477-482 Chambery, France.

Nasser J. (1988), Nuclear Power Plant Expert System Verification And Validation, Proc. Workshop on Validation and Verification of Expert Systems, IEEE Expert, August 1988, 26-41.

Ng, S.T. and Smith, N.J. (1998) Verification and Validation of Case-Based Prequalification System, Journal of Computing in Civil Engineering, 12(4), ASCE, 215-226.

O'Keefe R., Balci O. and Smith E. (1987), Validating Expert System Performance, IEEE Expert, Winter 1987, 2 (4), 81-90.

Preece A. (1990), Towards a methodology for evaluating expert systems, Expert Systems, 7 (4), 215-236.

Simoudis E. (1992), Using Case-Based Retrieval for Customer Technical Support, IEEE Expert, 7 (5), October 1992, 7-12.

Smith J. and Johnson T. (1993), A Stratified Approach to Specifying, Designing, and Building Knowledge Systems, IEEE Expert, 8(3), 15-25.

Yen J. and Lee J. (1993) A Task-Based Methodology for Specifying Expert Systems, IEEE Expert, 8 (1), 8-15.

Validation and Verification of Knowledge-Based Systems for Power System Control Centres

Jorge SANTOS; Carlos RAMOS
Polytechnic Institute of Porto, Institute of Engineering, Dept. of Computer Engineering

Zita VALE
Polytechnic Institute of Porto, Institute of Engineering, Dept. of Electrical Engineering

Albino MARQUES
REN - Portuguese Transmission Network, EDP Group

Key words: verification, validation, KBS, temporal reasoning, power systems

Abstract: During the last years, electrical utilities began to install intelligent applications in order to assist Control Centres operators. The SPARSE is a Knowledge-Based System used in the Portuguese Transmission Network for operator assistance in incident analysis and power restoration. The Verification and Validation (V&V) process must assure the reliability of these applications, even under incident conditions. This paper addresses the Validation and Verification of Knowledge-Based Systems (KBS) in general, focussing particularly on the V&V of SPARSE. Validation and Verification are presented in a complementary perspective, stressing its relation with the KBS developing stages. VERITAS is an automatic verification tool initially developed to verify SPARSE Knowledge Base. Although its initial goal was the SPARSE verification, the tool was developed with generic verification purposes and domain independent approach. Hence it is able to perform knowledge base structural analysis allowing the detection of knowledge anomalies at low cost, especially with big knowledge bases. VERITAS is currently being used in the verification of several Knowledge Based and Data Mining systems.

221

1.   INTRODUCTION

Quality is a concept that represents more than a goal itself, it is a fundamental path to the conception of better products/services in order to satisfy the final consumers. Quality management becomes an imperative question inside organisations and a wide range of tools is used in order to achieve this goal.

Information and software are intrinsically related to the management of organisation knowledge. In this scenario, software certification and verification plays a very important role. Knowledge Based Systems Verification and Validation is the paradigm of this concept.

This paper addresses the Validation and Verification of Knowledge-Based Systems in general, focussing particularly on the V&V of SPARSE, a KBS to assist operators of Portuguese Transmission Control Centres in incident analysis and power restoration.

Nowadays, Control Centres (CC) are of high importance for the operation of electrical networks. These Centres receive real-time information about the state of the network and Control Centre operators must take decisions according to this information. Under incident conditions, a huge volume of information may arrive to these Centres, making its correct and efficient interpretation by a human operator almost impossible. In order to solve this problem, electrical utilities began to install intelligent applications in their Control Centres. These applications are usually Knowledge-Based Systems (KBS) and are mainly intended to provide operators with assistance, especially in critical situations.

The correct and efficient performance of such applications must be guarantied through Verification and Validation (V&V). V&V of KBS are not so usual as desirable and when used are usually undertaken in a non-systematic way.

The systematic use of formal V&V techniques is a key for making end-users more confident about KBS reliability, especially when critical applications are considered.

It is known that knowledge maintenance is an essential issue for the success of a KBS, therefore, it must be guaranteed that the modified Knowledge Base remains consistent and will not induce incorrect or inefficient system behaviour. This issue leads to the problems of Validation and Verification (V&V).

Since there is no general agreement on the meaning of these terms, for the remaining of this paper, the following definitions will be used:

– Validation - Assure that the KBS provide solutions that present a confidence level as high as the ones provided by the experts. Validation is then based on tests, desirably in the real environment and under real circumstances. During these tests, the KBS is seen as a "black box" and only the input and the output are really considered important.

– Verification - Assure that the KBS has been correctly conceived and implemented and does not contain technical errors. Verification is intended to examine the interior of the KBS, hence the KBS is seen as a "glass box". Not only the input and the output are considered important but also the methods needed to compute results.

This paper is organised as follow: the following section describes the SPARSE system, namely, its architecture, reasoning model, rule selection mechanism, denoting its implications for Verification and Validation process. The third section describes the Validation stage of SPARSE development focussing on the field tests and on the need for applying formal methods in the V&V of SPARSE. The Verification section presents VERITAS, the tool initially used to verify SPARSE Knowledge Base and currently being used to perform knowledge base structural analysis in several systems. Finally, some conclusions and future work are presented.

2. SPARSE

SPARSE is a KBS developed for the Control Centres of the Portuguese Transmission Network This KBS assists Control Centres operators in incident analysis and power restoration (Vale and Moura 93) (Vale et al. 94).

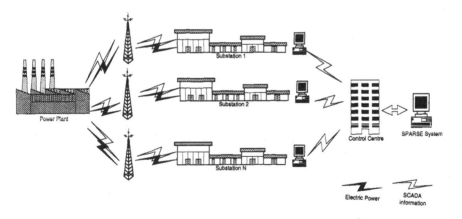

Figure 1. Power Network interacting with SPARSE

Real-time information is acquired through the Power Network by the SCADA (Supervisory Control And Data Acquisition) System. This information is sent to a Control Centre where decisions are take and the control actions take place (see Figure 1).

The development of SPARSE required several kinds of knowledge:
– knowledge about Power System elements and topology (e.g. power plants, substations and lines);
– knowledge about the alarms that are generated at each moment (alarm lists);
– knowledge about the information transmission system (e.g. how and what is transmitted);
– knowledge concerning alarm interpretation.

The first two kinds of knowledge are included in the Fact Base, under the form of PROLOG facts. The remaining knowledge is embedded in the Rule Base. A major issue in the knowledge included in the Rule Base concerns temporal aspects. In fact, temporal aspects are the key for alarm interpretation in what concerns the events occurred and the transmission of information to Control Centres. According to this, SPARSE rules include the required features in terms of temporal questions consideration (Vale et al. 96). SPARSE presents some features that make the verification work more difficult than for most KBS. These features include nonmonotonic behaviour, temporal reasoning and the meta-rules used by rule triggering mechanism.

Considering the following rule:

rule xx : 'EXAMPLE':
[
[C1 and C2 and C3]
or
[C4 and C5]
]
==>
[A1,A2].

The conditions considered in the Left Hand Side (C1 to C5 in this example) may be of one of the following types:
– A fact which truth must be proved (normally these facts are time-tagged);
– A temporal condition, used to define temporal relations between facts;
– Previously obtained conclusions.

The actions/conclusions to be taken (A1 to A2 in this example) may be of one of the following types:
– Assertion of facts (conclusions to be inserted into knowledge base);
– Retraction of facts (conclusions to be deleted from the knowledge base);
– Interaction with the user interface.

Temporal issues are also of major importance for the inference mechanism. The Inference Engine of our system has been completely developed in PROLOG, specifically for this application. It allows an efficient real-time processing of alarm messages (more than 1200 alarm messages per minute).

The main requirements that led us to develop our own Inference Engine were the following:
- the amount of the involved information is very large;
- the processing must be done in real time, according to the arrived information;
- the analysis involves complex temporal reasoning;
- the power system is a dynamically changing environment requiring nonmonotonic reasoning.

The Inference Engine of our system uses a forward chaining strategy of reasoning that triggers the appropriate rules when a new fact, external (alarm) or internal (conclusion) arrives, in order to derive new conclusions. The Inference Engine uses meta-knowledge in order to select the appropriate rules and guide the reasoning process, improving the system efficiency.

As Power Systems are dynamically changing environments, the corresponding information also changes dynamically. This requires dynamically changing knowledge bases for Intelligent Alarm Processors and inference engines supporting nonmonotonic reasoning. In fact, alarm messages reflect changes in the Power System and the arrival of a message may turn false conclusions previously achieved. The inference engine must be able to test the veracity of previous conclusions according to the most recent information.

The rule selection mechanism uses facts with the following structure:

trigger(Fact,
[
    (Rule-1,Tb-1,Te-1),
    ...,
    (Rule-n,Tb-n,Te-m)
])

where:

Fact – the arriving fact (external alarm or internal conclusion);

Rule1,...,n – the rule that should be triggered in first place when the fact arrives;

Tb1,...,n – the delay time before rule triggering, used to wait for remaining facts needed to define an event;

Te1,...,n – the maximum time for trying to trigger the rule.

3.   VALIDATION

The project team aimed to perform the validation of SPARSE using examples as close as possible to the ones that the application should face in the real environment. According to this, it was considered that validation should be based mainly on real information about the network.

When integration issues are not addressed in an early phase of the project, the changes that are required when the system is integrated in the real environment may be very significant and impose almost a complete rebuilding of the system. Hence, the experts should consider these issues during the knowledge acquisition phase.

REN's staff developed an application named TTLOGW (Rosado 93) to acquire real-time information from SCADA and to send it to SPARSE. It acquires information related to the state of electrical network equipment, which is used to generate material for the validation of SPARSE.

This application acquires the information related to the state of the equipment of the electrical network. This information includes, namely:
– state of breakers and disconnectors (open, closed, changing);
– mode of operation of substations (local or remote and automatic or manual).

Therefore, files concerning real incidents have been obtained and have been used in order to validate SPARSE conclusions. Experts involved in the project commented these conclusions and corrections in the Knowledge Base were made whenever necessary.

New validation techniques had to be applied after SPARSE being installed in the control centre, since then it received real-time information from TTLOGW. The validation of SPARSE considering real-time information was very important due to several reasons:
– Temporal reasoning should be tested under real situations in order to assure its correction;
– Consideration of multiple faults is an important aspect of SPARSE performance that is very dependent from the way information flows;
– Processing times should be tested in order to guarantee real-time performance, even under incident conditions.

As nowadays electrical networks are very reliable it was not possible to completely validate SPARSE with real incidents. A large number of different types of incidents had to be simulated to allow validation. As this simulation should be as accurate as possible, two different techniques have been used:
1. Simulation of incidents by operators located in chosen substations
2. Simulation of incidents using a programmable impulse generator and a Remote Terminal Unit (RTU).

These two techniques are complement to each other, allowing the complete validation of SPARSE.

The simulation of incidents by operators allowed real-time information to be obtained, that was forced to be generated, presented exactly the same characteristics as the information obtained during a real incident. During these tests, the operators, making the whole system act as if a real incident was taking place simulated the behaviour of the protection equipment. Therefore, the information used by SPARSE was generated, as it would be under a real incident.

Due to the difficulties of co-ordinating operators in several substations, the simulation is not always correct and the whole process may have to be repeated several times in order to obtain a good test case.

Regardless all the difficulties and costs involved, this kind of tests has been considered absolutely essential for the validation of SPARSE, increasing the confidence in its real-time behaviour.

In order to undertake a complete set of tests without the extremely high costs required by this technique, a different technique of test has also been used. This technique involves the use of a Remote Terminal Unit (RTU) and of a programmable impulse generator (PIG). The PIG generates impulses in order to force alarm messages creation by the SCADA system. This technique was used to simulate a wide set of incidents allowing a more complete SPARSE Knowledge Base validation with reduced costs.

These methods of validation have been considered sufficient to put SPARSE in service.

4. VERIFICATION

In the Portuguese Transmission network, the introduction of new substations, with different types of operation or layout, has already imposed some modifications to the SPARSE knowledge base. Under these circumstances, performing complete validation tests, as the ones described before, is not acceptable. Even if the costs were acceptable, the required time would oblige the Knowledge-Based System to be either out of service or to be in service without a validated Rule Base longer than desirable.

As formal methods of verification rely on mathematical foundations, they are able to detect a large number of possible problems. Therefore, it is possible to guarantee that a KBS that has passed through a verification phase is correct and efficient. Moreover, it is possible to assure that it will provide correct performance with examples that have not been considered in the validation phase. It seems obvious that it is impossible to carry out those tests after each knowledge updating so the developed verification tool offers an easy and inexpensive way to assure the knowledge quality maintenance.

A specific tool, named VERITAS (Santos 97) (Santos 99) has been developed for the verification of SPARSE, performing structural analysis and allowing knowledge anomaly detection.

VERITAS is knowledge-domain and rule-grammar independent. It has been developed with an open and modular architecture (see Figure 2) allowing user-interaction through all the verification process. Since the tool is independent of KB grammar, theoretically any rule-based system can be analysed by VERITAS.

The Converter module allows the representation of external rules in an internal canonical form that is recognised by the other modules. Notice that this module works in two directions. It can also convert the canonical form into an external KB, generating new rules during knowledge updating, after anomaly detection, using an external grammar.

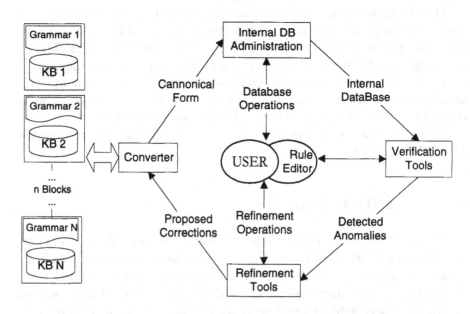

Figure 2. VERITAS Architecture

The Internal DB Administration module is responsible for the extraction and classification of all the information needed during the anomaly detection phase. In the first step all literals extracted from rules are classified according to the following schema:

– Fact – if it just appears in rule antecedents;

– Conclusion – if it just appears in rule consequents;

– Hypotheses – if it appears in both sides of the rules.

Notice that this classification is domain independent and just makes sense for verification procedures. This classification offers the advantages of a more compact knowledge representation and the reduction of the complexity of the rule expansion generating process. As it will be described later, this process corresponds to the analytical calculation of all possible inference chains. Another advantage is the reduction of anomaly detection complexity. For instance, if the Left Hand Side (LHS) is just composed by facts or if all literals of Right Hand Side (RHS) are conclusions (no hypotheses) no circularity could be entailed.

Afterwards, the Internal DB Administration module generates useful information about existing relations between previously obtained literals. That information is used not just to make the expansions generation process faster but also in the automatic detection of Single Value Constraints. VERITAS considers some type of constraints already described in the literature (Zlatareva and Preece 94), which can be classified in the following classes:

– Semantic Constraints – this type of impermissible set is formed by literals that cannot be present at the same time in the KB. Semantic constraints have to be introduced by the user.

– Single Value Constraints – this type of impermissible set is formed by only one literal but considering different values of its parameters. Notice that those potential constraints are automatically detected. After this, the constraint can be either confirmed or changed by users.

– Logical Constraints – there are just two types of logical constraints: **A and not(A)** (where **A** stands for a literal) and **A and notPhysical(A).** The designation of the second is obtained by analogy with logical negation and allows to represent the constraint defined by a literal and by its retraction from the KB.

The anomaly detection (performed by verification tools) is a heavy process that can be done in two modes: batch or interactive. In batch mode, the knowledge base is tested in a single block and all tests are carried out. In interactive mode, the verification tools are used by the rule editor. Nevertheless, the performed tests are not very complex, hence it is possible to verify the rule in question immediately and to assure the KB consistency after the insertion of that rule.

The rule editor shows the existing relations between the rules that are to be modified and the remaining existing knowledge in the KB. This information is supplied in a graphical interface using a directed hypergraph type representation. This technique allows rule representation in a manner that clearly identifies complex dependencies across compound clauses in the rule base. Furthermore, a unique directed hypergraph representation for each set of rules is obtained (Ramaswary and Sarkar 97).

When the verified Knowledge Base has large dimensions, the information generated during anomaly detection can be huge, implying that the detected anomalies have to be reported using a form suitable for easing its analysis. Special care has been put on this task, in order to reduce the time needed for the information analysis, hence it is possible to aggregate or select information by type of anomaly, number of rule or literal identification.

The anomaly detection relies on rule expansion and constraint analysis. This method is also used by some well known V&V tools, as KB-REDUCER (Ginsberg 87) and COVER (Preece 90). The used technique, due to SPARSE specific features, is a variation of common ATMS (Assumption-based Truth Maintenance System) (Kleer 86). Namely, the knowledge represented in the meta-rules had to be considered in rule expansion generation.

The rules expansion calculation method relies in the analytical determination of all possible inference chains of the analysed rule base. Consequently, evaluation of variables, specifically the temporal ones, was considered crucial.

As an example, the following rules are an extract of a larger knowledge base used for vehicle classification.

r1: **if** [type(VEHICLE,passengers) **and** class(VEHICLE,light)]
then light(VEHICLE,automobile).

r2: **if** [type(VEHICLE,goods) **and** class(VEHICLE,heavy)]
then heavy(VEHICLE,truck).

r3:   **if** [**not** passengers(VEHICLE,>,9)**and not** weight(VEHICLE,>,3500)]
then class(VEHICLE,light).

First one expansion is created for each rule with the following structure:

/* expF(#SeqNumber, RHS, LHS, Support Rules, Level) */

expF(1,c1,[f1,h1],[r1],1).

expF(2,c2,[f2,h2],[r2],1).

expF(3,h1,[not f3,not f4],[r3],0).

The "Level" field is obtained in straight manner:

Level 0: expansions which LHS are exclusively composed by facts;

Level n+1: where **n** is the highest existing level in LHS.

Afterwards new expansions are created based on the substitution of the hypothesis (since conclusions and facts are the inference chain boundary) by supporting literals. In the considered example **h1** is replaced by **[not f3,not f4]** resulting in the following expansion:

expF(11,c1,[f1,not f3,not f4],[r3,r1], 0).

During this process, another database is created with the original rules in order to allow variable evaluation and pattern matching. Notice that during the verification process (this type of verification is also called static verification) it is not possible to know all possible values that variables would take.

The detected anomalies are grouped in three major classes: redundancy, circularity and inconsistency, as presented in Figure 3.

This classification is based on Preece classification (Preece and Shinghal 94) with some modifications. First, since matching values are considered in rule analysis, a new set of anomalies will arise. Considering the following circular rules:

r1: t(a) and r(X) → s(a)

r2: s(a) → r(a)

   for **X=a** some inference engines could start an infinite loop.

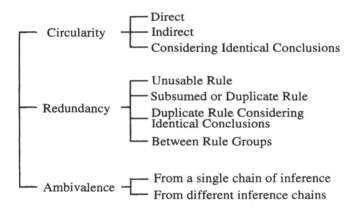

Figure 3. Anomaly Classification

Another situation concerns to redundancy between groups of rules. In the following example:

r1: a and b and c → z

r2: not a and c → z

r3: not b and c → z

rules **r1, r2** and **r3** could be replaced by **rx** rule:

rx: (a and b and c) or (not a and c) or (not b and c) → z

   Applying logical simplifications to rule **rx**, it is possible to obtain the following rule:

rx': c $\rightarrow$ z

Redundancy between groups of rules is a generalisation of the unused literal situation already studied by Preece (Preece and Shinghal 94). Notice that this type of redundancy could be desirable. VERITAS can detect these situations using an improved Quine-McCluskey method for logical expression simplification.

The rule selection mechanism not only avoids some run-time errors (for instance circular chains) but also introduces another complexity axis to the verification because the inference chains depend directly on the existence or not of this mechanism.

The following example intends to show how the analysis of the rule selection mechanism transforms the reported anomalies.

The following meta-rule used by SPARSE rule selection mechanism:

trigger(alarm(msgA, Instalation, Panel),

[(d1,50,50),(d2,51,51),(d3,52,52)]]).

means that when the **alarm/3** arrives to the system, rules d1, d2 and d3 should be tried in this order, according to intervals defined by second and third parameters of each triplet.

Consider also the following simplified rules:

rule d1:

IF

alarm(msgA, Instalation1, Panel1) at T1,

alarm(msgB, Instalation1, Panel1) at T2,

temporal_condition(T1,T2,<,30),

alarm(msgC, Instalation1, Panel1) at T3,

temporal_condition(T1,T3,<,40)

THEN

actionA.

rule d2:

IF

alarm(msgA, Instalation1, Panel1) at T1,

alarm(msgB, Instalation1, Panel1) at T2,

temporal_condition(T1,T2,<,30)

THEN

actionA.

Notice that rules **d1** and **d2** are redundant by definition, according to previously presented classification, hence the verification system should detect and report an anomaly named "Duplicate or Subsumed Rule". However, with a deeper analysis it is possible to notice that rule **d1** is a specialization of **d2** rule. If a KB presents some of these situations, the inference engine should be able to assure that shortcuts (specialists rules could be also referred as shortcuts) will be triggered in first place, avoiding the message absorbing for the most generic rule.

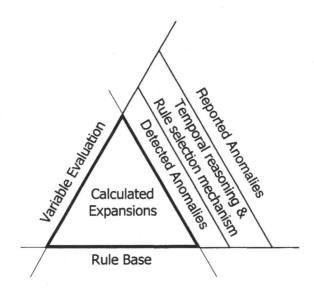

Figure 4. Rules Expansions Calculation Schema

VERITAS verification tool is able to detect KB existing anomalies, by using logic tests first. Later, the verification system performs meta-rule analysis allowing to filter previously detected anomalies, providing really accurate information, namely by preventing false anomaly reporting (see Figure 4)

5.   CONCLUSIONS & FUTURE WORK

This paper dealt with some important aspects for the practical use of KBS in Control Centres, namely knowledge maintenance and its relation to the Verification and Validation process.

The systematic use of Verification and Validation methods is very important for the acceptance of Knowledge-Based Systems by their end-users, especially when critical applications are considered. The use of Verification tools, based on formal methods, increases the confidence of the user and eases the process of changing KB, reducing the testing costs and the time needed to implement them.

The paper first presents SPARSE, a Knowledge-Based System used in the Portuguese Transmission Network for operator assistance in incident analysis and power restoration. Then its Validation phase is described, focusing on the field-tests and on the used techniques. Afterwards, the Verification of SPARSE is discussed, introducing a tool (VERITAS) that uses a formal verification method.

VERITAS is a verification tool that performs structural analysis in order to detect knowledge anomalies. We argue that the usefulness of VERITAS increases proportionally with KB size and the number of knowledge modifications, which must be undertaken.

Presently, VERITAS is being improved in order to allow the detection of anomalies related to temporal and nonmonotonic reasoning. VERITAS is starting to be used in Data Mining applications generated knowledge verification and as KB integrator for applications with multiple knowledge sources.

ACKNOWLEDGEMENTS

The authors of this paper would like to acknowledge PRAXIS XXI Research Program, FEDER, the Portuguese Science and Technology Foundation and Innovation Agency for their support of SATOREN Project and Project PRAXIS/3/3.1/CEG/2586/95.

REFERENCES

Ginsberg, A. (1987), "A new approach to checking knowledge bases for inconsistency and redundancy", In *Proceedings of the 3rd Annual Expert Systems in Government Conference*. 102-111. Washington, D.C., IEEE Computer Society.

Kleer, J. (1986), "An assumption-based TMS", *Artificial Intelligence* (Holland). 28(2):127-162

Preece, A. (1990), "Towards a methodology for evaluating expert systems", *Expert Systems* (UK). 7(4):215-223.

Preece, A; and Shinghal, R. (1994), "Foundation and Application of Knowledge Base Verification", *Intelligence Systems*. 9:683-701.

Ramaswary, M. and Sarkar, S. (1997), "Global Verification of Knowledge Based Systems via Local Verification of Partitions", In *Proceeding of the 4th European Symposium on the Validation and Verification of Knowledge Based Systems (Eurovav'97)* 145-154. Leuven, Belgium.

Rosado, C. (1993), "Process TTLOGW", EDP Technical Report, RESP/ SCDS 20/93, Electricidade de Portugal

Santos, J. (1997), "Verificação e Validação de Sistemas Baseados em Conhecimento – VERITAS, uma Ferramenta de Verificação", MSc Thesis diss., Dept. de Engenharia Electrotecnica e Computadores, Faculdade de Engenharia do Porto.

Santos, J; Faria, L.; Ramos, C.; Vale, Z.; and Marques, A. (1999), "VERITAS – A Verification Tool for Real-time Applications in Power System Control Centers", In

Proceedings of the Twelfth International Florida Ai Research Society (FLAIRS'99). 511-515. Orlando, Florida.

Vale, Z. and Moura, A. (1993), "An Expert System with Temporal Reasoning for Alarm Processing in Power System Control Centers", *IEEE Transactions on Power Systems* 8(3):1307-1314.

Vale, Z.; Faria, L.; Ramos, C.; Fernandes, M.; and Marques, A. (1996), "Towards More Intelligent and Adaptive User Interfaces for Control Center Applications", In *Proceedings of the International Conference on Intelligent Systems Applications to Power Systems (ISAP'96).* 2-6. Orlando, Florida.

Vale, Z.; Moura, A.; Fernandes, M.; and Marques, A. (1994), "SPARSE - An Expert System for Alarm Processing and Operator Assistance in Substations Control Centers", *Applied Computing Review.* 2(2):18-26. ACM Press.

Zlatareva, N.; and Preece, A. (1994), "An Effective Logical Framework for Knowledge-Based Systems Verification.

A priori Verification of Product Models in Mechanical Design

Florence SELLINI*, Pierre-Alain YVARS**
* PSA Peugeot Citroën, Knowledge Engineering, Florence.Sellini@wanadoo.fr

** ISMCM-CESTI, GRIIEM Research Team, payvars@ismcm-cesti.fr

Abstract :   The research work presented in this article covers the constitution and reutilization of technical memory (i.e. company know-how and skill). The aim of the work in progress is to verify knowledge models in design aid systems. The declarative product Model is explained in the first section. In the second one, we present the knowledge required for verification and, finally, the contents and consistency of the approach proposed for the verification of the Models.

1.   INTRODUCTION

This contribution concerns the verification of product modelling for design aid systems for mechanical sets, based on knowledge of expertise. The product model constructed using the knowledge of expertise acquired from a design office specialist is the basis for carrying out the design task. The designer, therefore, is induced to handle this Model directly and management of its operation is transparent using constraint propagation techniques.   In point of fact, this Model must be reliable, valid, well constructed, clear and comprehensible,...

When dealing with Knowledge Based System (KBS) design, conceptual model construction itself, often lacks any verification whatsoever.   As a consequence, the experts mostly have difficulties of using a rather abstract modelling formalism.   Some industrial experiences of KBS design for

237

guiding conception had been carried out at PSA. Our experience in this field brought us toward early to consider model verification in the KBS design process [16].

Even though quite a lot of work have been done on KBS validation through testing or inconsistency detection, on the contrary very few are centred on verifying the conceptual models on which the system is to be designed. However these models are the key in KBS design [16], and their verification is quiet important to build reliable systems [8]. Some works carried out simulations of the models in order to make them "running" using a typical instance case before coding them [2]. Other researchers use these models in order to validate the results of their KBS behaviour [7]. Assuming that the used models are valid as long as accepted by the expert and the knowledge engineers. Even if a complete validation does not exist [6], then it seems to us essential to partly automate the model verification early in the design process, in order to have any feasible guarantees on their validity.

The work presented is related to two problems involved in the creation of a verification process : What must we verify and Which verification strategy, implemented by which mechanisms?

The first aspect concerns the modelling structure. The structure stemming from research undertaken in the DEKLARE project [3 ; 13] has served as the initial basis for this work. We needed to develop it further in order to clarify the full extent of the knowledge supported by this Model. We have enhanced the expressivity of the application Models in order to make actual verification more efficient [15]. The second aspect concerns definition of a verification strategy and mechanisms for implementing it. Irrespective of the type, mechanisms require references in order to assess the consistency and accuracy of what is written. Rules governing writing and consistency were identified by means of model structure specification work. Then, using Model verification requirements, a set of mechanisms was identified and their consistency achieved : this resulted in a verification process forming an integral part of the application Model production activity [14]. This could constitute a first step towards the construction of a knowledge Model editing and maintenance workshop for use directly by the design specialist who would then be able to modify the knowledge represented in application Models and be certain of assistance with correct updating of the *Profession Knowledge Base*.

In the first section, there is a brief presentation of the structure of the Model used to model the expertise acquired (concerning the product to be designed). Then, we will review the contents of the Model of References for Verification (MRV). Finally, we will present the consistency of the various verification mechanisms.

2. PRODUCT MODELS

The description of the product is made from three basic viewpoints : structural, functional and geometric. The mechanical parts designer may thus use different approaches in his design task : specification of functions to be fulfilled, the choice of structure and the dimensions of a mechanical set that he is not going to reinvent ; he also has at his disposal a complete geometric representation. The set of parameter is manage with constraints programming techniques. The structural relations within the Model are supplementary constraints for the verification and implementation of the Model during the design operation.

2.1 Presentation of the Meta-Models

The functional Meta-Model describes the various functions which the entire product class must fulfil. This is a functional breakdown diagram. A structural Meta-Model is a structural breakdown diagram of the product which comprises the different variants existing in the product class.

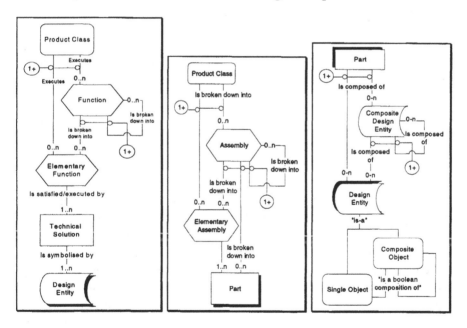

Figure 1. Product Meta-Models : Functional, Structural an geometrical viewpoints

Unlike other views, which are diagrams describing the overall product, the geometric viewpoint is used to construct the geometric representation of each component part of the product (parts defined in the structural view) by using Design Entities (functional surfaces defined in the functional view).

Structural and functional views are related to the geometric view by "link" elements. The link between the structural view and the geometric view is made via the *Part* entity which thus has a dual viewpoint. For the functional and geometric views, it is the Design Entity which serves as the interface.

2.2   **Declarativity of knowledge**

This paragraph relates to the principal enhancements made to the Models in [13] which contribute to a more extensive expressivity of knowledge. In order to improve verification of Models, the explicit nature of the knowledge represented must be consolidated. To do this, we have integrated cardinalities and meta-constraints called *relation connectors* to make structure relations explicit (composition hierarchy structure). This concept is similar to that of the association constraints in UML [12] or other entity/association formalisms.

The use of relation cardinalities seems to be doubly advantageous within the framework of the Models used. On one hand, it is possible to express the number of instances referenced to a composite object ; on the other hand, an existential dependence characteristic [5] of the component in relation to the composite can be expressed. Utilisation of cardinalities expresses :
- *the statement of possible* (whole) values (discreet or continuous) for the number of instances,
- *the optional or mandatory nature* of the relation, therefore the existence of the component entity.

To describe a product class, certain relations have to be expressed, defining how the components of the product are put together, or the various composition configurations for a product. In particular, to make this knowledge of the different variants within a *Product* class explicit, we have introduced the notion of *relation connectors*. These relation connectors are *meta-constraints*, managed like the other constraints expressed in the Model, by the propagation driver at the time of implementation [9]. These are **meta**-constraints since they are constraints that affect other constraints (profession constraints expressed in the form of relations between parameters). In fact, since they affect Model composition links, they condition whether certain entities exist or not and the association between other entities which themselves contain constraints.

Four basic connectors have been defined for our needs :

AND_Equivalent : (+)

"At least one" : (1+)

Mutual exclusion : (X)
Implication : (→)

These are not logic connectors but are rather similar to constraints. Their behaviour is governed by their semantics.

The connectors have two possible statuses in the implementation : *true* and *violation*. The *true* status *(1)* corresponds to a *success*, and indicates that the constraint imposed by the presence of the connector is respected. *Violation (0)* corresponds to a *failure*, and indicates that the connector has not been respected and this therefore corresponds to choices prohibited due to the presence of this connector. For example, let us look at the table (cf. *Table 1*) summarising the behaviour of the AND_Equivalent (+) connector (cf. *Figure 2*).

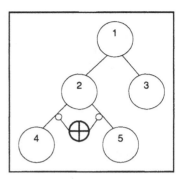

Figure 2. Presence of the connectors

node[1] 4	node 5	case in Figure 2
0	0	Violation
0	1	Violation[2]
1	0	Violation
1	1	true

Table 1. Behaviour of the AND Equivalent connector

Table 1 is not a truth table (or Karnaugh table) in the sense of Boolean algebra. It is a table summarising the couples of nodes allowed if the AND_Equivalent connector is present.

2.3   An example

The example in *Figure 3*, represents the Connecting Rod-Piston assembly (structural viewpoint). The various assembly possibilities must appear on the Model. The connectors and cardinalities allow this to be expressed clearly.

On the Model in *Figure 3*, an AND-Equivalent (+) connector has been added between the « Rod small end bushing » and "Snap ring" or "Circlips" elements so that choice and definition of these is dependent. The use of

---

[1] The value **0** corresponds to the **non-active** status of the node, whereas the value **1** represents the **active** status.

[2] The term violation indicates that the connector does not allow the choice of this configuration, it is a case of violation of the constraint.

cardinalities also allows part of the knowledge to be expressed. In the case of the parts of the Connecting Rod-Piston assembly, the cardinality (1) for the "Connecting Rod Body" gives information on the mandatory nature of this element. In the same way, the "Nut" part has as cardinality of (0-2), therefore it is optional. The notation used indicates a restriction to only 2 choices : 0 or 2 Nut instances. The integration of connectors on relations and cardinalities allows a maximum of information to be made explicit, which, in itself, contributes to the removal of ambiguity and makes verification when reviewed by the specialist that much easier.

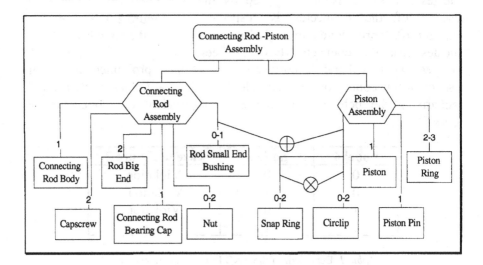

Figure 3. Structural model of the Connecting Rod-Piston assembly

It is important to emphasise that the designer has immediate visibility at his disposal as regards the choices and constraints that affect certain entities. If the same Model as the one in *Figure 3* were considered without the cardinalities or connectors, we would have a truncated perception of the product class knowledge. This approach gives a complete vision of the knowledge and interdependence between parts at the static level (without implementation of the Model), unlike Models [4 ; 13] in which the knowledge is totally expressed by the dynamic.

3.   THE KNOWLEDGE REQUIRED FOR VERIFICATION

The *Model of references for validation*, also called the *C-Model* by [1], contains all the knowledge required to undertake a verification of the conceptual Models that we use. It could also be called the *Validation knowledge Model* as some people term it [11]. This Model corresponds to the explicit, detailed description of the Meta-Models.

This knowledge could be classified in three different categories. Firstly, there is the knowledge which relates to the construction of the Model, the writing formalism. Then, there is the knowledge which allows the Model to be simplified during construction, thus preventing any unnecessary overload. Finally, there is the knowledge concerning Model consistency. It is principally relative to the presence of relations on connectors. Depending on the case, this knowledge is expressed in the form of definitions (« what must be»), or rules (« it is prohibited to.. »).

Definitions are *mandatory* since they refer to a writing syntax which covers the basic rules required for an unambiguous interpretation of the Model. These rules are of two kinds : those which *prohibit* in reference to an obvious inconsistency which can lead to an error of interpretation and those which give a *warning* in reference to a situation which is not inconsistent, i.e. which is not error-generating but which does not make sense in the context.

We are showing in this article some of this knowledge related to these three categories

3.1   Rules for writing connectors

A connector is a relations constraint which concerns a minimum of two relations (binary or n-ary constraint). The following definitions illustrate this :
– A connector must be placed on at least two different links in the diagram.
– A connector must not be created between two parent links.

3.2   Rules for simplification between connectors

In the case of redundancy or overload, a simplification must be made. The simplification can allow the number of connectors to be reduced, without modifying the semantics. The simplification will enable the following :
– firstly, the replacement of two or n connectors affecting two identical links by a single connector (cf. *Figure 4*),
– secondly, the merger of two connectors affecting a common link.

There is a third configuration relating to cases of redundancy, on one hand, and pertinent positioning of connectors, on the other hand. The number of connectors will not necessarily have to be reduced but they may sometimes have to be moved to make their impact in the diagram more obvious. We are only presenting the first configuration in this article.

Study of the coexistence of two (or n) connectors within this framework has enabled simplification rules to be stipulated as well as rules prohibiting connector associations.

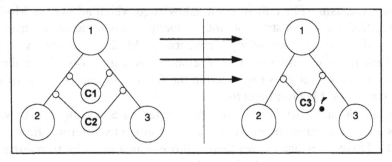

Figure 4. Simplification : two connectors affecting two identical links

3.3   Rules for consistency between connectors and cardinalities

On the one hand, this aspect of consistency is studied according to the semantics chosen for the composition link, namely that a composite cannot exist unless at least one of its components exists and, on the other hand, according to the presence of connectors that might impose a constraint to the existence of the components in question and, finally, according to any cardinalities which may be added to the composition links. A few of the flagrant cases of inconsistency or not making sense that we have identified are presented below.

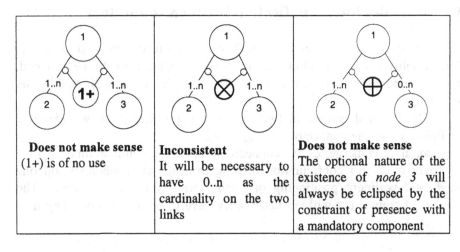

| **Does not make sense** (1+) is of no use | **Inconsistent** It will be necessary to have 0..n as the cardinality on the two links | **Does not make sense** The optional nature of the existence of *node 3* will always be eclipsed by the constraint of presence with a mandatory component |

In this section, we have just presented the elements needed to conduct a verification of application Models. These elements will serve as references for the assessment of the Models, in order to avoid writing errors and to determine whether there is any inconsistency. Validation knowledge is classified into three categories : knowledge describing « correct » writing of the Models, that which describes the simplifications possible to make the Model more powerful and, finally, that which describes the consistency standard or cases of generic inconsistency.

4. VERIFICATION MECHANISMS

A differentiation has to be made between two types of validation : macro-verification and micro-verification.

Macro-verification or verification of the macroscopic structure of the diagram, involves the consistency of the representation of concepts from a structure viewpoint and the consistency of interaction between objects. This verification is performed in reference to the syntax. We will first of all describe the verification of the structure of the diagram in the sense of relations between concepts, then turn to the verification of the integrity of the connected diagram with the presence of relations over connectors and, finally, we will address the overall necessary verification of the diagram.

Micro-validation particularly affects knowledge supported by the concepts. This is professional knowledge. This verification is performed in consistency with the syntax of each object defined at Meta-Model level and with the characteristics of the domain of expertise concerned. It involves considering why it is impossible to cover professional knowledge as a whole on an overall basis and how to generate the contexts into which the sets of concepts participating in the same design solution will be isolated.

4.1 Verification of the macro-structure

4.1.1 Verification of the structure of the diagram

Two important aspects must be verified when concepts are structured :
− That the concepts 'in relation' are those which should be.
− That the cardinality restrictions defined at Meta-Model level for the structure of the application Model are respected.

Concerning the first aspect, the Model of References for Validation (MRV) contains the authorised concept couples, that is to say, the valid composite/component couples. According to these defined types, the mechanism will prevent 'bad' associations when a composition relation is being created. The second preoccupation is to be put into relation with the semantics chosen for the composition relation, on the one hand, and with the cardinalities defined for the structure on the other hand. In point of fact, as long as an entity is not a leaf (terminal node), it is a composite entity and must, therefore, be in relation with its components. It will be essential to verify whether the Model is complete from this viewpoint. And, vice versa, that a leaf is attached to a composite of the Model.

4.1.2   Verification of the integrity of the diagram (connected)

Verification of the connected graph consists of studying the presence of connectors over relations. This verification is based on three complementary aspects :
– Simplification and completeness of the diagram from the viewpoint of the presence of these connectors
– Study of consistency between the connectors,
– Study of the consistency between the presence of the connectors and cardinalities

4.1.3   Overall verification of the diagram

To complete the procedure for the verification of the diagram macrostructure, the diagram must be considered as a whole, in order to verify some additional aspects. The principal motivation stems from the fact that the verification mechanisms previously mentioned only relate to the diagram piece-by-piece. To be completely sure, an overall analysis of the diagram should be performed to look at two particular things, at the least :
– Whether there is at least one valid diagram instance to describe the product to be designed (i.e. that it is still possible to link the root to one or several leaves of the diagram)
– Whether the full set of entities can be instantiated at least once in an execution context (i.e. whether the full set of entities participate in at least one design solution).
This overall verification is performed using a *simulation* aid. This is based on the statuses that can be adopted by each of the entities of the Model during execution : active, prohibited, not determined.

4.2   Verification of the micro-structure

Verification of the « micro-structure » consists of examining the knowledge supported by the concepts and relations.

Different aspects will complement this verification :
- verification of each concept as regards its internal structure (syntax) ;
- the construction of all the various contexts linked to the different design solutions (product variants) ;
- verification of the contextual constraint sets (expert knowledge) thus obtained.

As a reminder, *experts or "profession" relations* represent the designer's professional expertise. For this verification, you have to take into account the fact that a product class includes all the possible variants for the same type of product. Therefore, the diagram[3] executed is intended to represent knowledge of all these variants which are sometimes contradictory.

Within the framework of a general approach to verification of product Models, it is necessary to verify professional knowledge as far as possible. It is not our aim, with an automated approach, to certify that the knowledge expertise database is valid. We do not have the means to do this, particularly as the only judge of the validity of professional knowledge is the expert himself. The approach proposes to detect possible inconsistency and thus assist the expert, by means of the calculation power of the machine, to have an overall grasp of professional knowledge and indicate to him if any flagrant inconsistency exists. Professional knowledge is represented by constraints. It is true to say that, if there are inconsistencies, the constraints propagation mechanism will, to some extent, indicate this by not arriving at a solution. However, the expert does not have the possibility of knowing between which constraints there is inconsistency. Therefore, before activating constraint propagation and thus give enhanced assurance of success, it is useful to record the maximum number of contradictions in the knowledge expressed. Before envisaging verification of constraints, therefore, this verification action must be prepared by generating the contextual knowledge sets.

4.3   Consistency of verification mechanisms

We now present the interaction between various verification actions linked to the editing (writing) phase of the Model. The mechanisms defined are intended to be used during the application *Model editing phase,* which corresponds to the instantiation of the Meta-Model, in order to verify the representation of product knowledge before it is used during the design task. Two principles are proposed to make the array of actions consistent : real time verification when the Model is being written and an overall verification once the Model has been finished.

---

[3] The diagram is the application Model which will be instantiated during the design activity.

The first principle consists of providing for « *Editing of the Model under constraint* », which will act as a guide to ensure writing is correct. A few mechanisms will intervene during the construction of the Model to automatically prevent incorrect choices, indicate prohibited and inconsistent elements and, therefore, prevent anything that is prohibited from being recorded. For example, once the component or composite has been designated, when creating a composition link, prevention of inaccurate writing will consist of accepting the relation only if the two participants are mutually compatible.

For example, when a connector is created between two composition links and a connector already exists in the same place, the designer[4] will be informed of the result of a simplification between the two connectors if this is possible, or will be advised that this is prohibited if these connectors are incompatibles. The number of connectors in the diagram will be automatically reduced in real time. Using the same approach, when a connector is created a local verification will be performed on three levels of generation to indicate to the designer if there is something that does not make sense or is inconsistent with respect to the presence of the connector added. The Model will not be considered finished while composite elements without components exist or there are components (leaves) without a link to a composite.

Figure 5 indicates all the mechanisms used for this local consistency verification during the editing process.

The second principle provides for *overall verification of the diagram* which takes place once the Model has been written. This overall procedure occurs after the local verification aspects which have put constraints on the editing.

Figure 5 presents this activity in detail. Two principal aspects are managed : on one hand, the verification of professional knowledge which requires a general view of the diagram in order to generate contexts ; on the other hand, a simulation is performed as a final addition.

In this manner, the full set of actions makes sense within a coherent approach to the verification of these Models. These mechanisms principally intervene when the Model is edited and this gives certain guarantees of validity before exploitation using system-assisted design of the mechanical part. This type of mechanism contributes to a « clean », rigorous production of the Model, allows a certain number of inconsistencies in the Model to be eradicated, along with major or minor errors, which can be very useful in product representation Models, a fortiori multi viewpoint, for which it

---

[4] Here, the designer is the person who makes the application Model ; he may be a knowledge engineer, an expert or both.

rapidly becomes difficult to have an overall view of the scope of the knowledge.

It is satisfying to know that the solving of problems during the design process in order to achieve a product solution will be made more efficient. Furthermore, during the execution of the Model, i.e. during the instantiation of the Conceptual Model, a certain number of verification mechanisms stated are managed by the propagation of constraints. Indeed, within the framework of the implementation of the Model in a problem resolution environment using constraint programming methods and mechanisms, the behaviour of the elements of the Model and the connector type is driven by constraints.

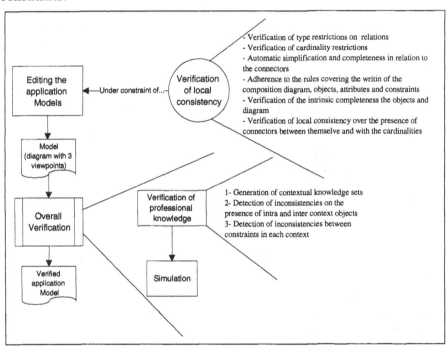

Figure 5. Interaction in the Model verification approach

5.   CONCLUSION

In this article, we have presented a contribution to *a priori* verification of product models in mechanical design. Three principal areas have been covered in detail : concepts and tools for the declarative modelling of product classes, specifically using connector or Meta-constraint ideas, the Model of References for Verification, adapted to our requirements, as well as the mechanisms to be implemented to put this approach into operation. The entire set of verification mechanisms demonstrated is in the process of implementation in the GRIIEM's KoMoD (KnOwledge MOdelling for Design) design-aid application development [17]. The Model of References for Verification has been formalised into a set of production rules, interpreted by an order one object-oriented inference engine [10]. The representation of product knowledge is performed by the cognitive scientist using KoMoD. The detection of inconsistency is done automatically in real time for each modelling action the scientist undertakes. The perspectives given to this work particularly concern integration of the entire set of verification mechanisms into one software environment.

REFERENCES

[1] **M. Ayel & M.-C. Rousset** - *La cohérence dans les bases de connaissances* pages. Paris, Cépadues Eds. (1990).

[2] **S. Boyera, S. Tourtier et O. Coray** - Simuler le comportement macroscopique d'un modèle conceptuel, *JAVA, 3ème Journées Validation des Systèmes à Base de Connaissances* (1994).

[3] **Consortium DEKLARE** - *Conceptualisation of Design Analysis Methodology,* , DEKLARE - Esprit Project 6522 (1993).

[4] **Consortium DEKLARE** - *DEKLARE Small Book - ESPRIT Project 6522*, Final Project Report, CEE (1995).

[5] **C. Djeraba** - Composite objects and dependency relationships in engineering, *Application of Artificial Intelligence in Engineering VI* , Vol. 1 : design, methods and technique, p. 67-82 (1993).

[6] **J. Guyot, J.-P. Vaudet et S. Petitjean** - Vers une caractérisation des outils de validation des systèmes à base de connaissances : application à deux outils, *11th International Conference in Experts Systems and their Applications* , Avignon, France (1991).

[7] **C. Haouche-Gingins & J. Charlet** - Une méthode pour tester les systèmes à base de connaissances par rapport à leur modèle conceptuel. *Revue d'Intelligence Artificielle*, Vol. : 11 - n°4 (, p. 463-487 (1997).

[8] **T. Hoppe** - Hypotheses Generation for Knowledge Validation, *9th European Conference on Artificial Intelligence - ECAI* , Stockolm - Sweden, p. 354-356 (1990).

[9] **ILOG** - *Solver C++ v. 4.0 - Reference Manual.* (1997).

[10] **ILOG** - *IlogRules, Reference Manual,* , Ilog SA, Paris (1998).

[11] **P. Lefevre** - *La validation vue comme une tâche de résolution de problème à part entière : contribution au projet AIDE*, PhD Thesis in Contrôle des systèmes, UTC, Compiègne (1997).

[12] **P.-A. Muller** - *Modélisation Objet avec UML*. Eyrolles ed, 421 pages. PARIS (1997).

[13] **A. Saucier** - *Un modèle multi-vues du produit pour le développement et l'utilisation de systèmes d'aide à la conception en ingénierie mécanique*, PhD Thesis in Mécanique, ENS de Cachan (1997).

[14] **F. Sellini** - *Contribution à la représentation et à la vérification de Modèles de connaissances produit en ingénierie d'ensembles mécaniques.*, PhD Thesis in génie industriel & informatique, Ecole Centrale de Paris (1999).

[15] **F. Sellini & P.-A. Yvars** - Modèles objet & représentation déclarative du produit en conception mécanique. *Revue L'Objet - Hermès*, Vol. : 4 (2) (1998).

[16] **F. van Harmelen & A. ten Teije** - Validation and Verification of conceptual models of diagnosis, *EuroVaV'97 - 4th European Symposium on the Validation and Verification of Knowledge Based Systems*, Leuven, Belgium, p. 117-128 (1997).

[17] **P.-A. Yvars & F. Sellini** - KOMOD : A constraint based design support system for mechanical engineering, *CIRP'99 - International CIRP Design Seminar*, Enschede - Netherlands (1999).

Verification of Business Processes for a Correspondence Handling Center using CCS

Michael Schroeder
City University London, Northampton Square, London EX1V 0HB, UK.
msch@cs.city.ac.uk

Abstract: In this research paper we develop a translation of business processes given in the process interchange format (PIF) to the calculus of communicating systems (CCS). Then we show how to verify properties such as deadlocks, livelocks, safety- and liveness properties. We demonstrate our results using examples taken from a scenario in work distribution in Correspondence Handling Centres.

Keywords: Verification, Process Definition, Workflow Management

1 INTRODUCTION

In the past few years, much research has been devoted to formal verification of business processes [14, 13, 11, 12, 10, 5]. As motivation for this strand of research Wodtke et al. point out that the only validation techniques for workflows currently available are animation and simulation, and argue that symbolic verification is a mature field that provides a number of results and tools appropriate for workflow verification [14]. There are several suitable approaches - the MENTOR project, for example, uses state charts [14, 13]; van der Aalst develops a framework based on petri nets [11, 12]; and process algebras, a prominent example of which being CCS, the calculus for communicating systems [8]. In this paper, we adopt CCS as the underlying language for the task of verifying process definitions.

The main contribution of this paper is an algorithm for the translation of business processes from the process interchange format PIF [7] to CCS. Properties of the translated process (such as deadlocks, livelocks and other safety and liveness properties [6]) can then be verified using CCS and the Edinburgh Concurrency Workbench [1, 9]. This approach was evaluated using a scenario based on the business process enacted by a typical Correspondence Handling Centre.

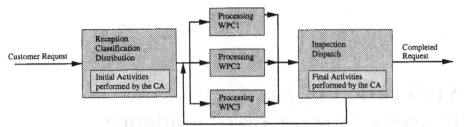

Figure 1. Simplified Business Process for a Correspondence Handling Centre

2 MOTIVATION

The domain adopted here is that of an enterprise receiving a stream of correspondence from its customers concerning its service offerings. These requests
are fed into the enterprise's Correspondence Handling Centre (CHC). This section describes the CHC and its business process.

The Correspondence Handling Centre   The Correspondence Handling
Centre is a logical entity that is composed of a number of Work Processing
Centres (WPCs) and a Central Administration (CA), as shown in Figure 2. A
CHC may handle all or part of the correspondence received by the enterprise it
serves. This correspondence is of many types, ranging from requests to quote for
new business, through complaints about existing goods or services, to requests
to modify or remove/cease goods or services already provided. The business
process used in our scenario is shown in Figure 2 and is a simplified version
of the process adopted by a typical Correspondence Handling Centre. This
CHC business process is defined in terms of six specific categories of activity,
namely Reception, Classification, Distribution, Processing, Minor Repair and
Despatch. Note that, of the six, only Processing is performed by the WPCs,
the rest being the concern of the CA.

The CHC Business Process   Each incoming work item is received and
classified by the CA, then distributed to one of the WPCs. The WPCs check
whether received work items are manageable and then either process them, or
reject them, in which case they are returned to the CA for distribution to a
different WPC. Processed work items are forwarded to the CA for checking. If a
work item needs minor adjustments, the CA carries them out prior to dispatch.
In the case of serious defects, the work item is returned to the WPC that
originally processed it. Completed items are dispatched to the customer and
records may be kept for future billing, customer query and auditing purposes.

Verification of Business Processes   When designing a business process
(such as the CHC process described above) several properties should be verified,

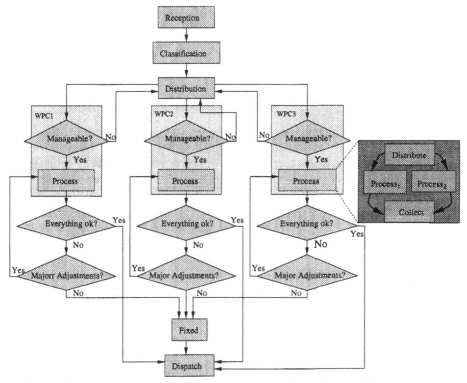

Figure 2. Correspondence Handling Centre business process (with sub-process detail)

prior to implementation. These properties include *deadlocks, livelocks, safety* and *liveness. deadlock:* Activity A requires Activity B to complete before it can proceed, but Activity B requires Activity A to complete before it can proceed. Hence there is an impasse, or deadlock.

livelock: Activity A passes work items to Activity B, Activity B passes the same work items back to Activity A without producing any observable results. This circularity condition is known as livelock.

safety properties: The business process will always satisfy a given property, e.g. it will always run to completion.

liveness properties: The business process will sometimes satisfy a given property, e.g. it will sometimes run to completion.

In order to formally verify our CHC business process we proceed as follows: First of all, we need a process definition, i.e. a representation of the business process that we can reason over. In this paper we use PIF, the process interchange format [7]. Other formalisms with equal expressiveness are also suited, but PIF was adopted due to its simplicity, ease of use, and extensibility. Secondly we extract, from the process definition, sufficient information to support checks for deadlocks, livelocks, safety and liveness. This information is translated into CCS notation, and fed into a verification tool. If any errors are detected by the verification tool, the process definition is modified and the 'design, test, debug' cycle is repeated.

3   PROCESS INTERCHANGE FORMAT

PIF, the process interchange format, is intended to provide a common ontology for the exchange of process definitions among a wide variety of business process modelling and support systems, including workflow management systems, flow charting tools, planners, process simulation systems, and process repositories [7]. Systems using PIF in this way only need implement a single translation service, i.e. from their system-internal representation of processes to PIF, and vice versa. In a BT project on in-service management for existing (software) agencies [2], PIF formed the basis of a content language used to exchange information between an agent-enhanced workflow management system [4] and a management agent which provided engineering and visualisation services for both agents and business processes.

A PIF process definition consists of a number of instances of a predefined set of frame definitions. The frame definitions are typed, and form a simple class hierarchy, rooted on *ENTITY*, which may be extended as required.

A PIF *ENTITY* is either an *ACTIVITY* with subclass *DECISION*, an *OB-JECT* with subclass *AGENT*, a *TIMEPOINT*, or a *RELATION* with subclasses *CREATES, MODIFIES, PERFORMS, USES, BEFORE, SUCCESSOR*, and *ACTIVITY-STATUS*. A *PIF-SENTENCE* is a logical expression that is used to represent various constraints for instances of PIF *OBJECT*s and *RELA-TION*s.

Example 3.1 If we represent an *ACTIVITY* graphically as a rectangle and a *DECISION* as a diamond, then Figure 2 is one possible visualisation of the PIF used to define the CHC business process described in section 2.   □

As depicted in Figure 3, a *DECISION* is an *ACTIVITY* with additional attributes 'If' (of type *PIF-SENTENCE*), 'Then' and 'Else' (both of type *AC-TIVITY*). This provides a simple mechanism for representing OR-splits and AND-joins. AND-splits and OR-joins can be represented using one-to-many and many-to-one *SUCCESSOR* relationships between instances of *ACTIVITY*, thus requiring no decision points.

Once we have produced a process definition using PIF, we want to check certain properties of the process. One approach to accomplishing this goal is the use of process algebras. Governed by a set of laws, these algebras allow us to manipulate processes and transform them into equivalent processes. Of course, the very notion of equivalence of processes is crucial - the most common being the notion of observational equivalence, i.e. whenever an observer cannot see a difference between two processes from the outside, then they are

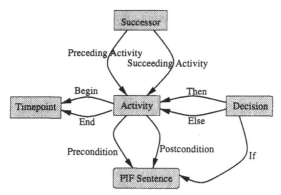

Figure 3. Relations between Activity, Decision, and Successor.

equivalent. Given a process algebra and a workbench to implement some of the transformations and checks, we show how to use it for verification of certain essential properties of process definitions. We translate from PIF to the process algebra and then use the workbench to analyse the process definition. In the next section, we give an overview of the process algebra CCS, then describe the translation from PIF to CCS.

4   CCS

CCS was introduced to verify concurrent systems [8]. From the beginning it has been widely adopted and is used (among other purposes) to specify and verify parallel imperative, logical, and functional programming languages and communication protocols.

Syntactically, CCS comprises of five basic operations:

- prefixing for sequential execution ($\langle Action \rangle.\langle Process \rangle$);

- summation for non-deterministic choice ($\langle Process \rangle + \langle Process \rangle$);

- parallel composition ($\langle Process \rangle | \langle Process \rangle$);

- renaming ($\langle Process \rangle[(\langle Action_1 \rangle / \langle Action_2 \rangle)^+]$);

- restriction ($\langle Process \rangle \backslash \langle Action \rangle^+$).

Besides the basic operations we need a set of actions (or ports) where we distinguish output and input - indicated by the use of overlining. There is also a special silent (or invisible) action τ which is created when two processes synchronise. The empty process is denoted by 0.

Definition 4.1 Syntax of CCS *Let Act be a set of actions such that α and $\overline{\alpha} \in Act$. Let $\tau \notin Act$ be a distinct symbol for the silent action, let $\alpha, \beta \in$*

$Act \cup \{\tau\}$, $Act' \subseteq Act$, and 0 be the empty process. Then 0 is a CCS expression and if P, Q are CCS expressions, so are $\alpha.P$, $P + Q$, $P|Q$, $P[\alpha/\beta]$, $P\backslash Act'$. $\square$

Example 4.1 For the sake of simplicity and clarity we explain the syntax and semantics of CCS expressions in this section by an example. This is based on the CHC example of section 2 but deviates from it to focus fully on the essentials needed to shed light on CCS. Consider a scenario where a Central Administration (CA) and a Work Processing Centre (WPC) do business. We may specify the CA as a process which promises to pay 5000 monetary units, receives the WPC's output and then either pays the WPC 5000 or nothing. This is expressed as

$$CA = promise5000.\overline{recvResults}.(pay5000.0 + pay0.0)$$

The WPC in turn receives an offer from the CA, carries out some work, sends the results to the CA and takes the expected payment:

$$WPC = \overline{recvOffer}.work.sendResults.\overline{take5000}.0$$

Now we want to express the fact that these are concurrent processes within the same Correspondence Handling Centre (CHC), so CA and WPC are composed in parallel. Furthermore, some restrictions apply if we observe the system from an external viewpoint. First of all, we need to rename some actions to identify the complementary pairs in the two processes. As the exchange of monetary units between the CA and the WPC is an internal matter, we use the neutral term *envelope*. Envelope env_1 is used for the offer, env_2 for the result and env_3 for the payment. The CHC is represented thus:

$$CA[env_1/promise5000, env_2/recvResults, env_3/pay5000]$$
$$WPC[env_1/recvOffer, env_2/sendResults, env_3/take5000]$$

The overall system looks like this:

$$
\begin{aligned}
CA &= promise5000.\overline{recvResults}.(pay5000.0 + pay0.0) \\
WPC &= \overline{recvOffer}.work.sendResults.\overline{take5000}.0 \\
CHC &= (CA[env_1/promise5000, env_2/recvResults, env_3/pay5000] \mid \\
& \quad WPC[env_1/recvOffer, env_2/sendResults, env_3/take5000]) \\
& \quad \backslash\{env_1, env_2, env_3\}
\end{aligned}
$$

where the final construct is used to render the envelopes themselves (and not just their contents) inaccessible to external viewpoints.

Whilst the behaviour of both CA and WPC is quite straight forward, it is by no means clear how the CHC behaves. Therefore we want to define the semantics of CCS expressions. $\square$

The semantics of a CCS expression is defined with respect to a labelled transition system which consists of a set of states, an initial state and a transition relation.

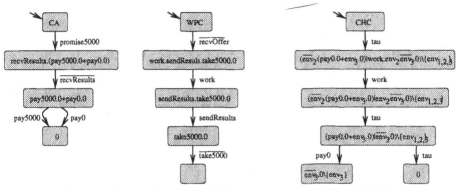

Figure 4. Semantics of the CCS expressions CA, WPC, CHC.

Definition 4.2 Transition System *Let S be a set of states, $t \in S$ an initial state, $Act \cup \{\tau\}$ a set of labels, and $\rightarrow \subseteq S \times Act \cup \{\tau\} \times S$ a labelled transition relation, then $(S, t, \rightarrow)$ is called a labelled transition system.* □

Example 4.2 Consider Figure 4. It shows transitions systems for the CA, WPC and CHC. Note that the states are CCS expressions themselves. The following definition shows how a transition system defines the semantics of a CCS expression. □

Definition 4.3 Semantics of a CCS expression *Let P, P', P'', Q', Q'' be CCS expressions and $(S, t, \rightarrow)$ a labelled transition system with $t = P$. We abbreviate a transition labelled α from state P to state Q by $P \overset{\alpha}{\rightarrow} Q$. Then $(S, t, \rightarrow)$ defines the semantics of P if*

- **Prefixing:** *P has the form $\alpha.P'$. Then it can perform an action α and then behaves like P', i.e. $\alpha.P' \overset{\alpha}{\rightarrow} P'$.*

- **Summation:** *P has the form $P' + Q'$. The summation expresses non-deterministic choice: the process $P' + Q'$ behaves either like P' or like Q'. I.e. $P' \overset{\alpha}{\rightarrow} P''$ implies $P' + Q' \overset{\alpha}{\rightarrow} P''$ and similarly $Q' \overset{\alpha}{\rightarrow} Q''$ implies $P' + Q' \overset{\alpha}{\rightarrow} Q''$.*

- **Parallel Composition:** *P has the form $P'|Q'$. The parallel composition $P'|Q'$ allows three options: if $P' \overset{\alpha}{\rightarrow} P''$ and $Q' \overset{\beta}{\rightarrow} Q''$ then $(P'|Q') \overset{\alpha}{\rightarrow} (P''|Q')$ and $(P'|Q') \overset{\beta}{\rightarrow} (P'|Q'')$, respectively. The third option is that P' and Q' synchronise. If β is the complement $\bar{\alpha}$ of α, then $(P'|Q') \overset{\tau}{\rightarrow} (P''|Q'')$, where τ is the invisible action. Intuitively, both actions are absorbed and an invisible τ is performed.*

- **Renaming:** *P has the form $P'[f]$. Actions can be renamed. If $P' \overset{\alpha}{\rightarrow} P''$ then $P'[f] \overset{f(\alpha)}{\rightarrow} P''[f]$, where f is a function over the set of actions.*

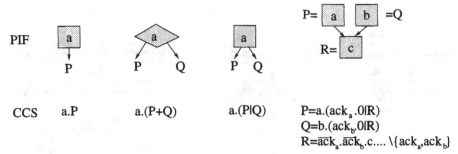

Figure 5. Schematic correspondence between PIF and CCS. Variables P, Q, R abbreviate processes.

- **Restriction:** *P has the form $P' \backslash L$. Actions can be restricted. If $P' \xrightarrow{\alpha} P''$ then $P' \backslash L \xrightarrow{\alpha} P'' \backslash L$, only if $\alpha \notin L$.*   □

Example 4.3 The transition systems in Figure 4 define the semantics for CA, WPC and CHC.   □

The expression describing the CHC in example 4.3 has a general form which is dubbed standard concurrent form:

Definition 4.4 *Synchronous Communication We can generalise the CHC example. Let P, Q be processes such that $P \xrightarrow{\alpha} P'$ and $Q \xrightarrow{\overline{\beta}} Q'$ and $\alpha, \beta, \gamma \in Act$, then the process $(P[\gamma/\alpha]|Q[\gamma/\beta]) \backslash \{\gamma\}$ is in standard concurrent form and performs a synchronised communication τ.*   □

The transition systems are an adequate representation for verification of processes. Besides using algebraic laws as defined in [8] to verify properties of the processes, we could apply temporal logic [3] with respect to the transitions systems of a CCS expression. For a comprehensive description of the calculus see Milner's *Communication and Concurrency* [8]. Now we want to use CCS to verify process definitions specified in PIF.

5 CONVERTING FROM PIF TO CCS

Interpreting PIF In order to check our process definition for deadlocks, livelocks, safety and liveness properties, we need information relating to precedence and synchronisation issues.

In practice, this requires the translation of PIF *ACTIVITY*, *DECISION* and *SUCCESSOR* instances into CCS expressions. *SUCCESSOR* relations are used to capture the ordering of individual process steps within a given branch, and *DECISION*s, as previously stated, provide a means of explicitly representing both OR-splits and AND-joins. Synchronisation is only an issue in the case of AND-joins.

If required, predecessor relations can be inferred from the *SUCCESSOR* relations. Additionally, we assume that there is only one initial activity. The case of more than one initial activity can be reduced to the case of a single activity, by introducing a new initial activity whose successors are the previous initial activities. Basically, the algorithm treats the process as a graph and traverses it depth-first, beginning with the initial activity, and maps PIF constructs to the corresponding CCS constructs. Figure 5 shows that the *SUCCESSOR* relationship in PIF is mapped to a dot (.) in CCS; a PIF *DECISION* (when used to represent an OR-split) corresponds to choice (+) in CCS; two concurrent PIF *ACTIVITIES* are parallel composition (|) in CCS. If they terminate in an AND-join they require synchronisation.

This last case is more complicated. Consider the rightmost case in Figure 5 where c has to wait for the completion of both a and b. This is represented in CCS by having a and b send acknowledgements upon completion. c waits on both acknowledgements (the order does not matter), and executes when the second one arrives.

The next step in the algorithm is a follows: the node's action (activity or decision) is carried out and then for each branch leaving the node the algorithm is called recursively. In the case of an AND-join, an acknowledgement is sent for the current node.

Example 5.1 Consider the following example to help understand the synchronisation of concurrent activities within CCS: the WPC's processing activity is composed of an AND-split, a pair of concurrent sub-processes and an AND-join. Figure 5 is a diagrammatic representation of the PIF that defines the WPC's processing activity on the left, and the generated CCS expressions on the right. The definition of the collect activity states that it has to receive acknowledgements (corresponding to the envelopes in example 4.1) from both sub-processing activities before it can execute. The sub-processing activities each send an acknowledgement upon completion, thus collection takes place when both sub-processes have finished.   □

Algorithm For convenience, CCS expressions are underlined. If a variable is not underlined and part of a CCS expression, it is replaced by its value, i.e. for example the variable $m = Reception_1$ in the expression $\underline{ack}_m$ stands for the action $\underline{ack_{Reception_1}}$. A plain plus-symbol denotes syntactical concatenation of expressions, e.g. does $CCS + \underline{0}$ stand for the CCS expression with a 0 added to its end.

Input: A set of nodes, i.e. decisions and activities, a set of decisions *decisions*, the successor and predecessor relations *succ* and *pred*, and an initial node n.

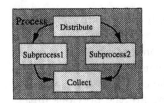

$$X_4 = \overline{ack_2}.\overline{ack_3}.collect_4.0$$
$$X_2 = subprocess1_2.(ack_2.0|X_4)$$
$$X_3 = subprocess2_3.(ack_3.0|X_4)$$
$$X_1 = (distribute_1.(X_2|X_3))\backslash\{ack_2, ack_3\}$$

Figure 6. PIF process-activity and translation to CCS including activity synchronisation.

Global variable: *Ack*, the set of actions to be acknowledged.

Initialisation:

- unmark all nodes

- $Ack := \{\}$

- call $PIF2CCS(n, true)$

Main body: $PIF2CCS(n, top)$ prints out CCS expressions. The parameter n denotes the current node and the boolean variable *top* indicates whether we are processing the topmost CCS expression where acknowledgements are forced to synchronise. The global variable *Ack* is used to accumulate the acknowledgements.

- **if** not marked(n) **then do**

    - mark n
    - $CCS := \underline{agent\ X_n\equiv}$
    - **if** $|pred(n)\backslash decisions| > 1$ **then**
        - $Ack := Ack \cup (pred(n)\backslash decisions)$
        - **for** all $n \in pred(n)\backslash decisions$ **do** $CCS := CCS + \overline{ack}_m.$
    - $CCS := CCS + n + .$
        - **if** $succ(n) = \emptyset$ **then** $CCS := CCS + \underline{0}$
        - **else for** all $m \in succ(n)$ **do**
            - $PIF2CCS(m, false)$
            - **if** $n \in decisions$ **and** m not last in $succ(n)$
              then $CCS := CCS + \underline{+}$
              else $CCS := CCS + \overline{|}$
            - **if** $|pred(m)\backslash decisions| > 1$
              then $CCS := CCS + \underline{(ack_n.0|X_m)}$
              else $CCS := CCS + \underline{X_m}$

- if *top* then $CCS := CCS + \backslash Ack$
- write(CCS)

Experiments For the example introduced in section 2, the algorithm described in section 5 generates the CCS expressions in Figure 5, and the ones shown in the rest of this section. Actions are indexed with an ID to identify actions with the same activity name.

Consider the sub-process in example 5.1. The algorithm translates it into the CCS expressions in Figure 5 which include two acknowledgements to ensure that collection is not carried out until both sub-processing activities have terminated. Using the concurrency workbench [1, 9] we want to verify some properties of this process. First of all, we would like to know whether items are *always finally* collected. The workbench provides the operator AF to check such a safety property (For a formal definition of AF as a fix-point see [3]). If we type $checkprop(X_1, AF(\langle collect_4 \rangle T))$ (note X_1 is defined in Figure 5, T stands for true) at the workbench's command prompt to see whether action $collect_4$ is *always finally* encountered, the workbench comes up with a positive answer. Next we check whether collection is carried out after the sub-processing. In terms of the AF operator, we want to know whether there is *always finally* a $subprocess1_2$ and then *always finally* $collect_4$. As we expected the command $checkprop(X_1, AF(\langle subprocess1_2 \rangle AF(\langle collect_4 \rangle T)))$ returns *true*.

Having considered the detailed WPC process (which contains an example of synchronisation) let us turn to the process described in section 2. The algorithm produces the expressions below:

$$
\begin{aligned}
\text{agent } X_{13} &= dispatch_{13}.0; \\
\text{agent } X_{17} &= fixed_{17}.X_{13}; \\
\text{agent } X_{14} &= major\_Adjustment?_{14}.(X_7 + X_{17}); \\
\text{agent } X_{10} &= everything\_Okay?_{10}.(X_{13} + X_{14}); \\
\text{agent } X_7 &= process1_7.X_{10}; \\
\text{agent } X_4 &= manageable?_4.(X_3 + X_7); \\
\text{agent } X_{15} &= major\_Adjustment?_{15}.(X_8 + X_{17}); \\
\text{agent } X_{11} &= everything\_Okay?_{11}.(X_{13} + X_{15}); \\
\text{agent } X_8 &= process2_8.X_{11}; \\
\text{agent } X_5 &= manageable?_5.(X_3 + X_8); \\
\text{agent } X_{16} &= major\_Adjustment?_{16}.(X_9 + X_{17}); \\
\text{agent } X_{12} &= everything\_Okay?_{12}.(X_{13} + X_{16}); \\
\text{agent } X_9 &= process3_9.X_{12}; \\
\text{agent } X_6 &= manageable?_6.(X_3 + X_9); \\
\text{agent } X_3 &= distribution_3.(X_4|X_5|X_6); \\
\text{agent } X_2 &= classification_2.X_3; \\
\text{agent } X_1 &= reception_1.(X_2)\backslash\{\};
\end{aligned}
$$

Here we are interested in the fix and dispatch activities. To find out whether items are *always finally* fixed, $checkprop(X_1, AF(\langle fixed_{17} \rangle T))$ comes up with *false*. If this safety property is not satisfied we want to ensure at least that the liveness property that there *exists finally* a fixed action, i.e. items are not always but sometimes fixed. Similar to the *AF* operator, there is an *EF* operator to check liveness properties. This time the workbench comes up with the positive result *true* upon typing *checkprop*$(X_1, EF(\langle fixed_{17}\rangle T)$. Thus, it is possible to reach the $fixed_{17}$ action, though it does not happen necessarily, which is exactly what we expect to happen.

For dispatching work items the situation is different. We want to make sure that items are *always finally* dispatched, however *checkprop*$(X_1, AF$ $(\langle dispatch_{13}\rangle T)$ does not lead to an immediate result. In fact, the workbench does not terminate. The reason is that the definitions of X_1 to X_{17} have an infinite transition system as semantics: If work is distributed (X_3) three processes (X_4, X_5, X_6) are invoked. First, they decide whether the work is manageable or not. If not the work is returned to distribution (X_3) which then distributes the item again invoking three fresh processes (X_4, X_5, X_6). Therefore jobs that are not manageable in principle lead to an infinite number of idling instances of units X_4, X_5, X_6 and thus a non-terminating concurrency workbench. Hence the process contains a livelock, i.e. the business process is internally busy forever, without any observable result from the outside. Unfortunately, this livelock is only indirectly verifiable. If we remove the possibility of an item being returned for re-distribution (i.e. we remove X_3 in definitions of X_4, X_5, X_6) then it turns out that our initial question is answered positively and jobs are always eventually dispatched.

Finally, we check a last property: freedom from deadlocks. There are two ways to check for deadlocks: First, by means of observational equivalence. The state of the process where the deadlock occurs is observationally equivalent to the empty process 0; second, by means of the operator *AG* checking that a formula is satisfied *always generally*, i.e. for every state of the transition system. Then deadlock-free states satisfy $AG(\langle *\rangle T)$ where $*$ is a wildcard. As it turns out the workbench detects a deadlock (which is however the last node where work items are dispatched) and therefore the whole process is fine and runs smoothly to the end.

6   CONCLUSIONS

As pointed out by Weikum et al. [13], formal verification of workflows is an important issue that needs to be investigated to complement existing validation techniques such as animation and simulation. Work has already been carried out to investigate state charts [14, 13] and petri nets [11, 12] for this purpose. We adopted a third formal verification framework: the process algebra CCS. The main contribution of this paper is the link between the verification tool and process definitions expressed in the process interchange format (PIF) [7]. We developed an algorithm that maps the necessary concepts from PIF to CCS and thus facilitates verification. A major issue is the synchronisation of activities. To represent an AND-join (i.e. that two or more concurrent, preceding, activities have to finish before the current one is carried out) we introduced acknowledgements, which are exchanged between the activities. To this extent petri nets [11] are more elegant since the synchronisation is automatically achieved by the use of tokens.

Our approach allows us to verify liveness and safety properties [6] such as, for example, ensuring that jobs are possibly fixed and necessarily dispatched. Furthermore, we showed how to check for deadlocks and livelocks. An advantage of CCS - also enjoyed by state charts [14] - is the ability to nest expressions, which allows one to represent a composition of several PIF Activities as a single activity. For example, the front end process in section 5 is defined by X_1, X_2, X_3 and the three work processing units by $\{X_4, X_7, X_{10}, X_{14}\}$, $\{X_5, X_8, X_{11}, X_{15}\}$, and $\{X_6, X_9, X_{12}, X_{16}\}$, respectively. This flexible hierarchy is a major advantage for complex verification tasks. We can verify a composite process on a detailed level as a white box, and then use a black box representation of it for subsequent verification in the context of other processes. This reduces the complexity of the verification task since process details are considered only locally, and are hidden in the context of other processes and activities. This compositional property is very important and van der Aalst [11] addresses it by providing translation rules between petri-nets which define an operational notion of equivalence. Compositionality is one of the major concerns in CCS and it provides (along with its notion of observational equivalence) a congruence allowing equivalent processes to be replaced by one another, independent of the context. Thus congruence in CCS is more expressive than in van der Aalst's notion. Another advantage of CCS - again, also enjoyed by state charts [14] - is that it permits multiple entry points for sub-automata.

In summary, the main contribution of this paper is an algorithm for the translation of business processes from the process interchange format PIF to CCS. Properties of the translated process can then be verified using CCS and the concurrency workbench. The approach was evaluated using a scenario based on a Correspondence Handling Centre.

ACKNOWLEDGEMENTS

The paper was written while I worked at BT Labs, Ipswich, UK. My special thanks go to Zhan Cui and John Shepherdson, whose comments substantially improved this paper.

References

[1] R. Cleaveland, J. Parrow, and B. Steffen. *The concurrency workbench: A semantics based tool for the verification of concurrent systems.* In Proc. of the WS on Automated Verification Methods for Finite-state systems, LNCS 407. Springer-Verlag, 1989. The workbench is available at http://www.dcs.ed.ac.uk/packages/cwb/.

[2] Z. Cui, B. Odgers, and M. Schroeder. *Distributed system visualisation and monitoring using software agents.* BT Labs, Ipswich, UK, 1998. Filed Patent.

[3] E. A. Emerson. *Temporal and modal logic.* In Handbook of Theoretical Computer Science, volume B, chapter 16. Elsevier, 1990.

[4] D. Judge, B. Odgers, J. Sheperdson, and Z. Cui. *Agent enhanced workflow.* BT Technology Journal, 16(3), 1998.

[5] M. U. Kamath and K. Ramamritham. *Corretness issues in workflow management.* Distributed Systems Engineering Journal, 3(4), 1996.

[6] L. Lamport. *Proving the correctness of multiprocess programs.* IEEE Transactions on Software Engineering, 3(2), 1977.

[7] J. Lee et al. *The PIF process interchange and framework version 1.1.* Technical report 194, MIT Center for Coordination Science, 1996. http://soa.cba.hawaii.edu/pif/.

[8] R. Milner. *Communication and Concurrency.* Prentice Hall, 1989.

[9] B. Steffen, R. Cleaveland, and J. Parrow. *The concurrency workbench.* ACM Transactions on Programming Languages and Systems, TOPLAS, 15(1):36–72, 1993.

[10] A. H. M. ter Hofstede, M.E. Orlowska, and J. Rajapakse. *Verification problems in conceptual workflow specifications.* In Proc. of the Intl. Conf. on Conceptual Modeling, pages 73–88. Springer-Verlag, 1996.

[11] W.M.P. van der Aalst. *Verification of workflow nets.* In Application and Theory of Petri Nets, pages 407–426. LNCS 1248, Springer-Verlag, 1997.

[12] W.M.P. van der Aalst. *The application of petri nets to workflow management.* Journal of Circuits, Systems and Computers, 1998.

[13] G. Weikum, et al. *Spezifikation, Verifikation und verteilte Ausführung von workflows in MENTOR.* In Informatik Forschung und Entwicklung. Springer-Verlag, 1997.

[14] D. Wodtke and G. Weikum. *A formal foundation for distributed workflow execution based on state chars.* In Proc. of the Intl. Conf. on Database Theory, 1997.

User Participation-Based Software Certification

Jeffrey Voas

Reliable Systems Technology Corporation, Sterling, Virginia 20166, USA
jmvoas@rstcorp.com

Abstract: Except for a couple of rigorous software certification schemes that are required for certain safety-critical software applications (e.g., RTCA DO178-B), there are no generally trusted software certification schemes. While there is no theoretical reason why these safety-critical standards could not be applied to all applications, there is a practical reason: cost. Estimates vary, but it is generally accepted that a line of safety-critical software costs between $500-$5,000 to design, write, test, and certify. Such levels of rigor and quality are excessive for most non-safety–critical applications.

Nonetheless, a ubiquitously accepted process which provides guarantees about software quality is still needed. These guarantees must be product-based and trustworthy. This paper presents a certification process we believe satisfies this need. Our process collects appropriate data that can then be used to stamp limited warranties onto commercial software.

Keywords: Certification, software warranties, residual testing, software users, software publishers

1   INTRODUCTION

Today, the number of approaches and standards for certifying software quality is increasing. These approaches either validate the integrity of the software product, development processes, or personnel [7].

The most popular approaches are process-based (e.g., ISO9000 and SEI-CMM). Here, software publishers usually take oaths concerning which development standards and processes were used. Also, auditors may be employed to "spot check" a publisher's project documentation and oaths [7]. Even if a certification auditor can verify that the software publisher was truthful, that alone does not guarantee high quality software. An analogy here is that dirty water can run from clean pipes [5].

We propose a certification methodology that does not employ auditors and publisher oaths. We believe that completely *independent* product certification is the only approach that consumers should trust. And demands for access to *independent* agencies that can play this role are being heard from both publishers and end-users.

Publishers prefer independent agencies since they then are not responsible for warranting their own software. By hiring a third party to grant software *certificates* (or *warranties*), publishers shift this responsibility onto someone else (much like when a doctor orders a second opinion or another test). End-users also benefit from independent agencies that offer unbiased assessments. Therefore the business case for creating independent agencies to certify software quality is strong.

We will refer to agencies that perform third-party, independent software certification as Software Certification Laboratories (SCLs). The beauty of having independent SCLs is that they provide a fair "playing field" for each publisher (assuming that each product under review receives equal treatment). A key reason, however, that SCLs have not become widespread can be attributed to the liability of being a certifier. When certified software fails in the field, the certifier bears some level of liability.

Why? Because SCLs represent themselves as experts. Courts in the United States are notorious for holding persons and organizations that represent themselves as professionals to unusually high standards. For example, suppose a surgeon, who never erred after 999 operations, makes a serious, *negligent* mistake during the 1,000th operation. The surgeon has a failure rate of 0.001. Even though the surgeon is highly skilled, very reliable, and has helped 999 patients, the surgeon could still be sued into bankruptcy because of one case of negligence.

SCLs bear a similar *liability* with similar consequences for mis-certification [6]. In order to reduce an SCL's liability, accurate methods for making certification decisions must be employed. Unfortunately, even the best static analysis techniques and testing techniques often fail to consider the actual stresses that software will experience when in the hands of users. Thus SCLs suffer from the problem of accurately determining how well-behaved a software system will be in the future. And that is the key piece of information we need from certifiers.

The certification process we will propose greatly reduces this liability quagmire while also eliminating the need to dispatch human auditors. Our process harnesses the testing resources of end-users. It is similar to the way in approach that made Linux the most popular and reliable of all Unixes [2, 4].

2   OUR SOFTWARE WARRANTY MODEL

Our interest is in certifying software applications and components with dual-use potential. We are interested in certifying applications such as Microsoft Word. And in fact, we are more interested in smaller components that could be embedded in a variety of applications. Our goal is to provide a certification process that fosters greater software reuse throughout different classes of applications.

Component-based software engineering (CBSE) is simply building software systems from software parts. By building from software parts, reuse is increased. This has the potential to substantially decrease the cost of development and decrease time-to-market.

But the virtues of CBSE have been touted for years. And there is *little* evidence that we are close to CBSE becoming the de facto standard for how software systems are built. Why is this when glue technologies (e.g., CORBA, ActiveX, COM, DCOM) for component interoperability and reusable component libraries already exist?

In our opinion, CBSE has not become ubiquitous because of: (1) widespread distrust of software components, and (2) a lack of knowledge about how to design-for-reuse. Any two components can be glued together rapidly, but that is not sufficient for popularizing CBSE. Integrators must have confidence that the right components were glued, they were glued together correctly, and the components are dependable. (Also, integrators must be able to find the components that they need, but we will assume that component visibility will eventually become a solved problem with the World-Wide Web.)

And as already mentioned, trust in a component's dependability must come from someone other than the software publisher. We have already listed two reasons for this: the liability associated with making claims concerning quality, and end-user distrust of publishers. Two additional reasons for not allowing the software publisher to be the person to assess the goodness of their products are: (1) software publishers are unlikely to have adequate resources to test to the levels that would justify software warranties, and (2) publishers are likely to make incorrect assumptions about how users will use the software.

Interestingly enough, SCLs that might hope to employ in-house testing as a means to certify software will suffer the same problems just mentioned: inadequate levels of testing and incorrect assumptions. In fact, the degree of testing that can be performed in a cost-effective manner at a SCL may be less than that already done in-house by the software publisher. Thus the idea then that SCLs can do in-house testing as a means for granting warranties is dubious.

In our opinion, software warranties must be the end-result of massive amounts of operational testing. Such testing will have demonstrated product stability in fixed environments and fixed marketplace sectors (embedded, desktop, Web-based, etc.). Without this, these limited warranties will either be too restrictive or unbelievable.

If SCLs and publishers cannot perform adequate product testing, who can? Our answer is the disorganized body of software testers known as the users. They can be unified to overcome this problem and do so in a way that is advantageous to them. The issue then is how to best tap into them in a manner that makes software warranties into a reality.

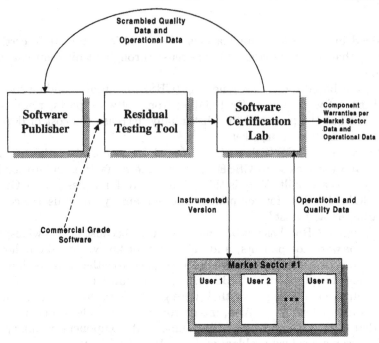

Figure 1. Basic Certification Process

We propose user-based product certification as a means for granting software warranties. Our approach collects valuable field data in a non-intrusive manner from the user's environment with their permission. Currently such data is rarely collected.

Our approach will exploit testing technologies similar to the *residual testing technologies* discussed by Pavlopoulou [3]. Residual testing is post-release testing that tests fielded software as it operates. Residual testing employs instrumentation that is embedded in operational software to collect information about how the software behaves. This information can reveal what software code is executed, whether assertions fail, and whether the software itself fails (e.g., if a limited regression testing capability is bundled with this instrumented version). We will also collect information on how the product is used. We can measure the frequency with which certain features are called, simply collect files of inputs (that later can be used to build operational profiles), etc. These sets of information will serve as the basis for issuing *limited* software warranties.

Our certification process is shown in Figure 2. Here, a software publisher subjects their finished product (i.e., the post-β version) to a residual testing tool which creates a fixed number of identical, instrumented copies (non-identical copies could also be built but that will make the tasks of the SCL more complicated). The copies are then supplied to the SCL. The SCL provides the instrumented versions to pre-qualified users from different marketplace sectors. Pre-qualified users will be those who will use the product in a manner consistent with how the SCL wants the product used. (Microsoft's beta-user program is an excellent example of how to screen possible users to those who will actually provide the greatest amount of information.) Periodically, the SCL gathers the information from the user sites.

All user information is merged and statistics are computed by the SCL. The SCL provides: (1) statistical data back to publishers concerning how their product was used, and (2) data telling publishers how their products behaved in the field (i.e., product quality). Statistics must be generated such that a backwards trace to any specific user is impossible. This is of paramount interest. (We will later look at why previous attempts by publishers to force users to reveal similar information were unsuccessful and how our model avoids those pitfalls.)

Recall that the goal of this process is for an SCL to confidently determine whether a product should be warrantied and what it should be warrantied for. That is, which platforms, which market sectors, and which environments? This is why we refer to our warranty as "limited." As an SCL gathers additional data over time, the SCL may be in a position to broaden a warranty, i.e., make it into a fuller, less restrictive warranty.

The motivation for our approach to software warranties stems from a client request some years back. They wished to employ the AIX operating system in a highly safety-critical environment. The client needed to know how reliable different AIX operating system and library calls were. The client could not find the information (nor did IBM know) even though thousands of AIX users worldwide had generated enough anecdotal evidence that when taken together, almost certainly would have answered our client's question. But because that information was lost, the client had to spend substantial resources re-testing each operating system and library call. And worse, it is possible that other organizations are redoing what our client did. This is clearly wasteful.

Note that we are not suggesting that you seek volunteers to fly uncertified software-controlled aircraft or use uncertified software-controlled medical devices in order to see if the software in them should be certified. Instead, what should occur is for the software to be first certified for non-critical market sectors. Then, if a supplier of a safety-critical product were to discover that this certified software utility was certified for an environment that mirrors the safety-critical product's environment, then the supplier has the option to employ it. (Thus all we have said here is that the operational profiles are equivalent between the non-critical and safety-critical environments.) If the software behaves well in this and other safety-critical applications, and if enough if this evidence can be collected demonstrating confidence in the software utility, then evidence will exist that warrants certifying the utility for the safety-critical market sector. Clearly much caution must be taken here, but recall that we are dealing with post-β software to begin with. We are never dealing with untested software, even when a piece of software is first embedded into a safety-critical environment.

3 KEY CHARACTERISTICS OF OUR MODEL

We have described our model. For our model to be acceptable to users, SCLs, and publishers, we deliberately built in the following characteristics:

1. Certification is performed on a stable, non-β version of the product.

2. Certification is not done by the software publisher. The publisher delivers a fixed number of versions of a product to the SCL. These versions have residual testing capabilities built-in. The SCL licenses the versions to pre-qualified users from various application domains (e.g., safety-critical, desktop, Web, etc.).

3. The testing methods and type of usage information collected must be determined by the SCL. This information should also be made available to users.

4. Certification decisions are based on significant operational experience created by the user base. This approach employs orders of magnitude more testing than the publisher or SCL could perform. Also, certification decisions are based on real operational scenarios as opposed to hypothesized scenarios. Hypothesized scenarios are usually the best that a SCL and publisher can base pre-release testing on. That will rarely be good enough, for example, to convince an actuary in an insurance company to insure a software product. Because our approach employs field data, the data an SCL will collect could be used by insurers that hope to insure software-based systems. Also, insurers may feel confident enough to indemnify an SCL against mis-certification since each warranty is based on historical data.

5. User data is collected by background processes that minimally interfere with users. Users expend no resources to trap and collect the information (other than the computer resources necessary to gather and store the information). Although users are not required to perform manual tasks to collect the information, their versions will have performance degradation due to the background processing cycles required to perform the post-deployment testing. Users that participate in this accelerated testing program will be compensated with reduced rate or free software.

6. All testing data collected from users is delivered exclusively to the SCL. The raw information does not go to the publisher. SCLs agree to legal confidentiality between themselves and users. Once the raw information

is scrubbed and user identities are not traceable from the composite information, the composite information is passed back to publishers. This allows them the opportunity to improve quality on future upgrades and focus in-house testing toward their user base.

7. A software warranty is limited to different market sectors (safety-critical, desktop, e-commerce) and different environments (Unix, Windows-NT, Macintosh). When enough data is collected from the field affirming that a component is working properly in a particular market sector, the SCL will provide software warranties specific to that market sector. For example, a SCL warranty might read as: software product X is warrantied to perform with a reliability of 99.9 in the Windows-NT desktop environment.

8. Users *consent* to participate. Users that do not wish to participate in this process do not have to. They are free to license non-β versions that do not undergo residual testing.

9. Publishers compensate SCLs for their services. The SCL will also own the collected data. This data has economic value. The laboratory will reserve the right to sell the data (possibly in a format like that found in *Consumer Reports* magazine). Recall our AIX story where a client had to re-test the software to get the data it needed on AIX's dependability, and other organizations will have to do the same. Why not create the information once and then sell it? Also, it is plausible that a non-profit company or government agency serve as an SCL.

10. No auditors are needed. Most existing certification models require that trained auditors visit publisher sites and sift through requirements documents, test plans, etc. Our scheme avoids the pitfalls associated with human auditor error.

11. Unlike ISO-9000 and CMM, our product-based certification allows innovative processes to emerge. If a developer organization can produce certifiably good products that conform to an in-house standard, then they have developed new processes that other development organizations should consider. After all, ISO and CMM may lock us into old process ideas prematurely.

12. And finally, this process forces publishers to define what is correct behavior for their software. This alone could result in higher quality software products.

Clearly there are benefits to our approach. But those benefits cannot be realized until we know precisely what data is sufficient to justify issuing software warranties. We envision it including reliability assessments, data from assertions, monitoring exception calls, data on operational usage, and code coverage analysis. But ultimately it depends on how strong of a warranty is sought.

Other analyses are possible, but these seem to be the more important indicators of whether a component has been exercised thoroughly enough to warranty it for specific environments and market sectors. This is a topic for future research. Our immediate plans are to work with technology insurers to select the residual testing technologies that provide data sufficient for offering software insurance premiums and software warranties.

4   RELATED APPROACHES

While our model for combining SCLs with residual testing technologies is unique, it admittedly leverages existing and previous ideas from other organizations. Here, we will compare our model with these other ideas.

Our first example is from a product called PureVision that was released in 1995. PureVision was offered by Pure Software. The product performed crude residual testing functions. It worked in a manner similar to how we have defined residual testing: a publisher produced copies of a product that were able to monitor themselves at user sites [1]. The copies sent back a report *to the publisher* concerning: (1) which user and user site were using the product, (2) the version number, (3) system configuration, (4) when the version started executing and stopped, (5) which program features were used, and (6) the amount of memory used at exit. If the product failed, exit codes and a stack dump were added to the report. Pure knew that users would be wary of publishers looking over their shoulders and thus included an option whereby a user could inspect a report before it was sent back. An option to not send a report back was also available. According to former Pure employees, speculation for why PureVision did not survive is that users were unwilling to provide such detailed, non-technical information (e.g., which user was using it, at what times, on which host, etc.). In contrast, the information we will collect is more technical; our information spies on the software and its correct behavior as opposed to spying on the user.

Our second example is similar to PureVision. Netscape 4.5 contains an option called The Netscape Quality Feedback Agent. The agent sends feedback to Netscape's developers concerning how the product is performing. The agent is enabled by default and is activated when Communicator encounters some type of run-time problem. When the agent is activated, it collects relevant technical data and displays a form in which a user can type comments. Netscape uses this data to debug known problems and identify new ones. Unfortunately, however, most users do not activate this feature for similar reasons to those for why PureVision did not survive.

Our next example is taken from the Software Testing Assurance Corporation (STAC) which was a for-profit venture started in 1997. STAC attempted to be the sole certifier for Year 2000 insurance on behalf of insurers. STAC's certification procedure was based on a public-domain testing standard (for Year 2000 remediated code) and STAC-approved auditors who were to make site visits to companies seeking Year 2000 software insurance. In the end, however, these insurance policies were never offered because insurers felt that the assessment approach for whether the software had been remediated correctly was too risky.

Microsoft has long employed beta-testing as a way to collect information on how their products perform in the hands of users. And for this information Microsoft compensates users. Pre-qualified users are given advanced copies of a product at reduced rates in exchange for feedback concerning product stability, usability, and reliability. Microsoft uses this information to decide when a product is ready for general release. This demonstrates user willingness to participate in exchange for discounted software.

And finally, consider Linux, a Unix operating system project that began in 1991 and today has nearly 8 million users. Linux is the product of hundreds of users, all of whom donated their time to write the system. Their efforts paid off: Linux is considered to be the most reliable of all Unix operating systems [4]. In fact, the success of Linux is often used as the argument for why products with open source are the only products that are trustworthy.

So what can we surmise from these anecdotes? From Microsoft and Linux, we see that users are willing to participate in efforts that result in improved software. From PureVision and Netscape, we see that publishers have a serious desire to attain field information. And from STAC, we see interest from industry in forming for-profit software certification corporations.

What still remains to be seen, however, is whether users will trust an SCL to act as an intermediary between themselves and a software publisher. As long as the confidentiality agreements between: (1) the SCL and publisher, and (2) SCL and user are binding, we believe users will.

5   SUMMARY

Demands for SCL services translate into business opportunities for those that can overcome the liability risks. In fact, several SCLs are already in existence today. For example, KeyLabs certifies language purity for Java but makes no promise about software quality. Because language purity is trivial to test for, the liability for KeyLabs is low.

Our approach dissolves the distrust associated with schemes that use auditors or measure process maturity. We capture user information that is traditionally discarded: (1) is the software behaving correctly?, and (2) how is the field using the product? Our approach does not invade user privacy; users agree to license instrumented versions from intermediaries who sit between them and the publishers.

Our approach has the potential to decrease the cost of software development by fostering CBSE. If software applications can be warranted under certain environments, then users with equivalent environments no longer need to guess at how a commercial product will behave. Nor do they need to invest heavily in re-testing the application.

And finally, the time it takes to get a limited software warranty can be reduced by offering more instrumented versions or only releasing instrumented versions to persons that are committed to seriously stressing a product. This will reduce the time until all users can enjoy un-instrumented, warrantied software.

ACKNOWLEDGMENTS

This work has been funded by Reliable Software Technologies in Sterling, VA, USA (http://www.rstcorp.com).

References

[1] Bingley, L. (1995). *PureVision: Shedding Light on Black Art Betas.* APT Data Services, Inc, New York, June, p17.

[2] Miller, B. P. et. al (1995). *Fuzz revisted: A re-examination of the reliability of* UNIX *utilities and services.* Technical report, University of Wisconsin, Computer Sciences Dept, November.

[3] Pavlopoulou, C. (1997). *Residual Coverage Monitoring of Java Programs.* Master's Thesis, Purdue University, August.

[4] Miller, B.P., Fredrikson, L., and So, B. (1990). *An empirical study of the reliability of* UNIX *utilities.* Communications of the ACM, 33(12), pp32–44.

[5] Voas, J. (1997). *Can Clean Pipes Produce Dirty Water?.* IEEE Software, 14(4), pp93–95.

[6] Voas, J. (1998). *Software Certification Laboratories: To Be or Not to Be Liable?* Crosstalk, 11(4), pp21–23.

[7] Voas, J. (1998). *The Software Quality Certification Triangle.* Crosstalk, 11(11), pp12–14.

Verification and Validation in Support for Software Certification Methods

Anca Vermesan, Per Martinsen, Jarle Sjøvaag and Keith Bell
Det Norske Veritas AS, Norway

Key words:

Abstract: Companies are introducing more and more intricate software into systems. In complex systems, regulatory or other considerations (such as potential financial losses) may require the software components to undergo a certain level of certification corresponding to its application and criticality. This paper presents an approach to certifying software contained within systems where its functionality is considered critical within the environment in which it is placed. Those software components implemented using the knowledge-base (KB) technology are highlighted and the role of verification and validation (V&V) in certification of KB components is emphasized. Within a certification model, two particular elements are presented in detail. Firstly, a categorization scheme based on V&V classes is described which has the potential for ensuring reproducibility of the results from software certification by different bodies. Secondly, a certification profile for a software component is described which aims to ensure repeatability of the results of software certification carried out by the same body. The approach presented here is based on the findings of the SafeKBS[1] European project.

[1] This project has been partially funded by the ESPRIT Programme of the Commission of the European Communities as project number 22360. The partners in the Safe-KBS project are Sextant-Avionique (F), Det Norske Veritas (N), Enel-Sri (I), Tecnatom (ESP), Computas Expert Systems (N), Uninfo (I), Qualience (F).

1. INTRODUCTION TO THE SOFTWARE CERTIFICATION CONTEXT

Certification is the process of issuing a certificate to indicate conformance with a standard, a set of guidelines or some similar document. Producers can choose to have their products certified because they believe that it will make the particular product more marketable. Producers may themselves declare that their product conforms to specified standards and issue a certificate accordingly; this is referred to as *self-certification*. In other cases, a particular buyer may require that products be submitted for certification by a specified body; this is referred to as *requested certification*.

In other cases, manufacturers of safety-critical systems may need certification of their products because this is a regulatory requirement. Many industries have a regulatory authority that oversees all projects. The industry's regulations may specify that the conformity of a product be demonstrated by an independent third party. In this case, certification is mandatory, including also the certification of the software components. This is referred to as third party certification. *Third party certification* is therefore when a body, independent of both the producer and the user, carries out the certification process [Vermesan et al.99].

Although all of these forms are important, major developments are in the realm of third party certification and it is this form of certification upon which this paper is focused. In such cases, software certification is not explicitly expressed, but results directly from the fact that the software is integrated into a wide range of products of various technologies, for which certification is requested.

In the maritime domain, for instance, Det Norske Veritas (DNV) has developed the DNV Rules for Classification of Ships, which together with other internationally recognized standards form the basis of DNV Conformity Certification Services. The Rules are aimed at ensuring safety against hazards to the ship, personnel, passengers and cargo, as well as hazards to the environment as a consequence of sea transport. The Rules define acceptance criteria for design, construction, survey and testing of ships, their machinery installation, systems and equipment, applicable to both the newbuilding and operational phases. DNV Rules for Classification of Ships [DNV Rules 97] require certification for all computer based systems which perform monitoring and control of functions, or when the installed systems may have an impact on the safe operation of the ship.

As in the maritime domain, there are many other application domains, where companies are introducing more and more intricate systems. Whether such systems are for monitoring and control or for safety protection, they are best realized with programmable systems. Some of the benefits offered by programmable technology are shown in *Figure 1*. It is often the new software features that distinguish these products in the marketplace.

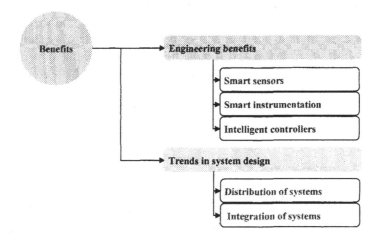

Figure 1. Benefits of the software technology

1.1   The KB technology

Software systems are proving themselves beneficial to monitoring and control systems by replacing human involvement:
- where speed and reliability of response is required over long periods of time,
- from tasks that the human finds repetitive and tedious, and
- from situations which place the human at high risk.

More and more often, knowledge-base (KB) technology is being applied to complex problem-solving and critical tasks in many application domains, implementing the software component of smart sensors and instrumentation, and intelligent controllers.

The need for assuring the quality of knowledge-based systems (KBS) is nowadays widely recognized among the research community and is steadily gaining acceptance by industry as a fundamental component of KBS development. This is due to the fact that new generations of KBS are beginning to appear. Previously, KBS were stand-alone applications built using special hardware with special software support and were mainly used to assist human operators by producing advice or recommendations. They act in a supervisory or advisory capacity to enhance an otherwise independent system. This was a common use of KBS, where their role in the larger system was in support of diagnostics (of a failure for instance) and predictions.

Today, KBS are more and more often found within another complex hardware/software system; they must interact with other hardware and software components, operate in a real-time environment and in some cases function without human intervention, especially in control systems that do not include the operator in the loop. The intelligent element performs an essential function within the system, and without which the system will not perform correctly. This use is however restricted to lower orders of machine intelligence, as the reliability and predictability of higher orders are difficult to assess. In such situations, KB components[2] are required to be highly dependable.

Research into the field of verification and validation (V&V) of KBS is intended to address issues associated with quality aspects of KBS and to ensure such applications have the same degree of dependability as conventional applications. V&V are terms that have been used for several years in knowledge engineering. Although V&V of KBS is still a maturing field, there are now many V&V techniques, methods and methodologies, plus considerable experience and expertise in using them [Coenen and Bench Capon 93],[Gamble and Shaft 96],[Vermesan and Bench-Capon 95]. Part of the knowledge and techniques developed are now ready to be transferred to industry for the implementation of software certification. Certification is probably the most advanced use of the V&V methods, techniques and knowledge that have been developed so far. As techniques for the evaluation of software systems develop in parallel with the systems themselves, certification bodies must constantly review the requirements that are required from software components in order to achieve safe and dependable systems.

1.2   Research initiatives - The European SafeKBS project

The practiced way to software certification has been to assess the development process of the software rather than the software itself. Software certification processes have become so intertwined with the development processes that true product certification, which should demonstrate that the software would behave appropriately, is almost never employed [Voas 98].

---

[2] In this paper we use the terms "knowledge-based systems" and "knowledge-based components" interchangeably. This is due to the fact that more and more often, the knowledge-based technology is used to implement not a whole system, but a component of a larger software system.

It is reasonable to assume that there is a relationship between the development methodologies and the quality of the final product. However, it is not always easy to clearly define the desired product quality attributes and their relationships to specific variables of the software development process. Where the KB component is employed in a system where its failure may be detrimental to the safety of the whole system, analyzing the development process of the software alone may not reveal hazards resulting from interactions of the component with its environment.

Although a lot of attention has been given to the software development process, software process improvement does not guarantee "fitness-for-purpose" of software products. Thus, the "process culture" of traditional software engineering may at last yield to the "product culture" in knowledge engineering. This is due to the fact that it is the functionality and other qualities of the knowledge base that identifies the "competence" of a KBS. Moreover, it is the correctness and validity criteria for the knowledge base that are more advanced and that may be translated to external requirements of the overall system [Vermesan 98b].

Therefore, other approaches have moved away from traditional practices. For instance in the US, in the approach described in [Voas 98], software certification becomes a software-centered activity as opposed to a development process-centered activity. The approach is independent of how the software was developed, although some evidence of the process is required. The aim is to separate the certification process from the development process. For safety critical software this is almost mandatory. Ideally, software certification schemes that are labeled to guarantee high assurance should be able to determine whether the software has the potential to exhibit undesirable behavior.

In Europe, some projects have taken place under the European Strategic Programme for Research and Development in Information Technology (ESPRIT). An example is the Safe-KBS project, which aims to demonstrate the feasibility of integrating software components incorporating knowledge-based technology into safety critical systems. It attempts to solve the issues governing safety and certification of such systems, with the appropriate links to software engineering, using real applications from maritime, avionics and nuclear domains.

The rest of this paper will describe the approach taken in the Safe-KBS project and how some of the results contribute to the development of software certification, emphasizing the role of V&V in support of certification methods. One of the main results of the project is a certification methodology, consisting of certification requirements and methods to demonstrate compliance with such requirements. The Safe-KBS

Certification Methodology is based on a model consisting of the following elements [SafeKBS 98]:

– **Certification methods** – they clearly identify the activities to be performed.
– **Certification components** – they are the elements on which the certification methods are applied.
– **Technological support** – is the element in-between, which implements the application of each certification method.

The model suggests an order in which the methods can be applied. Thus, a scenario for the certification process could be the following:

1. Assess the criticality of the software along the desired criticality dimension (safety in the case of SafeKBS)
2. Classify the software in order to define the rigorousness and completeness of the certification effort.
3. Identify those parts of the product to be evaluated and elements of the development process to be assessed.
4. Specify the product requirements useful to certification, i.e. build the certification profile of the software.
5. Select and apply the appropriate V&V techniques in order to arrive at a pass/fail decision.

Such a model can be the basis of a certification framework, methodology, or scheme as defined below:

– **Framework**: consists of certification methods and technological support for their application. The Safe-KBS project is mainly about developing the framework.
– **Methodology**: goes beyond a framework in the sense that it defines a philosophy (set of principles) behind the methods and imposes an order in which the certification methods are to be applied. The Safe-KBS approach suggests an order of the methods, but without being prescriptive.
– **Scheme**: goes beyond the methodology in the sense that it identifies the parties involved in the certification process and defines each party's role.

Whether we talk about the framework, methodology, or scheme, the methods themselves are an integral part of each of them. It is important, in order to obtain an objective and impartial scheme, that the certification methods are applicable and recognized by both the developers and users. Thus, the certification methods should be:

– **Repeatable**- repeated activities of the same product to the same certification requirements by the same authority should produce the same results.

– **Reproducible**- repeated activities of the same product to the same certification requirements by different authorities should produce the same results.

In this paper we focus on two such certification methods, i.e. classify the software component based on V&V classes and specify its certification profile. In order to satisfy repeatability, it is important to have well-defined certification requirements, while in order to ensure reproducibility it is important to have well specified V&V techniques to verify compliance with the requirements.

2. THE SAFE-KBS CERTIFICATION METHODS

This section approaches the two certification methods referred to in the previous section.

2.1 Categorization system

In its simplest form, the certification of a software product could consist of identifying those characteristics useful for certification, and then demonstrating their compliance with specific requirements. Based on a fail/pass decision, a certificate or letter of conformance may be granted, specifying explicitly the exact extent of the coverage performed, what attributes had been examined, etc. A more complex scheme, however, would characterize or classify the software before it is certified. Consequently, the type and amount of work to be done during the certification process would depend on how that product is to be classified.

– Categorization may be based on different factors, such as:
– Consequence of system failure
– Probability of system failure
– Levels of risks
– Criticality of system or operator response time
– Amount of autonomy of system or software
– Type of software application (active – directly controls hazardous functions vs. reactive- monitors and initiates fault recovery), real time, simulation, etc.

Although this approach highlights the difficulty of finding an appropriate categorization system, it is the most common approach for certification of systems operating in safety critical environments. For instance, the IEC61508 standard [IEC61508] suggests categorization based on safety integrity levels.

The Safe-KBS approach also proposes a categorization scheme along two critical dimensions: safety and complexity. The categorization scheme assigns combinations of various safety integrity levels and complexity into V&V Classes. This categorization scheme means that different software components in a complex system are to be assigned V&V classes.

2.1.1   The safety dimension

As we deal with safety critical systems, system safety integrity is a factor which needs to be considered in determining the extent of the estimated V&V required for the software. It is well known that software introduces specific difficulties along the safety dimension. In the Safe-KBS project, a categorization of the system has been proposed, compatible with the system integrity level of each application in the avionics, nuclear and maritime domains. Such a categorization allows the way the certification methodology develops to be tailored with respect to the criticality of the software. In the Safe-KBS project, safety integrity levels (SIL) were used to describe the criticality of the software module (from « light » requirements at level E to « strong » requirements at level A).

In the Safe-KBS project, the idea of SIL was seen to be an important factor in determining the rigorousness of V&V needed for a system in order to ensure its compliance with the relevant requirements and to focus attention on specific cases of the software where its correct functioning is of greatest importance.

2.1.2   The complexity dimension

From the point of view of V&V, the characteristics of a software system that define its complexity are of particular importance. These characteristics determine how hard the software will be to develop and analyze. Generally, the higher the complexity, the greater the opportunity for errors and the greater the need for V&V [Vermesan 97].

Many metrics have been developed, and the most common measures are size and complexity metrics. However, in the Safe-KBS approach, the complexity dimension does not stem from such software metrics. Of particular interest are problem domains whose complexity stems not so much from the size and structure, but from inherently difficult solutions such as those for fault tolerance, fault avoidance, parallel or distributed processes. The important aspect is what type of complexities the software technology introduces to the solutions of these problems. In other words, the complexity dimension here is connected with the complexity of the overall system.

A list of complexity factors for software systems has been suggested, and based on these factors, three complexity levels have been defined: low, medium and high. The average complexity level across the range of all existing conventional systems would probably be low to low-medium. However, new software is tending to move towards the higher-medium and even high complexity levels. This is particularly true when dealing, for instance, with knowledge-based technology. With the emerging software technologies, one can expect that more and more software systems will have higher and higher complexity characteristics.

2.1.3 The experiment and the V&V Classes

Utilizing the two dimension approach as presented above yields a 15-cell combination, i.e. a 5x3 table. The cell with the highest values for complexity and required safety integrity, should receive the most stringent application of V&V methods. The most extensive and thorough methods would be used for this situation. Similarly, the lowest complexity and required integrity cell, should receive only the minimum degree of V&V.

The Safe-KBS project required completing the categorization scheme for each of the three applications. An example from the maritime domain is given in *Table 1* (the example has been reduced to a 3x3 table):

Table 1. General bulk ship with engine with electronic cam shaft and highest Nautical Safety class notation.

Degree of required system safety	System complexity		
	LOW	**MEDIUM**	**HIGH**
SIL D	Main alarm system, auxiliary control system, power generation, etc.	Navigation system, main alarm system, auxiliary control system, power generation (if integrated), etc.	Automatic control of propulsion and steering
SIL B-C	Remote control of propulsion and steering	Propulsion	Not applicable
SIL A	Not applicable	Not applicable	Not applicable

The overall approach has been to provide a set of recommended V&V methods and techniques graded against safety/complexity classification scheme. The first dimension has been taken into account almost implicitly, since we deal with safety critical software. The second dimension, i.e. complexity, has also been included, since it is known that completeness of the V&V methods and techniques will depend upon the extent of the application complexity. It is important to mention that, for any given application, the safety dimension in the classification scheme will be domain-dependent, while the complexity dimension will always be application-dependent.

Based on the proposed classification tables and the experiment itself, three V&V classes have been defined. The meaning of the classes is as follows:

- V&V Class I receives the most stringent level of V&V
- V&V Class II receives a substantial degree of V&V
- V&V Class III receives the minimum degree of V&V

The concept of increasing stringency may imply several things such as greater thoroughness and completeness in testing coverage of the system, or greater effort to discover critical faults. The classification scheme can be summarized in a 3x3 table as given in *Figure 2* .

Degree of required system safety	System complexity		
	LOW	MEDIUM	HIGH
LOW	1 V&V Class III	2	3
MEDIUM	4	5	6
HIGH	7 V&V Class II	8	9 V&V Class I

Figure 2. The identification of V&V Classes.

It is important to mention that the grouping of SIL A-E into Low, Medium and High would be domain dependent. Also, the grouping of cell combinations into V&V classes should be seen as recommended and not prescriptive. The lower right cells, number 8 and 9, are the members of V&V Class I, the most stringent class; the upper left-most two cells, cells 1 and 2, constitute V&V Class III; and the remaining cells are in V&V Class II (cells 3-6). The meaning of the classes is as given above.

The reason that the classification has been defined as a certification method is that it usually should be an agreement between the developer and the certification authority on the following issues:

- The V&V methods and techniques employed by the developer
- The extent and completeness of the V&V performed by the developer
- The extent to which the certifier will be witnessing the developer's V&V

- The nature of fully independent V&V activities, performed by the certifier

The solution proposed by the Safe-KBS methodology is that:

- Having defined a classification system consisting of V&V classes and
- having identified the most appropriate V&V methods and techniques for each V&V class,

The remaining issue is that the developer and certifier agree to which V&V class the software to be developed belongs.

2.2 Safe-KBS Certification Profile

Requirements which apply to software whose failure could result in a risk or injury to persons or loss of property address the potential risk unique to equipment controlled by software. The software employed to perform critical functions will also need to comply with the basic construction and performance requirements contained in the applicable end-product or component/system standards.

Thus, according to the application, a lot can be said about a piece of software, as each application has an associated series of characteristics. However, not all of these characteristics are useful for certification. Therefore, it is important prior to development, to clearly define a quality profile for the software to be certified. When the certification requirements are domain specific, the meaning of the certificate is clear, it is "fitness for purpose" for the users in the specific application domain. Thus, the certification requirements focus mostly on the functional needs.

The Safe-KBS approach suggests the definition of a quality profile taking into consideration those properties that are useful for certification (see *Figure 3*), and differentiates between minimum and desirable properties in order to obtain a well defined quality profile. The following minimum requirements are defined as criteria for testing in the realm of certification:

- **Consistency**. This means the requirement specification or the implemented system is free of internal contradiction.
- **Accuracy**. This property refers to the requirement that the knowledge embodied into the system should reflect the domain.
- **Completeness**. The completeness of a system with respect to the requirement specification is a measure of the portion of specification implemented in the system.
- **Coverage**. This refers to the completeness of the problem space, thus concerns the relationship between the system and the application domain world.

- **Robustness.** The property refers to the requirement that the system gives an appropriate output to a problem which is outside the input domain.

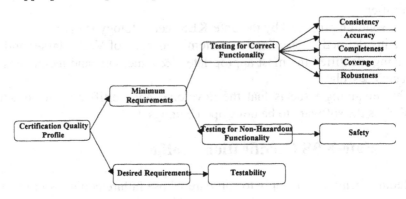

Figure 3. The SafeKBS Certification profile

It is important to observe that the minimum requirements relate to safety either directly or indirectly. The properties that are targeted at testing for correct functionality are indirectly related to safety, in the sense that their application will be dependent on the safety criticality. The safety property as a target for testing for non-hazardous functionality relates directly to the criticality along the safety dimension. As a desired requirement, testability has been specified, although the list may be extended.

3.   RESEARCH RESULTS

An important result of the project is the mapping between the two certification methods as described above, as shown in *Table 2*. Such a mapping gives indication and guidelines about what V&V techniques can be used for which V&V Class and to test which criteria as given by the certification profile.

Table 2. Dynamic Black-box testing techniques mapped against criteria and V&V classes

Technique/V&V Class and Test Criteria	III	II	I	TC1	TC2	TC3	TC4	TC5
Cause-effect testing	R	R	R	X	X	X		X
Equivalenece partitioning	R	HR	HR	X	X	X	X	
Boundary value testing	R	HR	HR	X	X	X		X
Specific functional testing	R	R	R	X	X	X		X
Stress testing	R	R	R	X	X	X		X
Random testing	R	R	R	X	X			

(R-Recommended, HR-Highly Recommended)
TC1-Consistency, TC2-Accuracy, TC3-Completeness, TC4-Coverage, TC5-Robustness)

The table gives the example of the dynamic black-box testing techniques. Similar mappings have been defined for larger groups of V&V methods and techniques. In this context, an experimental framework has been designed allowing conventional V&V techniques to be evaluated for application to KBS. The results of this work are reported in detail in another paper. This paper reports on the acceptability principles for KB components, derived from the Safe-KBS certification profile, as described earlier.

3.1 Acceptability principles for knowledge-based components

A key task in setting up a certification scheme is establishing pass/fail criteria based on the data obtained by certification methods. Correctness criteria have been considered for a long time the basis for verification and validation of KBS [Vermesan 98b]. In case of certification, the issue is whether the correctness view is still valid to be the basis of pass/fail decision, i.e. whether the system can be deployed in the application domain or not.

If the definition of correctness is applied, the system output is correct if it matches the output part of the test case exactly. However, the acknowledgement that safe software would not be achievable via the process assessment, caused correct outputs to be de-emphasized and "acceptable" outputs became the goal. Therefore, the pass/fail decision in certification should be based on acceptability principles rather than correctness principles. If the definition of acceptability is to be used, then domain-interpretation of what is "acceptable" needs to be defined. It will not be feasible to demonstrate that any KB component will always perform acceptably. Therefore, any certification scheme should impose realistic acceptability requirements, although in the case of KB software acceptability needs to be judged by experts from the domain in question.

Here we define the pass/fail decision as the process of determining the criteria underwhich the results of KBSs should be accepted, i.e. the KBS can be deployed in the application domain. Pass/fail criteria are especially important in domains where the consequences of faulty decisions are unacceptable. Thus, certifiers need a set of criteria to establish pass/fail; here referred to as pass/fail criteria. These criteria comprise both verification and validation. It is important to differentiate between issues of verification and validation. Verification shows that the resulting KBS meet a given specification - that one is building the system right. This definition has been extended to satisfy certain structural properties. Validation demonstrates that the system meets the user's requirements - that the right system was built. This demonstration goes beyond checking that the system reaches the correct conclusion. It is also important that the system addresses the right problem, i.e. the reasoning which leads to the correct answer is of importance.

The SafeKBS project has defined three acceptability principles:
- Non-redundancy
- Consistency
- Fitness for purpose

These are shown in *Figure 4*. The specification of the KBS is the core around which the system is developed further towards the final implementation represented by the space within the triangle. Everything outside the triangle then represents the problem space. Thus, the specification, originally abstract, is refined towards more concrete specifications. The refinement is guided by verification and validation. Verification is a matter of establishing that the refinement faithfully represents the specification, while validation checks that the right system is being specified and refined.

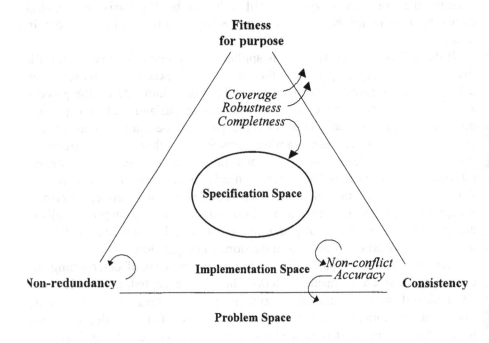

Figure 4. The three acceptability principles

Each principle is given one or several interpretations. Those interpretations represented by arrows oriented internally or towards the specification space are verification criteria, while those oriented towards the problem space are validation criteria. In the following, each principle is approached separately, and examples are given in the context of rule-based systems. A taxonomy of reasoning specific to rule-based and hybrid systems can be found in [Vermesan 98a].

3.1.1   Consistency principle

Two interpretations for the consistency principle are considered:
- **Non-conflicting knowledge**. Conflicts occur when more than one rule can fire, but with contradictory consequences.
- **Accuracy**. Refers to the requirement that the knowledge embodied in the KBS should correctly reflect the problem in the domain.

The second interpretation comes to support the requirement that the system must be assessed whether it is the correct system, rather than one that provides the correct answers. Thus, accuracy is a validation issue, while non-conflict is a verification issue.

In the context of rule-based systems, conflicting rules possess consequences that succeed, but introduce contradictory information. Therefore conflicting rules can yield an inconsistent state and should not be allowed in a KBS. A description of the verification criteria for the consistency principle is given in the Appendix.

3.1.2   Fitness for purpose

This principle is concerned with the performance of the KBS and the ability to generate useful answers. Three interpretations are considered:
- **Completeness**. This interpretation reflects the ability of the system to cover the specification space.
- **Coverage**. It is similar to completeness, but refers to the ability of the system to cover the problem space.
- **Robustness.** The property refers to the requirement that the system gives an appropriate output to a problem which is outside the input domain.

The first principle is not met when a system cannot achieve a goal state from a legal initial state. Conversely, a KB is complete if it consists of rules that can move the system from any legal set of initial states to a set of goal states. In the context of rule-based systems, two interpretations of completeness are considered:
- **Circularity**. A KB contains circularity if it is possible to enter an endless loop while following some chain of inference.

- **Missing rule**. This interpretation refers to deficiencies in the KB that may suggest that additional knowledge is needed in order to correct the deficiency.

A rule is considered missing if there is a range of possible data values for some attributes, but not sufficiently covered by the existing rules. This form of incompleteness can cause a reasoning process to stop before reaching a goal state. Coverage refers to the completeness of the problem space, thus concerns the relationship between the KBS and the application domain world. The primary concern is whether the KBS adequately covers the problem space. In order to meet these criteria, a clear understanding of the system intended purpose is paramount. A description of the verification criteria for the fitness for purpose principle is given in Appendix.

3.2   Certification of the knowledge base

The principles as defined by the SafeKBS certification methodology go beyond mathematical (logical) correctness. "Beyond" means that in addition to the verification aspects of these principles which form together the correctness criteria, the validation aspects are considered as well.

Based on the principles identified above, it seems that the certification of the knowledge base can be approached with the help of two techniques: syntax checking and semantic checking. *Syntax checking* is in fact anomaly detecting, and from the acceptability principles, deals with verification issues:
- non-redundancy criteria
- non-conflict criteria
- completeness criteria
  while the *semantic checking* deals with the validation issues
- the accuracy interpretation of consistency
- the coverage interpretation of fitness-for-purpose
- the robustness interpretation of fitness-for-purpose
  Within the SafeKBS certification framework we identify KB certification methods as those methods that are specific to KB technology. These refer mainly to the knowledge base which is the only component of a KBS which cannot be adequately certified using conventional methods.

It is important to mention that these criteria can be used by certification authorities when making pass/fail decisions. Depending on the nature of the system to be certified, these criteria may be relaxed. Nevertheless, as today certification is required especially in connection with safety critical systems, it is very much likely that these criteria should be met. In this respect, requirements tracing should be a mandatory procedure to investigate the completeness of the KB with respect to the safety requirements that were established at the beginning of the project. This is the technique used to check coverage, i.e. the completeness of the problem space.

4. SUMMARY AND DIRECTION OF FUTURE RESEARCH

In this paper, we have highlighted, from the perspective of a certification authority, some approaches and results from the SafeKBS project. To conclude, the main points of this paper are summarized below:
– V&V is one of the primary activities to be addressed by developers and certification specialists, and the rigorousness and completeness of V&V activities depend on the criticality and complexity of the software.
– Certification is probably the most advanced use of the V&V methods, techniques and knowledge that have been developed so far within software/knowledge engineering.
– Major developments are in the realm of third party certification, requiring not only objectivity, but also extensive expertise in the specific application domain. The need to have software certification schemes that are labeled to ensure fitness for purpose will hopefully move industry away from the "process culture" of software engineering towards a "product culture" in knowledge engineering.
– The pass/fail decision in certification should be based on acceptability principles rather than correctness principles. Domain-interpretation of what is "acceptable" needs to be defined.
– The V&V methods and techniques employed in the view of certification should ensure that the certification methods are repeatable and reproducible.
The continuing harmonization of technical regulations in Europe will require mature software certification technology. A common approach to testing and certification of software will secure mutual recognition arrangements, both inside Europe and between Europe and other countries, for test reports and certificates. Thus, accredited certification is, presently and in the years to come, an important service provided by third-party certification authorities.

Reproducibility is the major obstacle to accredited certification. The SafeKBS project has provided a set of well-specified V&V methods and techniques, leading to a basis for certification. Although these techniques are well-specified and many of them are currently used in software development, more experimentation is needed to demonstrate the feasibility of the certification methods as developed by the SafeKBS project. The Safe-

KBS approach was to use the best practices as reported today to arrive to a comprehensive set of useful certification methods. Future experimentation may reveal that additional certification methods are needed in order to develop a fully sufficient certification methodology.

The main contribution of this paper is its insight into the understanding of what the certification process should be when the software product is the target. It puts forward the approach and results of the SafeKBS certification methodology, emphasizing particularities when dealing with KB components. The V&V should support the certification process, the repeatability and reproducibility of its certification methods. In order to satisfy repeatability, it is important to have well-defined certification criteria, while in order to assure reproducibility it is important to have well-specified V&V methods and techniques to verify compliance with the requirements.

Finally, more work is needed to establish how the V&V methods as currently used in the development would be applied by an independent certification organization to arrive at a pass/fail decision. The existent V&V methods need to be better understood in order to answer the difficult questions of certification.

REFERENCES

Coenen, F. and Bench-Capon, T. (1993). *Maintenance of Knowledge-Based Systems*, Academic Press, London.

DNV-Rules (1997), Det Norske Veritas - *Rules for Classification of Ships*. Pt.4 Ch.5 Instrumentation and Automation.

Gamble, R.F. and Shaft, T.M. (1996). Eliminating concerns for redundancy, consistency and completeness. *International Journal of Software Engineering and Knowledge Engineering*, 6(4).

IEC 61508 -Functional Safety: Safety Related System, International Electrotechnical Commission.

Safe-KBS Certification Methodology. Task 5.3 Report. Esprit Programme Project No. 22360, 1998.

Vermesan, A.I. (1997). Quality Assessment of Knowledge-Based Software: Certification Considerations. In Proceedings of Third *IEEE International Software Engineering Standards Symposium* (ISESS '97) Walnut Creek, CA.

Vermesan, A.I. (1998) Foundation and Application of Expert System Verification and Validation, Chapter 5, pp.5.1-5.32, in *The Handbook of Applied Expert Systems*, CRC Press, 1998.

Vermesan, A.I. (1998). Software Certification for Industry – Verification and Validation Issues in Expert Systems. In Proceedings of the *Ninth IEEE International Workshop on Database and Expert Systems Applications* (DEXA'98), Vienna, Austria, August 1998.

Vermesan, A.I. and Bench-Capon, T. (1995) Techniques for the Verification and Validation of Knowledge-Based Systems: A Survey Based on the Symbol/Knowledge Level Distinction, *Software, Testing, Verification & Reliability*, John Wiley & Sons, Ltd, pp.233-271.

Vermesan, A.I., Sjøvaag, J. and Martinsen, P. (1999) Towards a certification scheme for computer software, *ISACC'99 International Software Assurance Certification Conference*, February 1999, Washington DC, USA.

Voas, J. (1998). A Recipe for Certifying High Assurance Software. Proceedings of *COMPSAC'98*, Vienna, Austria , August 1998.

APPENDIX

Non-Redundancy Principle		
Criteria	*Example*	*Description*
Duplication	$(r_1)\ l_1 \wedge l_2 \rightarrow m$ $(r2)\ l_2 \wedge l_1 \rightarrow m$	Either r_1 or r_2 is redundant.
Subsumption	$(r_1)\ l_1 \wedge l_2 \rightarrow m$ $(r_2)\ l_1 \rightarrow m$	r_1 is redundant.
Unusable consequence	$(r)\ ... \rightarrow m$	m is neither a goal nor there exist another rule in the system of the form $m \rightarrow ...$
Unfirable rule	$(r)\ l \rightarrow m$	The system has no way of establishing l, because l is not the output of any rule of the form $... \rightarrow l$ and l is not a system input either.
General redundancy	$(r_1)\ l \rightarrow m$ $(r_2)\ m \rightarrow n$ $(r_3)\ l \rightarrow n$	r_3 is redundant, since it can be inferred from the first two rules.

	Consistency Principle		
Interpret ation	*Criteria*	*Example*	*Description*
Non-conflict	*Direct conflict*	$(r_1)\ l_1 \wedge l_2 \rightarrow m$ $(r_2)\ l_1 \rightarrow \neg m$	Two or more rules fire with the same premises, but lead to conflicting information.
	Chained conflict	$(r_1)\ l \rightarrow m$ $(r_2)\ m \rightarrow n$ $(r_3)\ l \rightarrow \neg n$	It is similar to the direct conflict case in that the premises are identical, but it is through a series of deductions that the conflict states are reached.

	Fitness for purpose Principle		
Interpretation	*Criteria*	*Example*	*Description*
Completeness	*Circularity*	$(r_1)\ l \rightarrow m$ $(r_2)\ m \rightarrow n$ $(r_3)\ n \rightarrow l.$	a set of rules is circular if the chaining of those rules in the set forms a cycle
	Missing rules	$(r_1)\ ... \wedge l \wedge$ $... \rightarrow ...$ $(r_2)\ ... \rightarrow m$	Unused input: if l is declared to be input but there is no rule of the form (r_1). Unreachable goal: m is declared to be a goal, but there exist no rule of the form (r_2).

Validation, Verification and Integrity in Knowledge and Data Base Systems: Future Directions

Frans Coenen
Department of Computer Science, University of Liverpool, UK
frans@csc.liv.ac.uk

Barry Eaglestone
Department of Information Studies, University of Sheffield, UK
B.Eaglestone@shef.ac.uk

Mick Ridley
School of Computing and Mathematics, University of Bradford, UK
M.J.Ridley@scm.brad.ac.uk

Abstract: In this paper we consider possible future directions for rule base V&V on the presumption that many techniques developed by the rule base V&V community have come out of the "research domain" into what might be described as "the main stream". In particular we consider opportunities for possible "cross-overs" between database integrity checking techniques and a number of rule base V&V strands. Collectively we refer to these techniques as VVI (Validation Verification and Integrity) techniques. We commence by giving an overview of integrity issues, then go on to consider overlaps between database and rule base systems and finish with a discussion of "future directions" in VVI.

Keywords: VVI (Validation, Verification and Integrity)

1 INTRODUCTION

The database community has been concerned with the issue of data integrity almost since the conception of database systems. Codd's 1970 paper [10] includes a section on "Consistency" that covers this ground (and data integrity occurs in the article's key words and phrases) although it is perhaps not until Codd's 1979 paper [11] that integrity rules are explicitly formulated as *entity*

integrity and *referential integrity* in a way that will be familiar from Codd's 12
rules [12]. There is also now a considerable history of attempts to formalise
this area from Nicolas [31] onwards. Consequently work on data base integrity
issues considerably predates the work on rule base V&V.

It can be argued that the traditional view of rule base system V&V was established in the late 1980s/early 1990s and focussed on the static and dynamic
inspection of rule bases to identify anomalies and symptoms of errors. Examples of this work include: Preece and Shinghal's COVER tool which checked
KBSs written in a generic rule language ([33]), Suwas's rule checking program
developed as part of the Work on MYCIN ([37]), Cragen and Steudel's ECS decision table based KBS V&V program ([14]), and Ginsberg's KB-reducer ([20])
(there are many others). Although software verification and validation has always been perceived as being unglamorous, this initial work was prompted by
a clear requirement for rule base V&V tools as the KBS/expert system concept
moved from a research platform to a commercial one. To a large extent this
work is now generally accepted by practitioners and can be described as "main
stream" technology, rather than research technology.

Current work on rule base V&V (much of which can be traced back to the
earlier, now well established, work noted above) is concerned with the automated testing of systems and semi-automated revision of rule bases (KRUST-
WORKS — [15]), the testing of task specific properties of rule bases ([22]), V&V
at the formal specification level of KBS development (KIV — [19]), quality assurance ([39]) and the application of rule bases V&V tools to wider domains
such as the WWW ([35]).

On the face of it there is very little common ground between the integrity
considerations associated with databases and the V&V of rule bases. Integrity
is concerned with the ongoing validity of dynamic systems, i.e. a constantly
evolving database; while validation and verification are respectively concerned
with the truthfulness of a system with respect to its problem domain and the
correctness of its construction, i.e. whether a rule base is logically or structurally flawed. Integrity is not a concept with which KBS are generally concerned — possibly because such systems tend not to be dynamic. Conversely
the terms V&V are rarely used in the database literature ([18]). (Of course
in the broader sense, validation and verification forms an important part of
the traditional software engineering of the Data Base Management Systems
(DBMS) as it also does in the development of the inference engine component
of expert systems.)

There has always been some acknowledgement that there is a kinship between the relational model of databases and rule bases systems in that both can
be expressed in clausal form logic, however in the context of VVI (Validation,
Verification and Integrity) the two communities have rarely come together. In
more recent years, however, the establishment of alternative database models
has begun to alter this situation such that a significant overlap between the
two technologies can now be identified.

In this paper we firstly (Section 2) give an overview of the integrity issues that concern the database community (it is assumed that the intended readership of this paper does not require an overview of the concerns associated with KBS V&V). We then examine this growing overlap between the two genres in Section 3. Having established that significant overlap exists we then go on in Section 4 to identify opportunities (future directions) for the application of "cross-over" technologies — the aim being to widen the scope of rule base V&V to encompass VVI. Some conclusions are drawn in Section 5.

2 DATABASE INTEGRITY

Although, as noted above, integrity may have been a central concern to the database community and of database theory for many years, it also true to say that it has been poorly implemented in many database systems. Codd made the point:

> "It is ,however, vitally important to remember that the relational model includes three major parts: the structural part, the manipulative part and the integrity part ..." [12]

in the context of questioning the relational credentials of many systems. Similarly Date [16] in the mid 80s, in a standard introduction to database systems, said:

> "..no system, SQL-based or otherwise, currently provides very much in the way of integrity support."

The situation has improved since then and in this section we outline the main issues from a theoretical position and note that the techniques of implementing these vary considerably from system to system.

The integrity part of the relational model consists of two general integrity rules:

Entity Integrity: Enforcing entity integrity ensures that there is a unique name or identifier in each row in a table to distinguish the object being represented from any other object.

Referential Integrity: Referential integrity is concerned with maintaining cross references from object to object in a database. Much of the power of relational databases derives from their ability to connect the items of data held in separate tables on common values. Enforcing referential integrity means that those values which are keys in tables are kept consistent.

Although the above refers to the relational model the concepts of entity and referential integrity can be extended to other models.

2.1 What are we maintaining?

The constraint support from most RDBMSs will stop changes to an existing database that violate the rules, which may be held in a number of ways, but do not check the entire database so a previous consistency is assumed. This may be significant since databases can be set up with bulk loading utilities that do not obey integrity rules.

Without an extensible type mechanism many constraints that are really (or could be) domain constraints may be represented by referential integrity constraints. For example if we want a data item to be a day of the week it may only be possible to achieve this by checking that an instance of this data item occurs in a table that simply contains "Monday","Tuesday", etc.

2.2 How are we maintaining it?

In RDBMSs integrity constraints will be enforced in a number of ways. Entity integrity is generally better supported than referential integrity and is usually provided via a standard SQL command that creates a table and declares that a column or columns are the Primary key and must not be null. This is a case where support has improved; in the past for example the Ingres RDBMS provided this support not by specifying a primary key, and hence uniqueness, but by making the table's storage structure one that guaranteed uniqueness. This meant that there was no guarantee that the storage structure could not be changed in the future so that the constraint could then be broken.

Referential integrity is commonly implemented by database rules and procedures. These may take a form like the ECA format discussed in section 3.3.2 (active databases). This type of mechanism allows changes to be cascaded through the database so that an update to one table is propagated to all references to that datum throughout the database. Conversely it can also be used to block changes so that data may not be removed from a table if there are references to it in other tables.

Finally, simple domain constraints may be supported by an SQL "create integrity" statement, and other domain constraints may be supported by the type system of the DBMS itself.

3 THE VARYING RELATIONSHIPS BETWEEN DATABASE AND RULE BASE SYSTEMS

In this section we review the varying relationships between database and rule base systems. We commence by firstly considering the architecture of both; and then examining the interconnection between rule base systems and different DB models commencing with the relational model and then going on to consider the deductive, active, object-oriented, and constraint models which have been

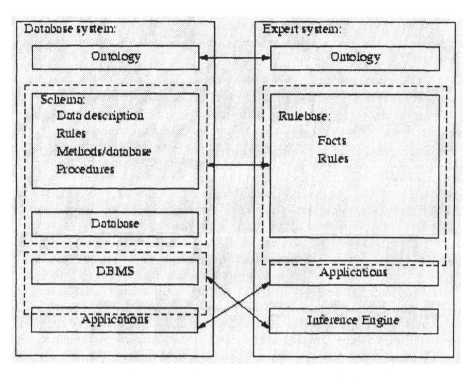

Figure 1. The mapping between DB and ES system components

proposed, with varying degrees of success, in more recent years. The objective of this section is to establish the nature of the overlap between the database and expert system technologies.

3.1   Architecture

Initially, the most obvious mechanism for high lighting the similarities between database and expert systems is to consider the components of such systems. A diagram is presented in Figure 3. Broadly both systems comprise some conceptualisation, both have what we might refer to as an "operating" systems, both have some form of "information repository", and both have an application domain. In some cases the boundaries between these component are not as clear as in other. This is particularly the case with respect to the application level. In the database community there is a definite approach of separating the database out from its applications (which may be varied), this distinction is not so clearly made in the context of expert systems that are often more closely linked to a key application. What ever the case, for discussion purposes, we can consider a hierarchy of:

— VVI **of** expert and database systems — the "operating" system level.

— VVI **in** expert and database systems, i.e. VVI **of** the knowledge/rule/data
  base — the "information repository" level and the main focus of this
  paper.

— VVI of expert and database systems applications

From the figure, at the conceptualisation level, in both expert and database
systems, we have the concept of an ontology, i.e. a common understanding and
vocabulary. In the case of expert systems an ontology is a set of definitions of;
(hierarchically ordered) classes, objects, attributes, relations and constraints.
It's main function is to provide a vocabulary for the expression of domain
knowledge, i.e. a knowledge level description ([30]). A similar conceptualisation
exists with respect to database systems — ontologies have been introduced for
DBSs as a conceptual layer above the schema ([29]).

The "operating system" component — the Data Base Management System
(DBMS) in the case of a database, and the inference engine in the case of an
expert system — are traditional software systems in the sense that they are
developed using "mainstream" software engineering tools and techniques.

The "information repository" in both cases provides the most fertile area
of interest with respect to this paper. In the case of a database we distinguish
between the database schema, which specifies the structure of the database;
and the database instance, which specifies its actual content (Abiteboul et al.
comment that the difference is analogous to the standard distinction between
the type of a data item and its values as found in imperative programming
languages). In the case of certain types of database further information in the
form of rules and constraints may be added consequently there is some shared
terminology. Inspection of the Figure also indicates that the concept of rules
can appear in both systems, there is also a correspondence between "database
facts" and "fact base data".

3.2   The relational model

From the above we can see that, in terms of architecture, there is a clear
mapping between the two systems which if nothing else at least hints at the
possibility of "cross-over" technology. A clearer overlap can be found if we
compare the relational model (still the most prevalent DB model in industry)
with rule base representations. The relational data model [10] represents data
as tables of atomic values and defines an algebra for set-oriented associative
manipulations. As note above it specifies two general integrity rules: *entity
integrity* prohibits null-valued keys, ensuring that all data objects include an
identifying name; and *referential integrity* prohibits foreign keys values which
do not also occur as primary keys, thus avoiding *dangling references*. Relational
databases ([17]) are the state of the art and benefit from the widely accepted
APIs, ODBC and JDBC, and an international standard language, SQL, which
provide the functionality of the relational algebra.

Given the above, identical relations can be specified as facts in a rule base which can the be queried in a similar manner to that provided by SQL, i.e. we can express a relational database using a clausal form identical to that used in rule bases. For example a PROLOG program can be viewed as a relational database where the specification of relations is partly explicit (facts) and partly implicit (rules). In addition most expert system environments provided mechanisms for updating, adding and removing facts (PROLOG provides the built in predicates `assert` and `retract` to do this).

3.3 Hybrid systems

A number of *hybrid* technologies have been developed which borrow from both the expert system and database domains. These include:

— Deductive databases

— Constraint databases

— Active databases,

all of which are supported by significant rule sets of a similar nature to that found in expert system rule bases. An overview of each of these hybrid models is presented below.

3.3.1 Deductive databases

If the relational model serves to bring the two technologies "in touch" the deductive model can be viewed as serving to merge the two technologies. Deductive database systems provide mechanisms for managing knowledge as well as data. They are a natural extension to the relational model. As such deductive databases are able to derive new facts using existing information explicitly stored in the database [32]. This is achieved by generalising the type of information that may be stored; in addition to simple facts it is also possible to store expert system style rule sets. This then produces a database system with similar properties to that of a logic programming environment. In some cases it is difficult to distinguish between what is a deductive database systems and a rule base system. The distinction between the two is that the primary concern of the first is the management of large amounts of data with the manipulation of that data as secondary [25]. Expert systems, on the other hand, are more concerned with the manipulation of "smaller" amounts of data and more complex amounts of knowledge, with the emphasis on manipulating that data in a manner that reflects the mode of working of a domain expert. We can also point to the mode of implementation and its manner of operation — DBMS or expert system language/environment, SQL or inference engine. The ratio of facts to rules may also be a useful indicator to distinguishing between an expert system and an expert database - an expert systems will (generally) contain many more rules than facts while an expert database system will contain many more facts than rules.

3.3.2   Active databases

Active databases support the automatic triggering of updates in response to internal or external events. This is generally achieved in an expert system like manner where forward chaining of rules is used to accomplish the update. Rules typically follow the ECA (Event-Condition-Action) format of:

```
on <event> if <condition> then <action>
```

The similarity between this and expert system style rules, especially in the case of production rule systems, is self evident. The distinction is that in a rule base the triggering event is user supplied rather than expressly included. In a sophisticated active rule base the action part of the rule may entail calls to further rules in a manner identical to that supported by expert system style rule bases. The overlap here is so close that the rule set that forms a component of an active database is generally referred to as a rule base [1].

3.3.3   Constraint databases

The constraint model ([24]) is an extension of research into Constraint Logic Programming (CAP) ([23, 21]) which itself is an extension of logic programming. In CAP constraint satisfaction is embedded into a logic programming environment/language, for example Sicstus PROLOG which is an extended version of traditional PROLOG which incorporates CLP features.

The basic idea of constraint databases is to replace the notion of a tuple in a relational database by that of a generalised tuple, i.e. a conjunction of constraints. For example given a tuple:

$$(a_1, \ ..., \ a_n)$$

this can be regarded as a generalised tuple of the form:

$$(x_1 = a_1) \wedge ... \wedge (x_n = a_n)$$

Of course this model also needs to be supported by an appropriate "constraint database" query language. The extension of both expert system and data base models to incorporate constraint satisfaction features may be viewed as another growing area of overlap.

It should also be noted here that the use of constraints is a recognised as an important tool for database integrity checking. In early work in this area constraints were expressed in terms of clausal logic. More recently much more sophisticated constructs have been adopted.

3.4   Emerging database models

The emerging third generation of DB technology is predominantly object and object-relational. Respective de facto standards, i.e. ODMG [8] and the SQL3 standard proposals [4], can be viewed as object-oriented programming languages with added database facilities and relational databases systems with added object-oriented features. Both are technology (rather than theory) driven and have emerged in response to the realization that the application of relational systems is impeded by a limited type system. Speculative requirements for these technologies were set out at the turn of the decade in the object-oriented and third generation database manifestos [5, 36].

The current predominance of object-oriented programming (Java, Etc.) has also led to the extension of expert systems into the OO domain ([34]). Much of this work is speculative, and thus it is difficult to say where the connection between OO databases and OO expert systems will be, however, it should not be forgotten that frame based expert systems were a feature of the 1980s (many written in LISP) and that the frame concept is not that different from the ideas associated with classes and instance of classes.

3.5 Summary

From the above we can identify a number of areas of overlap. We can summarize these as follows:

— There is a direct mapping between the architectural components of both types of system.

— Both systems have an underlying conceptualisation associated with them, which can be expressed using some common vocabulary using (i.e. the ontology concept).

— There is a clear overlap between the relational model and the clausal forms used in many rule based systems.

— Hybrid systems contain components borrowed from both domains.

— There is a close relationship between the validation and verification of the DBMS and Inference engine, but this is outside the scope/spirit of VVI as envisaged here.

We can also say that as soon as a rule base system starts to become dynamic, i.e. evolving with time, integrity becomes an issue.

A word of warning is also appropriate here, the relational model remains the industry standard, the remaining models at best are still regarded as experimental and at worst as "academic toys". Whether any of the alternative models will establish a firm place in industry remains a topic for debate and "wait and see".

4 FUTURE DIRECTIONS (AND "CROSS-OVERS")

In this section we consider a series of possible directions for future work. Some of these are directed at the areas of overlap identified above, others focus on some additional areas which may come under the remit of "cross-over" technology.

4.1 Conceptualisation

The ontology component is "an explicit conceptualisation of the domain" ([7]). Bench-Capon ([7]) has identified a number of areas where ontologies which conceptualise the problem domain can be used to support V&V of expert systems ([7]). It is suggested that the added coherence of an explicit domain conceptualisation gives a more motivated and focussed role for experts who are "signing off" a KB, reduces the scope for subjective interpretation which can mask errors, and provides the possibility of a test harness. More specifically, an ontology provides an agreed representation of the universe of discourse and hence support for validation and verification based upon real world semantics. Although Bench-Capon admits that an ontology is at present not usually defined for expert systems it can be argued that there are advantages in doing so. A similar case can be put for systems for database systems. It is likely that some advantage can be gained from the application of the ontologies concept for V&V at the conceptualisation level. There are already a number of practitioners carrying out V&V studies for expert systems at the conceptualisation level ([19]) although the term "ontology" is not explicitly used.

4.2 Relational models

The correspondence between schema/database and rule base is most apparent for relational databases, since they share a common theoretical foundation with expert systems, i.e. clausal form. This has been exploited, for example in deductive databases where relational DBMSs provide back-end fact storage. However, this correspondence has not been exploited practically to any extent for V&V of database systems or for integrity maintenance of evolving expert systems.

Given that a relational database can be represented in rule base terms (subsection 3.2) it should be possible to implement classic database integrity checking techniques in these terms. It may be that the "intelligent" features of these systems can then be used to enhance the "productivity" and capabilities of these techniques.

4.3 Hybrid systems

Although a correspondence can be established between relational data-base systems and expert systems the correspondence is much stronger in the context of the hybrid models that contain significant expert system components. For example the rule sets associated with deductive and active database systems are subject to identical anomalies and symptoms of errors that the expert system's V&V community have been concerned with for many years. Some work is already being undertaken in this area with respect to active databases. For example Aiken et al. ([3]) have suggested methods to identify infinite loops in active database rule sets using an approach known as the *trigger graph method*; similar work has also been undertaken by Lee and Ling ([26]).

4.4 The object-oriented model and frame based systems

The predominant expert system methodology is currently founded on the rule base approach, the alternative frame based approach has become unfashionable, instead this has been replaced by work on object oriented expert systems. For example Riley's CLIPS systems ([34]). To the best knowledge of the authors of this paper no work has been done with respect to V&V of object oriented expert systems; it is therefore not possible to make any predictions concerning the possibilities of "cross-over" in this context although it might be an interesting area for future investigation.

4.5 The application of database techniques to the expert system V&V domain

In the foregoing we have concentrated on areas where current V&V techniques as applied to expert systems may find a role on the context of various database models, especially where those models intersect with the expert system domain. However, at least in theory, the opportunity for crossover should be "two-way". For example if a relational database can be represented in a clausal form, it should be possible to represent a rule and fact base as a set of database tables. This is undoubtedly true but does it "buy" you anything? With respect to inferencing strategies probably not, but in the context of V&V this may well offer advantages. Support for the latter conjecture can be found in the many tabular techniques used by expert system V&V practitioners; truth tables ([38]), incidence matrices ([2]) and other tabular representations ([27]).

Another area where one might expect the application of DB theories to ESs (and by extension DDBs) is design theory. Normalisation is a formal approach to the refinement of relational DB design. (by ensuring no unnecessary replication of data). Normalisation, together with representational theory [28], provides a theory of "goodness of relational DB design". Again one would expect this to improve our ability to design good representations of facts within ESs (and DDBs). However, that is not the case, since normalisation is necessary for relational databases only because of the 1NF constraint which prohibits direct representations of complex objects. In DDB and ESs, complex structures can be modeled. For example, a list can be accommodated in a DDB fact (although physical storage may be harder if a relational DB is actually used for the fact storage).

4.6   Other possible opportunities

There are a number of areas of research that are currently under consideration within the expert systems V&V community which, although not directly applicable to the overlap identified here, have possibilities with respect to their application to database systems. Of note is Vermesan's work on the classification of KBS ([39]). Knowledge Base (KB) certification uses a number of different V&V methods such as static analysis, testing, inspection, and modeling to assess the quality of the KB component. This work is currently "on going". Although there is a perceived need for the certification of KBS (by for example marine classification societies such as Det Norske Veritas) does this also apply to database systems? and, if so how should this be undertaken?

A further consideration is that expertise is required by DB administrators and users, and thus expert system techniques may be appropriate to improve the quality of usage of DB technology by the non-skilled operator. Similar considerations may be appropriate to "intelligent querying".

Finally, although we have noted that the VVI of DBMS and inference engines is a subject for traditional software engineering techniques, a test suite of rules and or facts to test this level might be an attractive proposition, possibly providing a validity benchmark to put along side the performance benchmarks used with DBMSs. Clausal form providing a lingua franca across systems. The varied ways queries may be executed by a DBMS make this a more complex operation than might be at first assumed for database systems or hybrid systems that use DBMSs for fact or rule storage. Since most DBMSs use a query optimiser the way a query is executed may depend on a large number of factors, such as size of relations and statistics on that data, and its correct evaluation in all circumstances would be hard to test or guarantee. Errors in a B-tree algorithm might only come to light for example if an existing relation had its structure changed. [1]

5   CONCLUSIONS

From the foregoing it is clear that there is currently little common research effort or shared results between the database and expert systems communities,

---

[1] As an aside DBMSs have the notion of serializability in transactions (i.e. "isolation" — the I in ACID test) that aims to the same consistent end point no matter what the route through. Is there an expert system counterpart for rule firing?

despite the view held by members of both communities that dialogue and collaborations is long overdue. It is hoped that some of the ideas outlined in this paper will encourage this collaboration and that this in turn may result in some genuine technological advances that will benefit all concerned.

Some work has already been undertaken under the heading of VVI. The 1st International Workshop on Validation, Verification and Integrity Issues (VVI'98) to place in Vienna last year ([40]); a review of this workshop can be found in Bench-Capon et al. ([6]). It is intended to hold a second VVI workshop, in conjunction with DEXA, in the year 2000.

References

[1] Abiteboul, S., Hull, R. and Vianu, V. (1995). *Foundations of Databases*. Addison Wesley, Reading, MA.

[2] Agrawal, R.and Tanniru, M. (1991). *A Petri-net Based Approach for Verifying the Integrity of Production Systems*. Knowledge-Based Systems Verification, Validation a nd Testing Workshop Notes, AAAI'91, Anaheim CA.

[3] Aiken, A., Widom, J. and Hellerstein (1992). *Behavior of Database Production Rules: Termination, Confluence and Observable Determinism*. Proceedings ACM SIGMOD, International conference on the Management of Data, pp59-68.

[4] ANSI, (1998). *SQL3 drafts and discussion documents can be found at ftp://speckle.mcsl. nist.gov/isowg3/dbl.*

[5] Atkinson, M.P., et al., (1990). The Object-Oriented Database System Manifesto, in Kim, W., and Nicolas, J-M., and Nishio, S. eds., Deductive and Object-Oriented Databases, pp 223-239.

[6] Bench-Capon, T., Castelli, D., Coenen, F., Devendeville-Brisoux, L., Eaglestone, B., Fiddian, N., Gray, A., Ligeza, A. and Vermesan, A. (1999). *Validation, Verification and Integrity Issues in Expert and Database Systems*. Expert Update, Vol 2, No 1, pp31-35.

[7] Bench-Capon, T. (1998). *The role of Ontologies in the Verification and Validation of Knowledge based Systems*. In Wagner R. R, (ed), Proceedings DEXA 98 Ninth International Workshop on Database and Expert Systems Applications, IEEE Computer Society, pp64-69.

[8] Cattell, R. and Barry, D.K. (eds) (1997). *The Object Database Standard: ODMG 2.0*. Morgan Kaufman, San Fransisco.

[9] Coenen, F. and Bench-Capon, T. (1993). *Maintenance of Knowledge Based Systems:* Theory, Tools and Techniques. Academic Press, London.

[10] Codd, E.F. (1970). A Relational Model for *Large Shared Data Banks*. Communications of the ACM,13(6), pp 377-387.

[11] Codd, E.F. (1979). *Extending the Relational Database Model to Capture More Meaning*. ACM TODS 4 4 Dec.

[12] Codd, E.F. (1985). *Is Your DBMS really relational?* Computerworld, Oct 14.

[13] Cohen, J. (1990). *Constraint Logic Programming Languages.* Communications of the ACM, Vol 33, pp52-68

[14] Cragen, B.J. and Syeudekl, H.J. (1987). *A Decision-Table-Based Processor for Checking Completeness and Consistency in Rule-Based Expert Systems.* International Journal of Man-Machine Studies, Vol 26, pp633-648.

[15] Craw, S. (1998). *KRUSTWorks: Developing a Generic Refinement Toolkit.* Expert Update, Vol 1, No 2, pp35-47.

[16] Date, C.J. (1986). *An Introduction to Database Systems.* Vol 1 4th ed, Addison-Wesley.

[17] Eaglestone, B. (1991). *Relational Databases.* Stanley Thornes.

[18] Eaglestone, B. and Ridley, M. (1998). *Object Databases: A Introduction.* McGraw Hill.

[19] Fensel, D. and Schonege, A. (1997). *Specifying and Verifying Knowledge-Based Systems with KIV.* Proceedings EUROVAV'97, Katholieke Universiteit Leuven, pp107-116.

[20] Ginsberg, A. (1988). *Knowledge Base Reduction: A New Approach to Checking Knowledge Bases for Inconsistency and Redundancy.* In Proceedings AAAI'88, St. Paul, MN, Vol 2, pp585-589.

[21] Jaffar, J. and Maher, M. (1994). *Constraint Logic Programming: a survey.* Journal of Logic Programming, Vol19-20, 503-581.

[22] van Harmelen, F. and ten Teije A. (1997). *Validation and Verification of Conceptual Models of Diagnosis.* Proceedings EUROVAV'97, Katholieke Universiteit Leuven, pp117-128.

[23] Van Hentenryck, P. (1989). *Constraint satisfaction in Logic Programming.* Cambridge, MA: MIT Press.

[24] Kanellakis, P.C., Kuper, G.M. and Revesz, P.Z. (1995). *Constraint query languages.* Journal of Computer System Science, Vol 51, No 1, pp26-52.

[25] Kerschberg, L. (Ed.) (1986). *Expert Database Systems: Proceedings from the First International Conference.* Benjamin-Cummings.

[26] Lee, S.Y and Ling, T.W. (1997). *Refined Termination Decision in Active Databases.* In Hameurlain, A. and Tjoa, A.M. (Eds), Database and Expert Systems Applications, (Proceedings DEXA'97), Lecture Notes in Computer Science 1308, Springer Verlag, pp182-191.

[27] Ligeza, A. (1998). *Towards Logical Analysis of Tabular Rule-Based Systems.* In Wagner R. R, (ed), Proceedings DEXA 98 Ninth International Workshop on Database and Expert Systems Applications, IEEE Computer Society, pp30-35.

[28] Maier, D. (1983). *The Theory of Relational Databases*. Pitman Science Press, Maryland.

[29] Masood, N. and Eaglestone, B. (1998). *Semantics Based Schema Integration*. In Quirchmayer, G., Schweighofer, E. and Bench-Capon, T.J.M. (Eds), Database and Expert Systems Applications, proceedings DEXA'98 (Vienna), Lecture Notes in Computer Science 1460, Springer Verlag, pp80-89.

[30] Newell, A. (1982). *The knowledge level*. Artificial Intelligence, 18, pp87-127.

[31] Nicolas, J-M. (1982). *Logic for Improving Integrity Checking in Relational Data Bases*. Acta Informatica 18, pp 227-253.

[32] Paton, N., Cooper, R., Williams, H. and Trinder, P. (1996). *Database Programming Languages*. Prentice-Hall.

[33] Preece, A.D. and Shinghal, R. (1991). *COVER: A Practical Tool for Verifying Rule-Based Systems*. Knowledge-Based Systems Verification, Validation and Testing, Workshop Notes AAAI'91, Anaheim, CA.

[34] Riley, G. (1999). *CLIPS — A tool for building expert systems*. http://www.ghg.net/clips/CLIPS.html

[35] Rousset, M-C. (1997). *Verifying the World Wide Web: A Position Statement*. Proceedings EUROVAV'97, Katholieke Universiteit Leuven, pp95-104.

[36] Stonebraker, M., et al. (1990). *The Committee for Advanced DBMS Function*. Third Generation Database System Manifesto, SIGMOD Record, 19(3), 1990.

[37] Suwa, M., Scott, A.C. and Shortliffe, E.H. (1984). *Completeness and Consistency in a Rule-Based System*. In Buchanan, B.G. and Shortliffe, E.H. (eds), Rule-Based Expert Systems: The MYCIN Experiments of the Stanford Heuristic Programming Project, Addison-Wesley.

[38] Vanthienen, J. and Dries, E. (1993). *Illustration of a Decision Table Tool for Specifying and Implementing Knowledge Based Systems*. Proceedings 5th Int. Conf. on Tools with AI, pp198-205.

[39] Vermesan, A.I. (1998). *Software Certification for Industry — Verification and Validation Issues in Expert Systems*. In Wagner R. R, (ed), Proceedings DEXA 98 Ninth International Workshop on Database and Expert Systems Applications, IEEE Computer Society, pp3-14.

[40] Wagner R. R. (Ed) (1998). *Proceedings DEXA 98 Ninth International Workshop on Database and Expert Systems Applications*. August 26-28, 1988, Vienna, Austria. IEEE Computer Society.

Intelligent Data and Knowledge Analysis and Verification; Towards a Taxonomy of Specific Problems

Antoni Ligęza
Institute of Automatics AGH, Kraków, Poland
ali@ia.agh.edu.pl, ligeza@uci.agh.edu.pl

Abstract: This paper addresses the problem of intelligent analysis of data and knowledge. A common model for data and knowledge representation is proposed. The model takes the form of extended relational database table and it is provided logical interpretation. The main interest is in analysis of certain properties of such bodies of data and knowledge. In order to assure satisfactory performance of a system based on such data and knowledge several theoretical properties should be satisfied. The principal issue is then analysis and verification of these properties which are believed to constitute decisive factors for efficiency, reliability, quality and safety of operation. Several theoretical problems concerning data and knowledge are identified, defined and discussed. These problems cover adequate data and knowledge representation, completeness, consistency, correctness, equivalency, generalization and manipulation, similarity and inductive generalization. Influence of selected issues on system reliability, safety and quality is analyzed and a uniform logical framework for discussion is put forward.

Keywords: Data and knowledge representation and analysis, verification and validation, taxonomy of problems, completeness, consistency, correctness, equivalency, generalization.

1 INTRODUCTION

Growing complexity of advanced information processing, decision support and computer controlled systems together with the requirements for quality, reliability and safety standards of technical processes make necessary the application of advanced *data and knowledge* (D&K) processing systems. Such systems, constituting upper-level with respect to data bases (DBs), direct computer control level (the so-called DDC) or even some knowledge-based systems perform advanced and extended data processing, including process monitoring and knowledge based supervisory functions, extended data analysis, evaluation of quantitative and qualitative characteristics, verification of required properties, etc.

Obviously, information processing, control, decision making, supervision and diagnosis, etc. are performed to obtain certain results: the basic one being the final product or output (solution, decision, control) obtained with required quantity and quality. Further problems may also include limiting human effort, environment protection, cost minimization, optimal efficiency, etc. In fact, it is the *quality* of the output which seems to become a factor attracting most attention now. In information processing quality of data, considered both as input and output of information processing systems seems to be a crucial issue for satisfactory or optimal system performance. It is a straightforward conclusion that the data and knowledge constituting the input for information processing systems and the resulting output should be of highest quality. But what is the quality with respect to data and following it knowledge, then?

In order to be more precise, quality must be defined in terms of possible to evaluate characteristics, conditions to be satisfied, or comparative criteria. Several approaches are possible: unique numerical or symbolic quality index (or indices), multiattribute characteristics, specification of minimal requirements, ordering (linear or partial), satisfaction of constraints, etc. Only after introducing a way of quality evaluation one may speak about possibilities of quality verification and improvement.

In the case of D&K, the ultimate goal of analysis and verification can be achieved provided that factors influencing quality are identified, and their influence on the quality indices is learned or determined with use of models. Further, the scope of possible modifications must be specified and limiting constraints have to be provided. Only then search for improvement can be carried out.

In order to perform quality assessment, certain tools should also be available. These tools include, but are not limited to, general and domain specific languages, formalisms for data and knowledge representation, D&K models, D&K processing tools, and evaluation procedures.

This paper is concerned with analysis and verification of *data and knowledge*. Both data and knowledge (in restricted forms) are considered jointly; a common model, constituting an extension of the classical *Relational Database Model* is outlined. This model is both simple and transparent, yet powerful enough for realistic applications. Both data and knowledge are represented in a uniform tabular form following the database pattern. The difference between data and knowledge is subject to efface; to certain degree it becomes also a matter of interpretation. Data can be interpreted as precise, detailed knowledge (e.g. in case-based reasoning systems) and knowledge can be considered as data (e.g. intentionally specified data).

For the purpose of this paper the only criterion used to differentiate between data and knowledge is its intended interpretation: a data item (such as attribute value, record, table) is considered to be *data* if the main intended use of it is to provide static, detailed and precise image of some fragment of real world while a knowledge item (such as fact, simple conjunctive formula, DNF formula, and especially rules) is intended to provide more general knowledge defining universal or local properties of the world. From practical point of view, one can consider data to be the part of knowledge expressed with the *finest granularity* and unconditional. If the specification contains variables (e.g. universally quantified, or defining some scope ones) or it is true only under certain conditions (e.g. takes the form of rules, allows for deduction or any other form of inference), then it should be normally considered to be *knowledge*. However, in the uniform, simplified model proposed in the paper no explicit distinction is carried out.

The main focus of this paper is a *meta-level analysis* of D&K tables. Contrary to direct use of the data in database systems (operations like selection of interesting data or summary report generation) or direct use of knowledge-based systems (for example forward or backward rule interpretation), the main interest is in analysis of certain properties of such bodies of D&K. The underlying assumption is that such bodies should satisfy certain characteristics in order to assure satisfactory performance of the system which uses them. The principal issue is then analysis and verification of several theoretical properties which are believed to constitute decisive factors for reliability, quality and safety of operations based on such D&K. This kind of meta-processing is referred to as *Intelligent Data and Knowledge Analysis and Verification*.

In this paper seven top-level problems are identified; these are: adequacy of representation, sufficiency, consistency, correctness, equivalency, similarity and classification. Numerous subproblems are identified for each main problem as well. Further, some logical definitions are proposed within a unifying logic-based perspective. A taxonomy of problems proposed in this paper is aimed at providing a deeper theoretical insight at the D&K analysis and verification problems and establishing an initial platform for comparative analysis of some existing partial approaches and results. A proposal of a core, common D&K model constituting a starting point for further research on intelligent D&K analysis and verification tools is put forward. Concerning potential practical applications, the paper is oriented towards automatic analysis of D&K generated in monitoring and supervision of dynamic systems, especially control, diagnostic and decision support ones [Ligęza 95, Ligęza 97b].

The discussion presented in this paper follows the work on knowledge-based systems verification in AI, including [Andert 92], [Cragun and Steudel 87], [Nazareth 89], [Nguyen et al. 85], [Perkins et al. 89] and [Suwa 85]. On the other hand, it is biased towards the line of control applications [Laffey et al. 88], [Lunardhi and Passino 95], and [Tepandi 90]. It follows also the direction of uniform approach to database and knowledge-based system verification [Bench-Capon et al 98]. It is a continuation of the author's papers [Ligęza 93b], [Ligęza 94a], [Ligęza 94b] [Ligęza 95]. Recent paper on completeness verification is [Ligęza 97a] and recent results on verification of several issues are presented in [Ligęza 98]; there the tabular model for rule based systems is presented as well. The material concerning problems specific to knowledge-based process monitoring a nd supervision is presented in [Ligęza 97b]. Some other, approach to completeness verification can be found in [Preece 93, Preece 94]. Many technical details can be found in [Gouyon 94], [Famili 96], [Ligęza 97b].

2   A COMMON MODEL OF DATA AND KNOWLEDGE

In order to be more precise when speaking about data quality, a common model of *data and knowledge* (D&K) should be accepted for the sake of making the discussion well-founded. Below, a simple, commonly used approach based on attributes and relational databases in extended form is presented in brief. The core of the formalism is the essence of [Gouyon 94]; more detailed presentation can be found in [Ligęza 97b, Ligęza 98].

Let C denote a set of objects (elements, entities) of interest. The elements of C will be further described by providing values of some attributes applicable to their characterization. Let A denote a set of *attributes* selected to describe important features of the system under consideration, $A = \{A_1, A_2, \ldots, A_n\}$. For any attribute $A_i \in A$ let D_i denote a (finite) set of possible values of A_i, or in case of real domains some interval of real numbers. For avoiding triviality, one may assume that any set D_i contains at least two different elements. Further, extended functional character of the attributes is assumed, i.e. if $A_i = t$ and $A_i = t'$, then $t = t'$; here t and t' are either single elements of the appropriate domain or some subsets of it.

Attributes $A_1, A_2, \ldots, A_n$ denote some properties of interest, selected for expressing the domain knowledge of the analyzed system when operating in a specific local context. The values of an attribute can be just listed in a set, or some order of them may be established. If an attribute takes a set value (a subset of its domain), the semantics depends on the position of the term: if in conclusion (or an unconditional fact) then *all* the values are confirmed; if in preconditions (conditional), then *one* of the values is enough to confirm the fact.

A basic knowledge representation item consists of any element, its attribute and value of this attribute (if applicable) and constitutes a fact; in logical terms it constitutes an atomic formula. For intuition, the meaning of such a formula is that the value of the specified attribute for a given element is just the one provided; thus the basic relation here is equality, taken in the sense of assignment of a value to a function. Further, for simplicity, the name of the described object will not be specified explicitly; depending on interpretation, one may assume that each record describes a separate object, each record describes the same object at different time instant, etc.

In the basic statement, the structure of a single condition (atomic formula) is as simple as

$$p_{ij} \equiv (A_i = d_j),$$

where A_i is one of the attributes and d_j is its current value. In a more advanced formulation the following form can be admitted

$$p_{ij} \equiv (A_i = t_j),$$

where t_j is either a precise value from the domain of the specific attribute in use (A_i) $(t_j \in D_i)$, or a subset of the domain of A_i $(t_j \subseteq D_i)$, or just underscore ('_') to denote any (unspecified) value from the domain (as in logic programming the so-called *universal variable*). For simplicity, no variables are allowed here.

For example, `colour = red` denotes the fact that the value of attribute `colour` for the object of interest is `red`. For attribute `temperature` a fact like, for example, `temperature = upper_limit` might denote some dangerous situation when the temperature of cooling liquid reaches some predefined upper limit. For numeric variables, the representation is similar, e.g. in order to denote the fact that current speed amounts to 60 (typically written as $v = 60$), one can construct the description `speed_value=60`. An example of an attribute taking several values can be `languages= {English, French, Polish }` or `signal_on=[0,20]`, meaning that all the three languages are served and the signal was observed to be on in the whole time period from 0 to 20.

Further, the notion of *conjunction* of facts is imported from classical logic. To describe certain situations a set (logically: conjunction) may be necessary. Such a set of facts holding simultaneously will be called a *simple fact formula* or *simple formula* for short. Thus, if $p_1, p_2, \ldots, p_k$ are facts, any expression of the form $\phi = p_1 \wedge p_2 \wedge \ldots \wedge p_k$ is a simple fact formula.

Simple formulae characterize current state of the data or a single object. Since a simple formula constitutes in fact an abstract characterization (usually only selected parameters/features are taken into account), it can in fact refer to a situation including a great number of real states.

More complex formulae can be presented in *Disjunctive Normal Form (DNF)*, and are of the form $\Phi = \phi_1 \vee \phi_2 \vee \ldots \vee \phi_m$. Such a formula describing some set of objects or states (situation) may have a uniform array form as follows:

$$\Phi = \begin{array}{cccccc}
A_1 & A_2 & \cdots & A_j & \cdots & A_n \\
\hline
t_{11} & t_{12} & \cdots & t_{1j} & \cdots & t_{1n} \\
t_{21} & t_{22} & \cdots & t_{2j} & \cdots & t_{2n} \\
\vdots & \vdots & & \vdots & & \vdots \\
t_{i1} & t_{i2} & \cdots & t_{ij} & \cdots & t_{in} \\
\vdots & \vdots & \vdots & & \vdots & \\
t_{m1} & t_{m2} & \cdots & t_{mj} & \cdots & t_{mn}
\end{array}$$

The above table represents m simple formulae having the same structure and representing some data or knowledge. Since the terms may represent both single elements from the appropriate domains or their subsets, the presented formalism may be regarded as an extended database formalism. The table can present unconditional knowledge (e.g. records, facts), or it can be further structured into *rules*; then any record constitutes precodnditiosn and it must be assigned a conclusion.

Alternatively, formula Φ can be represented in a decision tree form. The tree is one with n branching levels (a level corresponds to an attribute), the root is normally assigned the attribute A_1, and the branches below correspond to the appropriate values of this attribute (these may be both elementary items and complex ones, such as subsets, intervals, etc.). Similarly, any node of depth i corresponds to attribute A_i, and the branches below such node correspond to different values of this attribute. Finally, the leaves represent ends of paths, where any path corresponds to a simple formula represented by a single row of the matrix and it defines some situation (context). If the leaves are assigned some output values, i.e. conclusions, decisions, actions, etc. the tree becomes a *decision tree*. Any path from root to a leaf node corresponds to one row of the appropriate matrix and thus it represents one rule of the system.

The form of presenting data in tables as above is a popular, widely accepted routine. It is easily understood by domain experts and, further, one can apply almost all the well-established notions and apparatus of *relational databases*. An advantage of this approach consists in the possibility of applying standard database operations for some data preprocessing steps.

3   PROBLEMS WITH DATA AND KNOWLEDGE: A TAXONOMY

Some most general classification of theoretical issues which undergo theoretical analysis can be one referring to the degree of influence they may have on system performance, and ranging from problems of *efficiency and elegance* of knowledge representation (e.g. redundancy and subsumption) to certain *critical errors* inside the encoded knowledge (e.g. *incompleteness* and *inconsistency* of specified knowledge). This point of view would be especially important when the analysis is to provide confidence about *reliability* and *safety* of an on-line (or even real-time) KBS working in safety-critical environment.

Note that *reliability* and *safety* are always to be considered w.r.t. KBS and its environment taken together. Note that, it is not the KBS itself, but always together with the controlled system and its environment which makes danger, crush or failure to occur. Thus, consideration of safety problems should be based on a more global analysis covering not only the software system but its potential interaction with its environment. For example, redundancy, which is normally considered harmless, may slow down operation of a real-time critical system and lead to some serious consequences since the output would be delayed; on the other hand, even inconsistent or incomplete system can work well for a long time, provided that no use of its knowledge leading to direct manifestation of inconsistency is done or the uncovered inputs do not occur.

Certain theoretical issues considered from the point of pure KBSs theory (such as correctness, incompleteness, inconsistency, consistency with reality, etc.) may appear "mathematically elegant" when analyzed at the level of theoretical definitions, but may turn out to become less attractive and hard to formalize when it comes to practical applications and efficient analysis. Especially purely logical approaches, e.g. ones based on automated theorem proving, would seem promising, but are hardly applicable for realistic systems. The same applies to software verification in general case, where proving consistency of final code with initial specification is a hard, tedious, usually not a realistic task. But even if performed successfully, it is not the end of the problems.

Below an attempt is made at presentation of working classification of general issues of interest with respect to theoretical analysis, each of them having relatively different origin and ways to detect and deal with it. Whenever possible, an idea of trouble detection procedure is outlined and suggestions about potential solutions are given. Further, the nature of potential problems is explained is case of omitting the analysis of a particular problem. In order to stay close to both engineering intuition and potential practical solutions, the discussion turns around simplified form of KBSs, i.e. the tabular form mentioned above. The proposed classification of theoretical issues pursued in this paper is as follows:

— **Problems of (adequate and minimal) data representation (redundancy, conciseness, adequacy)**, including:

  — duplicated information,
  — redundant information,
  — subsumption among information items,
  — reduction or partial reduction of records/rules (compression, gluing),
  — verification if all the attributes are necessary,
  — verification if all the necessary attributes and their values are present.

— **Problems of sufficiency of D&K (completeness)**, including:

  — specific (partial) completeness,
  — logical (total) completeness,
  — detection of incompleteness (holes), identification of gaps.

— **Problems of internal and external constraints satisfaction and consistency**, including:

  — satisfaction of internal/local constraints,
  — satisfaction of external/general constraints,

- determinism or uniqueness of data (in case of functional dependencies),
- conflict among data items,
- logical inconsistency of data,
- inconsitency of data with model.

— **Problems of correctness**, including:

- potential or partial correctness based on verification of specified external characteristics (e.g. as ones of the specified above),
- verification of consistency with specification (if applicable),
- verification w.r.t. real system (model), especially validation and testing on selected examples.

— **Problems of equivalency, generalization and manipulation of D&K**, including:

- comparison of two items (attribute values, records or tables) of D&K if they are equivalent,
- checking if one item (attribute value, record or table) of D&K (as above) is more general or specific than another one,
- algebraic manipulation, i.e. generation of intersection, sum, negation, etc. for two D&K items.

— **Problems of similarity and analogy of data**, including:

- comparison of two data items if they are similar,
- having a pattern, finding (the most) similar items in a table,
- defining and determining similarity between facts, records and tables;
- adaptation/modification of facts, records and tables (within predefined scope) so as to obtain analogous data item.

— **Problems of classification, generalization and learning**, including:

- induction from examples,
- induction from examples and background knowledge (*knowledge-based induction*),
- knowledge analysis and transformation.

The proposed classification is somewhat general, but it covers many detailed cases mentioned in the literature. For example, subsumption of rules covers some four subcases of *Redundancy in pairs of rules* [Nazareth 89]. The case of *unnecessary IF conditions*, as discussed in [Lunardhi and Passino 95], is a specific case of rule reduction discussed in this paper. On the other hand, as mentioned above, some checks requiring recursive analysis are not considered here. Note that in case of simple, reactive, forward-chaining systems it may be necessary to apply the same rule (or a sequence of rules) many times in turn, until external event changes the input. Further, a "circular" rule may in fact be equivalent to iteration which may be necessary to load a counter, etc. and finishes only after expected amount of repetitions. Thus, "circular" rules are not necessarily considered harmful.

4 LOGICAL ANALYSIS OF DATA AND KNOWLEDGE PROBLEMS

Let us briefly skim through the proposed taxonomy of anomalies. The first group refers to *inefficient* or *inadequate* representation, both with respect to the *structure* (i.e. the attributes) and the *data* (i.e. the records). It has mostly no influence on system correctness; certain systems can be *logically equivalent* (see the discussion below) but simultaneously their performance can be significantly different. Problems with inadequate representation can slow down system operation, and become a source of problems during modification or extension of the knowledge base. *Redundant rules* (not necessarily identical ones but semantically equivalent) can be detected and removed, leaving no more than one copy for each rule. *Subsumed rules* also can be eliminated, which has no influence on scope of representation or logical inference capability. However, in certain cases leaving a subsumed, more specific rule in knowledge base may be purposeful, for example it may affect the conflict resolution mechanism and inference control strategy [Lunardhi and Passino 95]. *Reduction of records/rules* means replacing two or more records/rules with a single, equivalent one by an operation resembling "gluing" the preconditions of them. Note that from logical point of view all of the activities referring to cleaning-up the above anomalies do lead to logically equivalent knowledge base, but a simpler (more elegant) one.

The problem of *completeness verification* consists in checking if all possible knowledge items (such as system inputs) are covered or served by at least one record or rule. Practically, this means that for any combination of input values and conditions, simple formula expressed with at least one matrix row (preconditions of at least one rule) should be satisfied. *Logical (total) completeness* means that the disjunction of preconditions of all the rules is tautology, i.e. no matter what input combination occurs, it will be served. In practice, not all such combinations may be admissible, or the system may be designed to work only for certain inputs. *Specific (partial) completeness* means that the scope of inputs such that the system is capable of dealing with is explicitly defined with a formula (restricting conditions) specifying the admissible input space. The logical definition of completeness of the D&K table Φ for some context (set of cases) defined with other formula Ψ can be defined as:

$$\Psi \models \Phi$$

In both cases, if the system does not satisfy completeness requirements, it may be of interest to determine gaps in the system input, i.e. generate a specification of unserved or uncovered input cases.

Problems of internal and external *constraints satisfaction* and internal *consistency* refer to verification if the D&K expressed in a table do satisfy certain imposed constraints. Such constraints usually specify restrictions imposed on the data or consistency constraints on the knowledge. For example, a case when consistent application of the rules may lead to ambiguous or inconsistent results may mean violation of such constraints. *Ambiguous results* may have place in case of *lack of determinism*, i.e. when two (or more) rules can be applied for the same input, but their outputs are different. It may be the case that such a result is harmless, or even intended, but in case of reactive control systems the situation like that should be carefully analyzed. A more dangerous case is the one of *conflicting records/rules*, i.e. when the simultaneously produced outputs cannot both be correct with respect to the intended interpretation (external world). For example, there are a number of devices which can be in one and only one state at a time, and concluding that such a device takes simultaneously two different states leads to physical inconsistency. Assuming that the constraints are specified with a formula Γ, the logical definition of constraint satisfaction can be stated as:

$$\Phi \models \Gamma$$

Inconsistency can become logical if some two conclusions are logically inconsistent, either in direct case (if one is the negation of the other), or in an indirect case (when assuming that both are simultaneously true allows for formal demonstration that there is logical inconsistency). For obvious reasons such problems should be detected and carefully analyzed.

Problems of *correctness* are not of direct interest here; the discussion of them goes far beyond the scope of this paper. Further, a general and satisfactory solution of such problems seems to be hard to achieve. Partial solution may consist in verifying *potential correctness* [Ligęza 95] through verification of some or all of the theoretical properties mentioned above. It is practically impossible to perform verification against specification since KBSs are close to what can be called *executable specifications*; this is so since they are often specified in high level declarative languages (and this is the case of tabular D&K specification considered here). Assuming that M denotes the model of real world, the correctness problem can be expressed as:

$$\models_M \Phi$$

On the other hand, limited testing can be performed (even on real plant or system), but this way of validation always leaves unanswered questions about the behaviour of the system in new, unexplored situations (e.g. unexpected faults). Some initial considerations referring to this issue are presented in [Tepandi 90].

Problems of *equivalency*, *generalization* and *manipulation* are important if two or more data items (attribute values, records or tables) are to be analyzed and compared. This may be the case of knowledge coming from different sources, comparative analysis of several systems or knowledge analysis, evaluation and manipulation in multi-agent systems. Two tables, Φ_1 and Φ_2 can be considered logically equivalent if $\Phi_1 \models \Phi_2$ and $\Phi_2 \models \Phi_1$. If only one of the conditions holds, then one table is more general than the other. The D&K representing intersection, sum, negation, etc. can be generated using "almost-standard" database operations (well, they must be extended because of the extended model used here).

Problems of *similarity* and *analogy* of the D&K appear in intelligent imprecise matching algorithms (e.g. when looking for "similar" items in a database) and find application in databases, case-based reasoning and reasoning by analogy. Since they may require enhancing knowledge representation with auxiliary mechanism (e.g. fuzzy linguistic variables) the model may become more complex. The precise discussion may require incorporation of technical details of the extended model and as such is beyond the scope of this paper.

Last but not least, and in contrast to classical understanding of *verification*, induction and learning (generalization) from a set of low-level records/rules were put together with other issues. This is in order to underline that *verification* should perhaps be considered jointly with D&K systems *synthesis*. In fact, it seems reasonable to attempt at direct synthesis of "correct" D&K systems rather then perform afterword verification and correction. These problems, however, are left for further research.

5   CONCLUDING REMARKS

In this paper formal logical bases for extended, intelligent analysis and verification of D&K systems are outlined. A single, uniform model for representing both data and knowledge is proposed. A taxonomy of theoretical problems is presented and discussed. The potential influence on system reliability, safety and quality is evaluated and some logical definitions of problems are provided. The discussed issues are embedded into a unifying logical framework – most of the checks can be reduced to (specialized) theorem proving [Ligęza 93b, Ligęza 95]. For the uniform tabular D&K model proof procedures can take the form of simplified, algebraic manipulations [Ligęza 97a, Ligęza 98].

ACKNOWLEDGMENTS

Research supported within AGH Internal Grant No. 11.11.120.44

References

[Andert 92] Andert, E.P. (1992). *Integrated knowledge-based system design and validation for solving problems in uncertain environments*. International Journal of Man-Machine Studies, 36, pp357–373.

[Bench-Capon et al 98] Bench-Capon T. et al. (1998). *Validation, Verification and Integrity Issues in Expert and Database systems*. Expert Update, Vol. 2, No. 1, pp31-35.

[Cragun and Steudel 87] Cragun, B.J., and Steudel, H.J. (1987). *A decision-table-based processor for checking completeness and consistency in rule-based expert systems*. Int. J. Man-Machine Studies, 26, pp633–648.

[Famili 96] Famili A., Shen, W.-M., Weber, R., and Simoudis, E. (1996). *Data preprocessing and intelligent data analysis*. Intelligent Data Analysis, 1, (http://www.elsevier.com/locate/ida).

[Gouyon 94] Gouyon, J.-P. (1994). KHEOPS *Users's Guide*. Report of Laboratoire d'Automatique et d'Analyse des Systemes, No. 92503, Toulouse, France.

[Laffey et al. 88] Laffey, T.J., Cox, P.A. Schmidt, J.L., Kao, S.M., and Read. J.Y. (1988). *Real-time knowledge-based systems*. AI Magazine, Spring, pp27–45.

[Ligęza 93b] Ligęza, A. (1993). *A note on backward dual resolution and its application to proving completeness of rule-based systems*. In: Ruzena Bajcsy (Ed.), Proceedings of the 13th IJCAI, 1, pp132–137, Chambery, France. Morgan Kaufmann Publ. Inc.

[Ligęza 94a] Ligęza, A. (1994). *Backward dual resolution. Direct proving of generalization*. In Hannu Jaakkola et al. (Eds.), Information Modelling and Knowledge Bases V: Principles and formal techniques. IOS Press, Amsterdam, pp336–349.

[Ligęza 94b] Ligęza, A. (1994). *Logical foundations for knowledge-based control systems. Part I: Language and reasoning*. Archives of Control Sciences, 3(3-4), pp289–315.

[Ligęza 95] Ligęza, A. (1995). *Logical foundations for knowledge-based control systems. Part II: Representation of states, transformations and analysis of theoretical properties*. Archives of Control Sciences, 4(1-2), pp27–63.

[Ligęza 97a] Ligęza, A.(1997). *Logical analysis of completeness of rule-based systems with dual resolution*. Proceedings of EUROVAV-97 - 4th European Symposium on the Validation and Verification of Knowledge Based Systems, Leuven, Belgium, pp19–29.

[Ligęza 97b] Ligęza, A. (1997). *An Introduction to Knowledge-Based Process Monitoring and Diagnosis. Basic Ideas, Problems and Theoretical Foundations*. Working notes (unpublished manuscript), Girona, Spain.

[Ligęza 98] Ligęza, A.(1998). *Towards logical analysis of tabular rule-based systems*. Proc. of Ninth Int. Workshop on Database and Expert Systems Applications at DEXA'98. Wien. IEEE Computer Society, Los Alamitos, CA, pp30–35. (extended version submitted to J. of Intelligent Systems).

[Lunardhi and Passino 95] Lunardhi, A.D., and Passino, K.M. (1995). *Verification of qualitative properties of rule-based expert systems.* Applied Artificial Intelligence, 9, pp587–621.

[Nazareth 89] Nazareth, D.L. (1989). *Issues in the verification of knowledge in rule-based systems.* Int. J. Man-Machine Studies, 30, pp255-271.

[Nguyen et al. 85] Nguyen, T.A., Perkins, W.A., Laffey, T.J., and Pecora, D. (1985). *Checking an expert system knowledge base for consistency and completeness.* In Proceedings of the 9-th IJCAI'85, 375–378, Los Angeles, California. M. Kaufmann Publ. Inc., Los Altos, CA.

[Perkins et al. 89] Perkins, W.A., Laffey, T.J., Pecora, D., and Nguyen, T.A. (1989). *Knowledge base verification.* In: G. Guida and C. Tasso (Eds.), Topics in Expert System Design, 353–376. Elsevier Science Publ. B.V. (North-Holland), Amsterdam.

[Preece 93] Preece, A.D. (1993). *A new approach to detecting missing knowledge in expert system rule bases.* Int. J. of Man-Machine Studies, 38, pp161–181.

[Preece 94] Preece, A.D., and Shinghal, R. (1994). *Foundation and application of knowledge base verification.* Technical Report, 26 pp. (postscript file).

[Suwa 85] Suwa, M., Scott, A.C., and Shortliffe, E.H. (1985). *Completeness and consistency in rule-based expert system.* In B. G. Buchanan and E.H. Shortliffe (Eds.), Rule-Based Expert Systems, pp159–170. Addison-Wesley, London.

[Tepandi 90] Tepandi, J. (1990). *Verification, testing, and validation of rule-based expert systems.* In Proceedings of the 11-th IFAC World Congress, pp162–167, Tallin.

[IJCAI-W23, 1993] IJCAI-W23. (1993). *Validation of Knowledge-Based Systems.* IJCAI'93 Workshop Notes W23, Chambery, 1993.

[ECAI-W2, 1996] ECAI-W2. (1996). *Validation, Verification and Refinement of Knowledge-based Systems.* ECAI-96 Workshop W2, Budapest.

Ontology-based Verification and Validation of Federated Database Systems

Nayyer Masood[1] and Barry Eaglestone[2]
[1].Department of Computer Science, Bahauddin Zakariya University, Multan, Pakistan
[2].Department of Information Studies, University of Sheffield, UK

Key words: Validation, verification, fedrated database system, schema integration, schema analysis, ontology, context, common concept model

Abstract: Validated and verifiable schema integration is critical to successful engineering of federated database systems. However, this is currently problematic because component database systems are not engineered to support future integration. To address this problem, a new conceptualisation of schema semantics is defined. The conceptualisation is based on the use of an ontology to represent real-world concepts. Schema semantics are then made explicit by mapping schema elements to the concepts, represented in the ontology, that they denote. Innovatory features are the definition of schema semantics both in terms of the intrinsic semantics of the schema elements, and their semantics in the contexts within which they are modelled. The paper also briefly overviews a semi-automated methodology for the schema analysis phase of schema integration based upon the ontology-based conceptualisation of schema semantics. This methodology is supported by software tools and an extended federated database systems architecture. Persistent representations of schema semantics provide a basis for formal validation and verification of schema integration within the federated database systems.

1. INTRODUCTION

This paper concerns validation and verification (V&V) issues of federated database systems (FDBS). An FDBS integrates pre-existing, geographically distributed, autonomous and heterogeneous database systems to provide new services based upon those of the component systems [PBE95]. Engineering, in general, involves constructing systems from validated and verified components such that the integrity of the component

327

systems is not violated. This is made easier if the engineering of components anticipates and supports future integration, for example, through rigorous definitions of system interfaces and their semantics as "open systems" interfaces. However, this is not the case for current database systems engineering methods. Interfaces are defined as database schemas, but these carry very little semantic information. Further, database systems are engineered in isolations and the consequential semantic heterogeneity (SH) between schemas can obscure semantic relationships and hence complicates definition and validation of the integrated system.

We have therefore researched a new approach to designing FDBSs, in which component systems are explicitly engineered for future integration. Specifically, we consider the problem of analysing component database schemas to determine those schema elements that must be integrated. To support this analysis, we propose a conceptualisation of schema semantics within the global context of the federated system. Innovatory features are the representation of both the intrinsic semantics of schema elements, and also their semantics within the various contexts within which they are modelled. This conceptualisation is based on the "common concept approach" [YSDK91]. In this, ontologies provide an explicit conceptualisation of the Universe of Discourse (UoD) and schema semantics are made explicit by mapping their elements to the concepts in the ontology that they denote. We have used this conceptualisation as the basis for a semi-automated schema analysis methodology, called Extended Common Concept-based Analysis Methodology (ECCAM). ECCAM is defined within an FDBS architecture which is extended to provide a persistent representation of schema semantics using our conceptualisation. The framework defined by the methodology, together with the persistent schema semantics enable verification of the schema analysis process. The use of ontologies also increases validity by supporting analysis on the basis of schema semantics, rather than schematic information.

This paper focuses on the ontology-based conceptualisation of schema semantics and the way in which it is used in ECCAM. In particular, we discuss how it provides enhances support for V&V of FDBSs. A full description of ECCAM, including details of a comparative evaluation with other schema analysis methodologies, can be found in [M99].

2.   V&V ISSUES OF MULTIDATABASE SYSTEMS

V&V has not been a major issue database research [ER98]. Instead, the focus has been on maintaining the integrity of databases by ensuring that instances continue to comply with formally defined integrity constraints after updates. This is to ensure that database instances provide plausible representations of the UoD. However, V&V issues are becoming more important because of a trend towards distributed multidatabase systems [ACM99]. Central to the task of engineering multidatabase systems is schema integration (SI), in which schemas are defined to provide integrated access to relevant parts of component databases. However, this adds complexity to database systems design by introducing the need to reconcile two conflicting requirements - maintaining autonomy of component database systems, while providing integrated access. A consequence of local autonomy is that component database systems are engineered in isolation, resulting in SHs between the schemas in different systems. SHs can be identified and reconciled only through human analysis of the real-world semantics of schema elements. This makes V&V of the correctness of SI difficult, since the process is predominantly intuitive. A more rigorous treatment requires a formal representation of the human analysts' conceptualisation of schema semantics, so as to facilitate formal analysis.

These observations motivation our research into SI, describe in the paper.

3.   SCHEMA INTEGRATION WITHIN AN FDBS

We have researched SI within the context of the de fact standard FDBS architecture [SL90] (Figure 1). In this, parts of component databases available to the federated system are represented as *component schemas*, using a canonical data model (the de facto standard in recent research [CEH+97] is the ODMG standard object model [C97]). Subsets of component schemas are specified in *export schemas*, to make them available for specific federations supported by the system. Export schemas relevant to a federation are then integrated within a *federated schema*. In this way each federated schema defines a virtual database relevant to a specific federation, and thus provide integrated access to relevant data stored in the component databases. Specific applications may then access the relevant definitions of a federated schema via an *external schema*. The SI task is therefore to define federated schemas which simultaneously represent relevant parts of component schemas.

Schematic aspect of SI concerns ensuring that the elements of the integrated schema correctly represent semantically similar elements of the schemas that they integrate. We believe this to be straight-forward once elements to be integrated have been identified, and are expressed within the same data model. For example, transformations involved can be formally verified using techniques similar to those in [CP98]. However, the semantic aspect, i.e., identification of semantically similar schema elements, is problematic. Three reasons are: (i) semantic integration requires knowledge of, and ability to capture and reason with real-world semantics of component schema elements, but data models currently lack the expressiveness to represent real-world semantics; (ii) SHs between schema elements can obscure semantic similarities between them - the SI process must therefore identify and resolve SHs; (iii) in the absence of tools for controlling the problem complexity, human integrators may be required to analyse and compare prohibitively large numbers of component schema elements within the context of the global UoD.

Early SI approaches [DH84, BL84, NEL86, M87] focus on schematic aspects, for example, by providing operators for schema integration. These approaches assume prior identification and resolution of SHs, and therefore side-step semantic difficulties. More recently, a schema analysis phase has been included [LNE89, YSDK91, GLN92, SGN93, NS96, GMS94, KS96, EM97, ME98] to address the semantic issue of identifying semantically similar schema elements. This requires formal representation of integrators' conceptualisations of schema semantics. The latter methods provide this mainly through semantic enrichment of schemas.

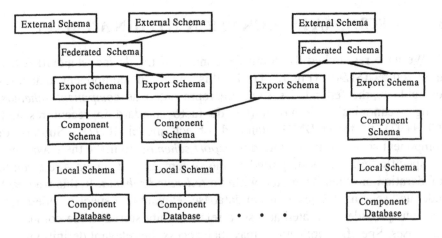

Figure 1. Sheth and Larson Federated Database System Architecture

Two main semantic enrichment approaches are metadata- and ontology-based. Metadata-based approaches provide semantic information in the form of meta-attributes or descriptors, which represent attribute characteristics, such as uniqueness, bounds and integrity constraints of attribute domains. The added information defines properties that are a consequence of semantics of schema elements. Semantic similarity can be inferred from these. For example, semantic equivalence is implied where a one-to-one mapping can be defined between the domains of two attributes [LNE89].

Limitations of this approach include the possibility of similarities between meta-attributes which are purely coincidental. Further, the task is made unnecessarily complex, for example, by defining mappings between domains prior to determining equivalencies. Ontology-based approaches (e.g., [YSDK91, FN92, BF94, EM97, ME98]) attempt to provide a direct representation of schema semantics by mapping schema elements to representations of concepts that they denote. This allows reasoning to be based upon semantics, rather than schema elements properties that are a consequence of semantics.

Most recent SI approaches [CHS91, YSDK91, SGN93, NS96, ME98] also support semi-automation of the integration process. Automation generally takes the form of software tool(s) which analyse semantically enriched schemas and generate assertions of semantic relationships between schema elements. Though full automation has been attempted (e.g., [GLN92, NS96]), it is generally accepted that human intervention is necessary to validate the assertions.

Schema analysis is therefore critical to the success of SI, but for it to be successfully achieved, it should be at least partially automated to reduce the complexity for integrators. Analysis should be based upon real-world semantics of schema elements to ensure validity of the analysis. The latter will reduce the impact of SHs, since many semantic similarities may then be apparent, even where there are schematic dissimilarities. Ontology-based approaches are promising in this respect. In particular, if component schema semantics are expressed in terms of a single "global" ontology, this will prepare them for, and establish a basis against which to validate future SI. A formal schema analysis methodology that can facilitate verification that the analysis has followed appropriate procedures is desirable.

The use of ontologies is also advocated for V&V of knowledge bases [B-CJ98, CER98]. However, the aim of database technology is more modest in that it seeks only to represent and efficiently manipulate information as data (facts), such that the database structures model corresponding information structures [ER98]. V&V issues therefore concern establishing the correctness of data types used with respect to the information they must denote. Knowledge bases currently have less advanced type systems, but greater deductive capabilities. Knowledge bases aim to represent and apply domain knowledge (rules) to given facts. The role of ontolgies in V&V of knowledge bases therefore also concerns the generation of cases with which to test validity of inferences that can be made from the represented knowledge, i.e., external consistency of the rule base. Given these differences in the roles of ontologies in these two technologies, there is also commonality in that both are concerned with using ontologies to provide an explicit conceptualisation of the domain such that experts do not have to rely on their individual interpretations. In this way, an ontology provides a standardised language with which to reason about correctness of a systems with respect to its real world requirements. Both areas benefit from advances in ontology engineering [JB-CV98] and the resulting resources of re-usable ontologies (e.g., the Ontology Page (http://www.medg.lcs.mit.edu /doyle/top); the yellow pages of ontologies (http://delicias.dia.fi.upm.es /REFERENCE. ONTOLOGY/).

We have therefore chosen to develop a semi-automatic methodology based on the ontology or Common Concepts approach [YSDK91]. Following sections, respectively, define our conceptualisation of schema semantics, and overview the schema analysis methodology (ECCAM) [EM97, ME98, M99] and an extended FDBS architecture based upon it.

4.   AN ONTOLOGY-BASED CONCEPTUALISATION OF SCHEMA SEMANTICS

In the common concept approach [YSDK91], an ontology is stored to provide an agreed representation of concepts of the UoD. Semantics of schema elements are made explicit by mapping them to concepts within the ontology that they denote. Thus, each schema element is given an interpretation. Our conceptualisation develops this approach. The principle refinement is to introduce the notion of *context*, and to provide interpretations of schema elements which represent their *intrinsic* meanings (independent of any context), and also their specific (*in-context*) meanings within the contexts in which they are modelled.

The ontology, or concept model, for a UoD is a set of tree structures in which nodes and edges respectively represent concepts and *is_a* relationships which associate them. Simple example concept trees, from a library system concept model [M99], are given in Figure 2. A concept hierarchies provide abstractions and a vocabulary for reasoning about the meanings of schemas in real-world terms within the wider context of the federated system.

Intrinsic semantics of each schema element are defined by a mapping to the most specific concepts that it denotes. These are defined as a function, *Int*, from schema elements to the powerset of concepts:

$Int(O_i) = \{c_i, i=1..m\}$ where c_i are the concepts denoted by O_i

Schema elements can be compared on the basis of their intrinsic meaning to determine if they are (shallowly) semantically similar.

Two schema elements, O_i and O_j, are **shallowly similar** if

$Int(O_i) \cap Int(O_j) \neq \emptyset$

However, shallow similarity can be misleading, since schema elements have more specific semantics if contexts within which they are modelled are taken into account. For instance, attributes, *Item.title* and *Person.name* denote the same concept, *name*. On this basis these attributes are semantically equivalent, but when viewed in the context of the respective classes, semantic differences become apparent - the name of a library item is not the same as the name of a person.

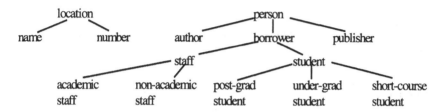

Figure 2. Example concept hierarchies

Contexts are represented as constructs in schemas, e.g., relationships, Set, Tuple. These denote semantic relationships (SRs), such as inclusion, aggregation and association, between schema elements. We therefore define *deep similarity* which takes into account context. Deep similarity is used as a basis for determining if schema elements are semantically similar. A schema element's contexts is defined in terms of the semantic relationships which associate it to other schema elements, as follows:

The **context** of a schema element O_i with respect to a structural schema element O_x is defined by the function, *context*, as:

$context (O_i, O_x) = O_x$ *where* $O_i = O_x$

otherwise

$context (O_i, O_x) = O_x$ $srel_{x, x-1}$ $context(O_i, O_{x-1})$

where $O_x, O_{x-1}, \ldots O_{i+1}, O_i$ denote the elements in the structural path from the context schema element O_x to the schema element O_i, linked with each other by semantic relationships $srel_{x,x-1}, \ldots, srel_{i+1,i}$.

A schema element may be interpreted as having different specific semantics, depending upon the contexts within which it is defined. These context-specific interpretations of a schema element are called its in-context semantics.

The **in-context semantics** of a schema element O_i in $context(O_i, O_x)$ is represented by concatenating the intrinsic meaning of the element O_i, the SR $srel_{x,x-1}$, and the in-context meaning of the element O_{i+1} in $context$ (O_{i+1}, O_x), i.e.,

$$ICMean(O_i, O_x) = Int(O_i) \quad \text{if } O_i = O_x$$

  otherwise

$$ICMean(O_i, O_x) = ICMean(O_{i+1}, O_x)\ srel_{x,x-1}\ Int(O_i)$$

where $O_x, O_{x-1}, \ldots O_{i+1}, O_i$ denote the structural path from the in-context schema element O_x to the schema element O_i.

To illustrate the above conceptualisation, consider the ODMG schema in Figure 3.

```
module UniversityLib                          }
class Item                                    class Person
(       extent items) {                       (       extent persons) {
        attribute unsigned short acc_no;              attribute String name;
        attribute String holding;                     relationship set<Book> bk_issued
        attribute String title;                               inverse Book::issued_to;
}                                             }
class Book extends Item                        class Publisher extends Person
(       extent books) {                       (       extent publisher) {
        attribute set<String> auth_names;             attribute String name;
        attribute String c_comp;                      attribute String address;
        attribute Publisher publ;             }
        relationship Person issued_to inverse         ...
                Person::bk_issued
```

Figure 3. A fragment of an ODMG library object database schema

In determining the semantics of this schema, we first define the intrinsic semantics of each schema element, i.e., those concepts denoted if we ignore the context within which the element is defined. The function *Int* is therefore defined to map each schema element to the most specific set of concepts represented in the concept model that it denotes. For example,

Int (Person) = {*author, publisher, academic staff, non-academic staff, under-grad student, post-grad student*}

Int (Person.name) = {*name*}

Int(publ) = {publisher, address}

Int must be defined explicitly by the human integrator. The purpose of *Int* is to formally represent the integrators' (intuitive) perceptions of the meanings of schema elements so that subsequent reasoning on the basis of those semantics can be semi-automated. Also, by making the integrators' analysis explicit, we provide a basis for verification of subsequent derivations.

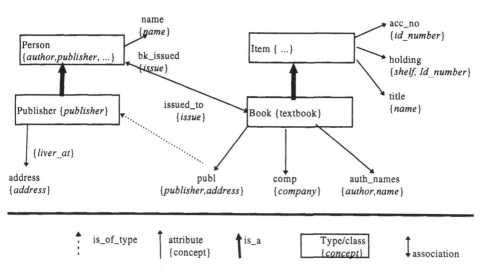

Figure 4. Schema Semantics represented as a Directed Graph

SRs are similarly defined by the integrators. The SRs denoted by structural schema elements, together with intrinsic semantics of schema elements can be represented as a directed graph, as in Figure 4. Intrinsic semantics can be defined for SRs by mapping them to concepts they denote, e.g. the *bk_issued / issued_to* relationship denotes the concept *issue*.

Note that schema elements can be specified within many contexts. For example, the attribute *publ* can be analysed within *context(publ, Book)*, i.e., *publ attribute_of Book*, and also within *context (publ, Publisher)*, i.e., *publ is_of_type Publisher*.

Making the semantics of a schema explicit goes some way towards validating the schema design, since it provide greater understanding of its actual (rather than intended) meaning. For example, schema semantics in Figure 4 reveal a design flaw - the association represented by the *bk_issued / issued_to* relationship is valid only between a book and a borrower, but the *Person* class also denotes the concepts, *author, publisher,* etc. This establishes a need, either for an integrity constrains to restrict instances of the relationship or for the schema to be refined to include a *Borrow* class to participate in the *bk_issued / issued_to* relationship.

Deep similarity can be computed between shallowly similar schema elements, and is based upon the in-context semantics of schema elements. Informally, we define deep similarity as follows:

two schema elements are **deeply similar** if there is a correspondence between the concepts that they model when compared in a particular context.

Defining correspondence between concepts is made complex by the existence of SHs, since these can result in semantically similar schema elements being defined in different structures. We therefore formally define deep similarity only for schema elements with contexts which have compatible structures, and separately consider the problem of reconciling structural SHs. Structures are compatible if they comprise the same number of structural elements, and corresponding SRs are of the same type.

Deep similarity between a pair of elements O_i and O_j, with respect to the contexts, *context*(O_i, O_x) and *context*(O_j, O_y), exists if the following conditions hold:

1. $Int(O_i) \cap Int(O_j) \neq \varnothing$, i.e., O_i and O_j are shallow similar
2. if $(O_i \neq O_x)$ and $(O_j \neq O_y)$ then $srel_{i+1,i} \approx srel_{j+1,j}$ i.e., the corresponding SRs are compatible
3. O_{i+1} and O_{j+1} are semantically similar respectively within *context*(O_{i+1}, O_x) and *context*(O_{j+1}, O_y)

where $O_x, O_{x-1}, \ldots O_{i+1}, O_i$ denote the structural path from the context element O_x to the schema element O_i, and $O_y, O_{y-1}, \ldots O_{j+1}, O_j$ denotes the structural path from the context element O_y to the schema element O_j.

In our conceptualisation we define and resolve one particular form of structural SH, *information dispersion*, which will potentially obscure a deep similarity between elements. An information dispersal exist between a context and a single element, if each element in the context is shallowly similar to the single element. An example of an information dispersion is given in Figure 5. Note that *publname* is semantically similar to both *name* and *Publisher*. Therefore the context (*name attribute Publisher*) is an information dispersion of *publname*.

Where information dispersions are detected during schema analysis, these can be replaced by a single (complex) schema element which maps to the union of the concepts denoted by the elements of the context. In the example, *Publisher* and *name* will therefore be treated as a single element *Publisher.name* (*Int(Publisher.name)* = {*publisher, name*}) when analysed for deep similarity with *publname*. In this way, structural differences between semantically similar schema elements can be resolved.

Figure 5. Information Dispersal

There can be variation in the strength of deep and shallow similarities, depending on the number of concepts that elements have in common. The metric that we use to compute the strength of similarity is based upon the proportion of concepts which are common to the elements being compared. The general formula for computing similarity between two objects, O_i and O_j, is that used in [YSDK91], i.e.:

$$sim(O_i,O_j) = \frac{CV_{oi} \cdot CV_{oj}}{\sqrt{CV_{oi} \times CV_{oj}}}$$

where CV_{oi} and CV_{oj} are concept vectors for elements O_i and O_j. Concept vectors comprise bits which correspond to the concepts in the ontology. A bit has the value 1 if the corresponding concept is denoted; otherwise 0.

The difference between computing strengths for shallow and deep similarity is in the construction of the concept vectors. For shallow similarity, the vectors represent the intrinsic semantics, i.e., concepts defined by *Int*. For deep similarity, the concept vector of an element being compared is formed by ORing its (intrinsic) concept vector with the concept vectors of its context elements.

5.   SCHEMA ANALYSIS USING THE ONTOLOGY-BASE CONCEPTUALISATION

ECCAM is a semi-automated schema analysis methodology in which the above conceptualisation of schema semantics (described in the previous section and illustrated in Figure 4) is used to determine those component schema elements that must be integrated within a federated schema. ECCAM prescribes the following framework of processes:

1. **Pre-Integration:** Concept hierarchies are developed for the UoD (as illustrated in Figure 2).

2. **Schema Interpretation:** The semantics of relevant schemas are defined as follows:
   - The semantics of each component schema are made explicit (as illustrated in Figure 4). This is done once, when the schema is included within the FDBS. In this way the engineering of component schemas anticipates and supports future integration.
   - The semantics of the federated schema that is to be defined are specified (as in Figure 4). The resulting directed graph acts as requirements, by specifying what the federated schema will mean when it has been defined. The elements for which semantics are specified are as yet virtual. This is performed once each time a federated schema is designed.

   Advantages of this approach are: (i) the proposed semantics of the planned federated schema and of the existing component schemas are directly comparable because they are both expressed in terms of the same ontology; (ii) the explicitly stated semantics provides a basis for formally validating the correctness of the federated schema that is derived.

3. **Schema comparison:** The is done automatically using a software tool. The tool compares elements of component schemas with the virtual elements of the specified federated schema, to determine is they are deeply similar. Thus, the semantics of the planned federated schema provide a context for the comparisons. Assertions of semantic similarity are generated. Each assertion is given a value (between 0 and 1) to indicate the strength of similarity.

4. **Similarity analysis:** Finally, assertions are ranked, according to their likelihood of validity (using heuristics described in [M99]).

The schema semantics used in the above methodology are made persistent within the FDBS architecture. This is to ensure consistent schema analysis over time, and facilitate verification that the SI process has been correctly applied. In addition, this allows integrated schemas to be validated with respect to the specified federated and component schema semantics. Accordingly, we have extended the FDBS architecture in Figure 1 (as shown in Figure 6), to include: (i) an ontology that represents the common concept model for the federated system; (ii) the semantics of each component schema and federated schema, in the form shown in Figure 4.

A prototype of the extended architecture has been constructed using object database technology, but with "schema element to concept" mappings defined in a separate file. However, [M99] describes how these extensions can be implemented within the ODMG object model, primarily using meta-attributes. ECCAM has been implemented and evaluated for case study schema integration scenarios. The prototype software tool, named KHOJI (Pakistani for "hunter"), for the schema comparison phase currently restricts comparisons for deep similarities to immediate contexts (i.e., those involving a single SR). This is to avoid a combinatorial explosion. A preliminary comparative evaluation is also documented in [M99]. The evaluation is on the basis of recall (the proportion of valid assertions generated) and precision (the proportion of generated assertions that are valid). Results indicates a significant improvement in both precision and recall over previous comparable methods [YSDK91].

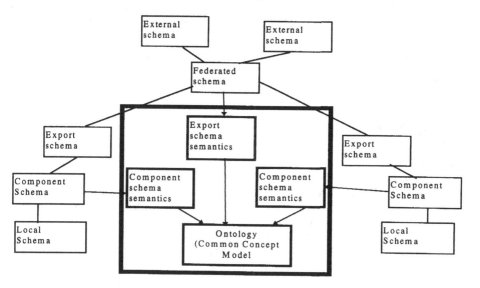

Figure 6. Extended FDBS Architecture

6.   CONCLUSIONS

In this paper we have identified a need for improved V&V methods to establish the correctness of SI within FDBSs. Specifically, we have identified the semantic aspects of schema analysis as being critical to successful SI, but problematic. There is a need for persistent semantic enrichment of the FDBS architecture to make explicit the integrators' perceptions of schema semantics, such that the analysis process can be formally defined and executed in a systematic semi-automated manner.

Our solution is a conceptualisation of schema semantics which develops the "common concept" approach. In this approach, an ontology provides an explicit conceptualisation of the UoD, and schema semantics are specified by mapping elements to concepts they denote. Our contributions are the representation of both intrinsic and in-context semantics, and shallow and deep similarity, respectively based upon these.

Early results indicate that ECCAM improves on previous comparable methods with respect to both recall and precision of assertions generated. Further, we have described how schema semantics based upon this conceptualisation can be made persistent within an extended FDBS, and thus provide a basis for formal validation and verification of federated schemas with respect to the component schema semantics and the required semantics of the federated schema. By mapping component schemas to a single ontology when they are added to the FDBS, we also prepare them for future integration.

The research described is preliminary work towards a framework for ontology-based V&V of databases, as suggested in [CER99].

REFERENCES

[ACM99] Special Section on Semantic Interoperability in Global Information Systems, SIGMOD RECORD, ACM, 28(1), March 1999.

[B-CJ98] Bench-Capon, T.J.M (1998) The Role of Ontologies in Verification and Validation of Knowledge Based Systems, Proceedings of the Ninth International Workshop on Database and Expert Systems, IEEE Press, Los Alamitos, pp 64-69.

[BL84] Batini, C., Lenzerini, M., A Methodology for Data Schema Integration in the Entity Relationship Model, IEEE Trans on Software Engineering, 10(4), pp 323-364, Dec, 1984.

[BF94] Bonjour, M., Falquet, G., Concept Base: Support to Information Systems Integration, CAISE'94, Utrecht, 1994.

[C97] Cattell, R.G.C., Barry, D.K., ed, The Object Database Standard: ODMG 2.0, Morgan Kaufman, San Francisco, 1997.

[CER99] Coenen, F., Eaglestone, B., Ridley, M., Validation and Verification and Integrity in Knowledge and Database Systems: Future Directions, EUROVAV'99, Oslow, 1999.

[CP98] Castelli, D. and Pisani, S. (1998) Ensuring Correctness of Personalised Schema Refinement Transformations, First International Workshop on Validation and Verification Issues of Expert and Database Systems, DEXA'98, Vienna, 1998.

[CEH+97] Conrad, S., Eaglestone, B., Hasselbring, W., et al., Research Issues in Federated Database Systems: Report of EFDBS'97 Workshop, SIGMOD, Vol 26, No 4, December, 1997, pp 54-56.

[CHS91] Collet, C., Huhns, M.N, Shen, W., Resource Integration Using a Large Knowledge Base in Carnot, IEEE Computer, Dec, 1991.

[DH84] Dayal, U., Hwang, H., View Definition and Generalization for Database Integration in a Multidatabase System, IEEE Trans on Software Engineering, pp 629-645, Nov, 1984.

[EM97] Eaglestone, B., Masood, N., Schema Interpretation: An Aid to the Schema Analysis of Federated Database Systems Design, First Int CAISE'97 Workshop on Engineering Federated Database Systems, Barcelona, Spain, pp 1-12, June, 1997.

[ER98] Eaglestone, B., Ridley, M., Validation, Verification and Integrity: A Database Perspective, First International Workshop on Validation and Verification Issues of Expert and Database Systems, DEXA'98, Vienna, 1998.

[FN92] Fankhouser, P., Neuhold, E.J., Knowledge based integration of heterogeneous databases, Proc IFIP Conf. DS-5 on Semantics of Interoperable databases Systems, Lome, Victoria, Australia, Nov, 1992.

[GLN92] Gotthard, W., Lockemann, P.C., Neufold, A., System-Guided View Integration for Object-Oriented Databases, IEEE Trans on Knowledge and Data Engineering, 4(1), Feb, 1992.

[GMS94] Goh, C.H., Madnick, S.E., Siegel, M.D., Context Interchange: Overcoming the Challenges of large-scale Interoperable Database Systems in a Dynamic Environment, Proc of Third Int Conference on Information and Knowledge Management (CIKM), Gaithersburg, Maryland, 1994.

[JB-CV98] Janes, D.M., Bench-Capon T.J.M, Visser, P.R.S. (1998) Methodologies for Ontology Development, Proc IT&KNOWS Conference of the 15th IFIP World Computer Congress, Budapest, Chapman-Hall.

[KS96] Kashyap, V., Sheth, A., Semantic and Schematic Similarities between Database Objects: A Context Based approach, 22nd VLDB, Bombay, 1996.

[LNE89] Larson, J.A., Navathe, S.B., Elmasri, R., A theory of Attribute Equivalence in Database with Application to Schema Integration, IEEE Trans on Software Engineering, pp 4490463, Apr, 1989.

[M99] Masood, M., Semantics Based Schema Analysis, University of Bradford Ph.D. Thesis, January, 1999.

[M87] Motro, A., Superviews: Virtual integration of multiple databases, IEEE Trans on Software Engineering, 13(7), pp 786-798, 1987.

[ME98] Masood, N., Eaglestone, B., Semantics based Schema Analysis, Proc of 9th Int Conf, DEXA'98, Vienna, Austria, LICS 1460, pp 80-89, Aug, 1998.

[NEL86] Navathe, S., Elmasri, R., Larson, J., Integrating user views in database design, IEEE Computer, 19(1), pp 3-31, Jan, 19986

[NS96] Navathe, S., Savasere, A., A Schema Integration Facility Using Object-Oriented Data Model, In Object-Oriented Multidatabase Systems: A Solution for Advanced Applications, PHI, 1996.

[PBE95] Pitour a, P., Bukhres, O., Elmagarmid, A., Object Orientation in Multidatabase Systems, ACM Computer Surveys, 27(2), Jun 1995.

[SGN93] Sheth, A.P., Gala, S.K., Navathe, S.B., On Automatic Reasoning for Schema Integration, Int Journal of Intelligent Co-operative Information Systems, 2(1), pp 23-50, Mar, 1993.

[SL90] Sheth, A. P., Larson, J. A., Federated Database Systems for Managing Distributed, Heterogeneous and Autonomous Databases, ACM Computing Surveys, 22(3), pp 183-236, Spt, 1990.

[YSDK91] Yu, C., Sun, W., Dao, S., Keirsey, D., Determining Relationships among Attributes for Interoperability of Multi-Databases Systems, Proc. First International Workshop on Interoperability in Multidatabase Systems, IMS, Kyoto, Japan, pp 251-257, April, 1991.

[RN95] Stuart J. Russell, Peter Norvig. *Artificial Intelligence: A Modern Approach*. Prentice Hall, 1995.

...

Applicability of Conventional Software Verification and Validation to Knowledge-Based Components
A Qualitative Assessment

Anca Vermesan and Frode Høgberg
Det Norske Veritas AS, Norway

Key words:

Abstract: Verification, validation and testing techniques developed for use with conventional development practices, are not always applicable when developing knowledge-based software. This paper presents an experimental framework to determine whether a technique is applicable or not, based on concepts from mutation testing. The framework itself comprises of a number of steps guiding the researcher/practitioner in the assessment process. Mutation testing is used to simulate faults in an example programme to determine the technique's ability to detect them. The framework has been applied to two techniques: control-flow analysis and cause-effect graphing. The conclusion is that the framework gives a good basis for a qualitative assessment of the applicability and efficiency of applying specific traditional VV&T techniques to knowledge-based components.

1. INTRODUCTION

The need for verification, validation, and testing (VV&T) of software is driven by society's increasing dependency on computer-based systems, and in particular its use in safety critical environments such as transportation and nuclear power generation. There is a wide range of techniques available for VV&T. Techniques such as inspections, cause-effect analysis and testing, control flow analysis and testing, and data flow analysis and testing have been around for a long time and are now (to a larger or lesser extent) part of industrial practice.

However, most of the techniques have been developed for conventional software. The essential differences between conventional and KB technology suggest that, although V&V techniques work very well for conventional systems, applying V&V techniques to KBS is not straightforward. The specific KB software characteristics require slightly different components of the developing system to be considered and the traditional ones to be extended and adapted. A detailed comparison between V&V as found in traditional software engineering and KBS can be found in [Vermesan and Bench-Capon 95]

Research in the V&V of KBS has emerged as a distinct field only in the last decade and is intended to address issues associated with KBS quality aspects and to credit such applications with the same degree of dependability as conventional applications. Some projects have taken place under the European Strategic Programme for Research and Development in Information Technology (ESPRIT). An example is the Safe-KBS[1] project, which focused on demonstrating the feasibility of integrating software components incorporating knowledge-based technology into safety critical systems. It looked at solving the issues governing safety and certification of such systems, with the appropriate links to software engineering using real applications from the maritime, avionics and nuclear domains. One of the results of the project has been experimenting with adapting traditional VV&T techniques to the development of knowledge-based systems. The experimentation has taken place in a methodological framework of our own design, utilising concepts from mutation testing [Budd et al. 80].

The rest of this paper describes the approach taken in the Safe-KBS project. In the next section we define a few key terms and give a short account of mutation testing before presenting the assessment framework. Thereafter, we demonstrate how we have used this framework to experiment with two selected VV&T techniques, evaluating their applicability to the development of knowledge-based systems. Finally the main results are presented along with some suggested directions for future research.

2.   FAULT, FAILURE, ERROR AND MUTATION TESTING

Failure of a computer programme is the observed discrepancy between actual and intended behaviour. The failure is caused by a *fault* in the

[1] This project has been partially funded by the ESPRIT Programme of the Commission of the European Communities as project number 22360. The partners in the Safe-KBS project are Sextant-Avionique (F), Det Norske Veritas (N), Enel-Sri (I), Tecnatom (ESP), Computas Expert Systems (N), Uninfo (I), Qualience (F).

program, the fault being the difference between the actual programme text and the text as it should have been for the programme to behave correctly. This fault may have been introduced at the coding stage or have been present already in the requirements or design document. The fault is introduced and caused by a human *error*, either in reasoning or inadvertently. Reasoning errors include misconceptions about the nature of the problem domain, not properly understood requirements, misunderstandings relating to the semantics of the specification or programming language, errors in transforming from one representation to another and many more. A typical inadvertent error is making a typing mistake. Not all faults cause a failure.

In [National Bureau of Standards 81], *mutation analysis*[2] is defined as "a method to determine test set thoroughness by measuring the extent to which a test set can discriminate the programme from slight variants [mutants] of the program". The idea of mutation analysis is to produce a number of incorrect variants, *mutations,* of a software component or program. A mutant is created by breaking the original programme into syntactic tokens and then changing a single token by applying a *mutation operator.*

If, when executing the test cases on the mutant, the programme fails (i.e. that the output when running the mutant is different from the expected output), the test cases have been shown to be able to reveal the fault introduced. The mutant is said to have been *killed* and has become a *dead mutant.* If no fault is discovered, the mutant is a *live mutant*, the reason being that it is either functionally *equivalent* to the original programme or that the coverage of the test cases is not satisfactory. If the mutant is functionally equivalent to the original program, no set of test cases will be able to distinguish between the two programme variants. The challenge is thus to determine that this is the case or else extend the set of test cases to improve coverage.

The rationale for doing mutation analysis is that the improvements made to the set of test cases will not only discover the artificially introduced faults, but also still hidden faults in the original program. Mutation testing is based on two hypotheses: 1) that the programme is nearly correct, and that a correct programme can be created by simple syntactic changes to the code (competent programmer hypothesis), and 2) that revealing simple faults will also reveal complex faults (coupling effect hypothesis). The distinction between simple fault and complex fault recognises the fact that some kinds of faults can only be simulated by higher order (compound) mutation operators. In our approach we have only considered simple mutation operators.

---

[2] The terms *mutation testing* and *mutation analysis* seem to be used interchangably in the literature.

Mutation testing can be used on its own, requiring test data to be selected so as to achieve mutation coverage. More often, mutation testing is used to assess the effectiveness of other test techniques. It may give an idea of the capabilities of a specific testing technique, or it may be used to compare several different techniques. In this sense, mutation testing is a second order testing technique.

3.   EXPERIMENTAL FRAMEWORK

The experimental framework is a methodology that describes the steps we take when trying to apply a traditional VV&T technique to knowledge-based components. It is a practical methodology for guiding the work, and does not represent a formal approach.

Input to the method is a VV&T technique; output is a KBS-adapted version of the technique, as well as some indication of how well the technique performs at revealing some specific kinds of faults.

Usage of the experimental framework assumes that one has chosen one or a set of VV&T techniques for further investigation and that the language of the specification/implementation to which the techniques will be applied has been decided upon.

The methodology consists of the following basic steps:

Table 1. Experimental framework steps

Step	Description	Comment
1	Depending on the intended usage of the VV&T technique, **select specification / programme example** (product) on which to perform analysis / testing.	Some techniques are applicable to only one phase of the software development process, others are very generic. The purpose of this step is to select or design example products to which the technique can be applied. The number and type of products selected depends on the scope of the evaluation effort, both with respect to range of techniques and depth of assessment.
2	**Adapt VV&T technique** to the kind of product being assessed	This is the step requiring the most ingenuity. Some VV&T techniques may be used as described, others may need adaption or even a major reinterpretation. Some may not be applicable at all for the specification / implementation technology used.
3	Define a set of **types of faults** relevant for the type of product	We will test the adaption of the VV&T technique by introducing faults into the products selected in Step 1 and determine whether these faults are detected when applying the technique. The purpose of this step is to decide on which

Step	Description	Comment
		types of faults will be injected. Although ultimately every fault is unique, attempts at classifying faults have been made [IEEE Standards Board 93]. The types of faults are in part dependent on the language used for specification or implementation and this must be taken into consideration when defining fault classes. An overview of faults in rule-based systems can be found in [Vermesan 98]. Consideration should also be given to the fact that not all kinds of faults can be expressed by a simple mutation operator.
4	Define a set of **mutation operators** corresponding to fault types of product	The mutation operator is a syntactical transformation operator and as such closely linked to the language of the product to which it is applied. Having made a selection of fault types in the last step, the challenge is now to design a mutation operator that can simulate this fault.
5	**Create mutants** from original specification / programme by applying mutation operators	A mutant is created by applying *one* of the mutation operators defined in Step 4 *once* to *one* of the products selected in step 1. Doing this for a large set of products and mutation operators will require automation support; for just a few it may be done manually.
6	If the testing technique is dynamic, **create test data** to be used during test execution	This is an optional step. Many verification and validation techniques do not require test data at all. With respect to testing techniques that have coverage requirements, the test data must be selected so that these coverage criteria are met.
7	**Execute testing / analysis** by applying VV&T technique to original as well as to mutants	At this time, the technique is applied. Depending on the technique, this may or may not involve execution using test data from Step 6. The technique is applied both to the original products (selected in Step 1) and their mutants (created in Step 5). When applying the technique, it is important to have in mind the rationale and methodology of the technique and not be distracted by the knowledge of the faults which have been injected.
8	**Analyse testing results**	Having executed the testing or analysis it is time to evaluate the results. Did the technique reveal all the faults injected? Were there some faults that went undetected? Why were they not detected?

4.   EXPERIMENTATION

We have applied the framework to two selected testing techniques:
- control-flow analysis and
- cause-effect graphing.

In the rest of this section, we follow the steps of the framework to see how it is applied to determine whether these two techniques may be used for analysis and testing of a rule-based program.

4.1   Selection of Specification / Programme Examples

Within the context of Safe-KBS, some of the partners have provided for experimentation, example applications within the targetted application domains. It proved difficult to isolate smaller parts of the code for reporting in this paper, thus for simplicity we created a small *Example Expert System* using the rule-based and object-oriented language CLIPS [CLIPS 97]. The specification of the example programme can be found in the appendix[3]. The programme consists of 8 rules of the type below:

```
(defrule r1
   (a3)
=>
   (assert (e1))
   (assert (e2))
)
```

The rule named *r1* specifies that if the fact *a3* is defined then facts *e1* and *e2* shall be defined. The same programme example will be used for assessing both VV&T techniques.

4.2   Adaption of VV&T Technique

4.2.1   Control Flow Analysis

In *procedural* programming languages, the solution to a problem is described in terms of sequential steps of computation, with control flowing from the first statement of the programme to the last. Such languages also have constructs for decision and looping to enable alternative and repeated computation. These fundamental concepts of procedural programming are reflected in the *control flow graph model*. The control flow graph can be

---

[3] The listing of the programme has been omitted for brevity.

analysed statically to check the correctness of branching or to detect anomalies such as unreachable ("island") code.

Many knowledge-based systems are implemented in a rule-based language. It seems difficult to impose a *control flow graph model* on this paradigm, since the flow of control is implicit rather than explicit[4].

One approach to describing the structure of a rule base has been given in [Preece et al. 93] and [Preece et al. 98]. This approach views a rule-based system in terms of a state space model, which during execution progresses from state to state, some of which are *goal states* providing a solution or a partial solution to the problem being solved. The rule base is modelled as a set of execution *paths*, where each "path" is a *network* of interdependent rules and facts, giving the sequence of rule-firings necessary to achieve a certain goal state. The goal state is defined as a conjunction of predicates called a *logical completion*. The logical completions must be defined by the user and act as meta-knowledge to the path analysis tool extracting paths from the rule base.

4.2.2   Cause-Effect Graphing

Cause-Effect Graphing is a functional testing technique used both for static analysis and dynamic testing.

The aim of cause-effect graphing is to determine the logical relationships between causes (a distinct input condition or an equivalence class of an input condition) and effects (an output condition of a system/programme state change) and represent them by a combinational network (graph). As a static technique, the construction of the graph may help to discover ambiguities and incompleteness of a specification. Based on the graph it is also possible to derive a set of high-yield test cases that may be used for dynamic testing. The cause-effect graph is usually derived from a requirements specification.

Being a functional (black-box) testing technique, the structural characteristics of the implementation language are of less concern when applying cause-effect graphing.

In one way it may even be more useful for knowledge-based systems than traditional ones, since knowledge-based systems frequently provide an explicit trace of reasoning, thus enabling the demonstration of the premises and intermediate reasoning steps required to reach the resulting conclusion. This trace (as in the control-flow graph of knowledge-based systems previously described) can also be compared to the internal nodes and edges of the cause-effect graph to establish whether reasoning proceeds as

---

[4] Flow of control is explicit within the action part of rules but not at the rule level.

expected or not. Such intermediate steps may be more difficult to verify when problems are solved algorithmically.

4.3   Investigate Typical Faults

To some degree, the type of faults occurring in software development is dependent on the implementation technology used [O'Keefe and O'Leary 93]. Examples of typical faults of rule-based systems include:
– Unfireable rule
– Duplicate rules
– Subsumed rules
– Redundant rules
– Conflicting rules
– Ambivalent rules
– Circularity
– Missing rule*
– Incorrect rule triggering (condition too lax)*
– Incorrect rule action (no actions)*

While all of these faults relate to rules, some are more specifically related to syntactical elements than others. For our investigation we will concentrate on the types of faults marked with an asterisk above (*).

4.4   Mutation Operator Definition

Now, we need to find mutation operators that will simulate these types of faults. A basic requirement is that application of the mutation operator must yield a syntactically correct program.

Below is a list of mutation operators, classified on the basis of which type of lexical element is being modified. Note that this by no means is a complete list.

Table 2. Mutation operators and corresponding faults

Lexical element	Mutation Operator		Fault Type
Rule	Remove rule	RUR*	Missing rule
	Duplicate rule	RUD	Duplicate rule
Rule condition part (LHS)	Falsify condition (AND FALSE)	RCF	Unfireable rule
	Remove condition	RCR	Incorrect rule triggering (always triggers)
Conditional element (LHS)	Remove conditional element	CER*	Incorrect rule triggering (condition too lax)
	Negate conditional element (not)	CEN	Incorrect rule triggering (inverted condition)

Lexical element	Mutation Operator		Fault Type
Rule action part (RHS)	Remove action part	RAR*	Incorrect rule action (no actions)
Action (RHS)	Remove action (not entire action part)	ACR	Incorrect rule action (missing action)

The mutation operators corresponding to the faults we selected in the last step are marked with an asterisk (*).

4.5   Generation of Mutants

The mutation operators CER, RUR, and RAR were applied to the *Example Expert System* to create three different mutants. The same mutation operator could also have been applied to different places of the original programme to create multiple mutants with the same type of fault in different places.

4.5.1   Mutant 1

Applied operator CER (Remove conditional element).

```
(defrule r5
   (a2)
   (a4)
=>
   (assert (e4)))
```

4.5.2   Mutant 2

Applied operator RUR (Remove rule).

```
(defrule r8
   (a1)
   (a6)
=>
   (assert (e1))
   (assert (e5))
)
```

4.5.3   Mutant 3

Applied operator RAR (Remove action part).

```
(defrule r4
```

```
    (c1)
=>
    (assert (e3))
)
```

4.6   Creation of Test Data

Since we only consider control flow *analysis* and not control flow *testing*, there is no need for test data when we apply this technique.

For cause-effect graphing, we intend to simulate execution of the program, so in this case test data are required.

There are two input parameters to the *Example Expert System*:
- *i*: which takes on positive integer values (including 0)
- *k*: which is of an enumerated type with values Low, Medium and High

Both input parameters have three equivalence classes. For parameter *i* we select the following representative test values:

Table 3. Test values for parameter i

Equivalence Class	Test value (i)
$0 <= i < 20$	5
$20 <= i < 50$	25
$50 <= i$	100

The expected output consists of two variables with two and four equivalence classes respectively. All of these equivalence classes are discrete and singular.

For parameter *k* there is only one value in each equivalence class. Only considering the input we thus get the following test data set:

Table 4. Test data and expected results

Test Case	Input i	k	Expected result Output Message	Alarm
1	5	L	Normal system state A	Off
2	5	M	Normal system state A	Off
3	5	H	Hazardous system state	On
4	25	L	Normal system state B	Off
5	25	M	Hazardous system state	On
6	25	H	Hazardous system state	On
7	100	L	Illegal value for *i*	On
8	100	M	Illegal value for *i*	On
9	100	H	Illegal value for *i*	On

This also covers all the *possible* combinations of output values. The expected result here is based on the specification in the appendix.

4.7   Execution of Verification/Validation Process

4.7.1   Control flow analysis

The rule graph corresponding to the *Example Expert System* is shown below:

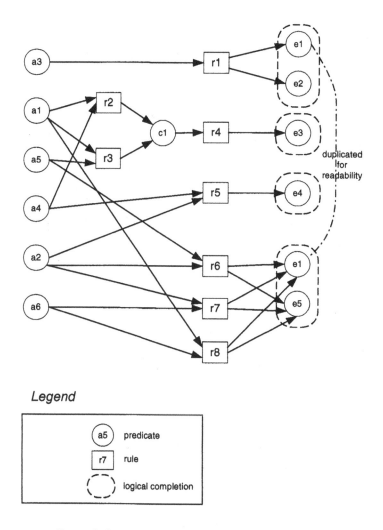

Figure 1. Control-flow graph of Example Expert System

Predicates are represented by rounded boxes and rules by rectangles. Note that this control structure is not directly comparable to the control structure of procedural languages. Although processing may be associated with the rules, there is no "control" exercised by the facts. The arrows do not, then, signify transition of control, but visualise the dependency relation holding between rules and the predicates involved relation. It is a network of potential causes and effects (a causal network).

Figure 1 is actually a composition of all the paths in the system. The individual paths are shown below:

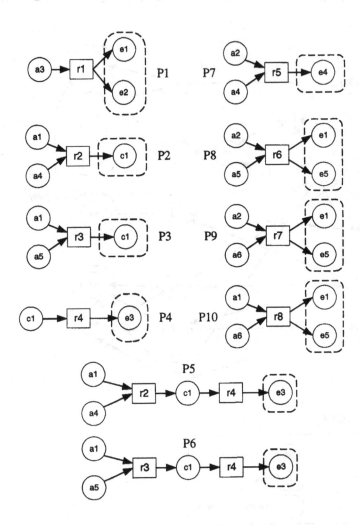

Figure 2. Individual paths of control-flow graph

Depending on whether we consider c1 a logical completion or not we get 7 or 8 paths. The alternative set of paths consists of (P1, P7, P8, P9,P10) and either (P2,P3,P4) or (P5,P6).

4.7.2   Cause-effect graphing

To apply cause-effect graphing to the example, we first assign node numbers to the predicates previously defined (see appendix) and classify them into causes and effects.

Table 5. Nodes representation of predicates

	Node #	Predicate
Causes	1	a1
	2	a2
	3	a3
	4	a4
	5	a5
	6	a6
Effects	91	e1
	92	e2
	93	e3
	94	e4
	95	e5

Based on the specification we are now able to derive a cause-effect graph:

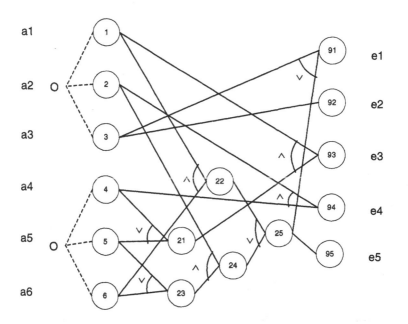

Figure 3. Cause-effect graph for Example Expert Program

The nodes represent causes (left side) or effects (right side). Causes are input or stimuli to the system, while effects are function outputs, changes to the system state or any kind of observable output. The description of causes and effects must be a statement that is either true or false. There may also be "intermediate nodes" representing "intermediate" causes/effects. The edges connecting a node on the right side with one or more nodes on the left side determine the conditions required for the effect to take place. The relationship may be a simple one, like that between nodes 3 and 92 above, in which case the effect follows when the cause occurs. The relationship could also be negated (not/~), or depending on one of (or/∨) or multiple (and/∧) causes. The 'O' on the left hand side connecting (1,2,3) and (4,5,6), states that one and only one of the causes within the same group will occur at any time.

From the cause-effect graph we can derive the decision table. Note that although there are 6 inputs and thus $2^6 = 64$ potential test cases, constraints on the inputs mean that we need to consider only 9.

Table 6. Decision table derived from cause-effect graph

Nodes	1	2	3	4	5	6	7	8	9
1	1	1	1	0	0	0	0	0	0
2	0	0	0	1	1	1	0	0	0
3	0	0	0	0	0	0	1	1	1
4	1	0	0	1	0	0	1	0	0
5	0	1	0	0	1	0	0	1	0
6	0	0	1	0	0	1	0	0	1
21	1	1	0	1	1	0	1	1	0
22	0	0	1	0	0	0	0	0	0
23	0	1	1	0	1	1	0	1	1
24	0	0	0	0	1	1	0	0	0
25	0	0	1	0	1	1	0	0	0
91	0	0	1	0	1	1	1	1	1
92	0	0	0	0	0	0	1	1	1
93	1	1	0	0	0	0	0	0	0
94	0	0	0	1	0	0	0	0	0
95	0	0	1	0	1	1	0	0	0

Translating this table into test input data and expected output gives the following result:

Table 7. Input and expected output according to decision table

Test Case	Input i	k	Expected result Output Message	Alarm
1	5	L	Normal system state A	Off
2	5	M	Normal system state A	Off
3	5	H	Hazardous system state	On

Test	Input		Expected result	
Case	i	k	Output Message	Alarm
4	25	L	Normal system state B	Off
5	25	M	Hazardous system state	On
6	25	H	Hazardous system state	On
7	100	L	Illegal value for i	On
8	100	M	Illegal value for i	On
9	100	H	Illegal value for i	On

4.8   Analysis of Results

4.8.1   Control Flow Analysis

Both the original and the mutant versions of the *Example Expert System* are analysed in the same way. The point is not to compare the results of analyses of different versions *with each other*, but to carry out the analysis on the premises of the technique itself. With respect to control flow analysis, this means that each of the programme versions have to be represented by a control flow graph that is inspected for internal inconsistencies as well as compared to the specification.

4.8.1.1   Mutant 1
The first mutation affects one of the paths of the control graph, removing the dependency on a2.

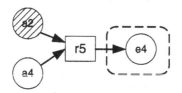

Figure 4. Path P7

The complete graph is still valid. There are no facts (predicates) that are not being used. There are no rules that are not included in any path. However, inspecting the graph above yields the meaning that "given a *k* value of L (regardless of value of *i*!), a message 'Normal B' should be output". This is not in accordance with the specification, which describes at least two different responses for a *k* value of L.

4.8.1.2   Mutant 2

The second mutation affects path P10 of the control graph, which is simply removed. Since all of a1, a6, e1, and e5 are used in other contexts, the error will not be revealed because of unused input or missing goals. Determining that the rule is missing by studying the control graph seems difficult.

4.8.1.3   Mutant 3

Given that c1 is a sub-goal only path P4 is affected by this mutation.

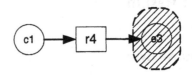

Figure 5. Path P4

In fact, P4 is no longer a path, meaning that r4 is not included in any path - which is clearly an anomaly. Also, the subgoal c1 is not used by any rule, nor does any rule produce the goal e3.

4.8.2   Cause-Effect Graphing

The cause-effect graph itself has been derived from the specification of the program. Introducing mutation operators at the requirements specification level could have been done, but would have required a more formal specification language. Since the faults we introduce are faults of the code rather than of the specification, we do not have multiple versions of the specification, nor of the cause-effect graph. What we are assessing is thus *cause-effect testing* rather than *cause-effect analysis*. Test data input as well as expected output are derived from the cause-effect graph. The testing consists of running all of the programme versions with the same test data and comparing the actual output with the expected output.

4.8.2.1   Mutant 1

Running the mutated expert system with the test data set yields the following result[5]:

---

[5] Deviation from expected output is marked with inverse; additional or changed output is marked with italic, missing with strike-through

Table 8. Output from running mutant 1 with cause-effect graph test data

Test Case	Input i	k	Expected result Output Message	Alarm
1	5	L	Normal A Normal B	Off
2	5	M	Normal A	Off
3	5	H	Hazardous	On
4	25	L	Normal B	Off
5	25	M	Hazardous	On
6	25	H	Hazardous	On
7	100	L	Normal B Illegal i	On
8	100	M	Illegal i	On
9	100	H	Illegal i	On

The table shows that for 2 of 9 test cases, actual output deviates from expected.

4.8.2.2 Mutant 2

Running the mutated expert system with the test cases yields the following results:

Table 9. Output from running mutant 2 with cause-effect graph test data

Test Case	Input i	k	Expected result Output Message	Alarm
1	5	L	Normal A	Off
2	5	M	Normal A	Off
3	5	H	Hazardous	Off
4	25	L	Normal B	Off
5	25	M	Hazardous	On
6	25	H	Hazardous	On
7	100	L	Illegal i	On
8	100	M	Illegal i	On
9	100	H	Illegal i	On

The table shows that for 1 of 9 test cases, actual output deviates from expected.

4.8.2.3 Mutant 3

Running the mutated expert system with the test cases yields the following results:

Table 10. Output from running mutant 3 with cause-effect graph test data

Test Case	Input i	k	Expected result Output Message	Alarm
1	5	L	Normal A	Off

Test Case	Input i	k	Expected result Output Message	Alarm
2	5	M	Normal A	Off
3	5	H	Hazardous	On
4	25	L	Normal B	Off
5	25	M	Hazardous	On
6	25	H	Hazardous	On
7	100	L	Illegal i	On
8	100	M	Illegal i	On
9	100	H	Illegal i	On

The table shows that for 2 of 9 test cases, actual output deviates from expected.

4.8.3   Assessment Conclusion

We have applied two different VV&T techniques to a number of variants of an example expert system in which faults have been artificially injected. The matrix below summarises the result of this experiment:

Table 11. Summary findings of applying VV&T techniques to mutants

VV&T Technique	Expert System Variant applied to		
	Mutant 1 (CER)	Mutant 2 (RUR)	Mutant 3 (RAR)
Control-flow analysis	Analysis likely to reveal fault	Analysis NOT likely to reveal fault	Analysis likely to reveal fault
Cause-effect graphing	2 of 9 TCs fail	1 of 9 TCs fail	2 of 9 TCs fail

The black-box cause-effect graphing testing techniques reveal all the three mutants as erroneous. The faults injected into mutant 1 and 3 are also likely to be discovered by control-flow analysis. Mutant 2 demonstrates how difficult it is to spot missing information when only looking at the structural properties of a system.

5.   CONCLUSION

This paper has presented a framework for assessing the applicability of a traditional VV&T technique in the development of knowledge-based systems. The framework is a 7 or 8 step methodology that gives practical guidance to the researcher or practitioner employing it.

Assessment answers the two questions:

- What kind of adaptation is required if the method is to be used in the new context?
- How efficient is the technique in discovering certain types of faults?

The first question is answered in the sense that doing the exercise of adapting the technique will give an impression of how easily it can be done, if at all. The approach will vary considerably with the technique assessed, and for this reason the framework itself gives little guidance as to how it should be done. [Preece et al. 98] have shown that a *reasonable adaptation* of control-flow analysis exists for knowledge-based systems although the term "control-flow" must be re-interpreted. The commonality between traditional control-flow analysis and the one suggested for KBSs is that they both focus on structure. Cause-effect graphing is more readily adaptable, the reason being simply that it is more specification-oriented and less implementation-oriented than control-flow analysis.

The answer to the second question, regarding efficiency, is given by the mutation-based experiments. For dynamic testing techniques, we are able to count the number of testcases failing; for other VV&T techniques, judgement of whether a fault is discovered or not may not be that easy (especially not when the person applying the technique is the same as the one generating the mutants). In addition, the result of manually applied analysis techniques is highly dependent on the skills of the person performing the analysis. There is of course a human element in dynamic testing techniques as well, e.g. in the selection of test data. However, the rules for doing test data selection are probably fewer and more rigid than the ones guiding an analysis process. That is why, for control-flow analysis, the results of the analysis is stated in terms of "likely to reveal fault" and "not likely to reveal fault".

What we have described is a qualitative assessment. A quantitative assessment would require a much larger number of example programs, mutants, test data sets (in the case of dynamic testing techniques) and human testers (for selection of test data or for analysis) to yield meaningful statistical results. Generating a large number of mutants is easily automated and the automatic generation of test data is also possible. The most time consuming activity is probably the manual performance of analysis techniques. This effectively limits the number of samples that may be made, at least for techniques that cannot be automated.

The aim of this qualitative approach was not to conclude whether a given technique will reveal a certain kind of fault with a certain probability. The few samples we have can only *hint* at the efficiency of a technique. The strongest statement that can be made is that the technique will discover the fault in some cases. However, even such a statement adds to our understanding of a technique being applicable for knowledge-based systems. An experimentation measuring effectiveness of various verification tools for KBS can be found in [Preece et al. 97]

Thus, we subjectively classify techniques as either *highly applicable*, *applicable*, *low applicability* or *not applicable* according to the schema below and based on the answers attained for the two questions formulated above.

Table 12. Categories for classifying applicability of VV&T techniques KBSs

Category	Description
HA (Highly Applicable).	The technique can be applied straightforward.
A (Applicable).	The technique's concept applies but some adaptations are necessary.
LA (Low Applicable).	The technique's concept applies but extensive adaptations are necessary.
NA (Not Applicable).	The technique's concept does not apply.

The conclusion for the two methods assessed is that *Control Flow Analysis* has *Low Applicability* and that *Cause-Effect Testing* is *Applicable* to knowledge-based systems. The reason for the low score of the first technique is the extensive adaptations required.

Possible extensions to our work includes the implementation of a mutation generator for a rule-based programming language that would allow us to perform a quantitative assessment of techniques. We would also like to extend the number of VV&T techniques assessed, and build up a library of multiple, different, more meaningful example specifications that could serve as a standardised library for the assessment framework.

ACKNOWLEDGEMENTS

The contribution of Antoine Mensch and Jean-Marc Meslin from Sextant Avionique and Encarna Mesa from Tecnatom, all partners in the SafeKBS project, is kindly acknowledged.

REFERENCES

Budd, T.A., R.A. DeMillo, R.J. Lipton, and F.G. Sayward. 1980. "Theoretical and empirical studies on using program mutation to test the functional correctness of programs" *Conference Record of the Seventh ACM Symposium on Principles of Programming Languages (POPL '80)*. ACM Press, pp. 220-233.

CLIPS. 1997. *CLIPS Reference Manual Version 6.05 - Volume I: Basic Programming Guide.*

IEEE Standards Board. 1993. "IEEE Standard Classification for Software Anomalies". In: *IEEE Standards Collection - Software Engineering*, ed. IEEE Standards Board. IEEE.

National Bureau of Standards. 1981. *Validation, Verification and Testing of Computer Software*, Special Publication 500-75, National Bureau of Standards.

O'Keefe, R.M. and D.E. O'Leary. 1993. "Expert system verification and validation: a survey and tutorial" *Artificial Intelligence Review*, vol. 7, pp. 3-42.

Preece, A.D., P.G. Chander, C. Grossner, and T. Radhakrishnan. 1993. "Modeling Rule Base Structure for Expert System Quality Assurance" International Joint Conference on Artificial Intelligence Workshop on Validation of Knowledge-Based Systems., pp. 37-49.

Preece, A.D., S. Talbot, and L. Vignollet. 1997. "Evaluation of verification tools for knowledge-based systems" *International Journal of Human-Computer Studies*, vol. 47, pp. 629-258.

Preece, A.D., C. Grossner, P.G. Chander, and T. Radhakrishnan. 1998. "Structure-based validation of rule-based systems" *Data and Knowledge Engineering*, vol. 26, pp. 161-189.

Vermesan, A.I. and T. Bench-Capon. 1995. "Techniques for the Verification and Validation of Knowledge-Based Systems: A Survey Based on the Symbol/Knowledge Level Distinction", *Software, Testing, Verification & Reliability*, John Wiley & Sons, Ltd, pp.233-271.

Vermesan, A.I. 1998. "Foundation and Application of Expert System Verification and Validation". In: *The Handbook of Applied Expert Systems*, ed. J. Liebowitz. Boca Raton: CRC Press LLC., pp. 5.1-5.32.

APPENDIX - EXAMPLE EXPERT SYSTEM

We have defined an example expert system that does not belong to any domain. However, in order to be able to do any testing on this system, we will have to define the inputs and expected outputs.

The purpose of our expert system is to provide an interpretation of the state of a system (e.g. in the nuclear domain) based on measurement of two variables. These form the input parameters i, and k to the system. The first parameter is a positive integer parameter, the second takes on discrete values.

Table 13. Variables and legal values

Variable	Values	Comment
i	$0 <= i < 20$	Legal range R1
	$20 <= i < 50$	Legal range R2
	$50 <= i$	Illegal
k	L	Low
	M	Medium
	H	High

There is no way a negative i-parameter may be given. The three categories of values for i and k constitute equivalence classes. In logical terms (i.e. for the diagnosis) all values of the same class are equivalent.

The resulting outputs, *message* and *alarm* depend on the combination of values for i and k. We will assume that the system responds by displaying a message and optionally by sounding an alarm or both. The following responses may be given:

Table 14. Output

ID	message	alarm
o1	Illegal value for *i*	On
o2	Normal system state A	Off
o3	Normal system state B	Off
o4	Hazardous system state	On

The relationship between input and output can be described as follows:
- If *i* is illegal then output o1
- If *i* is less than 20 and *k* is L or M then output o2
- If *i* is in the range [20..50) and *k* is L then output o3
- Otherwise, if none of the above is valid, then output o4

Transforming this little specification into a rule-based programme, we will first define some predicates that make the interface with both input and output devices simpler. When the condition given is present, the corresponding predicate is asserted as a fact:

Table 15. Predicates for condition

Predicate	Condition	
Input	a1	$0 <= i < 20$
	a2	$20 <= i < 50$
	a3	$50 <= i$
	a4	$k = L$
	a5	$k = M$
	a6	$k = H$
Output	e1	ring alarm[6]
	e2	display "Illegal i"
	e3	display "Normal A"
	e4	display "Normal B"
	e5	display "Hazardous"

Note that (a1,a2,a3) are mutually exclusive. The same is true for (a4,a5,a6) and (e2,e3,e4,e5).

[6] If e1 is not asserted the alarm is OFF